THE MAKING OF BRAHMANIC HEGEMONY

Studies in Caste, Gender and Vaiṣṇava Theology

THE MAKING OF BRAHMANIC HEGEMONY

Studies in Caste, Gender and Vaiṣṇava Theology

SUVIRA JAISWAL

Tulika Books

Published by
Tulika Books
44 (first floor) Shahpur Jat, New Delhi 110 049, India
www.tulikabooks.in

First edition (hardback) 2016
Second edition (paperback) 2018

ISBN: 978-81-939269-1-8

Printed at Chaman Offset, Delhi 110 002

In memory of

VIRENDRA BHAIYA

This Dharma of Manu, by reason of the governing force which it has had for centuries, has become an integral and vital part of the customs and tradition of the Hindus. It has become ingrained and has given colour to their life blood. As law it controlled the actions of the Hindus. Though now a custom, it does not do less. It moulds the character and determines the outlook of generation after generation.

– B.R. AMBEDKAR

(*Unpublished Writings, Dr Babasaheb Ambedkar: Writings and Speeches*, vol. 5, pp. 284–85)

Contents

Acknowledgements

This volume consists of essays, some published and some unpublished, written for different occasions. Ostensibly centring on different themes, these nonetheless have a thematic unity as they attempt to delineate the historical circumstances in which certain societal and theological structures develop, leading to a hegemony of brahmanic ideology.

Chapter 2 is substantially my address to the 68th session of the Indian History Congress as its General President. It was held at Delhi University in December 2007. The section on the 'Cultic Worship of Rāma Dāśarathī', forming part of Chapter 6, is my S.C. Misra Memorial Lecture delivered in March 2007 at the 27th session of the Indian History Congress held at Farook College, Calicut University, under the title 'The Making of a Hegemonic Tradition: The Cult of Rāma Dāśarathī'. Chapter 5 is an enlarged version of the Professor Mamidipudi Venkata Rangayya Memorial Lecture given on 5 January 2002 at Anaparthi (East Godavari district), on the occasion of the 26th annual session of the Andhra Pradesh History Congress. The Appendix to Chapter 1 ('Reconstructing History from the *Ṛgveda*: A Paradigm Shift?') was originally published in *Social Science Probings*, vol. 18, no. 2, December 2006, pp. 1–17; the article on 'Female Images in the *Arthaśāstra* of Kauṭilya' was published in *Social Scientist*, vol. 29, nos 3–4, March–April 2001. Chapter 8, 'The Demon and the Deity: Conflict Syndrome in the Hayagrīva Legend', was published in *Studies in History*, vol. I, no. 1, new series, 1985. I am thankful to the journals where these articles appeared in the first instance for permission to reproduce them.

I wish to record my most sincere thanks to Dr Ranjan Anand of Zakir Husain Delhi College (Evening) of Delhi University for helping me with the proofs. My daughter Neeraja Jaiswal undertook the work of getting the manuscript typed and helping me with the nitty-gritty of publication. Without her active interest and assistance I could not have managed to accomplish this task, particularly in view of my indifferent health. I also wish to thank my grandsons Nishant and Avinash for their keen interest and moral support. Thanks are also due to

Mr Shad Naved for copy-editing, organizing the end-notes, preparation of the Bibliography and Index, and to Tulika Books for publishing this volume.

I dedicate this work to the memory of my late brother Dr Virendra Kumar, M.A., D.Phil. (Alld), who unhesitatingly supported the higher education of his sisters at a great deal of personal cost.

Hyderabad
June 2016

SUVIRA JAISWAL

Introduction

The discipline of history in India is under severe attack, not only from those who adopt a pseudo-historical mode to popularize a mythically coloured version of the past with an ill-concealed political objective, but also from those who pose methodological challenges through unbridled theoretical relativism emphasizing cultural specificity and difference to the extent that it can only be termed as a reorientalization of the Orientals. Thus Ronald Inden, in his well-known work *Imagining India*,[1] attempts to seek the 'rationalities' of ritual practices of early India in terms of a metaphysical perspective that theorizes them as integral to a 'theophanic polity' totally opposite to the 'scientifically grounded politics' of the west. Aijaz Ahmad has called it 'orientalism-in-reverse'.[2] There are others who extol 'ahistoricity' of discourses in India in the name of celebrating indigenous knowledge systems,[3] apparently taking it as an attribute of the Indian mentality which needs no further explanation. The problem is further compounded by the elevation of an obscurantist discourse made fashionable by the votaries of postmodernism, particularly in the fields of cultural history and anthropology. Whereas Inden claims to have restored the 'agency' of the Indian (read 'Hindu') people – hitherto ignored by historians and Indologists – by locating their rationality in the way they 'reconstituted' or 'reproduced' their polity through the annual *abhiṣeka* (royal bath) ceremonies at royal courts, religious processions, rituals, etc., announcing the western socio-economic categories of analysis, systems of production, distribution, etc., as irrelevant for them,[4] Richard H. Davis attributes 'agency' to deities and idols[5] who supposedly issue commands as rulers and masters to subordinate humans, and are able to specify their own identities in case of a dispute. Indeed, he explains in the Introduction that he adopts the Hindu theological view that images established in temples through the complex ritual of 'establishment'[6] are living beings as a useful 'organising trope' for sketching the biographical case studies of Indian religious images. Nonetheless, he carries his imaginative theological reading too far when he criticizes Krishnaswamy Ayyangar for reducing to a historical event the way Rāmānujācārya resolved the dispute between the Śaivas and the Vaiṣṇavas about the identity of the image at Tirupati, 'without granting the image any agency'.[7] Apparently, 'agency' – a much abused word – even when attributed to gods and idols, should carry the meaning of 'capacity to act purposefully to change their own circumstances'.[8] Ascription of such functions to images of deities neatly camouflages the role of priests and rulers who made use of religious symbols in their class interests, for which a large amount of evidence is provided in this monograph.

We have also the phenomenological approach to religion, which argues for treating religious myths and 'visions' as supramundane phenomena, unique and irreducible, which have to be understood on their own plane of reference and apart from their material setting.[9] Millions in India still believe in miracles of idols drinking milk and shedding tears, and sea water becoming sweet through saintly agency. The Prime Minister of India, in all earnestness, tells an audience of doctors, scientists and celebrities that in ancient India plastic surgery was so advanced that the head of an elephant was fitted on to the body of a human being whom we all worship as Gaṇeśa.[10] In such a situation, to argue for a rational, scientific interpretation of India's cultural heritage is a hazard which historians and academics have to face if they wish to remain true to their discipline. The present volume is a collection of articles – both published earlier and unpublished – which have the underlying aim of unfolding the creation of Brahmanical hegemony through the institutions of caste, gender and religious ideology.

The concept of hegemony implies domination – which may be achieved not only through force, although the role of violence and coercion cannot be underplayed. However, in the long-term suppression of the oppressed, the impact of economic and socio-cultural factors too has to be taken into consideration, particularly if these take the form of a religious ideology. It is necessary to investigate the role of its agents and the material environment in which they operate. There is no doubt that in the creation of a Vedic–Brahmanic tradition the brāhmaṇas played an important part, but they alone were not responsible for its spread over the entire subcontinent. It was readily internalized by the dominant classes and the emerging elite groups who patronized Brahmanical institutions and helped in its spread, as it met both their material and metaphysical needs by giving legitimacy to their dominant position in a hierarchy of castes through the doctrine of *karma*. The doctrines of *karma* and rebirth were not exclusive to Brahmanism; these were fundamental to Buddhist and Jaina philosophies too. But in Brahmanism these were intertwined with the notion of 'pure' and 'impure' births, providing a religious rationale for the inequality of statuses and occupations, thus erecting a hierarchical society which served the interests of the dominant classes. The close collaboration of religious and temporal authorities is evident from the very inception of the *varṇa–jāti* system, which continues to this day. D.D. Kosambi was very explicit about the class role of the brāhmaṇa caste. 'This class was perhaps the most convenient tool of the ruling power, whether indigenous or foreign, in the enslavement of the Indian people', he wrote.[11] The Purāṇas repeatedly exhort that the king be imbued with divinity and that he should be worshipped daily (*bhaktiśca bhūpatau nityam*).[12] Caste ideology also limited the options available to the brāhmaṇa intelligentsia for earning a living. It had to be forever in search of patronage, or it would be reduced to pitiable poverty.[13] Nevertheless, as Kosambi pointed out, as a class auxiliary to the ruling class, its literary creations show a preoccupation with the interests and inclinations of the upper classes and not of the masses. Sanskrit was the language of ritual and of the upper classes, and it was kept alive by the brāhmaṇa priests and poets who wrote voluminous books on ritual, theology and philosophy, and developed intricate literary forms for the amusement of the leisured classes. But 'there is no Sanskrit work of any use to the blacksmith, potter, carpenter, weaver, ploughmen'.

While the caste system is said to constitute the structural basis of Brahmanism, to me it seems that caste was the main plank on which the entire edifice of Brahmanism was built. There is enough justification for the view that the present-day 'global Hindu religious identity',[14] into which Brahmanical Hinduism is trying to reinvent itself, is a late nineteenth-century phenomenon. B.R. Ambedkar rightly asserted that the only 'principle in Hinduism [to] which all Hindus, no matter what their other differences are, feel bound to render willing obedience . . . is the principle of caste'.[15] The much-acclaimed pluralistic toleration and acceptance, *swikriti* as Amartya Sen puts it,[16] of divergent religious beliefs, forms of worship and customs in the Brahmanic tradition has its roots in the Brahmanical mode of social integration, which allowed freedom of thought, rituals and practices so long as it was possible to absorb outsiders or non-conformist groups as 'castes', whether they were incoming foreign groups, marginal tribal communities or rebellious reformist groups from within. The ultimate triumph of Brahmanism was rooted in this paradigm of social integration.[17] It adopted a rigid stance against deviation from the customary socio-religious praxis of every community or caste, while making doctrinal issues a matter of individual choice. There was scope for intense debate and even the formation of different *sampradāyas* or sects. Evidence shows that the living together of sects has not always been smooth and non-violent.[18] Basically, it was conformity to caste/community-specific social and religious customs that was held as unquestionable, the violation of which invited severe punishment, even excommunication, and not the holding of non-orthodox concepts of the divine or a divergent world-view. The hegemonic character of this type of ideological symbiosis should not be ignored. Divergent and contradictory beliefs and customs posed no threat if the practitioners could be fitted into a hierarchical structure in which power, rank and 'purity' went hand in hand, in opposition to those who were considered dependent, subaltern and 'impure'. Exclusivity and fragmentation were enforced at the social level even when it is asserted[19] that as late as the nineteenth century almost all religions in India had no rigid boundaries, so much so that some elements of the Hindu and Muslim faiths too could be shared. The plethora of religious beliefs and practices led the philosopher and former President of India, Sarvepalli Radhakrishnan, to remark:

> At the outset one is confronted by the difficulty of defining what Hinduism is. To many it seems to be a name without content. Is it a museum of belief, a medley of rites or a mere map, a geographical expression? Its content if any has altered from age to age, from community to community.[20]

But this diversity was provided not by the universal acceptance of the authority of the Vedas – as is often assumed[21] – nor any specific notion of the divine or the cosmos, but by the recognition and acceptance of a community's identity as a 'caste' in the Brahmanical hierarchy.[22] The flexible umbrella of Hinduism, a term popularized in the late medieval and colonial times, has led to its being likened to a jungle.[23] Friedhelm Hardy, in his *The Religious Culture of India*, remarkable for its meticulous and erudite scholarship, likens the cultural scene of India to a 'chaotic jungle',[24] as none of the major religious systems of India – Jaina, Buddhist, Vedic, Upaniṣadic, Puranic or Tantric – denotes a coherent system of ideas. There are within each of them doctrines, principles, alongside antinomian features, presenting a bewildering variety of ideas and practices as well as a profusion of literature. Hence, Hardy organizes his study not under Vedic, Jaina, Buddhist or Tantric labels, which he regards merely as 'secondary divisions', but along the three themes of Power, Love and Wisdom, which find their powerful expression in all these religious streams, curiously, at about the same time. Nevertheless he has to admit that this 'extremely rich and varied manifestation of the religious' comes at a price, that is, of social conformity. 'While the latitude on a purely doctrinal or typological level is enormous, how one actually behaves in society is an infinitely more tightly-controlled affair, and this not necessarily through religion but through social consensus.'[25] I wonder how it is possible to dissociate and admire the plurality and freedom of thought and religious beliefs without taking note of its base, the *varṇa–jāti* system, which itself is a product of specific material and historical conditions, as I have shown elsewhere.[26] The superabundant manifestation of the religious has its counterpart in the multitudinous castes.

Current definitions of caste place its essence in endogamy.[27] Its role in the occupational system is not denied, and its past links with the form of the 'labour process' is duly underlined in Marxist historiography.[28] But assigning a foundational role to endogamy makes caste a transhistoric institution, a continuation of old clan and tribal units pre-dating the state.[29] Moreover, it supplies grist to the mill of those who trace its origin in the Aryan/non-Aryan dichotomy, to the desire of the conquering Aryans to keep the subjugated communities at a distance. However, a careful scrutiny of our sources reveals that it was not the enduring grip of the custom of tribal endogamy which was at the root of the caste system, but the emergence of a class society in which patriarchal control played an important role in securing the rights and privileges of the elite on a hereditary basis. It evolved a ranking system based on birth and control of female sexuality promoting endogamy. Our sources suggest that in the earlier phase of the *varṇa* system, hypergamy was widely practised. Citing textual as well as epigraphical evidence, P.V. Kane remarks[30] that *anuloma* (hypergamous) marriages were frequent down to the ninth–tenth centuries CE. We may add that elaborate rules about the shares of property to be inherited by the sons of wives belonging to different *varṇas* lower than that of the father are laid down in the Smṛti structure, including the *Manusmṛti*[31] and the *Arthaśāstra* of Kauṭilya.[32] These cannot be dismissed simply as intellectual exercises having no relation to the actual state of affairs.[33] However, hypergamy underscores the lower status of wife-givers; and this would naturally propel towards endogamy, particularly in fluid situations, later becoming the norm. In a later chapter, I discuss the origin and functioning of patriarchy in the caste-based Vedic–Brahmanic tradition.

In the making of Brahmanic hegemony, religion and mythology have played an important role in reducing the potency of counter-hegemonic forces and in providing an important means of communication with the subaltern, creating social ties between the dominant and the depressed. It was a complex process in which politics and economy played an important role. Myths reveal the stories of domination and resistance if we give attention to the processes of their production, and not take them as factual historical narratives. The question is not of dismissing myths as 'false, distorted or bad history'[34] but of examining the kind of reality they represent, in order to delve into the dynamics of their formation and their impact, and to account for the elements of continuity and change in them. I had adopted this approach in my monograph, *The Origin and Development of Vaiṣṇavism*. The articles on Rāma, Narasiṃha and Hayagrīva are further studies on the same lines.

Notes

[1] Ronald Inden, *Imagining India*.

[2] Aijaz Ahmad, 'Between Orientalism and Historicism', p. 163.

[3] Vinay Lal, *The History of History*, pp. 14, 271 note 79.

[4] Suvira Jaiswal, *Caste*, pp. 18–19, 31, 107.

[5] Richard H. Davis, *Lives of Indian Images*.

[6] Described as *prāṇa pratiṣṭhā*.

[7] Richard H. Davis, *Lives of Indian Images*, p. 292 note 1. This is with reference to S.K. Aiyangar's *A History of Tirupati*, vol. I, pp. 265–67.

[8] Aijaz Ahmad, 'Between Orientalism and Historicism', p. 160.

[9] The leading proponent of this view is Mircea Eliade; cf. his *Yoga: Immortality and Freedom*. David R. Kinsley adopts this approach in *The Sword and the Flute*. (Also see Suvira Jaiswal, 'Review of *The Sword and the Flute*'.)

[10] 'Speaking at the inauguration of the Sir H.N. Reliance Foundation Hospital and Research Centre last Saturday, he [Mr Modi] said: "*Mahabharat ka kahna hai ki Karn maa ki godh* [*sic*] *se paida nahi hua tha. Iska matlab yeh hai ki us samay* genetic science *mojud tha. . . . Hum Ganeshji ki puja kiya karte hain, koi to* plastic surgeon *hoga us zamane main jisne manushya ke sharir par hathi ka sar rakh kar ke* plastic surgery *ka prarambh kiya hoga*." (It is said in the *Mahabharata* that Karna was not born from his mother's womb. This means in the times in which the epic was written genetic science was very much present. . . . We all worship Lord Ganesha; for sure there must have been some plastic surgeon at that time, to fit an elephant's head on the body of a human being).' Karan Thapar, *The Hindu*, Saturday, 1 November 2014.

[11] D.D. Kosambi, *Exasperating Essays*, p. 87.

[12] *Viṣṇudharmottara Purāṇa*, II.80.3.

[13] D.D. Kosambi, *Combined Methods in Indology and Other Writings*, p. 332. This view has been criticized by Sheldon Pollock, but see Suvira Jaiswal, 'Kosambi on Caste', pp. 146ff. Goodwin Raheja's field work in a North Indian village has shown that the politically and economically dominant non-brāhmaṇa caste of Gujars treats brāhmaṇas in the same way as other service castes; see Goodwin Raheja, *The Poison in the Gift*.

[14] D.N. Jha, 'Looking for a Hindu Identity', p. 17.

[15] B.R. Ambedkar, *Dr Babasaheb Ambedkar: Writings and Speeches*, vol. III, p. 336. This attitude has begun to change in the educated upper crust of Hindu society in recent decades, but they still form an infinitesimal minority.

[16] Amartya Sen, *The Argumentative Indian*, p. 35.

[17] Suvira Jaiswal, 'Semitising Hinduism'.

[18] D.N. Jha, 'Looking for a Hindu Identity', pp. 30–39.

[19] Harjot Oberoi, *Construction of Religious Boundaries*.

[20] S. Radhakrishnan, *The Hindu View of Life*, p. 11.

[21] For this assumption of Brian K. Smith (*Reflections on Resemblance, Ritual and Religion*, pp. 13–14), see Suvira Jaiswal, 'Semitising Hinduism', pp. 21–23.

[22] Smith's argument that caste is not exclusive to Hinduism in India (the institution exists among Buddhists, Muslims and Christians too) is not valid, as among the non-Hindu Indian communities caste is an aberration, a surviving practice among converts fostered by the existing socio-economic relations. As for the Jainas, early Jainism contested the higher status of the brāhmaṇas, but accepted the *varṇa–jāti* system and developed its own priest-caste. In actual practice it functions almost like a sect of Hinduism; hence there are numerous instances of the same family having both Jaina and Hindu members and commingling without any restrictions on inter-marriage. See Suvira Jaiswal, *Caste*, p. 28 note 90.

[23] Ronald Inden, *Imagining India*, pp. 86–87.

[24] Friedhelm Hardy, *The Religious Culture of India*, chapter 24.

[25] Ibid., p. 545.

[26] Suvira Jaiswal, *Caste*.

[27] André Béteille, 'The Reproduction of Inequality'.

[28] Irfan Habib, *Essays in Indian History*, pp. 161–79.

[29] Morton Klass, *Caste*.

[30] P.V. Kane, *History of Dharmaśāstra*, vol. II, part I, pp. 447–51.

[31] *Manusmṛti*, IX.149–55.

[32] *Kauṭilīya Arthaśāstra*, III.6.17–22.

[33] Inter-*varṇa* marriages were considered legal by the Brahmanical law-givers. The *Bṛhannāradīya Purāṇa* (tenth century CE) states that there are a number of forms which, although legal, should not be practised. Among these practices is marriage of a 'twice-born' man with a girl not belonging to his own *varṇa* (*asavarṇā*). *Bṛhannāradīya Purāṇa*, XXII.12–13, quoted by R.C. Hazra, *Studies in the Upapurāṇas*, vol. I, p. 327. A rule quoted in the *Smṛticandrikā* from the *Ādi Purāṇa* lays down that a brāhmaṇa might take his meal in the company of his brāhmaṇa wife; but if he does so with his wife from a lower *varṇa*, he would instantly lose his caste. Ibid., p. 294 note 87. The *Smṛticandrikā* further states that it is unnecessary to discuss the case of sons born of *anuloma* as such marriages are no longer in vogue. P.V. Kane, *History of Dharmaśāstra*, vol. III, p. 599.

[34] Vinay Lal, *The History of History*, p. 123.

PART I

1

Power, Status and Ethnicity in Caste Formation

The view that the Indian caste system and its social inequality have a racial origin continues to find favour in many journalistic and academic writings[1] despite the outright rejection of the concept of race by most anthropologists and geneticists, particularly in the post-Second World War period.[2] Hence, it may not be inappropriate to examine the basis of such assumptions. Historiographical evaluations[3] attribute this view to colonial–Orientalist misrepresentations of Indian history in the nineteenth and twentieth centuries, but its continued acceptance is not merely due to its political use in Dalit assertion, but also because of the simplistic, uncritical readings of the Ārya–Anārya (Arya–non-Arya) conflicts and the *varṇa* differentiation mentioned in the *Ṛgveda*, the earliest literary source for South Asian history. India is a land of long continuities and the hierarchical nature of the caste system is generally traced to the *varṇa* hierarchy of the Vedic age.

The *Ṛgveda* applies the term *varṇa* to two groups of people, Ārya[4] and Dāsa,[5] whose relations with each other are clearly hostile. Their difference is perceived by the Ṛgvedic poets in the colour of their respective skins, use of language and worship of gods. In other words, the two *varṇas* are seen as two different ethnic communities.[6] It is contended[7] that Ārya as an ethnic term of self-reference is found in ancient linguistic materials from Iran and India; hence it should be confined to the speakers of Indo–Iranian and not used for Indo–Europeans. This does not, however, explain the derivation of the Finnish word '*orja*' meaning 'slave' from the Finno–Ugric *Orja equated to proto-Indo–Iranian *arya, which suggests that there were people known as Ārya living in the Russian steppes, in the vicinity of Finno–Ugric peoples. They were captured in war and enslaved in sufficient numbers by the latter to make their ethnic name mean 'slave' in the languages of the captors. The historical process was apparently similar to the one which gave the word 'slave' to English and *dāsa* to Sanskrit from the defeat and enslavement of the ethnic Slav and Dāsa communities, respectively.[8] The attempt to deny altogether any ethnic significance to the notion of

Ārya – even in its initial uses – seems to be influenced more by an awareness of the pernicious role played by the concept of the 'Aryan race' in the politics of the nineteenth and twentieth centuries than any critical–historical evidence.[9] The concept of a biologically determined 'Aryan race' may be a 'factoid',[10] 'a speculation repeated so often that it is eventually taken for hard fact', but it does not invalidate the notion of ethnicity or gainsay clear textual evidence that the Ṛgvedic Aryans did have a sense of their separate ethnic identity, deriving from a common linguistic and cultural tradition and from interaction with the indigenous Dāsas and Dasyus, whom they perceived as the 'other'.[11] Should we then trace the emergence of a hierarchical society in the form of *varṇas* to the Aryans' desire to retain the purity of their 'blood' by maintaining social distance through prohibitions regarding *connubium* and commensality, as has been assumed by the Census Commissioner Sir H.H. Risley?[12]

It is important to note that the *Ṛgveda* does not apply the term *varṇa* to the brāhmaṇa, kṣatriya and vaiśya categories, although these are mentioned at several places and in a hierarchical order in at least two hymns.[13] The śūdra is mentioned only once in the late *Puruṣa-sūkta* hymn, which attributes the origin of all the four groups to the various bodily parts of primeval man, making them constituents of one civil society, but does not use the term *varṇa* for them. Thus, there is hardly any justification for regarding the fourfold social stratification that emerged towards the close of the Ṛgvedic period, and seen by Risley and Louis Dumont as the root of caste hierarchy, as an extension of the binary opposition between the Ārya and Dāsa communities simply because the four orders are described as *varṇas* in later literature. The term soon came to mean 'class, kind, species', and even 'quality' and 'property', and was applied to letters of the alphabet and various objects both animate and inanimate.[14] It has been convincingly argued[15] that the Vedicists, particularly British Sanskritists, such as A.A. Macdonell and A.B. Keith, whose *Vedic Index* has been and continues to be used widely as an authoritative work, minimized the evidence which showed the Dasyus/Dāsas as wealthy, powerful opponents living in forts, and represented them as marginal, barbarous hill tribes subjugated by the more civilized, fair-complexioned Aryan invaders, as their interpretation of the Vedic data was influenced by the racial attitudes of whites towards blacks in South Africa and the United States. Apparently the fourfold *varṇa* hierarchy of later Vedic times was not an extension of the Ārya–Dāsa dichotomy, which had an ethnic hue.

The irrelevance of a racial dimension in the emergence of the *varṇa* system is revealed by the fact that the fourth *varṇa* is consistently described as 'śūdra', with the term *dāsa* reserved for slaves. No doubt, many of the defeated Dāsas must have been reduced to the rank of śūdras, but their presence was not the main factor in the categorization of the fourth *varṇa*. R.S. Sharma, whose *Śūdras in*

Ancient India[16] is undoubtedly the most important work on the subject, held the view that the defeated and dispossessed sections of the Aryan and non-Aryan tribes were reduced to the position of śūdras by the end of the Ṛgvedic period, but originally a considerable number of śūdras had been part of the 'Aryan Community'.[17] At any rate, had racial or ethnic discrimination been the prime mover in the crystallization of *varṇa* stratification, it would be difficult to explain how Kauṭilya could speak of a śūdra as an Ārya by birth, and prescribe a penalty for his sale or mortgage.[18] Patañjali too, while commenting on Pāṇini (II.4.10), speaks of śūdras who were Āryas and lived within the boundary of the village. In fact later Vedic texts, which evince the consolidation of the *varṇa* system, also indicate a shift in the meaning of the term Ārya, which was now increasingly used to mean 'noble' or 'high-born' and later came to be applied to any member of the four *varṇa* orders. The *Manusmṛti* states, 'Those communities in the world which are not included among the communities born from the mouth, arms, thighs and feet of the Creator (i.e. four *varṇas*) are all considered to be non-Aryan, irrespective of whether they speak an Aryan or non-Aryan language.'[19] Thus, according to Manu, the śūdra, born from the Creator's feet, is an authentic Ārya.

The defeat and subjugation of the Dāsa and Śūdra tribes, however, did play a catalysing role in accelerating the process of differentiation within Aryan tribes and their disintegration into a *varṇa*-divided class structure.[20] The tripartite functional grouping of tribesmen into priestly, warriors/rulers and commoners perhaps goes back to an Indo–European past, as has been argued by Georges Dumézil, and is characteristic of the ecology of pastoral tribes[21] among whom emerged two types of specialists: those who claim to increase the cattle wealth of the tribe by pacifying and pleasing the gods with their knowledge of rituals, and those who carry out cattle raids and defend the cattle of their own tribe through their martial prowess. Initially, the two privileged categories were not closed genealogically and were open to any tribesmen who had the necessary expertise. This is true of both the *brahma* (priestly)[22] and the *kṣatra* (ruler–warrior) groups. Sometimes members of the same lineage took on the office of the priest and of the chief.[23] Moreover, we also come across brāhmaṇa sages,[24] composers of Ṛgvedic hymns named after their Dāsī mothers (women of Dāsa tribe and not female slaves as interpreted by later Brahmanical writers), and some of the famous Ṛgvedic chiefs, patrons of brāhmaṇas, had Dāsa ancestry.[25] As D.D. Kosambi remarks,[26] purity of blood did not mean much in the life of the tribes, and there was assimilation of the Aryans and pre-Aryans at various levels. There is evidence of the absorption and remodelling of pre-Aryans in Vedic society in the later sections of the *Ṛgveda* and later Vedic texts,[27] but the major consequence of the Aryan–non-Aryan confrontation was the emergence of a stratified society in the form of four *varṇas*, with the addition of the servile category of 'śūdra' to the earlier three functional groups.

Unequal distribution of cattle wealth captured in cattle raids, sedentary agriculture and the availability of servile labour of the defeated Dāsa and Śūdra tribes contributed to the deepening of social differentiation among the Vedic tribes,[28] and the later Vedic sources reflect consolidation of the priestly and warrior groups into the hereditary brāhmaṇa and *rājanya*–kṣatriya *varṇas*, expropriating the surplus produced by the vaiśya commoners and depressed śūdras. This hierarchical fourfold *varṇa* organization provides the framework in which later *jātis* are embedded; hence, Indologists and historians have frequently used the term 'caste' for both *varṇa* and *jāti*. Sociologists, on the other hand, deriving their perception from contemporary realities, draw a clear distinction between *varṇa* and *jāti* concepts. They assert that *varṇas* were 'orders' or 'estates', theoretical constructs superimposed on the empirical realities of *jātis*, and that the term 'caste' should be applied to *jāti* alone. Nevertheless, indiscriminate and almost synonymous use of the two terms has a long history, going back to the law books of the early centuries of the Common Era. Early medieval records speak of villages inhabited by 36 *varṇas*, and the *Varṇaratnākara*, a fourteenth-century text from Mithila, describes 96 communities which were apparently as many *jātis* and not *varṇas*. Even today, both *varṇa* and *jāti* in popular parlance are used to identify the social identity of a person or community among the Hindus.[29] Hence, without adopting an essentialist definition of caste, which generally places its essence in the practice of endogamy, it may be more meaningful to consider how this kind of social structure evolved, and to enquire into its inner dynamic which has enabled it to survive through the ages and in changing social formations.

Célestin Bouglé's definition of the caste system, that it was a social organization which divided and at the same time held together multitudinous communities within its fold on the basis of three fundamental principles – hereditary division of labour with each group's occupation fixed by tradition from which little divergence was possible and only to a limited extent, gradation of communities in a system of ranking, and the 'repulsion' or isolation of one group from another through restrictions over *connubium* and commensality – is broadly valid for the pre-colonial period.[30] But far from being a product of an Indian mentality, which explains nothing, these principles have taken centuries to evolve, and strict adherence to them, their modification or rejection has been largely determined by the strength of the material factors in which they are rooted. Hence, it is not surprising that only those elements of the system which are incompatible with the capitalist mode of production are now withering away with the system adapting itself to a new social formation.

To begin with, certain kinds of caste principles such as the principle of 'repulsion', or separation of each community through restrictions on contact and acceptance of food, water, etc., from members of other communities, particularly lower-ranking ones, have visibly slackened in towns and practically disappeared in metropolitan cities. As for the persistence of endogamy, I have argued that only those features of the caste system need to undergo change or modification which are in conflict with the existing mode of production.[31] But endogamy subsists on the customary pattern of arranged marriages and subordination of the female sex, and the entire system is permeated with the capitalist value system. Hence, it has now become the 'essence' of the caste system.

Various attempts have been made to explain the origin of endogamy. Louis Dumont has argued that status gradation of castes into an integrated hierarchy is the core principle of the caste system, and endogamy is a corollary or natural consequence of it; castes have to be self-reproducing for the application of the hierarchical principle.[32] If this were correct, it would follow that once hierarchy is dissolved, endogamy too should disappear. Hierarchy of castes matters little today, at least among a substantial portion of the urban population, which continues to practise caste-based endogamy. Confronted with this reality, Dumont remarks that modernization has affected the politico-economic domain, which, in any case, in his conception of the caste system, is 'encompassed in an overall religious setting'. Hence, there is no essential transformation of the system, only a change involving minor areas.[33] This is a strange argument. For, he clearly defines hierarchy as a religious principle 'by which the elements of a whole are ranked in relation to the whole'.[34] If the notion of hierarchy is undermined, what remains of the 'religious setting' as he conceived it?

Moreover, the entire edifice of *Homo Hierarchicus* is built on the notion of graded ranking of 'pure' and relatively 'impure' hereditary groups, with the brāhmaṇa at the top and the 'untouchable' groups at the bottom. Dumont rightly holds that this theory presupposes the theory of *varṇas*, which not only separated priesthood from royal power but also ascribed to the latter an inferior rank, establishing the principle that religious status is superior to secular power. But, is it not necessary to examine the historical environment within which such concepts took root and gained wide acceptance, rather than attribute them to the hierarchical mentality of the Hindus? Dumont speaks of them as homologous with the theory of the *varṇas* laying stress on the function, and the theory of *jātis* (castes) on the heredity of social groups in terms of the 'pure' and the 'impure'. But, in fact, the latter concept evolved out of the former theory, which was a representation of the realities of the small-scale societies of the later Vedic age that came to be modified later in order to keep the continuity of tradition and suit the material realities of the expanding post-Vedic society. It is the Brahmanical perspective which leads to such assertions that the idea of *varṇa* lays more emphasis on function or 'duties' rather than on heredity and 'privileges of birth'.[35] The securing of the rights and privileges of the brāhmaṇa and kṣatriya lineages on a hereditary basis was no less a motivating factor for the birth of *varṇa* stratification than any notion of functional divisions among the Vedic peoples. In early Buddhist literature the hereditary basis of *varṇa* is taken for granted, although the Buddha tries to refute it. In the *Saṃyukta Nikāya* (I.98f), King Pasenadi, a contemporary of the Buddha, remarks that he would not hesitate to employ in his army a youth from any *varṇa* if he 'was trained and skilled, expert and practised, drilled and bold of steady nerve and undismayed and incapable of cowardly flight'.[36] The statement would make no sense if *varṇas* at the time were not based on birth. Dumont's argument, that it was because of the emphasis on social function in the *varṇa* scheme, and not heredity, that the Rajputs and dynasties of different origins unconnected with the ancient kṣatriyas could claim kṣatriya status,[37] ignores the fact that the ascription of kṣatriya status to rulers of 'low' or unknown origins was itself dependent upon their achieving putative hereditary links with the older kṣatriya dynasties through invented genealogies; and those who did not seek such validation continued as members of the lower *varṇas*, such as the vaiśya king Harṣavardhana of Kanauj and the Reḍḍi kings of Āndhra, who proudly proclaimed their śūdra status.

In the early stages of the *varṇa* stratification, both hypergamy and endogamy were practised. However, in a patriarchal society where wife-givers are deemed to be of lower status than wife-takers, the trend is towards endogamy. This was particularly so in fluid situations of changing power relations when new tribal groups were brought within the vortex of the *varṇa* system, which played an important role in facilitating the processes of state formation and the stabilization of a class society. Kosambi writes that the fusion of tribal elements into a general society lies at the very foundation of caste, 'the great basic fact of ancient Indian history'.[38] While there is no doubt that the proliferation of śūdra castes was largely due to such assimilation, this cannot be regarded as the reason for the emergence of the caste system. As Hutton observes,[39] when primitive tribes come within the Hindu fold they form outcastes or depressed castes, which, we may add, is a consequence of the deprivation of their earlier means of production, as they encounter the more advanced socio-economic and political system of the *varṇa* society and become dependent on it. But this cannot be regarded as the foundation of the caste system; status gradation, occupational division and endogamy-cum-hypergamy were already features of the *varṇa* system from later Vedic times. Kosambi regards *varṇas* as castes and tries to explain their evolution into endogamous units by suggesting that the Aryan ruling (kṣatriya) class adopted the 'ritually superior priesthood of the Indus culture',[40] which, recombining with the Aryan priesthood, gave rise to the brāhmaṇa caste, carrying over pre-Aryan *gotra* organization of exogamy. This was also at the root of 'the separation of the Brahmin in function and discipline from the kṣatriya and setting of both above the householder vaishya, after the *dāsas* had been conquered . . . for otherwise there is no reason for demarcation into endogamous castes'.[41] Kosambi is right in ascribing a catalytic role to the availability of *dāsa* labour in the acceleration of *varṇa* formation. But it should be noted – leaving aside the doubtful thesis of Aryan–Harappan confrontation – endogamy does not demarcate the Aryan and the non-Aryan priests who combine to form one caste; rather, it separates the brāhmaṇa, kṣatriya and vaiśya who had been members of the same tribe. Endogamy is clearly indicated in such later Vedic texts which assert that a brāhmaṇa is born of a brāhmaṇa, and a *rājanya* from a *rājanya*, and a vaiśya from a vaiśya.[42]

There is strength in the argument that the endogamous brāhmaṇa caste was formed by the assimilation of the Aryan with the non-Aryan, whether or not they were survivors from the Harappa culture. Madhav M. Deshpande[43] cites Patañjali's *Mahābhāṣya* (on Pāṇini, II.2.6), which says that no dark person ('of the colour of the heap of Urad lentils') sitting in the marketplace would normally be identified as a brāhmaṇa; and a brāhmaṇa is expected to be 'fair' (*gaura*), of clean conduct and tawny-haired (*piṅgalakeśa*). It is true that complexion is not race, though it is often taken to be a sign of race. Nevertheless, as against this passage, Kosambi quotes the *Bṛhadāraṇyaka Upaniṣad* (VI.4.16), which prescribes a certain type of diet to be taken by those brāhmaṇa parents who desire to have a black (*śyāma*) complexioned son with red eyes and have the ability to recite the three Vedas.[44] The text also contains prescriptions for having a daughter or a son of fairer complexion, and suggests that there was an uninhibited blending of Aryan and non-Aryan elements in the formation of the brāhmaṇa caste. Such assimilation has taken place in later times too. The fragmentation of brāhmaṇa *varṇa* into a number of endogamous subcastes is a development that took place in early medieval times in a different socio-economic and political set-up.[45]

The emergence of a large, ritually superior caste of brāhmaṇas in later Vedic times was mainly due to their control over Vedic sacrifices, which had by then become a highly specialized affair and required the services of a large number of ritual specialists, particularly for the performance of the *sattra* and *soma* sacrifices, such as the *rājasūya* and the *aśvamedha*. The role of Vedic ritual and Brahmanical ideology in legitimizing the aggrandizement of the kṣatriya chief over his own *rājanya* kinsmen as well as over the common tribesmen or the *viś* is openly proclaimed in later Vedic texts, which emphasize the interdependence of the priestly class and the ruling groups, and their combining against the vaiśya and śūdra producers. The brāhmaṇas even claimed to be the *bhūdevas*, or gods on earth, with such magical powers at their command that a priest, if so desired, could even ruin his patron – for whom he was officiating – by deliberately committing an error in the performance of the sacrifice.[46] Such exaggerated claims did not go unchallenged and although the Upaniṣads are mainly the works of brāhmaṇa thinkers, and, on the whole, propagate *varṇa* hierarchy and Brahmanical values, the kṣatriyas were seen as challenging their supremacy in the field of knowledge and the brāhmaṇas seeking instructions from them.[47] But the real challenge to their supremacy and hierarchical position was articulated in the early texts of Jainism and Buddhism, which not only rejected the cult of sacrifices but also gave precedence to kṣatriya *varṇa* while enumerating the *varṇa* orders.[48]

Several factors contributed to the strengthening of the *varṇa* stratification and pre-eminent position of the brāhmaṇas. The shift from Vedic ritualism to Puranic religion, which meant an appropriation of popular cults and heroic legends, such as those of Vāsudeva–Kṛṣṇa[49] and Rāma Dāśarathi, and making them the vehicles for propagation of Brahmanical ideology through the remodelling of the *Bhārata* epic and the composition of numerous Purāṇas and similar texts, provided an effective ideological tool for the perpetuation of the *varṇa*–caste system. No less significant was the part played by the brāhmaṇas in early medieval polity. The collaboration of the brāhmaṇa and the kṣatriya that exists in the later Vedic age continued in early medieval times, not only ideologically but also functionally, in the administrative and political set-up of various regional kingdoms, particularly those ruled by the 'improvised kṣatriyas' in an erstwhile tribal region where Brahmanical expertise was needed not only for fabricating genealogical myths but also for providing the details of administration. Attention has been drawn[50] to the Śāsana brāhmaṇas of Orissa, who were not only experts entrusted with the performance of foundational sacrifices of the great temples and other ritual matters, but were also entrusted with specific administrative functions such as supervising revenue administration, and helping in the defence and expansion of the kingdom in the name of Lord Jagannātha whose earthly representative was the king. Some of the brāhmaṇa clans belonging to the *Atharvaveda* school were responsible for the police and spy network, activities considered somewhat 'polluting'. That this was a pan-Indian phenomenon is clearly brought out by an inscription from Karnataka issued by king Mādhavavarman II of the Talakad branch. It records the gift of five villages and a tenth share of taxes of Kirumundaniri *nagara* to twenty-two brāhmaṇa families, described as follows:

Versed in the six duties, the study of the Vedas and employed within the palace enclosure (*prasāda prākāra baddhodyogāṇām*), they were adept in counsel and the determination of usage to be followed; acted as envoys; advised on making alliance and wars; determined with whom to ally and when to keep quiet after proclaiming war (*vigrahyāśana*) and how to march forth to battle in combination with others and how to attack the enemy in the rear. They were equally skilled in the protection of the kingdom (*maṇḍala*), in wielding the implements of war, in the construction of fortresses; in governing rural (*janapada*) and urban (*paura*) areas and in managing the treasury (*kośa*). They were lords over men, protectors of the brahmanical social order (*varṇāśramadharma*), chief and lords over the Maṇigrāma Śreṇis and the citizens of the four subordinate districts (*catuḥ sāmanta deśa*) of Tegure, Amaniya, Nandyala and Simbala. Adept in sacrifices to the gods and the manes, they were deeply versed in the *Ṛg* and *Yajur Vedas* and in uttering the words purified by sacred formulae. They engaged in congregational services and were lords over the merchants of the Tuviyal group.[51]

Thus there is no doubt that the practice of making land grants to brāhmaṇas in the tribal areas and the establishment of brāhmaṇa settlements – known as *agrahāras* – served multiple purposes: extending the area under cultivation, creating a class of loyal intermediaries, and restructuring the tribal population into castes with division of labour suited to petty production in a natural economy. The system was so useful to the ruling classes that whether they were inside it or outside it,[52] whether they were ascribed the status of 'kṣatriya' or 'śūdra',[53] they supported the *varṇa-dharma* and the Brahmanical institutions enthusiastically.

The spread of Brahmanical culture in the tribal areas was not always through the agency of brāhmaṇa migrants. K. Suresh Singh has drawn our attention to the movement of the 'non-tribal communities' and the 'functional castes', that is, the agricultural and artisan communities, into tribal regions and the penetration of cultural influences through them. Comparing the nomenclature and the nature of tools and implements used by the tribal and non-tribal peasants and artisans in Bihar and central India, he asserts that 'the diffusion of technology is more a function of tribe and peasant interaction and tribe and artisan interaction rather than a Brahmin–tribe contact'.[54] The chiefs of the tribal kingdoms of middle India, such as the Cheros, the Nagabanshis and the Gonds, invited the non-tribal peasantry and artisans from the plains to settle and cultivate tribal lands and generate surplus with their superior agricultural technology, and thus 'spared their own tribal people the strains of surplus production'. Apparently, the process was linked to the rise of states in the tribal areas with dominant lineages benefiting from such arrangements. It is well known that many of these chiefs forged links with established kṣatriya families and claimed kṣatriya status. But the effect of such migrations on the lower-ranking tribal segments needs to be explored further.[55]

However, the spread of *varṇa* ideology to different regions in divergent circumstances modified the orthodox model of the notion of *varṇa* categories formulated in the later Vedic texts, and gave rise to the division of the śūdra *varṇa* into *sat* (pure) and *asat* (impure) śūdras, as well as a change in the signification of the vaiśya category – issues that I have discussed in detail elsewhere.[56] In the later Vedic times, the third *varṇa*, vaiśya, was almost synonymous with peasantry, but it came to denote almost exclusively the merchant communities from the early centuries preceding the Common Era. This development is related to the depression of the peasantry and the widening gulf between those who were actual producers engaged in manual labour, and those who were able to extract surplus through various means and constituted the ruling aristocracy and ritual specialists. The hunting and food-gathering tribes, living on the margins of the agrarian society and dubbed as *hīna* (low) *jātis* in the early Buddhist sources, were condemned as 'impure' śūdras, for the orthodoxy regarded the *varṇa* categories as a god-created universal order in reference to which the existence of all communities had to be explained. This led to the invention of the theory of *varṇa-saṃkara*. The concept of a fifth (*pañcama*) *varṇa* did not find much favour, so a shift of emphasis took place from the hierarchy of functions to a hierarchy based on the notion of pure/impure birth. I have argued that it was not the pursuit of 'impure' occupations which led to the relegation of certain communities to 'impure' or 'untouchable' status.[57] Just the opposite. Those who were depressed and marginalized were condemned to carry out what were considered impure tasks. The exploitative nature of the whole system does not really need much elucidation.

Could such a system of exploitation endure merely on its ideological strength, without being buttressed by political power? Kosambi has indicated the way religious beliefs were used to minimize violence in its maintenance, but he adds that ultimately class structure is maintained by force and caste was class at the primitive level of production. However, the underpinning of force is undisguised in the Dharmaśāstra literature and the claims made by the kings in their inscriptions. It is repeatedly enjoined in Brahmanical 'law books' that the maintenance of *varṇa-dharma* is the sacred duty of the king; and a number of early medieval kings proclaimed themselves as defenders of the *varṇa* order, ruling in accordance with the laws of Manu. In case of dispute or confusion they were called upon to regulate or systematize the caste hierarchy,[58] and could even change the caste of a group or person, which would amount to severe punishment.[59] In the Brahmanical theory of the origin of kingship, the office of the king was created specifically for the upholding of the *varṇa* system[60] and this task was performed in many kingdoms through the office of the *dharmādhikārī*. The crucial role of the state in the construction of caste structure has been convincingly indicated in a number of competent studies of the medieval period.[61] In view of all this, it is difficult to agree with Dumont that in India power became 'secular' at a very early date, and that there was a complete disjunction between power and status. In fact, by acknowledging that in contemporary India the 'royal function' is being reproduced by the dominant castes in rural areas, Dumont concedes, in a way, that it is not ritual status but power and dominance that are decisive in the perpetuation of the system.[62]

With the changeover in the character of the ruling class from a hereditary dynastic nobility to a democratically elected elite, the earlier tendency of fission or fragmentation of castes for the sake of mobility has been replaced now by a movement towards forming broader coalitions and even amalgamation of castes, standing at the same level of ranking and socio-economic development within the region and sometimes even across the regions – a process facilitated by the awareness created by Census Reports. This is apparently because of the realization that in a democratic set-up, access to power and political opportunities is to be gained through mobilization of greater numbers of people, for which caste solidarities provide a readymade platform. Sociologists have noted that the endogamous boundaries between the subcastes are not so rigid now,[63] but this cannot be interpreted as a loosening of the caste system, for endogamy persists at the broader caste level. Caste is no longer tied to occupation and notions of hierarchy are visibly undermined, at least in the urban populace. Hence, whereas Dumont speaks of its 'substantialization', D.L. Sheth speaks of its 'secularization' in a different, 'newly emergent system of social stratification', surviving as a 'kinship based cultural community' whose members 'negotiate and own larger and multiple local and political identities'.[64]

But can it be said that 'caste has ceased to "reproduce" itself as it had in the past'?[65] Perhaps not with all the features that characterized it in the pre-colonial period, but the process of its reproduction continues unabated primarily for two reasons. There is still a broad congruence between caste and class, particularly in rural India. It has been pointed out that the pre-colonial structure of domination in the countryside has changed and a new, much broader class of prosperous farmers has emerged, which maintains its dominance through a mix of financial power and caste solidarity.[66] One may add that the oppressed subaltern castes too have acquired a new sense of awareness, benefiting to some extent from the state policy of affirmative action and the modern politico-economic system. So, caste conflicts have increased and have added to the intensification of caste solidarity. Associated with this phenomenon is the deployment of caste in electoral politics through which caste is reinventing its relations with the state.

The other and perhaps the most potent reason for the survival of caste is the practice of endogamy through which it reproduces itself. It is important that one should not confuse caste endogamy as a residue of tribal identities, related to the incomplete fusion of tribes in the Brahmanical *varṇa* order. Caste endogamy is a gendered device which had its origin in the desire of the upper *varṇas* to perpetuate and monopolize their class privileges on a hereditary basis, and it demarcated at its inception not tribes but the newly emerging classes of Brahmanical society. It is for this reason that the higher castes in general did not have caste assemblies or caste panchayats of the kind found functioning among the lower-ranking castes, which seem to have a guild or tribal origin. Caste exploitation has three dimensions: religious, politico–economic and gender. In my opinion, only those aspects of the system which are in conflict with the capitalist mode of production and democratic polity are being modified or eliminated. Traditions of long standing may originate in a specific material milieu, but once they have gripped the masses their hegemony is not easily subverted, unless they become totally untenable in the new social formation. But, as noted earlier, the custom of arranged marriages on which endogamy survives is quite in harmony with the values of a capitalist society and patriarchal mentalities, which have a long history. Unless a strong movement takes place to emancipate Indian women from patriarchal control, the transition from caste to class will remain elusive and caste ideology will continue to impede the unity of the exploited classes. Ambedkar had remarked: 'caste system is not merely division of labour. It is also a division of labourers.'[67] The principle enforcing the division of labour on a hereditary basis has been abolished by the Indian constitution; but the division of labourers continues as caste, basically being a system of exploitation, has been able to adjust itself in the new social formation.

Notes

[1] For example, Justice Markandey Katju, 'Looking Back on the Caste System', p. 8; Shrirama, 'Untouchability and Stratification in Indian Civilisation'.

[2] Nancy Leys Stepan, '"Science" and Race'.

[3] R.S. Sharma, 'Historiography of the Ancient Indian Social Order'; Romila Thapar, 'The Historiography of the Concept of Aryan'; Ronald Inden, *Imagining India*, pp. 56ff.

[4] *Ṛgveda*, III.34.9.

[5] *Ṛgveda*, II.12.4. The verse has been misinterpreted to argue that the Ārya and Dāsa already constituted categories of a hierarchical, stratified society. But for its correct interpretation, see Suvira Jaiswal, *Caste*, p. 178 note 105. For a close approximation and occasional identification of the Dāsas and Dasyus, see ibid., pp. 144–46, 177 note 91.

[6] Ibid., pp. 132–204; P.V. Kane, *History of Dharmaśāstra*, vol. II, part I, pp. 54–55; Madhav M. Deshpande, 'Aryan Origins'; Madhav M. Deshpande, 'Vedic Aryans, Non-Vedic Aryans, and Non-Aryans'; Suvira Jaiswal, 'Reconstructing History from the Ṛgveda' (reprinted below as an Appendix to this chapter).

[7] Madhav M. Deshpande, 'Aryan Origins', p. 99; Irfan Habib, *The Indus Civilization*, pp. 97–98.

[8] Asko Parpola, 'The Coming of the Aryans to Iran and India and the Cultural and Ethnic Identity of the Dāsas', p. 123. A.L. Basham (*The Wonder that Was India*, p. 29) points out that *Eire*, the name of the most westerly land reached by Indo–European peoples in ancient times, is a cognate of Ārya.

[9] Romila Thapar, *From Lineage to State*, pp. 43ff.; Romila Thapar, 'The Historiography of the Concept of "Aryan"', pp. 1–40.

[10] Jonathan Mark Kenoyer, 'Cultures and Societies in the Indus Tradition'.

[11] Suvira Jaiswal, *Caste*, pp. 132–204; also see chapter 5 below.

[12] For a critique of Risley's views, see Thomas R. Trautmann, *Aryans and British India*, pp. 198–204.

[13] *Ṛgveda*, VIII.35.16–18, X.90.12.

[14] *Mahābhārata*, XII.188.9, 10. V.S. Apte, *Sanskrit–English Dictionary, s.v. varṇa.*

[15] Thomas R. Trautmann, *Aryans and British India*, pp. 206–11.

[16] First edition, 1958. References are to the second revised edition, 1980.

[17] Ibid., pp. 33, 314ff. However, the *Taittirīya Brāhmaṇa* describes the śūdras as born of Asuras. See chapter 2 below.

[18] *Kauṭilīya Arthaśāstra*, III.13.1.

[19] *Manusmṛti*, X.45, quoted in Madhav M. Deshpande, 'Vedic Aryans, Non-Vedic Aryans and Non-Aryans', p. 78. In the Dharmaśāstra literature, Ārya is used in linguistic, ethnic, moral and territorial contexts too. Madhav M. Deshpande, 'Aryan Origins', pp. 102–03.

[20] See chapter 2 below.

[21] Suvira Jaiswal, *Caste*, pp. 146–54.

[22] *Ṛgveda*, VIII.31 mentions that any pious worshipper, the institutor of sacrifice (*yajamāna*) and not the professional priest, is *brahman*, and pleases Indra by performing worship, sacrificing, pouring libation and preparing the (sacrificial) meal. For further references, see Suvira Jaiswal, *Caste*, chapter 3.

[23] For example, Devāpi and Śantanu, Devaśravas and Devavāta, and Sumitra and Divodāsa. The elder brother functions as the priest and the younger acts as the tribal chief. In the *Viṣṇu Purāṇa* (IV.2.10), the Angirasas, one of the ancient brāhmaṇa clans, are said to have been born from a descendant of the kṣatriya ruler Nābhāga. Hence, it is said that the Angirasas are known as *kṣatropetā dvijāti*, brāhmaṇas possessed of *kṣatra. Viṣṇu Purāṇa* (Gita Press edition), p. 285.

[24] For example, Kavaṣa, son of Ilūṣa and Mahīdāsa, son of Itarā. The latter is said to be the author of the *Aitareya Brāhmaṇa.*

[25] The Dāsa chief Balbūtha Taruṣka gifted a hundred (cattle and horses) to the *vipra* (brāhmaṇa) Vasa Aśvya, the composer of *Ṛgveda*, VIII.46. Kosambi suggests that the famous king Divodāsa seems to have been a Dāsa adopted into the Aryan fold. D.D. Kosambi, *An Introduction to the Study of Indian History* (second edition), p. 94. If so, he must have been an adversary of Śambara and had joined the Aryans. Several hymns praise Indra for protecting Divodāsa from Śambara, killing the latter and bestowing his wealth on the former. *Ṛgveda*, I.51.6, 112.14, 130.7; IV.26.3; VI.26.5, 43.1. *Ṛgveda*, I.53.10 states that Indra made Atithigva (another name of Divodāsa) subordinate to king Suśravas.

[26] D.D. Kosambi, 'Indo–Aryan Nose Index', p. 533.

[27] Hyla Shuntz Converse, 'The Agnicayana Rite'; D.D. Kosambi, *An Introduction to the Study of Indian History* (second edition), pp. 86, 94ff.; infra, pp. 35–36.

[28] R.S. Sharma, *Material Culture and Social Formations in Ancient India*, chapters 2–5; D.D. Kosambi, *An Introduction to the Study of Indian History* (second edition), pp. 97–144.

[29] It is interesting that despite making a clear distinction between *varṇa* and *jāti*, Dumont remarks that the touchstone of a theory must always be 'what the people themselves think and believe'. Louis Dumont, *Homo Hierarchicus*, p. 37.

[30] Célestin Bouglé, *Essays on the Caste System*.

[31] Suvira Jaiswal, 'Caste in the Socio-Economic Framework of Early India', pp. 23–48.

[32] Louis Dumont, *Homo Hierarchicus*, p. 115.

[33] Ibid., p. 228.

[34] Ibid., p. 33.

[35] Kane writes, 'The ideal of varṇa even in the smṛtis lays far more emphasis on duties, on a high standard of effort for the community or society rather than on the rights and privileges of birth. The system of jātis (castes) lays all emphasis on birth and heredity.' P.V. Kane, *History of Dharmaśāstra*, vol. II, part I, p. 54. Apparently, Dumont is influenced by such views. But, Kane admits, by the time of the composition of the Brāhmaṇa texts, brāhmaṇas, kṣatriyas and vaiśyas had became separate groups 'more or less dependent on birth', and the brāhmaṇa had come to be regarded as superior to the kṣatriya by virtue of birth (ibid., p. 48).

In this connection, one may also note that the oft-quoted *Bhagavadgītā*, IV.13, which states that God created the four *varṇas* in accordance with their qualities (*guṇa*) and actions (*karma*), is cited to prove that the *varṇas* were originally functional depending on merit and not heredity. But *Bhagavadgītā*, XVIII.41 makes it clear that the *guṇas* of respective *varṇas* are natural and inborn (*svabhāvaprabhavairguṇaiḥ*), that is, hereditary, and hence they have been assigned different functions. Also see Suvira Jaiswal, 'Caste: Ideology and Context'.

[36] Quoted by Sarva Daman Singh, *Ancient Indian Warfare with Special Reference to the Vedic Period*, p. 16.

[37] Louis Dumont, *Homo Hierarchicus*, p. 74. Irfan Habib (*Essays in Indian History*, p. 167) points out that 'the one segment of caste structure most vulnerable to change was that of the ruling and warrior class. . . . Thus where the caste system should have been strongest, in actual terms, it was the weakest – namely the stability of the ruling community.' I would like to add that this was in fact the revitalizing feature of the system; it could accommodate changes in the contemporary power structure without affecting its fundamentals.

[38] D.D. Kosambi, *An Introduction to the Study of Indian History* (second edition), p. 27.

[39] J.H. Hutton, *Caste in India*, p. 171. He attributes this to the Hindu prejudice against the occupations and food of these aboriginal tribes, but adds that 'the socially superior individuals of these identical tribes are very frequently able to get themselves incorporated into the Hindu system as Rajputs or kṣatriyas, though their fellow-tribesmen may remain exterior.'

[40] D.D. Kosambi, *An Introduction to the Study of Indian History* (second edition), p. 102.

[41] D.D. Kosambi, 'Origin of Brahmin Gotras', p. 50. Compare this with Romila Thapar (*From Lineage to State*, p. 53), who argues that the brāhmaṇa and the śūdra were addenda to the lineage of the Aryan tribes.

[42] *Śatapatha Brāhmaṇa*, XIV.4.2.37.

[43] Madhav M. Deshpande, 'Aryan Origins', p. 103.

[44] D.D. Kosambi, *An Introduction to the Study of Indian History* (second edition), pp. 134–35. In the *Ṛgveda*, I.117.8, the gods, Aśvins, are described as presenting fair-skinned (*ruśatim*) women to the dark-coloured (*śyavāya*) sage Kaṇva.

[45] On the formation of 'subcastes' among the brāhmaṇas, see Suvira Jaiswal, *Caste*, pp. 57–66.

[46] V.M. Apte, 'Religion and Philosophy', p. 447. The exaggerated claims of the brāhmaṇas in the ritualistic Brāhmaṇa texts appear so 'filthy and repulsive' to B.K. Ghosh that he finds them to be of interest only to students of abnormal psychology (B.K. Ghosh, 'Language and Literature', p. 422). Also see, Suvira Jaiswal, 'Change and Continuity in Brahmanical Religion with Particular Reference to Vaiṣṇava Bhakti', pp. 9–11.

[47] For example, king Pravāhaṇa Jaivali instructs the brāhmaṇa Gautama Āruṇi; *Chāndogya Upaniṣad*, V.3.7.

[48] Cf. the Buddhist theory of creation given in the *Aganna Suttanta* (The Book of Genesis) in the *Dīgha Nikāya*, cited in U.N. Ghoshal, *A History of Indian Political Ideas*, pp. 62–63.

[49] Suvira Jaiswal, *The Origin and Development of Vaiṣṇavism*.

[50] G. Pfeffer, in Anncharlott Eschmann, Hermann Kulke and Gaya Charan Tripathi, eds, *The Cult of Jagannath and the Regional Tradition of Orissa*, p. 426.

[51] Cited in Malini Adiga, *The Making of Southern Karnataka Society, Polity and Culture in the Early Medieval Period*, p. 107.

[52] Irfan Habib has convincingly argued that the caste system reduced the cost of peasant subsistence by securing cheap labour and artisanal products from the menial castes in conditions restricting mobility. This allowed the rulers to mop up the larger surplus from the peasantry. Hence, the criticism of Muslim rulers and intellectuals was directed against Hindu polytheism and idol worship, but did not extend to the inequities of the caste system despite its being alien to Islamic law. Irfan Habib, *Interpreting Indian History*, pp. 19–21.

[53] The Reḍḍi king Vema, born 'in the fourth caste which originated from the feet of Viṣṇu', proudly proclaims that he restored all the brāhmaṇa *agrahāras* which had been taken away by the *mleccha* kings. Madras Museum Plates of Vema, inscription no. 3.

[54] K. Suresh Singh, *Tribal Society in India*, chapter on 'Technology and Acculturation'. Singh even speaks of the reverse process of 'tribalization' of non-tribal caste communities in tribal areas. For a critique of this view, see Suvira Jaiswal, 'Tribe–Caste Interaction'.

[55] In an interesting article, 'The Bodos' (in Dev Nathan, ed., *From Tribe to Caste*, pp. 432–45), Sujit Chowdhury demonstrates that the 'Hinduized' dynasties of Kāmarūpa, the Bhauma–Naraka, the Śālastambha and the Pālas, ruling the Brahmaputra valley roughly from the tenth to the twelfth century CE, seem to have been of tribal origin, and they made liberal land grants to brāhmaṇas as were being made by other royal houses of early medieval India. However, in Kāmarūpa the donated lands were located in settled riverine tracts which had been in the possession of Bodo tribals, so they were displaced and pushed to submontane and low hilly regions as they did not take to, or were 'excluded' from, plough agriculture. But the brāhmaṇa donees could not cultivate the land themselves, which led to the immigration of Kaivartas and perhaps also Kālitas, who constituted the peasantry (apparently dubbed as śūdra castes), and some artisanal castes from the neighbouring regions. The details of tribe–caste interaction and its consequences must vary in different regions depending upon the structural adjustments made in accordance with the production process.

[56] Suvira Jaiswal, 'Caste in the Socio-Economic Framework of Early India', pp. 33–48, 70–88; also see chapter 2 below.

[57] Ibid., for the Chamar caste. The Caṇḍālas are described as fallen kṣatriyas in the *Mahābhārata* and were initially a fierce aboriginal tribe. So were the Mātaṅgas, the present-day Mangs and the Doms. Suvira Jaiswal, *Caste*, p. 88. Przyluski identified the Doms with the Odumbaras; cited in J.H. Hutton, *Caste in India*, p. 30.

[58] In the seventeenth century, Narasimha III, the Raja of Khurda, regulated the hierarchical differentiation among the brāhmaṇa subcastes. Hermann Kulke, in Anncharlott Eschmann, Hermann Kulke and Gaya Charan Tripathi, eds, *The Cult of Jagannāth and the Regional Tradition of Orissa*, p. 332. Tradition credits king Ballālasena for systematizing the caste hierarchy in Bengal.

[59] For the order of a Tughlaq king dated 1414 CE relegating a group of kṣatriyas to the goldsmith caste, see R.K. Chaube, *Proceedings of the Indian History Congress*, 1938, pp. 147–48. F.A. Marglin (*Wives of the God–King*, p. 149) mentions several such cases.

[60] *Mahābhārata*, XII.59.114. In the *Manusmṛti* (VIII.148), the king is asked to use force to compel the vaiśyas and the śūdras to perform their respective tasks.

[61] Hiroshi Fukazawa, *The Medieval Deccan*; Nicholas B. Dirks, *The Hollow Crown*; Uma Chakravarti, *Rewriting History*.

[62] Louis Dumont, *Homo Hierarchicus*, p. 367.

[63] Ibid., p. 222.

[64] D.L. Sheth, 'Caste and the Secularization Process in India'.
[65] Ibid., p. 257.
[66] David Hardiman, *Histories for the Subordinated*, p. 16.
[67] Ambedkar, *Annihilation of Caste*, p. 47.

Appendix

Reconstructing History from the *Ṛgveda*: A Paradigm Shift?*

In 1981 H.D. Sankalia regretted the fact that the 'pastoral nature of the early Vedic civilization has been so much dinned into our ears during the last hundred years or more' that scholars have refused to consider the possibility of looking at the Harappa culture 'from the Vedic point of view'.[1] R.N. Nandi and V.K. Thakur do not think that the Harappan culture synchronized with that of the Ṛgvedic Aryans; nevertheless, they seriously question the pastoral nature of the Ṛgvedic society. In a recent publication edited by Irfan Habib and V.K. Thakur, it is categorically stated that there are numerous references in the *Ṛgveda* to agriculture; and contrary to a widespread characterization, the Ṛgvedic society was 'not essentially pastoral. Rather, the pastoral sector was important because of the requirements of agriculture.' The large herds of cattle constituted 'a means by which surplus extracted out of agriculture was stored'.[2] Whereas V.K. Thakur is convinced of the centrality of agrarian activities in Ṛgvedic economy,[3] R.N. Nandi is more circumspect.[4] He begins by referring to 'the diversity of the forms of life, the distinctions between the primitive and advanced stages of social development and transitions undergone by groups of Vedic speakers. Nevertheless, his main argument is that even the so-called early portions of the *Ṛgveda* – the family books – reflect a sedentary peasant society with a well-developed social differentiation between the non-kin-dependent labour force and 'owner-possessor householders', a view reiterated by Thakur *in toto*. As these assertions are made in opposition to the generally accepted view that Ṛgvedic tribes were mainly pastoral practising a little agriculture on the side, and have a critical bearing on the question of social stratification,[5] it is necessary to examine their validity and look into the text and context of the *Ṛgveda*.

Much has been written on the structure, organization and relative dates of Ṛgvedic hymns, and it is generally conceded that a wide gap separates the composition of individual hymns and their redaction into a *saṃhitā* for hieratical purposes. Even the redaction and collation was done in several stages, as the addition of the Vālakhilya hymns at the end of Book Eight shows. Moreover, the family books (i.e. Books II–VIII), although compiled earlier than Books I, IX

*Originally published in *Social Sciences Probings*, vol. 18, no. 2, December 2006, pp. 1–17.

and X and attributed to specific priestly families, contain hymns composed by several generations, both young (*nūtana, navya*) and old (*pūrva*),[6] which means that they may not present a static picture. It has been pointed out that the order of arrangement is not always indicative of the relative age of a hymn and that there are older hymns even in Book X, which is called the great appendix to the *Ṛgveda*. Hence, as Michael Witzel cautions, judgement must be exercised for every individual hymn.[7]

Nevertheless, it is clear that notwithstanding the time gap between the composition and redaction of the Ṛgvedic hymns, the text, even in its available form, still ante-dates the other *saṃhitās* and later Vedic literature by several centuries. Linguists regard the language of the *Ṛgveda* as the most archaic, a little different from the other Vedas and also from the form of Sanskrit out of which later classical Sanskrit developed.[8] Hence, extrapolation of evidence derived from later Vedic sources for reconstructing society in early Vedic times is not appropriate unless backed by other weighty considerations. The case for the pastoral economy of Ṛgvedic tribes is based on overwhelming internal evidence indicating a pastoral way of life, desire for cattle and pastures, etc., far in excess of references to agriculture and agrarian practices. This is not just an empty refrain of the Vedicists but is backed by solid studies[9] that cannot be dismissed simply as biased or inspired by a romanticized notion of nomadic pastoral Aryans. It is generally acknowledged that apart from cattle-breeding and food-gathering, hunting and limited agriculture contributed to the dietary requirements of the Ṛgvedic tribes. In arguing for a nomadic pastoral background of Ṛgvedic peoples, who gradually evolved into a peasant society after coming in contact with the speakers of non-Sanskrit languages, the evidence is mainly from philology, as it has been shown that most of the words related to agriculture in the *Ṛgveda* are loanwords borrowed from Austro–Asiatic and Dravidian (or a postulated proto-Elamo–Dravidian) languages whose presence at the Indo–Iranian borderlands before the influx of the speakers of Indo–Aryan is well attested by linguistic survivals in this region. The degree and nature of non-Aryan influences in the *Ṛgveda* need careful study, which are crucial for our understanding of the processes of transition affecting the Ṛgvedic peoples. And I agree with M.M. Deshpande's view[10] that the authors of the *Ṛgveda* are largely Aryan, in linguistic, ethnic and cultural terms, mixed with a small number of 'Aryanized' non-Aryans.

R.N. Nandi and V.K. Thakur criticize D.D. Kosambi and R.S. Sharma for speaking of the nomadic and pastoral character of the Ṛgvedic people. But the writings of these scholars also underline the transition to sedentary agriculture in the later Ṛgvedic phase. Referring to the Indo–European parallels of the term *pastya*, Sharma argues that initially this word had the sense of a 'pasture' or 'stall' but later it came to mean a 'house'; hence in the *Ṛgveda* a householder is described as *pastyavant*.[11] Kosambi too speaks of new social and economic developments in the 'later Ṛgvedic stage', when a recombination of Aryans with the pre-Aryans or non-Aryans took place.[12] He stresses the need for the stratification of Ṛgvedic hymns on the basis of language alone, much of which, he points out, had become obscure and was misinterpreted by later commentators. The perspective of these scholars becomes evident from the way they have explained the change in the meaning of the word *grāma*, which, according to them, was initially a mobile kin group led by the *grāmaṇī* but later acquired the meaning of 'village' when such groups took to agriculture and constituted a settlement. In a hymn of the third *maṇḍala* of the *Ṛgveda*[13] (III.33.11–22), the *grāma* of the Bharatas desirous of kine is said to have crossed the river. Kosambi writes that there was always trouble when two *grāmas* even of the same tribe confronted each other, which led to the coinage of a new word, *saṅgrāma*, meaning 'battle' in Sanskrit.[14] However, *grāma* had already acquired the meaning of a village in the later Ṛgvedic phase and is contrasted from *araṇya*, i.e. forest, at several places.[15] Nor is it correct to hold[16] that this generalization is based on a single passage of the tenth *maṇḍala* (X.27.19), which speaks of the sighting of a *grāma* moving without wheels from a distance. *Ṛgveda*, II.12.7 praises Indra as having under his control horses, cattle, *grāmaḥ*, all the chariots, the Sun, the Dawn, and also as the One who leads the waters. All the things mentioned in this verse are characterized by movement; apparently the *grāma*, mentioned here in plural, also denoted mobile bands of people who may or may not have been kin-related. As R.S. Sharma points out,[17] people of different stocks too could have come together to earn subsistence through hunting and other collective economic activities. At another place in Book I (I.100.10), Indra is said to have obtained treasures with the help of *grāmas* (*grāmebhiḥ*) and chariots, defeating those who hated him. Here too the interpretation of *grāma* as a warrior-band would be more suitable than as a village settlement. References indicating the evolution of the meaning of the term *grāma* from a 'horde of migrating cattle-breeders' or a 'band of warriors' to a settled village community have been analysed by Wilhelm Rau in his oft-quoted work,[18] published in 1956. The *Ṛgveda* provides much evidence for the entire process.

In his anxiety to prove the existence of a highly stratified society in the *Ṛgveda* with rich landowning householders having their fields cultivated by non-kin servile 'servitors', Nandi translates[19] '*nṛ*' as a 'servitor' and '*narāḥ*' as 'workpeople' or labourers. None of the Vedicists, to my knowledge, have given this meaning to the word. In this regard, in *Ṛgveda*, I.22.11–12, the goddesses Indrāṇī, Varuṇānī and Āgneyī are described as *nṛpatnīḥ*, the wives of *narāḥ*. Does it mean that they are being described as wives of servitors? In the preceding verse, Agni is exhorted to bring the spouses of gods. Obviously the correct translation of *nṛpatnīḥ* is 'wives of heroes'. *Nṛ*, like the word *vīra*, means 'man' or 'hero'.[20] Hence, in *Ṛgveda*, I.8.6, Indra is described as granting sons to the *naras* who come to the battlefield, just as he grants holy thoughts to the singers (*viprasāḥ*). The description of the tribal chief as *nṛpati*, 'lord of the people', confirms this.[21]

Similarly, Nandi translates[22] the word *prajā* as 'labourers' or 'workpeople', for which there is no justification. Derived from *prajan* in the *Ṛgveda*, the word signifies 'progeny', 'offspring', 'descendants', 'people' or 'creatures'. Later, with the emergence of the state, it also comes to mean 'subjects', but this is not applicable to Ṛgvedic passages. In *Ṛgveda*, II.3.9, the composer prays to Tvaṣṭā that he may 'give us *prajā* and thus increase our kindred' (*prajāṃ-tvaṣṭā-vi-syatu-nābhiṃ-asme*). Nandi himself is not consistent and translates *prajā* as 'kinsfolk' and *nṛ* as 'a group of servitors' in *Ṛgveda*, I.92.7, citing it as an example of a passage distinguishing between kinsmen (*prajā*) and servile non-kin (*nṛ*).[23] The arbitrary nature of such interpretations is obvious.

The most glaring example of a fanciful interpretation put forward by Nandi is provided by his explanation of *Ṛgveda*, II.13.4. According to him,[24] this 'refers to the people setting alignments of cultivated fields (*asinvan*) as managing the food (*bhojanam*) offered by the masters (*pituratti*) with their teeth (*daṃṣṭraiḥ*)'. Nandi does not explain how the term *asinvan* can be interpreted as 'setting alignment of cultivated fields'. It is a formation from the adjective *asinva*, meaning 'insatiable'.[25] In *Ṛgveda*, X.89.12, Indra's weapon is described as *asinva* and elsewhere *asinvam* stands for the demon Vṛtra (V.32.8). Perhaps Nandi has relied on the commentary of Sāyaṇācārya who glosses *asinvan* in this verse as *setubandhādikaṃ karmakurvanlokaḥ*. But neither the context nor the wording justifies this explanation, and Griffith is right in suggesting that it refers to the fire god Agni, who is described as consuming greedily the offerings made to him. It may be noted that the terms *asinvan* and *atti* (eats) are in the singular. It will be logical to infer that the verse in question speaks of the distribution of food among the people (*prajābhyaḥ*) after it has been offered to the god Agni, the Insatiable One, who devours it with his teeth. This kind of imagery relating to Agni is found at several other places: Agni Jātavedas having metal teeth (apparently copper, *ayodanṣṭro*) is invoked to burn down the evil spirits (*yātudhānān*) with his flame (*Ṛgveda*, X.87.2–3). He has both upper and lower teeth and may attack the wicked ones with his jaws (*jambhaiḥ*). Agni has a resplendent row of teeth (*bhrajate śreṇidan*, X.20.3) and his white teeth (*dantam śukram*) are sharp like an axe (IV.6.8).

Moreover, if Nandi had examined the hymn in an unbiased manner, he would have noted that the preceding verse (*Ṛgveda*, II.13.3), although somewhat cryptic, seems to refer to the institution of sacrifice. It says, 'one recites (*eko vadati*), the other gives (*yat-dadāti*), one shakes up the form (*rūpā minan*), another removes patiently (*vinudaḥ titikṣate*) the faults'. According to Sāyaṇa, the verse refers to the Hotā, Adhvaryu and Brahman priests, which seems plausible. The verse in question (*Ṛgveda*, II.13.4) may be interpreted as follows: they (the tribesmen) sit distributing the nourishing food (*puṣṭim*) among their progeny (*prajābhyaḥ*), the wealth ((*rayim*, which at this stage consists of food mainly) which is greater or more than the back can carry (*prabhavantaṃ*).[26] The Insatiable One comes (*āyate asinvan*) and with his teeth devours or eats (*atti*) the food offered by the leader or the chief (*pituḥ*).[27] The words *asinvan*, *atti* and *pituḥ* are in the singular, the first two referring to the fire god and the last one to the sacrificing chief. The verse ends with the refrain in praise of Indra. 'Thou [Indra] did these deeds first and hence are worthy of our praise.'

Nandi writes that the term *kṣetrapati*,[28] 'Lord of the Field' already occurs three times in Book IV of the *Ṛgveda*, and this is taken as a proof of the centrality of agricultural production.[29] What the reader is not informed of is the fact that all the three references to *kṣetrapati* are to be found in the same hymn (IV.57) composed in his honour. Hopkins regarded it as a late interpolation in Book IV, which itself, in his view, was later than the other family books.[30] More important, Oldenberg has made an exhaustive study of the hymns which violate the order of arrangement in the *Ṛgveda* and are thus clearly later insertions. According to him, verses 4–8 of IV.57, which mention the agricultural terms *lāṅgala*, *varatra*, *śunā*, *sīra* and *sītā*, were added later.[31] No doubt references to fertile fields captured from enemies, particularly the Dāsas and the Dasyus, and their distribution among Aryan tribesmen, and a few words related to agriculture are to be found in the family books,[32] and although such passages cannot be regarded as later additions, their number should not be inflated to give a distorted picture of the Ṛgvedic economy. Thakur refers to *Ṛgveda*, V.62.7 to prove the 'existence of bountiful *kṣetras*'.[33] But the verse does not refer to cultivated fields at all. The hymn is in praise of Mitra–Varuṇa, and the verse in question describes the chariot of the two gods as adorned with gold having columns made of *ayas* metal. 'May it be established on the field which is well oiled' (*bhadrekṣetre nimitā tilvile*). Sāyaṇa explains *kṣetra* here as the sacrificial ground which is well-oiled with clarified butter, *soma* juice, and the Vedicists generally accept this interpretation.

In fact, most of the references cited by Thakur are quite unreliable and have to be rechecked carefully for their meanings and contexts. He speaks of 'repeated references to the yoking of ox to the plough', but cites verses which refer to the yoking of the horse to the chariot.[34] *Astra* is not necessarily the 'ploughman's goad', as Thakur describes it. With the exception of the late IV.57 discussed above, it generally figures as a goad wielded by the god Pūṣan to drive cattle, goats, etc., and as such is associated with pastoral activities rather than the plough in the *Ṛgveda*.[35] Thakur writes that the fields 'were cultivated with the help of leather (*druti*) [*sic*] and wooden (*camasa*) pots'.[36] One could agree that *dṛti*, i.e. leather bags holding water and other fluids, may have been used for irrigating fields as well, but *camasa* was a kind of flat dish, cup or ladle, generally of a square shape, made of wood and furnished with a handle.[37] It was a vessel used at sacrifices for drinking *soma* and can hardly be taken to mean a pot used for irrigating fields.

One could go on pointing out such distortions and misinterpretations.[38] If a 'paradigm shift' is sought to be brought about in reconstructing the economy and society of Ṛgvedic tribes, more reliable and convincing arguments will have to be provided than produced by these scholars. It is unfortunate that a historian of the stature of Irfan Habib has also chosen to lend his weight to such a shift forcefully asserted in a work meant for general readers and students without fully examining various questions connected with the issue, and merely on the basis of some late Ṛgvedic passages and discovery of a ploughed field datable to eleventh century BCE at Aligama (Swat Valley). But the assumption that this piece of archaeological evidence has to be attributed to Indo–Aryans whose presence in this region is attested by the internal evidence of the *Ṛgveda*, does not take into account the fact that apart from the speakers of Indo–Aryan, there was also a strong substratum of non-Aryan speakers, Dravidian and Munda, in this region, from whom the Indo–Aryans picked up many words relating to agriculture and plant life. The non-Aryan contribution to the development of agriculture in North India may be well established through an analysis of the agricultural vocabulary.[39] As archaeological datum does not reveal the language of its creators, one will have to examine carefully the text of the *Ṛgveda* to match the linguistic and textual evidence with the archaeological, keeping in view the important fact that the *Ṛgveda* contains hymns composed around 1500 BCE (some may be even earlier) as well as late additions made in 1000–800 BCE. So it would be misleading to take a static view of the society and economy reflected in the text.

A number of Ṛgvedic myths refer to events which seem to have taken place in northern Bactria, even before the Indo–Aryans entered the Gāndhāra region. Such are the myths related to the battles against the Dāsas and Dasyus, and the destruction of their *purs* or 'forts'. Wilhelm Rau, through an analysis of the relevant Vedic passages, has shown that the Dāsa 'forts' were circular or had multiple concentric walls, quite unlike the rectangular layout of the Indus cities.[40] The Dāsa *purs* were not city structures under regular occupation, but temporary shelters for the protection of cattle. These were made of mudstone, a far cry from the brick buildings and citadels of the Harappans. Parpola locates the Dāsa, Dasyu and Paṇi peoples in northern Bactria, connecting them with the Bactria–Margiana Archaeological Complex datable to 1900–1700 BCE.[41] These people were defeated, killed or enslaved by the incoming Indo–Aryans whose god Indra earned the epithet of Purandara, destroyer of 'forts'. Parpola shows that etymologically, the ethnic names Dāsa, Dasyu and Paṇi are Indo–Iranian. Earlier, Bailey too had argued that in Old Iranian *daha* meant 'man', and he cited several examples of words meaning 'man' or 'hero' giving rise to ethnic names.[42] According to him, *dahyu* in Old Iranian meant 'land' or 'country'. The Indo–Aryan equivalents of *daha* and *dahyu* are *dāsa* and *dasyu*, the latter being the habitat of *daha/dāsa*, i.e. an enemy country. However, the Ṛgvedic poets often treat the two terms synonymously and '*dasyu*' as an enemy. '*Daha*' as an ethnic name figures in an inscription of Xerxes. 'Ptolemy's *Geography* locates this tribe in Margiana on the modern river Murghab and this is also mentioned by the historians of Alexander.'[43] Hence, it is difficult to accept the suggestion that these names were imposed by the speakers of Indo–Aryan, particularly in view of the fact that in the *Ṛgveda*, Dāsa was initially clearly an ethnic category and only later came to mean a slave, the change in meaning brought about by the defeat, capture and subordination of the majority of the Dāsa tribe.

According to Parpola, the Dāsas represented an earlier wave of Aryan immigrants who spoke an old Indo–Aryan dialect which was more archaic than the Ṛgvedic dialect, but which gave rise to classical Sanskrit. The Dāsas lived in close contact with the Harappans who spoke a Dravidian language, and hence their speech had words borrowed from the Dravidian; the Dravidian language structure had influenced their dialect. The Ṛgvedic Aryans scornfully spoke of the language of the Dāsas as *mṛdhra-vāc*, which, according to this view, does not mean 'unintelligible' but 'uncouth' or 'hostile'.[44] Parpola traces the occurrence of retroflexion and Dravidian loanwords in the *Ṛgveda* to the interaction of Ṛgvedic Aryans with the Dāsas who were eventually assimilated in the Vedic society.

Parpola's thesis and his identification of the Harappan script as Dravidian has not found general acceptance. But the recent discovery[45] of a Neolithic celt with four signs of the Harappan script at Ṣembian-Kandiyur village in Tamil Nadu proves, according to Iravatham Mahadevan, that the Neolithic peoples of Tamil Nadu shared the same language family with the Harappans, which could only be Dravidian. He dates the artefact, a polished hand-held axe, between 2000 BCE and 1500 BCE. The finding lends strong support to the identification of Harappans as speakers of a Dravidian language, but does not solve the problem of the nature and timing of interaction between Dravidian and Indo–Aryan speakers. Madhav M. Deshpande has forcefully argued that the retroflexes found in the available recension of the *Ṛgveda* are due to the changes that crept in because of the oral transmission of the text in the later centuries in the north-eastern regions of the subcontinent, and phonologically the text has not come down to us in its original form. However, this does not explain the presence of Dravidian loanwords in the text, even though they are only a few and their frequency increases in later texts. There seems to be a general consensus[46] that a proto-Dravidian or proto-Elamite Dravidian language was spoken in the Indo–Iranian borderlands and the Indus valley in prehistoric times, but there are indications that the Ṛgvedic peoples had also come in contact with the speakers of Munda, an Austro–Asiatic language.

Referring to the work of Küiper,[47] Witzel points out that almost all the words relating to agriculture in the *Ṛgveda* have non-Sanskritic origin, with very few of these (such as *yava* and *sītā*) traceable to Indo–European roots.[48] To explain the phenomenon of a large-scale borrowing of agricultural vocabulary from non-Indo–Aryan sources, he suggests that the Vedic tribes concentrated their energies on raising cattle, leaving the tedious work of cultivation to the local, non-Sanskrit-speaking population, and this kind of social interaction was built on relationships of dominance and subordination. The theory of Aryan invasion is discounted; and it is argued that the speakers of Indo–Aryan and Indo–Iranian dialects moved into South Asian regions in several waves. There are hardly any takers today of the theory propounded so forcefully by Mortimer Wheeler, that the horse-riding Aryan invaders had destroyed the urban Harappa culture. But the view that the chariot-riding pastoral Aryan tribes encountered and subjugated the indigenous agricultural population of the north-west cannot be wished away, as it rests on strong internal evidence of the *Ṛgveda*.

However, in an attempt to unfold the identity and motives of those who collected and arranged the hymns of the *Ṛgveda*, Witzel comes up with a highly speculative thesis that the *Ṛgveda*, above all, represents the history of two royal lineages, the Purus and the Bharatas, particularly from the middle Ṛgvedic period. The two dynasties are represented in the corpus roughly in equal proportions; and the text has acquired a unified appearance as most of the early material was recast in the Puru–Bharata mould.[49] He even goes to the extent of suggesting that the account of 'the battle of ten kings' was the prototype of the *Mahābhārata*.[50] However, I would like to point out that whereas the *Mahābhārata* had a heroic tale at its core and became a religious text, a *dharmagrantha*, through various accretions and later redactions,[51] the *Ṛgveda* was a hieratic text from the very beginning and it has retained this character throughout, the incorporation of a few *dāna-stuti* hymns celebrating generous patrons notwithstanding. This is not to deny that it contains allusions to certain historical events, lineages and personages, but its compositions were meant for ritual use even if in some cases that is now forgotten or the original ritual replaced by later inventions.[52] Hence, the text is more amenable to social and cultural probing than to questions pertaining to dynastic polity.

The earlier perception that the Aryan immigrants had led a semi-nomadic pastoral life[53] and made a transition to sedentary agriculture in the 'land of seven rivers' is now questioned,[54] on the grounds that although the Aryans raised cattle, goats and other animals, they also practised agriculture, which is inconsistent with nomadism; hence they may be described as pastoral but not nomadic. As we have seen, the adoption of agricultural activities increasingly through interaction with the indigenous non-Aryan population is reflected in the various layers of the Ṛgvedic text; yet the question arises, how does one explain traces of nomadism in certain Vedic passages which suggest that at least at some stage, nomadism was a way of life for some Aryans? In the *Atharvaveda* (IX.3.13–14)[55] we have a vivid picture of a moveable dwelling (*śālā*), which provided shelter not only to the household fire and members of the household, but also to cattle, horses and other animals. The *śālā* was fastened to the ground with fetters, and could be unfastened and carried with all its belongings to a different place. In verse 24 of the same hymn (IX.3.24) the poet specifically says, 'Like a bride (*vadhu*) O dwelling (*śālā*), we carry you wheresoever be our will.' The *Atharvaveda* is undoubtedly later than the *Ṛgveda*; nevertheless, it contains a few hymns which reflect an earlier way of life. The *śālāpati* of this hymn (V.12) was the master of a *śālā*, which could be shifted to another site, if necessary, for better pasturage, availability of water resources, etc. In the *Ṛgveda*, too, a hymn (VI.15.19) describes the entire household gear (*gārhapatyāni*) as *asthuri*, a cart driven by more than one horse. Evidently the Ṛgvedic *gṛhapati*[56] of this hymn, like the *śālāpati* of the Atharvavedic hymn, had a *gṛha*, which was a mobile unit.

However, two hymns of Book VII of the *Ṛgveda* (54 and 55) are dedicated to Vāstoṣpati – the tutelary deity of the homestead. One of these (55) is shown to have been a later addition.[57] It begins with an invocation to Vāstoṣpati but the remaining verses are addressed to the god Indra. Nonetheless, the hymn provides an interesting description of a homestead which housed not only the father and mother, but also kinsmen (*jñātayaḥ*) and the head of the clan or settlement (*viśpati*). The women of the kin unit are described as sleeping on the bench (*proṣtheśayā*), in the carriage (*vahyeśayā*) and on the bed (*talpaśīvarī*). That women could be sleeping inside the vehicle too does not support the assumption that *vāstu* here referred to a permanent residential building.[58] The *harmya* in this hymn (V.6) does not denote a mansion but domestic hearth or fireplace, an essential attribute of any abode, and Vāstoṣpati was invoked to bless any dwelling place at which the kin unit was residing at the time. He was requested to nourish the inmates, not only humans but also cattle and other domesticated animals.

There are two other hymns addressed to the all-gods (*viśvedevas*), among whom is included Vāstoṣpati (V.41.8; X.61.7). A third reference (VIII.17.14) is of a doubtful nature as the hymn is addressed to Indra; and, according to

Sāyaṇa, Indra himself is addressed here as Vāstoṣpati.

This is not to argue that pastoral nomadism continued to characterize the immigrant Aryan tribes in a significant way even after their arrival in the region of the seven rivers. My attempt is to show that vestiges of a nomadic past are embedded in certain hymns which have perhaps survived owing to their connection with some rituals. It may be still debatable whether the Vedic hymns were composed and compiled originally to meet the 'literary' or 'archaeological' needs outside of Vedic ritual, as has been asserted by Louis Renou,[59] or are hieratic compositions invented for liturgical purposes. The text, however, does have a blend of the old and the new, a fact admitted not rarely by the composers themselves.[60] Evidently new situations required fresh compositions, and interaction with the non-Aryan local population led to the creation of such hymns as the one attributed to Apālā (*Ṛgveda*, VIII.91).

Examining in detail the *Apālā-sūkta* and various references to it in later works, Hanns-Peter Schmidt states conclusively that the hymn celebrates a female puberty rite involving ritual purification of the female body in order to make it nubile.[61] Apālā is the prototype of a girl on the verge of puberty. She prays to Indra to make her mature by making her pubic hair grow. She also prays for the growth of corn on the field and hair on the head of her father. Most interpreters take it as a reference to the bald head of Apālā's father, but Schmidt's suggestion that it refers to the shaven head of her father as the ritual trimming and regrowth of the sacrificer's hair is connected with ideas of abundance and fertility, makes better sense. Apālā's body is purified by Indra by dragging her successively through the nave holes of a chariot and a cart and the pinhole of a yoke, which makes her skin glow like the Sun (*Ṛgveda*, V.7). Schmidt feels obliged to explain how a female puberty rite could find a place in an 'Indo–European' and predominantly patrilineal pastoral tradition. So he suggests that the initiation of girls into adulthood must have been connected with the marriage ritual. He also tries to explain the name Apālā as a phonetic variant of *apāra*, meaning 'boundless', as '*apālā*' cannot stem from Indo–Aryan roots. Indra is described as *apāra* in terms of strength and greatness, so Schmidt argues that *apālā*, being a variant of *apārā*, was the name of Indrāṇī, the wife of Indra. However, none of these far-fetched explanations are necessary, for the hymn on its own reflects an agricultural and not pastoral environment. Book VIII of the *Ṛgveda*, as Küiper has shown,[62] contains a few other myths which are Aryanized versions of Austro–Asiatic myths. The story of Apālā too falls in the same category. The name Apālā, like the name of sage Kaṇva, to whom is attributed the authorship of Book VIII, is non-Aryan, and was retained as such evidently because it was a crucial part of the puberty spell. I have argued elsewhere that the pre-Aryan Dāsa culture had certain matrilineal traits;[63] the women among them played a greater public role and fought against the enemies along with their men. Evidently the Apālā hymn derives from the same source. And it is pertinent that the hymn, cited as a proof of the agrarian nature of Ṛgvedic tribes and the existence of private property in land, reflects a non-Aryan culture.

Habib and Thakur repeatedly state that the importance of cattle in Ṛgvedic society arose from the fact that it constituted 'capital', yielding regular income through bartering oxen for grain from the peasants. But the few Ṛgvedic verses which refer to cultivated land speak of its capture from enemies, and there is no indication of pastoralists entering into a relationship of barter for receiving grain from agriculturists. The subordination of the non-Aryan population and capture of their land and kine undoubtedly led to the rise of inequalities and a deepening of the process of social differentiation among the Aryan tribes; but *varṇa*/class divisions emerged in Vedic society with the assimilation of the Aryan and non-Aryan peoples at every level, a process I have discussed in detail elsewhere.[64] It is also plausible that the captured Dāsa population was employed as manual labour in agricultural fields and not simply as domestic labour. But it is important to note that the *viś* or vaiśya of later Vedic times is primarily an Aryan peasant and not a pastoralist, as is the case in the *Ṛgveda*. This is clear from *Ṛgveda*, VIII.35, cited by Habib and Thakur to show that Vedic society was characterized by class differentiation. In verses 16–18 of the hymn, the poet prays to the twin-gods Aśvins to

> promote (*jinvatam*) our *brahma* (prayer), animate our intellect (*dhiyaḥ*), kill the demons (*rakṣāṃsi*) and drive away disease . . . promote our *kṣatra* (heroic valour or ruling power), give strength to our heroes (*nṛṛn*), kill the demons and drive away disease, promote our milchkine (*dhenurjinvatam*), give strength to our *viśaḥ* (common tribesmen), kill the demons, drive away disease.

Thus the *brahma*, *kṣatra* and *viś*, which later constituted the *varṇa* divisions, are mentioned here presumably in an hierarchical order, and it is not without significance that the Aryan *viś*, the common tribesman in this hymn, is linked with an increase in cattle farming, and not the growth of crops and fertility of fields. Just as the *brahma* is connected with intellect and valour, and the ruling power with heroes, the common tribesmen are connected with kine and not agriculture, suggesting that even at this stage agriculture must have been a minor activity. I have shown that a threefold functional division is not uncommon among the pastoral tribes.[65] This is true of the Nilotic tribes of East Africa as well as the Semitic societies depicted in the Old Testament. But these divisions are functional at this stage and not genealogical. Social organization rested on a different type of classification, that of family, clan and tribe in the manner of concentric circles. It is only towards the close of the Ṛgvedic period that a fourfold hierarchical stratification based on the principles of heredity crystallizes, and an ancient myth of the ritual sacrifice of the primordial man for the fashioning of the cosmos from his dismembered body is remodelled, in order to justify the new social order.[66]

Notes

[1] H.D. Sankalia, '"The Aryan Enigma"'.

[2] Irfan Habib and V.K. Thakur, *The Vedic Age*, pp. 6, 11–12.

[3] V.K. Thakur, 'A Note on Vedic Agriculture', pp. 140–51.

[4] R.N. Nandi, *Aryans Revisited*. Also see R.N. Nandi, 'Anthropology and the Study of Veda' and 'Archaeology and the *Ṛgveda*'.

[5] For example, R.S. Sharma, *Material Culture and Social Formations in Ancient India*, chapters 2 and 3; Romila Thapar, *From Lineage to State*; Michael Witzel, 'Early Indian History'; George Erdosy, 'Ethnicity in the *Ṛgveda*, and Its Bearing on the Problem of Indo–European Origins'.

[6] Madhav M. Deshpande, 'Vedic Aryans, Non-Vedic Aryans and Non-Aryans'. Also Madhav M. Deshpande, 'Genesis of Ṛgvedic Retroflexion'.

[7] Michael Witzel, 'Early Indian History', p. 310.

[8] Ibid., p. 96. Also see K.R. Norman, 'Dialect Variation in Old and Middle Indo–Aryan'. J. Gonda (*Vedic Literature*, vol. I, pp. 15ff.) writes that a good deal of the contents of the *Ṛgveda* is separated from the remaining Vedic literature by a comparatively wide chronological distance.

[9] Wilhelm Rau (*Staat und Gesellschaft im alten Indien*) has discussed in detail the material culture of Vedic Aryans. Also see R.S. Sharma, *Material Culture and Social Formation in Ancient India*, chapters 2 and 3; Michael Witzel, 'Early Indian History', pp. 101ff.

[10] Madhav M. Deshpande, 'Vedic Aryans, Non-Vedic Aryans and Non-Aryans', p. 80. He quotes Sjoberg who remarks, 'the *Ṛgveda* stands somewhat apart from the others in terms of its mainly Aryan (i.e. Indo–European) content. Some non-Aryan (mainly linguistic) influence in the *Ṛgveda* can be discerned, but a non-Aryan component seems more apparent in the later Saṃhitās.' A. Sjoberg, 'The Dravidian Contribution to the Development of Indian Civilization', p. 49. Earlier, Frits Staal's studies too had led him to the conclusion that there was a long time gap between the *Ṛgveda* and the *Yajurveda*. 'The former is largely Indo–Iranian, the latter only to a small extent.' Frits Staal, 'The Science of Ritual', pp. 48ff.; also see Suvira Jaiswal, *Caste*, pp. 194–95, 202 note 34.

[11] R.S. Sharma, *Material Culture and Social Formation in Ancient India*, pp. 26–27.

[12] D.D. Kosambi, *An Introduction to the Study of Indian History* (second edition), pp. 86, 94ff.

[13] I have consulted the following editions of the *Ṛgveda*: *Ṛgveda Saṃhitā* (with the commentary of Sāyaṇa), Vaidika Saṃśodhana Maṇḍala; *Ṛgveda Saṃhitā* (Hindi translation), edited by Pandit Ramgovind Trivedi.

[14] D.D. Kosambi, *The Culture and Civilization of Ancient India in Historical Outline*, p. 88.

[15] *Ṛgveda*, X.90.8, 146.1, 149.4; R.S. Sharma, *Material Culture and Social Formation in Ancient India*, p. 47.

[16] R.N. Nandi, *Aryans Revisited*, p. 37.

[17] R.S. Sharma, *Material Culture and Social Formation in Ancient India*, pp. 47–48.

[18] Wilhelm Rau, *Staat und Gesellschaft im alten Indien*. Referring to Rau's work, Sontheimer suggests that possibly the term *kula*, from which *go-kula* is formed, had a similar origin. Gunther-Dietz Sontheimer, *The Joint Hindu Family*, p. 9 note 2.

[19] R.N. Nandi, *Aryans Revisited*, pp. 36ff.

[20] Suvira Jaiswal, *Caste*, pp. 151–52, 162.

[21] *Nṛpati janānām*, ruler of the people among tribes; *Ṛgveda*, X.107.5. In *Ṛgveda*, II.1.1, *Agni* is described as *nṛṇam nṛpate*.

[22] R.N. Nandi, *Aryans Revisited*, p. 32.
[23] Ibid., p. 36.
[24] Ibid. Also see p. 31.
[25] V.S. Apte, *Sanskrit–English Dictionary, s.v. asinva.*
[26] Monier-Williams, *Sanskrit–English Dictionary, s.v. prabhu.*
[27] *Agni* is often described as the 'guest of men' invited to come; *Ṛgveda*, II.4.1.
[28] R.N. Nandi, 'Archaeology and the *Ṛgveda*', p. 46; R.N. Nandi, *Aryans Revisited*, p. 33.
[29] V.K. Thakur, 'A Note on Vedic Agriculture', p. 142.
[30] E.W. Hopkins, 'Numerical Formulae in the Veda and Their Bearing on Vedic Criticism'; E.W. Hopkins, 'Pragāthikāni, I', p. 85; Suvira Jaiswal, *Caste*, p. 136.
[31] For Oldenberg's list, see Michael Witzel, 'Early Indian History', p. 311.
[32] R.S. Sharma, *Material Culture and Social Formation in Ancient India*, pp. 24–26, 42.
[33] V.K. Thakur, 'A Note on Vedic Agriculture', p. 142.
[34] Ibid., p. 144. Thakur writes, '*yūpa* which denotes yoke, not plough, occurs frequently in the family book as well as in the later portions of the *Ṛgveda*'. This is not surprising, for *yūpa* is a sacrificial post to which the victim is fastened at the time of immolation. It does not mean 'yoke'. Among the references to this word as listed by Thakur in note 53 page 150, figure *Ṛgveda*, IV.115.2 and IV.184.3. But the fourth book of the *Ṛgveda* has only 58 hymns.

Thakur cites (note 54) *Ṛgveda*, III.33.13 and V.33.2 to show the occurrence of *yoktra*, which means 'yoking'. But both the verses refer to the yoking of horses. *Ṛgveda*, III.33 describes the Bharatas crossing the river Vipāśā with the help of Viśvāmitra's prayers. The Bharatas cross the river along with their *grāma* (V.11), which shows that *grāma* was a mobile unit, a band. *Ṛgveda*, V.33.2 uses *yoktra* in connection with the horses driving Indra's chariot. Again, *śamyā* in III.33.13 is a wooden pin used for yoking a horse to a cart or chariot, and is used in the same sense elsewhere too. See M. Sparreboom, *Chariot in the Veda*.
[35] See, for example, VI.53.9 and VI.58.2. Both hymns are addressed to Pūṣan who is specially associated with cattle and journeys. In VI.53.1, Pūṣan is Lord of the Roads (*pathaspate*), and verse 9 speaks of his *astra* (goad) guiding cattle and animals. In VI.58.2 also, Pūṣan is described as the protector of goats and animals (*ajāśvaḥ paśupā*), apparently cattle, and brandishing his goad. It is strange that Thakur cites these verses as referring to the ploughman's goad.
[36] V.K. Thakur, 'A Note on Vedic Agriculture', p. 145. He lists five references to *dṛti* (note 53), of which only three mention this word.
[37] Monier-Williams, *Sanskrit–English Dictionary, s.v. camasa.*
[38] For example, according to Nandi and Thakur, *Ṛgveda* VI.20.1 refers to 'corn-land providing subsistence to a thousand people' reflecting a well-developed 'peasant mode of production' (R.N. Nandi, *Aryans Revisited*, p. 33; V.K. Thakur, 'A Note on Vedic Agriculture', p. 142). But the verse in question, as interpreted by Sāyaṇa, is a prayer to god Indra to grant a son who may overcome the enemies just as the Sun (or Sky, *dyauḥ*) overcomes the earth, and who may win wealth in thousands as well as fertile lands. 'Bring or bestow wealth in thousands' is an oft-occurring expression in the *Ṛgveda* (cf. VIII.34.15) where the poet prays that wealth be brought to him in thousands, ten thousands and hundreds (*sahasraśobharāyutāni śatāni ca*). By misinterpreting *sahasrabharam* in *Ṛgveda*, VI.20.1 as 'providing subsistence to a thousand people', an exaggerated picture of agricultural production is presented, whereas the passage merely speaks of winning fertile lands. Thus, a few genuine references to agriculture and agricultural practices are subjected to baseless overestimation. For references to wealth, mainly cattle and horses, in thousands, refer to *Ṛgveda*, VIII.4.20, 5.37, 21.3, 46.22; IX.58.3.
[39] C.P. Masica, 'Aryan and Non-Aryan Elements in North Indian Agriculture'.
[40] Wilhelm Rau, *The Meaning of Pur in Vedic Literature.*
[41] Asko Parpola, 'The Coming of the Aryans to Iran and India and the Cultural Ethnic Identity of the Dāsas'; Asko Parpola, 'The Problem of the Aryans and the Soma'.

[42] H.W. Bailey, 'Iranian Arya and Daha'.

[43] Asko Parpola, 'The Coming of the Aryans to Iran and India and the Cultural Ethnic Identity of the Dāsas', pp. 120–28; Suvira Jaiswal, *Caste*, pp. 44–46.

[44] George Erdosy, 'Language, Material Culture and Ethnicity', p. 3 note 5.

[45] As reported in *The Hindu*, Monday, 1 May 2006.

[46] Irfan Habib, *The Indus Civilization*, pp. 96–97.

[47] F.B.J. Küiper, *Aryans in the Ṛgveda*.

[48] Michael Witzel, 'Early Indian History' (p. 103) translates Indo–European *kṛṣṭi* as 'furrow'. But it is doubtful. For its original meaning, see R.S. Sharma, *Material Culture and Social Formations in Ancient India*, pp. 24–25.

[49] Michael Witzel, 'Early Indian History', pp. 337–40.

[50] Ibid., p. 339 note 100.

[51] Suvira Jaiswal, *The Origin and Development of Vaiṣṇavism*, pp. 8–16.

[52] Suvira Jaiswal, 'Change and Continuity in Brahmanical Religion with Particular Reference to Vaiṣṇava Bhakti'.

[53] Hermann Kulke and Dietmar Rothermund, *A History of India*, p. 38.

[54] Thomas R. Trautmann, *The Aryan Debate*, p. xxxvii.

[55] I have consulted *Atharvaveda* (Śaunaka), edited by Vishva Bandhu, translated by W.D. Whitney, vols 7 and 8.

[56] For the changing role of the *gṛhapati* from the leader of a band to the head of a complex patriarchal household, see Suvira Jaiswal, 'The Changing Concept of Gṛhapati'. It is also incorporated with some additions in Suvira Jaiswal, *Caste*, chapter 4.

[57] The hymns figure in Oldenberg's list of later additions cited above in endnote 31. Also see V.S. Ghate, *Lectures on the Ṛgveda*, p. 69.

[58] It is curious that this hymn is cited by Nandi and Thakur as evidence of the sedentary nature of Aryan settlements.

[59] Louis Renou, *The Destiny of the Veda in India*, p. 5.

[60] To cite a few examples, the composer of *Ṛgveda*, IX.91 prays to Soma Pavamāna to make his new hymn (*navyase . . . sūktāya*) to go forward on the same path as of old, and grant him water, cows, offspring, many sons and ample land (*kṣetra*). The author of another hymn (*Ṛgveda*, I.105) not only acknowledges that he is reciting a 'new hymn' (*navyaṃ tat ukthyam*) in honour of Viśvedevas (verse 12), but also laments the disappearance of the ancient law (*ṛta*) (verse 4) and prays for the rise of a new order *(navyaḥ jayataṃ ṛtam*) (verse 15). Also see I.61.13 and I.62.11 for the newly fashioned hymns by the seer Nodhas. Also see IV.16.2.

Ṛgveda, III.31 provides an interesting example of the mixing up of the old and the new. Verse 19 of this hymn claims to renovate the old song (*navyaṃ kṛṇomi sanyase*) for the ancient god (Indra) who is to chase away godless creatures, and in verse 15, Indra is said to have shone with heroes (*nṛbhiḥ*) and given rich land (*mahikṣetram*) to his friends (*sakhibhyaḥ*). But the first two stanzas of this hymn are so archaic and baffling that different scholars have offered differing explanations. Quite unrelated to later verses, some have interpreted them as referring to ritual incest, some others with reference to the later institution of *putrikā-putra*. Hanns-Peter Schmidt is of the view that so far no plausible explanation has been offered. The second verse of this hymn uses *mātaro* for father and mother, which is an archaic feature. See Hanns-Peter Schmidt, *Some Women's Rites and Rights in the Veda*, pp. 196–97.

[61] Ibid., pp. 1–29.

[62] F.B.J. Küiper, 'An Austro–Asiatic Myth in the Ṛgveda'.

[63] See chapter 4 below.

[64] Suvira Jaiswal, *Caste*.

[65] Ibid., pp. 146–47.

[66] Ibid., pp. 135–36.

2

Caste, Gender and Ideology in the Making of Traditional India*

The resurgence and reinvention of caste identities in the post-Independence scenario is paradoxical in the face of the considerable modernization in many spheres, such as technology, industrialization and urbanization, in India. The annihilation of caste discrimination has been one of the main priorities of the national agenda against the highly exploitative and undemocratic system of social stratification. Nevertheless, it continues to impact in a major way not only the personal and inter-community relations, but also the various aspects of the public sphere – legal, political and economic – including access to land and water resources.[1] In order to understand the reasons behind its stranglehold, it is important to probe into its historical roots and the inner dynamics, which have rendered it a unique system of class and gender exploitation.

The postmodern and neo-colonial critiques of caste visualize it as a relatively modern phenomenon, a product of the British colonial rule (and the colonial Census Reports), delinked from the ancient, so-called Hindu period of Indian history or to the *Puruṣa-sūkta* of the *Ṛgveda* and the *Manusmṛti*.[2] Hierarchy-cum-interdependence, occupational specialization, endogamy and commensal restrictions, which the earlier Indologists and sociologists regarded as the defining features of the caste system, are, from this point of view, Orientalist–colonial readings motivated by the desire to systematize diverse forms of local social realities and identities into a holistic theory, 'essentializing' it as unique to Indian culture. Despite this criticism of 'essentialization', endogamy is recognized, implicitly or explicitly,[3] by these scholars as the essence of the caste system, without which the formation of 'discrete categories' or the allegedly modern process of 'ethnicization' or 'substantialization' of caste – which,

*This is an enlarged version of my address to the Indian History Congress as General President of its 68th session held at the University of Delhi on 28–30 December 2007. I am thankful to Professor Kunal Chakrabarti, Dr Rakesh Batabyal and Dr Ranjan Anand for helping me in various ways in the preparation of this lecture.

according to Nicholas B. Dirks, makes it 'a worthy synonym of community in the best sense'[4] – would not have taken place. The question arises: is endogamy an irreducible transhistoric phenomenon embedded in the psyche of the Indian people, or did it evolve through a historical process and continues to survive through the ages in a favourable material environment?

In the first decade of the twentieth century, Sir Herbert Risley, the British Census Commissioner, ascribed the origin of an endogamous caste structure to the desire of the Aryan conquerors to maintain their racial purity against the blood of defeated aborigines. A hierarchical gradation of people born of mixed unions is said to have evolved in proportion to the admixture of aboriginal blood in them, with the brāhmaṇas at the top representing the purest of the Aryan blood. Later, the principle of endogamy was

> strengthened, perpetuated and extended to all ranks of society by the fiction that people who speak a different language, dwell in a different district, worship different gods, eat different food, observe different social customs, follow a different profession, or practise the same profession in a slightly different way, must be so unmistakably aliens by blood that inter-marriage with them is a thing not to be thought of.[5]

The Aryan invasion thesis and racial origin of caste are no longer subscribed to, but the impact of Risley's ideas may be still seen in the explanations offered for the prevalence of endogamy.[6] Thus, according to Dipankar Gupta, the caste system may be defined as a form of differentiation in which the constituent units justify endogamy 'on the basis of putative biological differences which are semaphored by the realization of multiple social practices'.[7] Risley's notion that castes (i.e. *jātis*) considered each other 'aliens by blood' was an elaboration of his racial theory on the origin of the caste system. It is curious that although the theory of racial origin is no longer accepted, the perception that there exists a 'mythical notion of biological differences'[8] in the ideologies of all castes has been retained. It is argued that because of this notion, castes highly value the principle of endogamy.[9] However, I may point out that the idea that there are innate biological differences which distinguish one *varṇa* or *jāti*[10] from the other is a typically Brahmanical concept invented to justify the hereditary nature of varṇas,[11] and cannot be regarded as part of all caste ideologies, particularly of the subaltern castes, which, in the myths of their origin, almost invariably trace their descent from a brāhmaṇa or a kṣatriya ancestor. It is not the biological difference but the fact that their original ancestor was cheated, or he had violated some rule inadvertently, which is regarded as the reason for the present predicament of his descendants.[12] Moreover, the rise of a new endogamous unit through the processes of fusion and fission, owing to the adoption of some new technological, professional, religious or cultural practice, and the emergence of a new social group in the medieval times, is a feature well known to historians and sociologists – but this alone cannot explain the origin of caste endogamy.

Nevertheless, the view that caste endogamy is a residue of the tribal past of communities integrating with an expanding Aryan society is quite common,[13] perhaps because history does provide many instances of tribal groups being transformed into endogamous castes. But this only goes to show that, as a rule, assimilation into a caste society could take place only on a group or community basis with the new entrants retaining their distinctive identities, for the general society was already fragmented into social groups differentiated on hereditary principles. Attributing the origin of endogamous customs to incomplete fusion of tribal elements would imply that caste identities were biologically constructed, but, in my view, caste society was not a biological but a social construct.

I have argued elsewhere that caste endogamy was not a borrowing or survival of aboriginal practice.[14] It evolved and consolidated itself in the process of regulating hierarchical subordination of social groups and the reproduction of patriarchy. It is not possible to agree with Dumont's strongly idealistic view[15] of caste, which makes it, 'above all, a system of ideas and values' embedded in the Indian mind, the *Homo Hierarchicus*, presenting a perfect contrast to the western *Homo Aequalis*.[16] In my view,[17] hierarchy, defined as separation and superiority of the pure over the impure, of the priest (*brahma*) over the warrior–ruler (*kṣatra*), which forms the keystone of Dumont's model, derives from the material context of the ecology of cattle-keeping tribes, among whom emerge two groups of specialists: one claiming to mediate with the gods through specialization over rituals and thus increase the cattle-wealth of the tribes and ensure success in tribal wars, and the other the warriors who provide protection and increase the wealth of the tribe through cattle raids. Both groups, initially functional, claim and are able to acquire privileged positions. Caste ideology evolved gradually in consonance with the changing material conditions, and is not a mental invention unrelated to material roots. Nevertheless, I agree with Dumont that 'endogamy is a corollary of hierarchy, rather than a primary principle',[18] although, for me, caste hierarchy is not simply a matter of superiority of the pure over the impure but a form of exploitation which evolved in the process of enforcing subjection of women and weaker social groups.

II

The beginnings of the twin processes may be seen in the *Ṛgveda*. D.D. Kosambi, in a perceptive article, 'Urvaśī and Purūravas',[19] analysed a number of Ṛgvedic hymns containing traces of a matriarchal culture which was suppressed and superimposed by Aryan patriarchy. In his view, the conflict and transition is reflected in the earliest stratum, the matriarchal elements came from a pre-Aryan culture, and early Ṛgvedic society was formed from a combination of the conquered pre-Aryans and their Aryan conquerors. Kosambi identifies the pre-Aryans as survivors of the Harappa culture, not elite trading or ruling classes but 'women with their cults . . . either as wives or slaves, which would account for all the traces of their cults'. He adds that in any case 'Aryan' means a particular manner of life and speech, and not a race.[20] The thesis of direct confrontation and conquest of the Harappans by the Ṛgvedic Aryans is now generally discounted,[21] but there are strong grounds to believe that pre-Vedic elements were accommodated in the later sections of the *Ṛgveda*, particularly in Book VIII, which is supposedly authored by the sage Kaṇva and his lineage.[22]

Although it is plausible that certain external matriarchal components crept into Ṛgvedic narratives through absorption of pre-Aryan elements – the *Apālā Sūkta* (*Ṛgveda*, VIII.91), which is a female puberty spell,[23] being a case in point – not all traces of women's autonomy and subjectivity need to be attributed to external sources. There is a general tendency to force interpretations suited to patriarchy even when hymns suggest more equitable gender relations[24] owing to the presumption that patriarchy was deep-rooted among the warring 'bronze-age pastoral invaders'. Generally speaking, the Ṛgvedic poet does reflect a patriarchal attitude and speaks contemptuously of his adversaries as having been deprived of their manliness (e.g., *Ṛgveda*, X.48.2). Nevertheless, the systematic displacement of women from *Śrauta* rituals and the appropriation of their role by male priests in later Vedic texts has been pointed out by a number of scholars,[25] and it is difficult to attribute all traces of earlier practices to a non-Aryan/pre-Vedic source. The apologists of Vedic tradition have argued that marginalization or the exclusion of women is only one side of the story; in fact women were central to Ṛgvedic concerns, the desire for progeny, material wealth, etc. The Vedic *yajña* ritual required the presence of the wife of the sacrificer too, and much of the Hindu women's deep identification with religion, her 'positive self-image . . . stemmed from the Ṛgvedic Age'.[26] Such an essentialist, ahistorical approach, apart from creating a homogenized category of 'Hindu women' regardless of their caste, marital status, etc., ignores the material environment which may have induced women to internalize the patriarchal values of Brahmanical culture. Moreover, one cannot ignore the fact that stereotyping women as only sensual creatures lacking in wisdom and self-control, and acting as temptresses to reluctant males devoted to higher moral and ascetic goals, has its beginnings in the hymns of the *Ṛgveda*, as illustrated in the dialogue between Yama and Yamī (X.10), and Agastya and Lopāmudrā (I.179).

III

However, the consolidation of patriarchy and a hierarchically differentiated society comprising four *varṇa* divisions is an ongoing process in later Vedic texts, and the two developments were closely linked. Sedentary agriculture and availability of servile labour of the defeated and enslaved Dāsa and Śūdra tribes made it possible for the elite men and women to withdraw from manual labour, and become contemptuous of those who had to serve others and perform physical work. They were categorized into a distinct śūdra *varṇa* in later Vedic times. The *Puruṣa-sūkta* hymn, which is undoubtedly a late insertion in the *Ṛgveda*,[27] ascribes the lowest position to the śūdra in an organic conception of society which traces his origin from the feet of the same cosmic being whose mouth, arms and thighs produce brāhmaṇa, *rājanya* and vaiśya respectively. But several later Vedic texts attribute a divine origin to only the three upper *varṇas*. The *Taittirīya Brāhmaṇa* states that the śūdras sprang from Asuras or demons.[28] The same text at another place observes that the śūdra sprang from 'untruth' or 'non-existence' (*asat*).[29] Emphasis on the 'otherness' and the evil character of the śūdra may have been partly due to ethnic prejudice, but also because of a dependence on manual slave work. It is generally held that the śūdra *varṇa* arose out of defeated Dāsa, Śūdra and other aboriginal non-Aryan tribes reduced to various degrees of servitude. The Śūdra tribe is not mentioned in the *Ṛgveda*,[30] though it speaks of the capture and enslavement of a large number of Dāsa men and women,[31] with the result that the tribal name 'Dāsa' became a signifier of 'slave'. Ṛgvedic chieftains made liberal gifts of male and female slaves to priests and composers of the hymns, and, as Kosambi has argued,[32] the assignment of slave labour to the priestly and warrior lineages by the tribal chieftain catalysed the growth of social differentiation within the Aryan tribes and the emergence of a class structure in the form of four original castes, i.e. the *varṇas*. Kosambi explains that the subjugation of the Dāsa, Śūdra and other tribes gave rise to a generalized form of servitude in the form of the śūdra *varṇa* and not chattel slavery, for the tribal influence was still strong and individual property had not developed sufficiently. Internal differentiations among the Vedic tribes emerged with the priestly and warrior lineages uniting to exploit both the 'Aryan peasant (vaiśya) and non-Aryan helot (śūdra)'.

The cooperation and interdependence of the priestly and ruling groups and their exploitation and subjugation of the vaiśya and śūdra producers is a well-known feature of the later Vedic epoch. What deserves to be noted is the fact that the *varṇa* ideology from its inception plays a political and not just religious role in the hierarchical structuring of social relations. The *varṇa* system, and later its expanded version, the *jāti* system,[33] regulated the class structure of early

India, and as such was a powerful instrument functioning in the interest of the ruling classes. Its strong links with contemporary political powers and politics have been maintained, as we shall see, throughout its long history.

Here it is necessary to examine carefully historical evidence relating to the evolution of the concepts of *varṇa* and *jāti* in order to comprehend the reasons for their enmeshing in defining the same social structure. It is not without significance that the two terms have been used indiscriminately in Brahmanical law books composed in the first decade of the Common Era, as well as in medieval works such as the *Varṇaratnākara* of the fourteenth century, written in Mithila. To consider this as a 'puzzling error' is to look at the issue through the modern prism, which is anachronistic.[34] If we apply the touchstone that a theory must always be 'what the people themselves think and believe', as Dumont asserts,[35] we may note that in common parlance the Hindus apply the term *jāti* to all levels of the caste system, beginning with *varṇa* to what is described as 'sub-caste' by the sociologists.[36] The interchangeability of the *varṇa* and *jāti* in our sources derives from the fact that both the terms demarcated and were defined on the same principles: hereditary occupation, exclusiveness in matters of *connubium* and commensality and hierarchical gradation. Hence, even Manu uses the term *jāti* when he means *varṇa* and vice versa. He asserts that there are only four *jātis*, that there is no fifth, and goes on to describe the fifteen lowly 'mixed castes' as fifteen *varṇas*.[37] I have shown elsewhere that Dumont's argument that heredity was less important than function in the *varṇa* scheme is not sustainable.[38] The desire to secure and preserve the rights and privileges of the priestly and warrior elites on a hereditary basis was the prime mover in the crystallization of these *varṇa* categories among the Vedic tribes, and the word *varṇa*, which has been used in the *Ṛgveda* to draw a sharp distinction between the Ārya and the Dāsa tribes, began to be applied to the emerging four social classes in order to emphasize their disjunction and distance from each other. As long as the raising of cattle-wealth and other occupations, priesthood or warfare, were not genealogically closed professions, the term *varṇa* was not used in relation to them. Even the precedence of the priestly category over all others – which became the norm in later times – was not observed in the initial stages, as is evident in *Ṛgveda*, I.113.6. However, with the transition in the organizing principle from 'kinship to territory', the latter as 'dominion', the realm of 'sovereign power', to use the language of Marshal Sahlins,[39] and the emergence of territorial states in later Vedic times, a fourfold class structure evolved. The elaboration of Vedic sacrifices into rituals of great complexity made them a preserve of specialist lineages, and the teaching of ritual to only one's descendants and disciples gave rise to the brāhmaṇa *varṇa*.[40] The Vedic ritual specialists played a crucial role in providing religious justification for the superior claims of the Vedic chieftain and his *rājanya* kinsmen over the *viś* commoners, reducing the need for the use of force which undoubtedly underpinned such claims.[41] As the tribal structure disintegrated and socio-economic disparities grew, the *rājanyas* emerged as a separate privileged group and formed alliances with similar groups of other tribes, giving rise to the kṣatriya *varṇa*. There is enough evidence to show that the brāhmaṇa and kṣatriya *varṇas* did not originally come from prehistoric separate marriage circles, as suggested by some sociologists, but through the integration of priestly and warrior lineages of different tribes into close-knit, hereditary high-ranking groups in specific historical conditions.[42] The constitution of a brāhmaṇa *varṇa* through the assimilation of Aryan and non-Aryan elements may be inferred from a passage of the *Bṛhadāraṇyaka Upaniṣad* which recommends different types of diet to brāhmaṇa parents depending on their desire to have a black-complexioned (*śyāma*) son with the ability to recite the three Vedas, or a tawny (*kapila*) son with reddish brown (*piṅgala*) eyes having similar proficiency.[43]

The oligarchical lineages of the *gaṇa-rājyas* of the age of the Buddha claimed to belong to the kṣatriya *varṇa* although their lineages were described as *jātis*, to wit, Śākya *jāti*, Licchavi *jāti*, Jñatrika *jāti* and so on. But these were not *jātis* in the modern sense of the term, constituting separate endogamous units. Endogamy was practised within the kṣatriya *varṇa* with marriage across the *jāti* boundaries.[44] The term *jāti* was used initially in the literal sense to emphasize birth in a particular group. Hence we have references to *hīna jāti* and *ucca jāti*, birth in a low or a high social group. But the operation of the principle of heredity in establishing the identities of the brāhmaṇa and *rājanya* categories is clearly indicated in the *Śatapatha Brāhmaṇa* and early Upaniṣads such as the *Chāndogya*.[45] The latter text links it to the doctrine of transmigration and *karma*. It is said that those who have pleased the gods with their pleasant conduct enter a 'pleasant womb' and are born either as a brāhmaṇa, a kṣatriya or a vaiśya. But those whose conduct has been evil enter a 'stinking womb', such as that of a bitch, a pig or a Caṇḍāla.[46] Thus, birth in higher *varṇas* was considered the fruit of meritorious acts performed in the previous life.

IV

In an illuminating lecture published posthumously, A.L. Basham meticulously examines the Upaniṣadic passages which reveal the gradual evolution of the doctrine of rebirth from inchoate speculations into a well-developed ideology.[47] He shows that this doctrine was first adumbrated by the brāhmaṇa and kṣatriya intellectuals in an age characterized by great material progress, but also with the disintegration of tribal life and the rise of *varṇa* divisions. These developments created a sense of insecurity and pessimism among many thinkers, who opted out of society and became ascetics and wanderers trying to discover 'the ultimate meaning of existence'. To this one might add that the emergence of wide socio-economic disparities must have caused disillusionment. It is said in the *Chāndogya Upaniṣad*[48] that in this world, one's greatness depends on cattle, horses, elephants, gold, female slaves, fields and houses. The doctrine of *karma*, rebirth and *mokṣa* – the idea that the individual soul keeps on passing from one body to another to reap the fruits of the good or bad deeds – refers to an unending cycle from which one can be released only through realization of the impersonal *brahma* or Truth. The significant point is that it was an ideology that germinated among the elite. Not being rooted in early Vedic thought, it was taught initially as secret knowledge discussed by a few, but later became the basic principle of an ideological explanation of the cosmos (*saṃsāra*) preached by the brāhmaṇas, wandering ascetics and mystics, filtering down from them to the lower orders. Basham is quite emphatic that it was not the borrowing of a pre-existing idea from non-Aryan, indigenous peoples of animistic beliefs, as was suggested by earlier scholars, but an invention of the Upaniṣadic thinkers. It had its sceptics in the form of Cāravākas, Lokāyatikas and Nāstikas, but soon became the ideology of the mainstream, and was accepted widely at the time of the rise of Jainism and Buddhism.

However, the extant texts are documents of the upper castes and it is difficult to infer on their basis the extent to which this ideology was internalized by the depressed groups. Max Weber writes that the inexorable logic of this doctrine reconciled the poor to their lot in the hope that through good conduct they could improve their destiny in their next birth.[49] But field studies conducted among the 'untouchable' castes by a number of sociologists show that although the ideas of transmigration and *karma* – sins committed in previous lives being the causes of misfortunes in the present one – are accepted generally, the low status of their caste are not explained in this fashion.[50] Their origin myths ascribe their present degraded social ranking to some historical accident or the trickery of the high castes played on their ancestors or their genealogical founder. We shall be doing less than justice to the common sense of the exploited if we imagine that there could have been no resistance in thought, let alone in practice.

Despite the nature of our sources, traces of resistance are not altogether lacking. These have been overlooked because of the preconceived notions of the Orientalist and nationalist historiographies. If colonial reconstructions emphasized the static, stagnant nature of Indian society, immune to changes owing to a rigid caste structure rooted in religions beliefs, the nationalists presented an idealized picture of social harmony and contentment, with castes engaged in their traditional occupations unhindered by social conflicts.

However, R.S. Sharma's analysis of the Kali age crisis, mentioned in the *Mahābhārata*, *Rāmāyaṇa* and some early Purāṇas, clearly shows that the *varṇa* order and its ideology faced serious challenges in the early centuries of the Common Era from the lower orders, and although the upsetting of the social order is generally attributed to vaiśyas and śūdras, the same passages also speak of *antyas* or untouchables in this context.[51] The earliest reference to a revolt by menial labourers pertains to the slaves of the Śākyas who carried away 'married women, unmarried girls and daughters-in-law of high families of their masters'. Dev Raj Chanana is of the view that the way the Buddha reacted to this incident suggests that it was not the only occurrence of its kind.[52] One may presume that since the slaves acted collectively against their exploitation they formed a collectivity, perhaps a defeated and enslaved tribal population, but their integration as a depressed caste within the *varṇa* framework cannot be taken for granted, for the *dāsakammakaras* of the Pali sources constituted an economic category. Although the *varṇa* categories had hardened into an exclusive hereditary status in the age of the Buddha, the *jāti* structure within the *varṇa* framework was yet to develop. The category of untouchables grew rather slowly,[53] and the first untouchable groups seem to have been food-gatherers and hunters living on the periphery of agrarian settlements. In the listing of social groups in early Buddhist sources they are mentioned separately and not as a part of the śūdra *varṇa*. The *Jātaka* tales depict Caṇḍālas engaged as musicians, watchmen, executioners, corpse removers and street sweepers, but not engaged in agricultural work.[54] They were kept away from Aryan homes as their presence and proximity were considered polluting.[55] However, in Brahmanical perception they all formed part of the śūdra *varṇa*; for Pāṇini, who is generally assigned to the fourth century BCE, speaks of two groups of śūdras, the 'excluded' and the 'unexcluded' (*śūdrānāṃ aniravasitānām*; *Aṣṭādhyāyī*, II.4.10), and Patañjali's comment implies that the former included Caṇḍālas, Mṛtapās, etc.

V

Contrary to ideological interpretations which attribute the caste system's origin to the Indian psyche, a careful scrutiny of our sources shows that condemnation of certain peoples as having despicable and impure birth (*jāti*) begins much earlier than the formulation of religious concepts ascribing permanent impurity to certain occupations and practices. The most polluting task, according to the Hindu notions of impurity, is the cleaning of human excrement, a task imposed upon the lowliest of the untouchables known by different names in various regions, such as Bhangi, Vālmīki, Chuhrā, Pākī, Hādī, etc. Dumont argues that the Hindu belief in the desecrating effect of organic activities makes the Hindu of a good caste temporarily impure and leads to attribution of massive impurity to those categories of people who have specialization in impure tasks, *in practice or in theory*.[56] In other words, even without being actually engaged in 'polluting' occupations, theoretically they are associated with such tasks and hence regarded as permanently impure. However, we may point out that in Brahmanical theory impurity does not arise from specialization in impure tasks but from impure birth. Those whose putative ancestors are deemed to have violated the *varṇa* norms and contracted mixed '*pratiloma*' unions or marriages are condemned to subsist on 'impure' vocations, and their impurity is not removed even when they are not engaged in occupations ascribed to them by the Brahmanical tradition. Dumont completely ignores the instrumental nature of the ideology of purity/impurity invented by the Brahmanical ideologues for justifying a system of class exploitation. This becomes evident from the fact that from the early medieval to late medieval times, 'manual scavenging' in elite houses[57] was done by domestic slaves who were of 'clean' castes,[58] and the same person had to do other types of housework as well, such as fetching drinking water, grinding corn, cooking, etc., without any prejudice[59] – a situation unthinkable in modern-day Hindu homes. This shows that notions of purity could be modified or elaborated to suit the convenience of the exploiting classes. The creation of a caste of manual scavengers is linked with the growth of towns[60] and closed dwellings without open spaces; the process seems to have accelerated in the nineteenth century, perhaps aided to some extent by the Government of India Act V of 1843 abolishing slavery, despite the opposition of the landed aristocracy on the grounds that it was an ancient custom for slaves to do all manual labour for respectable people.[61] Moreover, army cantonments too required such services, and the municipalities and cantonments officially created the posts of manual scavengers. It is true that the British did not invent the caste of manual scavengers, they intervened to institutionalize it;[62] 'the technology of sanitation was structured to deepen social prejudice in India'.

A similar inference can be drawn from an enquiry into the emergence of a caste of Chamars (cobblers). In the early Buddhist sources, leather work is regarded as *hīna* (low) *sippa* (craft or occupation),[63] of low status value, but the leather worker or Carmakāra does not figure in the list of *hīna jātis* enumerated in the Vinaya texts. The repeatedly mentioned *hīna jātis* or *nīca kulas* (low lineages)[64] are Caṇḍāla, Neṣāda, Veṇa, Rathakāra and Pukkusa, who, with the possible exception of Rathakāra,[65] seem to have been aboriginal tribes living on the margins of the Aryan settlements. Although the tanning of hide is an ancient profession and is mentioned in the *Ṛgveda* and the later Vedic texts,[66] there is nothing to show that leather or leather workers were considered polluting even in later Vedic times. We have references to leather bags filled with milk and clarified butter (*ghṛta*) for use in sacrificial ritual.[67] According to Vivekanand Jha,[68] the Carmakāra, the Rajaka (washerman) and similar craftsmen and manual workers appear as untouchables only in texts datable between 600 and 1200 CE. The *Manusmṛti* refers to the mixed caste of leather workers with three different names, Carmāvakartin,[69] Dhigvaṇa[70] and Karavara,[71] which indicates the existence of subcastes among leather workers. But the dating of these passages is problematic. R.S. Sharma suggests a time bracket of 220–400 CE with later portions added in the fifth century or even later.[72] A Buddhist Prakrit inscription from Amaravati speaks of a Cammakāra (Carmakāra) Vidhika, who describes himself as the son of an Upājhāya (Upādhyāya, apparently a brāhmaṇa teacher) Nāga.[73] He made the gift of a slab with a filled vase. Paleographically the inscription is assigned to the early centuries of the Common Era and it shows that in the Deccan leather work was still a respectable profession. Patañjali, commenting upon Pāṇini's *sūtra* as mentioned above, assigns Caṇḍālas and Mṛtapās the lowest position, and places the carpenters, washermen, blacksmiths and weavers above them,[74] but does not speak of the Carmakāra in this connection. It appears that the association of untouchability/impurity with leather work is a later development.

VI

Notwithstanding the evidence of the Amaravati inscription, it is not possible to accept B.R. Ambedkar's thesis that the Chamar and other Dalit communities of modern India had been originally Buddhists, and were degraded as untouchables by the brāhmaṇa law-givers as they continued to eat beef even after it was given up by the brāhmaṇas and Brahmanical communities.[75] The Brahmanical law-givers, poets and playwrights continued to countenance the eating of animal flesh, including that of cow, till the end of the first millennium CE,[76] and in the sixth century Varāhamihira especially recommended the king to eat the flesh of the bull, buffalo and other animals on ceremonial occasions.[77] But references to 'untouchable' communities have been traced to sources datable several centuries earlier and the crystallization of social groups earning their living by leather work as specific castes of low status may be seen in the *Manusmṛti*.[78] In the later Smṛtis the *carmakāra* is clearly an untouchable.[79] So, leather work, beef-eating or eating carrion cannot be regarded as having given rise to the phenomenon of untouchability, although such practices were undoubtedly condemned later in order to relegate large sections of the lower classes and aboriginal communities to an untouchable status.[80] This is obvious in the case of present-day Chamars. This large caste living in a vast area of Northern India seems to have been formed through assimilation of a number of tribes, artisanal groups, local castes, etc. Only a small proportion of this caste lives on leather work; the rest subsists on agricultural labour in rural areas.[81]

However, following Ambedkar's theory, a number of Dalit scholars have visualized a glorious Buddhist past for the ex-untouchables. The more cautious among them do not attribute the origin of untouchability to the Brahmanical ostracization of the Buddhists, but argue that the revival of Brahmanism under the Guptas and the persecution of the Buddhists was largely responsible for the large increase in the number of untouchable castes in Gupta and post-Gupta times.[82] The thesis is emphatically espoused by Gail Omvedt[83] who asserts that the 'defeat of Buddhism in India' was the result of alliances between the brāhmaṇas and the kings, and the violent persecution of the Buddhists. She hypothesizes that the Caṇḍālas were indigenous to Bengal; they had been speakers of a proto-Munda language, their name being strikingly similar to the Mundari-speaking Santhals. The Caṇḍālas had spread out from Bengal to central India and into the regions of the Gangetic plains, where, under Brahmanical hegemony, they were defeated and reduced to untouchable status. In Bengal, communities like the Kaivartas and the Caṇḍālas have been supporters of Buddhism, 'imbibing its equalitarian high tradition'. Later many of them converted to Islam to avoid persecution and being labelled untouchables. However, those who were unable to convert, for whatever reason, were reduced to the untouchable rank. Omvedt does not accept Basham's explanation that the decline of Buddhism may be attributed to the decadence of Buddhist monasteries, the hold of the brāhmaṇas on the performance of life-cycle rituals, the reformed character of Brahmanism with the adoption of the *ahiṃsā* doctrine and its syncretistic attempts at the appropriation of the Buddha as the ninth incarnation of Viṣṇu. She is also critical of Kosambi's view that the individual Brahmanical priests were more suited to meet the needs of the self-contained villages of the agrarian economy rather than the large Buddhist monasteries, which had become uneconomic and dependent upon the patronage of higher classes and out of touch with the common people, and were now 'mired in wealth and superstition'.[84] Omvedt argues that Buddhist monasteries were not any more unproductive or 'parasitical than the Brahmanic priests living off innumerable gifts from believers'. In her view, Buddhism did not 'decline' but was 'defeated' and eliminated by the brāhmaṇas in collusion with the kings.

This is not the place to go into the causes of the decline of Buddhism, which is no doubt an important question and needs separate treatment notwithstanding the meticulous work of R.C. Mitra.[85] But it needs mentioning that the attitude of the early Buddhist and Jaina writers towards the Caṇḍālas as well as all those dubbed as *hīna jātis* was no different than the Brahmanical authors of the Dharmasūtras. This is amply shown by Richard Fick, Dev Raj Chanana,

Vivekanand Jha and Uma Chakravarti in their studies cited above. The theory of *karma*, which is taken for granted by Jainism and Buddhism, could be used effectively to rationalize discriminations on account of birth in a family or caste,[86] and, as Irfan Habib has argued[87] in his President's Address to the Indian History Congress in 1982, the principle of *ahiṃsā* could legitimize the hostility of the land-based peasantry towards hunting tribes of the forest living on the borders of agrarian settlements and thus justify their ostracism providing the basis for untouchablility. The hatred towards such communities is fully reflected in the early Jaina and Buddhist sources.

The myth of a harmonious and conflict-free golden age of India has been exploded in a number of studies,[88] and there is clear evidence of tensions, conflicts and also a few instances of persecution of Buddhists in the early medieval times.[89] For instance, Bhūdeva, a king of the Katyūri dynasty ruling over the regions of Kumaun and Garhwal in the tenth century, took pride in describing himself as a great enemy of Buddhist monks (*paramabuddhaśramaṇaripu*) and a great patron of the brāhmaṇas.[90] Several rulers of this region assumed the title of *paramabrahmaṇya*,[91] which, according to D.C. Sircar, should be translated as 'highly devoted to brāhmaṇas'.[92] We have also sculptures from Bihar and Orissa depicting Buddhist deities trampling the Brahmanical gods under their feet,[93] an unmistakable reflection of acute hostility between Buddhism and Brahmanism.

However, it is a mistake to think that sectarian conflicts, denunciations and violence were directed against the Buddhists alone. The *Periya Purāṇa* speaks of the impalement of 8,000 Jainas at the instance of the Śaiva saint Nānāsambandār, and a festival to commemorate the gruesome event is observed to this day at the Madura temple.[94] Even if the story is the invention of a sectarian mind, it reflects extreme hatred. The Tamil Āḷvār and Nāyanār saint–poets denounced both Jainism and Buddhism, but the attacks on the former were particularly vehement. Attempts were made to appropriate the worship of Jina Rṣabha too, while imprecating against the Jaina *śramaṇas* at the same time.[95] According to a Śaiva hagiographical work, the god Śaṅkara incarnated himself as the philosopher Śaṅkarācārya to destroy heretics, particularly the Jainas, who were massacred and their books and temples destroyed.[96] The *Basava Purāṇa* and the *Paṇḍitārādhya caritra* too speak of the Jaina's severe persecution and destruction of their temples.[97] Inscriptions from the tenth–eleventh centuries testify to the persecution of the Jainas in the South. Around 973 CE, Tailapa II of the Cālukya family overthrew the Rāṣṭrakūta dynasty, persecuted the Jainas and destroyed their shrines in the process.[98] Later the Coḷa armies overran the Cālukya country, destroying Jaina temples.[99] The causes may have been political, but greed for the wealth stored in religious institutions was no less a motivating factor. The *Rājataraṅgiṇī* narrates the iconoclasm of several kings:

Śaṅkaravaman,[100] Kṣemagupta,[101] Kalaśa[102] and his son Harṣa who, astonished at the amount of wealth stored in a deserted shrine, was tempted to loot the rich temples of the gods and appointed, especially, an 'officer for uprooting the gods'.[103] Religious literature of this period gives expression to acrimonious theological disputes among the Jainas, Buddhists, Śaivas and Vaiṣṇavas denouncing each other in strong terms.

If there are traces of conflict,[104] there are also many examples of syncretism[105] and veneration of deities of different and opposing religions,[106] giving grist to the mill of those who wish to paint a picture of a tolerant, harmonious and homogeneous 'Hindu' India; although it is possible to argue that, in many cases, these may have been attempts at reconciliation and resolution of conflicts. Nevertheless, the crucial question is: faced with similar challenges, why did Buddhism decline whereas Jainism was able to survive and retain its social base?

It seems to me that the answer lies not in the conspiracy theory of the brāhmaṇa–king collusion,[107] but the way the two 'heterodox' religions responded to the caste system. Both Jainism and Buddhism denounced the cult of Vedic sacrifices and challenged the superior position of the brāhmaṇas in the *varṇa* system, but did not reject the division of society into *varṇa* categories.[108] The fourfold division of society is a regular feature of the early Buddhist texts.[109] However, Buddhism was more liberal towards the śūdras and untouchables, and allowed them admission into its monastic organization. Although the majority of the monks mentioned in the early Buddhist sources came from the brāhmaṇa and kṣatriya backgrounds, quite a few, such as Upāli and Subhadda (barbers), Canna (*dāsīputra*), Talaputa (*naṭa*), Dhaniya (potter) and Sāti (fisherman), were born in *nīca kulas*.[110] In the *Theragāthā*, the monk Sunīta speaks of his birth in a 'low family' of sweepers (*pukkusa*).[111] It has been argued that the Buddha could not bring about a radical change in society owing to the limitations of the existing mode of production. But he tried to create an egalitarian order of monks which was open to all irrespective of rank or *varṇa*, to even those who had been slaves.[112] The *Jātaka* stories tell us of the Bodhisattvas born in the 'low' families of potters and Caṇḍālas.[113] Buddhism as a religion retained its catholicity and criticism of the caste system even in its later phases, despite the fact that Buddhist kings of the early medieval period, such as Dharmapāla and Vigrahapāla of the Pāla dynasty of Bengal, took credit in their inscriptions for re-establishing the *varṇāśramadharma* and barring any deviation from it, apparently because caste provided a useful mechanism for controlling and regulating economic and political resources. However, Buddhism seems to have had a large following among the lower classes. Kumārila Bhaṭṭa (eighth century CE) writes that the Buddha's teachings were followed by those who belonged to the fourth *varṇa*, i.e. śūdras or outcastes (*niravasitas*).[114] The Purāṇas denounced the Buddhists as *pāṣaṇḍins* who were adept in argumentation and wilfully transgressed the duties arising out of the distinctions of caste and the established order of life.[115] The example of Rāhulabhadra, the disciple of Āryadeva, shows that even a śūdra monk could rise to the position of the abbot of the Nalanda monastery and control immense amounts of wealth.[116] The *Vajrasūcī* of Aśvaghoṣa[117] makes a trenchant criticism of the caste system and the selfishness of the brāhmaṇas. In the *Laṭakamelaka* of Śaṅkhadhara, a Buddhist monk rejects the idea expressed by a Digambara monk that anyone can become polluted by the touch of somebody who is of a 'dissimilar caste' (*asadṛśa-jāti-sparśa*).[118]

Contrary to the Buddhist attitude, the Jainas fully endorsed the caste system. Raviṣeṇa in his *Padma Purāṇa*, which is the Jaina version of the *Rāmāyaṇa*, written in Sanskrit in 676 CE, credits Ṛṣabhadeva for creating the four *varṇas* from different parts of his body and assigning them their respective duties.[119] The theme is further developed in the *Ādi Purāṇa*[120] of Jinasena (ninth century CE) and *Ādīśvaracarita*[121] of Hemacandra (eleventh century CE) with some variations. The Jaina texts condemn the intermixture of *varṇas* as strongly as the Brahmanical law books.[122] Somadeva Sūri (tenth century CE), in his *Nītivākyāmṛta*, recommends that everyone should stick to one's hereditary occupation determined by one's caste,[123] and restricts religious initiation to the upper three *varṇas*.[124] Jainism also evolved rituals for its laity. Jaina domestic rituals were similar to Brahmanical ones officiated by the Jaina brāhmaṇa priests.[125] Kosambi's pithy comment on the survival of Jainism and the decline of Buddhism is typical of his deep understanding on these matters. 'Jainism survives in India to this day for the same reasons that prevented its spread outside the country . . . it soon came to terms with caste and ritual, as Buddhism did not.'[126] The caste system ensured the structured dependence of agricultural and artisanal labour, which was to the great advantage of the landowning and ruling elite.[127] Movements of protest could not be sustained for long without basic changes in the material conditions.

VII

The upper-class contempt for manual labour has been one of the basic organizing principles of the *varṇa–jāti* hierarchy. It is held that the Buddha forbade the monks manual labour in order to free them from worldly preoccupations.[128] The prohibition could also have been influenced by the doctrine of *ahiṃsā* (non-violence), as levelling the soil, watering fields, gardens, etc., destroyed 'lives'.[129] Hence, Buddhist monasteries were gifted *ārāmikas* (monastery slaves) and to supervise their work, a monk was elected as *ārāmika-pessaka* (supervisor of *ārāmikas*).[130] Manual work was avoided by the nuns too and domestic work was declared an offence by a *pācittiya* rule.[131] Such a negative attitude distanced the philosophers–monks of Mahāyāna Buddhism from physical work to such an extent that they developed a philosophy which acknowledged only the 'mental' nature of our experiences, arguing that everything is essentially no more than a 'mental construction' (*prajñaptimātra*).[132] Debiprasad Chattopadhyaya describes it as a revolutionary philosophy passing into its opposite.[133]

In material terms, the effect of this ideological turn of Buddhism was to further devalue and depress those who earned their living through physical labour; ultimately, this gave rise to the Sahajayāna form of Buddhism, popular among the lower castes.[134] In Jainism too there was an excessive emphasis on not killing any form of life, leading to the prohibition of agriculture and other manual activities from the very beginning. I have shown elsewhere that in post-Vedic times, with the depression of the peasantry, the well-to-do members of the *viś* community became traders and adopted Jainism in order to emphasize their dissociation from agriculture, with the result that in course of time, only merchants and traders came to be known as vaiśyas.[135] The shift from the later Vedic to the post-Vedic connotation of the term is indicative of the decline in the status of those communities which were engaged in the cultivation of soil and artisanal activities involving manual work. In Brahmanism, as we have seen, the servitude of the śūdra was the foundation of the *varṇa* system. Disdain towards the śūdra was extended to cover all *jātis* subsisting on manual work and primary production in post-Vedic times; the attitude was further hardened with the adoption of the principles of *ahiṃsā*[136] in neo-Brahmanism, and its use in ascribing impurity to menial occupations and communities. The *Manusmṛti* not only ranks hunters and gatherers as low-born outcastes, but also lays down that if a brāhmaṇa or kṣatriya is unable to earn a livelihood by his own specific vocation, he may earn it by the vocation of a vaiśya by trading in uncondemnable wealth-increasing articles but must not practise agriculture: '(Some) declare that agriculture is something excellent (but) that means of subsistence is blamed by the virtuous; (for) the wooden (implement) with iron point injures the earth and (the beings) living in the earth.'[137]

This ideology had serious implications for women. According to Manu, the householder (*gṛhastha*) has five 'slaughterhouses' (*pañca sūnā*): fireplace (*cullī*), grinding stone, broom, pestle and mortar, and water pot. Their use binds him with the fetters of sin, and so he should expiate by performing the five great sacrifices (*pañca mahāyajñas*) daily.[138] But these are the 'sinful' sites around which revolves the life of a common housewife. It is not surprising that women were regularly clubbed with the śūdras in Brahmanical texts.[139] The pain and drudgery of a life around the 'pestle and mortar' is vividly expressed in some songs of the Buddhist nuns included in the *Therīgāthā*.[140] Manu's attitude to work presents a striking contrast to the Ṛgvedic poet who worshipfully invokes the mortar set to work in every house to give a clear loud sound like the drum[141] of conquerors, and compares the mother goddesses Uṣas (in plural) with women singing as they perform *viṣṭi*, apparently working in the fields.[142] In later medieval literature, the term *viṣṭi* came to mean forced labour, but in the Ṛgvedic hymn it is a collective activity with no trace of scorn.

VIII

Attribution of impurity to manual labour gave religious sanction to the exploitation of the working classes, and helped in the evolution of a Brahmanical paradigm of social integration of diverse communities into a highly stratified caste society with an ideological tool with which to measure and justify the ranking of a particular social segment.[143] The role of brāhmaṇas in spreading of this ideology from its home in the Gangetic valley to the various regions of the subcontinent is duly stressed, and R.S. Sharma has laid particular emphasis on the consequences of land grants given to brāhmaṇas in the tribal areas in early medieval times. However, brāhmaṇas alone were not the carriers of caste ideology which was useful in the restructuring of tribes into a hierarchical society, legitimizing the claims of the tribal elites as superior status groups based on heredity. It may be noted that in Sri Lanka, the caste system developed under the influence of the Buddhist monks[144] who had carried with them the theory of *karma* and a notion of the functional hierarchy of social groups based on birth. But, as there were no brāhmaṇas or a caste of priests, castes were not defined in terms of pure/impure communities. The Sri Lankan example shows that the opposition of brāhmaṇa and untouchable, i.e. the 'pure' and the 'impure', is not the founding principle of the caste system as assumed by Dumont. Rather, it is the result of a superimposition on a structure of rigid class differentiations; in other words, castes can exist without the help of the ideology of pollution.

The expansion of caste society in various regions of India took place through multiple processes;[145] a few studies have underlined the role of tribal chieftains who emulated the kṣatriya model in order to legitimize their political power and control over community resources, and took initiative for the diffusion and broad acceptance of the Brahmanical norms in Orissa in early medieval times.[146] In some regions, the dominant ideology could have been disseminated through Jaina and orthodox Śaiva monastic orders. It has been argued that in the backward tribal territory of Rayalseema in south-western Andhra Pradesh, the transition from tribe to state took place in the sixth–seventh centuries CE when this area was exposed to outside influence owing to its strategic importance in the power struggle between the Cālukyas of Bādāmi and the Pallavas of Kañcī.[147] The region did not attract any brāhmaṇa settlements (*agrahāras*) but was penetrated by Jaina monks and Śaivas of the Kālāmukha sect who used the local vernacular to spread their message. They were patronized by the emerging local elite and chieftains who also showed their preference towards the local language in their inscriptions in order to assert their separate ethnic identity and local roots vis-à-vis the Cālukyas and the Pallavas.

These developments contributed not only to the growth of Telugu language and its literature, but also integrated this region with pan-Indian culture through ideologies opposed to the caste system. While I agree with the broad generalizations of this argument, it must be noted that neither the Kālāmukhas – who are wrongly confused with the Kāpālikas[148] – nor the Jainas in these centuries were opposed to the caste system. In fact the Kālāmukhas were thoroughly imbued with the dominant ideology and many of them became the preceptors of kings (*rājaguru*) or family priests for village headmen (*gāvuṇḍas*). They actively promoted the construction of temples, which, apart from being places of worship, also imparted Brahmanical education to people and received grants for that purpose.[149] It is not surprising that a Kaḷacūri inscription of the twelfth century CE praises Vimalaśiva, the Śaiva *rājaguru* of king Jayasiṃha, as one whose counsel had made even more distant regions pay taxes.[150] Nevertheless, the basic point that the initiative of the brāhmaṇa caste is not an essential condition for the spread of the Brahmanical ideology of caste is substantiated by the example of the numerically large Kallar caste residing in the southern districts of Tamil Nadu. Hutton describes it as a cultivating and predatory caste notable for their efficient agriculture, expert thieving, cattle-lifting, etc.[151] Dumont did intensive field work among the Pramalai Kallar, a subcaste of the Kallars, and published a monograph about them from a social anthropological point of view.[152] He writes that the Kallars are relatively unaffected by Brahmanic ideas and customs. They bury their dead, and although they have martial pretensions, they willingly allow themselves to be classed among the śūdra.[153] However, in the local hierarchy they occupy the middle rung of the caste ladder. They seem to have migrated from the Andhra country and founded the kingdom of Pudukkottai – between Tanjavur and Madurai – in the last quarter of the seventeenth century. Nicholas B. Dirks, who has made a detailed study of the kingdom of Pudukkottai,[154] compares them with the Rajputs of northern India and cogently argues that the assumption of power led to a restructuring of the Kallar caste, which got divided into a number of subcastes graded hierarchically, not on the basis of their 'purity /impurity but with reference to their relative proximity to royal power and control over land.[155] Pramalai Kallar is the royal subcaste. It is endogamous and is also known as Thevar (from the Sanskrit *deva*), originally a political designation but now a general title. The domination of the Kallars in the areas occupied by them manifested itself in the imposition of extremely humiliating and discriminatory prohibitions upon the 'exterior' castes who worked on their fields as labourers living in 'serf-like' conditions. Dumont describes these impositions upon untouchables as 'customary', but, as recorded by Hutton,[156] the prohibitions had nothing to do with the notions of purity and merely expressed arrogance of power. Dirks speaks of the increasing trend towards patriarchy and the adoption of some of the Brahmanic practices by the royal family of Kallar, such as seclusion of women, disapproval of widow marriage, etc. But the field work of Dumont shows that widow marriage prevails among the Kallar and that divorce is extremely easy.[157] The latter could be based on nothing more than the desire of one of the spouses. It follows that the Brahmanical influence was confined to the royal family and sanskritizing efforts had a very limited impact on the caste. Dirks' assertion that caste as a social system, whether in the political milieu of the pre-British period or in its 'increasingly Brahmanical forms under colonial rule', was a most pervasive form of oppression directed against women, is valid in general; but as far as the Kallar women are concerned, the impact of caste formation is yet to be worked out.[158]

Nevertheless, the twin pillars that support the caste system are first, the subordination of women, and second, its capacity to reinvent itself in changing social formations in the service of the powerful and the dominant. It has been shown that in spite of its apparent rigidity, the system was able to enrol new members and create new caste categories at various levels. There was scope for political or economic mobility through the processes of fission and fusion, as exemplified by the formation of the Rājput and Kāyastha categories. In these processes, control over woman's sexuality was critical; endogamy as well as hypergamy was used to create a distinct caste identity and raise its status. In the pre-British period, fission rather than fusion was adopted for upward mobility, but the trend in modern India has been towards fusion, in order to form numerically large caste groups by integrating subcastes and groups having parallel positions.[159] It is argued that the Census Reports have played a crucial role in this development by generating greater caste consciousness and an awareness of the bargaining possibilities of larger solidarities. Whatever the case may be, a change of trend underlines the real nature of this form of social stratification, which is its capacity to reconstruct itself as an instrument of power for the new elite in a different political formation. It is being argued that caste should not be disavowed or sought to be erased as a 'site of identity and power', for it has possibilities of political mobilization that would transform the prevailing relations of state and society in favour of the oppressed, and it provides a potent ideological tool for the assertion of Dalit identity.[160] Such postmodernist arguments are in fact arguments in favour of the status quo, pleading for the replacement of one set of power-elite with another without bringing about any revolutionary change in the politico-economic patterns of domination and exploitation. These do not take into consideration the fact that caste is no longer tied with occupation. Post-independence changes in the political and economic set-up and industrialization have impacted the internal homogeneity of castes, which have thrown up their own elite who may use the ideology of caste for narrow political interests without effecting any radical transformation in the condition of their caste in general. It is not without significance that the caste wars are fought these days on issues of reservation in jobs and institutions of higher education, but there is no strong movement around the questions of land reform and primary education which could transform the lives of the Dalit masses. Dr Ambedkar seems to have foreseen this possibility when he criticized the view that abolition of subcastes should be the first step towards caste reform. He categorically wrote, 'abolition of sub-castes will only help to strengthen the castes and make them more powerful and therefore more mischievous'.[161] He argued for the annihilation of caste,[162] for which he thought the real remedy lies in inter-caste marriages. The fact that he taught the Dalit communities self-respect and organized them for collective political action does not mean that he wanted to nurture caste identities. For Ambedkar, social and cultural emancipation of women and men was as important as political and economic empowerment. It is unfortunate that in the unabashed pursuit of political power today, this vision of Ambedkar is completely forgotten and, consequently, the pernicious strength of caste and patriarchal mentalities in our society is not seriously challenged.[163]

Notes

1 On 19 and 20 June 2007, the television channel *Aaj Tak* showed a Dalit man named Ramlal of Tonk, Rajasthan being badly beaten up, resulting in multiple fractures. He was apparently punished by the upper-caste villagers for his 'crime' of drinking water from a nearby borewell. This is not an isolated case. Incidents of this nature are frequently reported from various parts of the country.

More recently, *The Hindu* (20 October 2014) reported that a Dalit youth, Mehul Kabīra, of Bhayla village in the Ahmedabad district of Gujarat, was beaten up by some youth of the Darbar community for the 'crime' of attempting to ply an autorickshaw to earn his living instead of following his traditional occupation of sweeping and scavenging, as he belonged to the Valmiki (Bhangda) caste. He had to be hospitalized and his family had to flee the village. The attackers said that he and his community members were fit only for scavenging and work in fields belonging to the caste Hindus. The matter was reported to the police but 'with no strong action', the Dalits continue to live in constant fear.

It may be noted here that the issue is not of ritual purity but of caste-based prejudice and economic exploitation.

2 Ronald Inden, 'Orientalist Constructions of India'. As Aijaz Ahmad remarks, 'Colonialism is now held responsible not only for its own cruelties but, conveniently enough, for ours too.' Aijaz Ahmad, *In Theory*, pp. 196–97. Inden, however, in a later work, *Imagining India* (p.

82) has modified his position a little by linking the formation of the 'modern form' of caste to 'the collapse of Hindu kingship' in the thirteenth or fourteenth century. For a devastating critique of Inden's book, see Aijaz Ahmad, 'Between Orientalism and Historicism'.

[3] In her essay titled 'The Changing Caste System in India', Pauline Kolenda writes, 'the persistent feature of Indian society, its basic building block, is the endogamous group, which has now become a segmentary one rather than an organic one'. Pauline Kolenda, *Caste, Cult and Hierarchy*, p. 83. Dipankar Gupta speaks of castes as 'discrete categories' which 'value the principle of endogamy very highly', without explaining that these discrete categories could not exist without practising endogamy. Dipankar Gupta, *Interrogating Caste*, p. 70. For a detailed discussion, see Suvira Jaiswal, *Caste*, Introduction.

[4] Nicholas B. Dirks, *Castes of Mind*, pp. 7–8.

[5] H.H. Risley, *Census of India*, vol. I, p. 1, 1901, quoted in ibid., p. 222.

[6] For references, see Suvira Jaiswal, *Caste*, pp. 40–41.

[7] Dipankar Gupta, 'Continuous Hierarchies and Discrete Castes', reprinted in Dipankar Gupta, ed., *Social Stratification*, p. 137; also see Dipankar Gupta, *Interrogating Caste*, pp. 70, 84.

[8] Ibid., p. 70. However, earlier Gupta ascribed the origin of the *varṇas* to the attempt of the Aryans to maintain a social distance from the indigenous community. See Dipankar Gupta, 'From Varna, to Jati'.

[9] Ibid.

[10] I have shown that the two terms are used interchangeably in early Indian texts. Suvira Jaiswal, *Caste*, pp. 42–43.

[11] Kane quotes *Sūta Saṃhitā*, Śiva Māhātmya khaṇḍa, 12.51.52, which states that 'a man belongs to a caste by birth and no action of his can alter that fact, that several castes are like the species of animals and that caste attaches to the body and not to the soul'. P.V. Kane, *History of Dharmaśāstra*, vol. II, part II, p. 52. The *Bhagavadgītā* (XVIII.41) clearly says that owing to their natural (inborn) qualities (*guṇas*), the four *varṇas* have been assigned different functions. For a detailed discussion, see Suvira Jaiswal, 'The Making of a Hegemonic Tradition', pp. 26–27 note 54. For the implication of the theory of *guṇas* for the hereditary nature of *varṇa* organization, see Suvira Jaiswal, 'Caste: Ideology and Context', p. 611.

[12] See the origin myths current among Chamars, Dacca Cāṇḍāls, Kāyasthas, Vaniyans, Bhaṅgis, etc., cited by Dipankar Gupta to show that there were many and not one caste ideology. Dipankar Gupta, *Interrogating Caste*, pp. 73–77.

[13] D.D. Kosambi, *An Introduction to the Study of Indian History* (first edition), p. 25; Morton Klass, *Caste*, p. 175; Irfan Habib, *Essays in Indian History*, p. 17.

[14] Suvira Jaiswal, *Caste*, pp. 9ff., 157–58.

[15] Louis Dumont, *Homo Hierarchicus*.

[16] Suvira Jaiswal, *Caste*, pp. 34–38, 103 note 54, 118 note 207; Suvira Jaiswal, 'Caste: Ideology and Context'. Also see Gerald D. Berreman's excellent critique, 'The Brahmanical View of Caste'.

[17] Suvira Jaiswal, 'Varna Ideology and Social Change', pp. 41ff.

[18] Louis Dumont, *Homo Hierarchicus*, p. 113.

[19] D.D. Kosambi, *Myth and Reality*, pp. 42–81.

[20] Ibid., pp. 68, 76.

[21] Romila Thapar, *Ancient Indian Social History*, p. 18; R.S. Sharma, *Material Culture and Social Formations in Ancient India*, p. 157; D.N. Jha, *Ancient India in Historical Outline*. For the latest summing up of the archaeological and linguistic arguments respectively, see Jonathan Mark Kenoyer, 'Culture and Societies of the Indus Tradition' and Madhav M. Deshpande, 'Aryan Origins', pp. 41–97, 98–156.

[22] Suvira Jaiswal, *Caste*, pp. 136–37, 195.

[23] See Appendix to chapter 1 above.

[24] For example, see Hans-Peter Schmidt on *Ṛgveda*, X.27.12, which speaks of a beautiful woman choosing her spouse among the suitors of her own free will (*svayam sa mitram vanute jane cit*). According to Schmidt, the hymn shows the prevalence of bride price and the girl goes to the highest bidder. Hans-Peter Schmidt, *Some Women's Rites and Rights in the Veda*, pp. 76–77. But for a detailed discussion, see chapter 4 below.

[25] S.A. Dange, *Sexual Symbolism from Vedic Ritual*, pp. 73–74; Frederick M. Smith, 'Indra's curse, Varuna's Noose, and the Suppression of Women in the Vedic Śrauta Ritual'; Kumkum Roy, *Emergence of Monarchy in North India*, p. 67.

[26] Katherine K. Young, 'Hinduism', p. 64. M.N. Srinivas (*The Changing Position of Indian Women*, pp. 17–18) speaks of the considerable empowerment of high-caste women through their meticulous observance of purity–pollution rules, performance of periodical rituals, etc., which are considered necessary for the material and spiritual welfare of the household. Nevertheless, the high-caste woman's assertion or celebration of self-worth through the performance of Hindu rituals can hardly be linked to the Ṛgvedic vision. Women were debarred from listening to the recitation of the Vedas. The *Bṛhannāradīya Purāṇa* (XIV.144) says, 'A man who reads the Vedas in the proximity of women and śūdras goes to hells successively during thousands of crores of *kalpas*'; quoted in R.C. Hazra, *Studies in the Upapurāṇas*, vol. I, p. 325. The prohibition is restated in the *Rāmacaritamānasa* of Tulasīdāsa (I.109.1, p. 107).

[27] For the remodelling of an ancient myth regarding the creation of the cosmos through the original sacrifice of the primordial being to justify the fourfold social differentiation, see Suvira Jaiswal, *Caste*, pp. 135–36.

[28] *Taittirīya Brāhmaṇa*, I.2.6.7, quoted in U.N. Ghoshal, *A History of Indian Political Ideas*, p. 31.

[29] *Taittirīya Brāhmaṇa*, III.2.3.9, quoted in Jogiraj Basu, *India of the Age of the Brāhmaṇas*, p. 12. Other texts speak of the birth of the śūdra from Evil: *Kāṭhaka Saṃhitā*, XXXI.2, *Maitrāyaṇī Saṃhitā*, IV.1.3, quoted in U.N. Ghoshal, *A History of Indian Political Ideas*.

[30] For the name of the Śūdra tribe becoming a generic term for the fourth *varṇa*, see R.S. Sharma, *Śūdras in Ancient India*, pp. 34ff.

[31] *Ṛgveda*, I.126.3 speaks of chariots carrying *vadhus* given to Kakṣivān as part of his *dakṣiṇā*. These were apparently women captured from defeated alien tribes, presumably the Dāsas. *Ṛgveda*, VIII.19.36 mentions a gift of 50 *vadhus* given to the composer of the hymn by king Trasadasyu. Griffith translates the term as 'female slaves'. For women of the Dāsa tribes participating in wars against Aryan enemies, see chapter 4 below. Also see *Ṛgveda*, VIII, Vālakhilya 8.3, X.62.10. In *Ṛgveda*, I.92.3, the poet beseeches the dawn goddess to grant him ample wealth in the form of brave sons (*suvīrāḥ*), horses and troops of slaves (*dāsa–pravarga*).

[32] D.D. Kosambi, *An Introduction to the Study of Indian History* (first edition), pp. 93, 104.

[33] Suvira Jaiswal, *Caste*, pp. 167, 196–97.

[34] P.V. Kane, *History of Dharmaśāstra*, vol. II, part I, p. 55; Kumar Suresh Singh, 'Tribe into Caste', p. 32.

[35] Louis Dumont, *Homo Hierarchicus*, p. 37.

[36] Adrian C. Meyer, 'The Indian Caste System', p. 340.

[37] *Manusmṛti*, X.4; 31.

[38] Suvira Jaiswal, *Caste*, p. 103 note 54.

[39] Marshal D. Sahlins, *Tribesmen*, pp. 5–6.

[40] Suvira Jaiswal, *Caste*, pp. 146–62.

[41] *Ṛgveda*, VII.6.5 describes *agni* using force (*baliniruddhya*) to make *viś* give tribute to Nahuṣa. R.S. Sharma, *Aspects of Political Ideas and Institutions in Ancient India*, pp. 178–80. Sharma cites several passages from the *Mahābhārata* and *Manusmṛti* that recommend coercion against

the lower *varṇas* to discharge their *varṇa* duties and thus ensure the stability of the *varṇa* order. R.S. Sharma, *Early Medieval Indian Society*, pp. 63–65.

42 R.S. Sharma, *The State and Varṇa Formation in the Mid-Ganga Plains*, pp. 62ff.

43 *Bṛhadāraṇyaka Upaniṣad*, IV.4.14–16, quoted in D.D. Kosambi, *Combined Methods in Indology and Other Writings*, p. 320. Also see Suvira Jaiswal, *Caste*, pp. 59–61, and chapter 1 above.

44 According to a Tibetan tradition, the Śākyas and the Licchavis were branches of the same tribe. The origin myths of both groups attribute brother–sister marriage to the founders, and the origin of the Koliyas of Rāmagāma too is traced from a Śākya girl in such texts as *Sumaṅgalavilāsinī* and *Mahāvastu*. (Quoted in S.N. Misra, *Ancient Indian Republics*, p. 46.) Śuddhodhana, the father of the Buddha, is said to have married two Koliyan princesses, Māyā and Mahāpajāpati Gotamī. Kosambi discounts this tradition on the ground that the Śākyas were too proud to marry outside their tribe. He cites the story of Pasenadi, the king of Kosala, who was tricked into marrying Vāsabhakhattiya, the daughter of Mahānāma Śākya, by a slave girl Nāgamuṇḍā. However, this only shows that the Śākyans did not want to displease Pasenadi who had asked for the hand of a Śākya girl, but, at the same time, they did not wish to give a girl of pure Śākya lineage in marriage to him who belonged to the lowly Mātaṅga *kula*. The tribe of Mātaṅgas was later equated with Caṇḍālas. In the *Dīgha Nikāya*, the Buddha tells the brāhmaṇa Ambaṭṭha that the *khattiyas* (kṣatriyas) are more rigid and refuse to accept in their own group a man who is not pure by birth for seven generations on both his parents' lineages, but the brāhmaṇas accept sons born of partial non-brāhmaṇa origin on either side and allow them to participate in *yajña, śrāddha, sthālīpāka* and other rituals. *Dīgha Nikāya*, vol. II, pp. 92–97, quoted in N. Wagle, *Society at the Time of the Buddha*, pp. 101–13.

However, the Licchavis and the Jñātrikas, both members of the Vajjian confederacy, are known to have had marriage relations. The Licchavi chief Cetaka's sister Triśalā was married to Siddhārtha of the Jñātrikas, the father of the Jaina *tīrthaṅkara* Mahāvīra. Cetaka's daughter Cellanā was married to Bimbisāra, the king of Magadha, and Ajātaśatru was her son. Cetaka had several daughters whom he gave in marriage to kṣatriya rulers of the time. No doubt kings took wives from other *varṇas* too, but the mother of the heir-apparent or claimant to the throne had to be of kṣatriya lineage, as is shown by the story of Viḍūḍabha, son of Vāsabha-khattiya. Also see Suvira Jaiswal, *Caste*, pp. 15, 27 note 83. Wagle speaks of the Śākyas, Licchavis etc., as extended kin groups which ossified into castes by the time of the *Manusmṛti*. That the kṣatriyas too had become a caste like the brāhmaṇas is shown by the fact that an inscription from Andhra Pradesh palaeographically assigned to the early centuries of the Common Era speaks of kṣatriya merchants. K. Gopalachari, *Early History of the Andhra Country*, p. 91. The *Manusmṛti*, X.43–44 speaks of kṣatriya *jātis* in the plural, indicating the existence of a number of kṣatriya castes within the broad *varṇa* category.

45 *Śatapatha Brāhmaṇa*, II.1.4.4; XI.5.7.1; XII. 4.4.6; 4.4.7; XIII.19.1–2.

46 *Chāndogya Upaniṣad*, V.10.7, p. 233.

47 A.L. Basham, *The Origin and Development of Classical Hinduism*, chapter 3.

48 *Chāndogya Upaniṣad*, VII.24.2.

49 Max Weber, *The Religion of India*, p. 122.

50 Pauline Kolenda, 'Religious Anxiety and Hindu Fate'; Joan P. Mencher, 'The Caste System Upside Down, or the Not-So-Mysterious East'; Eleanor Zelliot, *From Untouchable to Dalit*, p. 74 note 5; Robert Deliège, 'The Myths of Origin of the Indian Untouchables'.

Following Jan Vansina, one may assume that these oral myths had been a part of the consciousness of the oppressed castes for a long time. But these have to be distinguished from caste histories written in response to the colonial documentation project. See V. Geetha, 'Rewriting History in the Brahmin's Shadow'; Badri Narayan, *Women Heroes and Dalit Assertion in North India*, pp. 170ff. However, the Mahar saint Chokhamela (thirteenth–fourteenth centuries) accepted his birth in a low caste as a consequence of his *karma*. Eleanor Zelliot, *From Untouchable to Dalit*, p. 7.

[51] R.S. Sharma, *Early Medieval Indian Society*, pp. 50–51, 53.

[52] *Vinaya Piṭaka*, vol. IV, p. 181, quoted in Dev Raj Chanana, *Slavery in Ancient India*, p. 62. Uma Chakravarti notes that this is one of the first written records which shows that women were the obvious targets in case of antagonism between two social groups. Uma Chakravarti, *Social Dimensions of Early Buddhism*, p. 27 note 145.

[53] Vivekanand Jha, 'Stages in the History of Untouchables'; Vivekanand Jha, 'Caste, Untouchablilty and Social Justice', p. 24.

[54] Vivekanand Jha, 'Stages in the History of Untouchables', p. 22.

[55] Richard Fick, *The Social Organization in North East India*, pp. 43ff. For the evidence of early Dharmasūtras, see Vivekanand Jha, 'Caṇḍāla and the Origin of Untouchability', pp. 4–7.

[56] Louis Dumont, *Homo Hierarchicus*, p. 47 (emphasis added). Similarly, the view that primitive notions about accepting food from non-kin causing pollution are the rationale for untouchability cannot be sustained. Restrictions on inter-dining and acceptance of cooked food from various categories of people have evolved gradually, much later than the emergence of untouchability. Suvira Jaiswal, *Caste*, pp. 86–87, 125–26 note 285.

[57] Ordinary people of the 'clean' (*śuddha*) castes must have used open spaces.

[58] Hiroyuki Kotani cites a document from the eighteenth century (quoted in G.S. Sardesai, ed., *Selections from the Peshwa Daftar*, pp. 43–92) mentioning that a female servant employed in the house of a brāhmaṇa family turned out to be of the Chambar caste. Hence, all those who had come in contact with her had to undergo various degrees of purification. Another instance cited by him shows that a female slave belonging to a family of the Prabhu caste committed adultery with an *antyaja* (*ati*-śūdra), which made all the members of the Prabhu family impure. H. Kotani, 'Ati-śūdra castes in the Medieval Deccan', pp. 56–57.

[59] For fair-looking Rājaputra (Rajput) girls sold into slavery and obliged to do all kinds of pure and 'impure work', see Pushpa Prasad, 'Female Slavery in Thirteenth Century Gujarat'; Suvira Jaiswal, *Caste*, pp. 84–85. The *Nāradasmṛti*, written perhaps in the fourth century CE, clearly specifies that while a hired servant (*karmakara*) is supposed to do only pure work, slaves are to do all kinds of impure work. P.V. Kane, *History of Dharmaśāstra*, vol. II, part I, pp. 184ff. Also see Prabhati Mukherjee, *Beyond the Four Varṇas*, p. 75.

[60] This does not, however, mean that the institution of untouchability can be traced to the Harappan culture, as was done by Christoph von Fürer-Haimendorf. See Suvira Jaiswal, *Caste*, pp. 78–79.

[61] T.R. Sareen, 'Slavery in India under British Rule, 1772–1843'.

[62] Gita Ramaswamy, *India Stinking*, p. 6.

[63] Uma Chakravarti, *Social Dimensions of Early Buddhism*, p. 104.

[64] N. Wagle, *Society at the Time of the Buddha*, pp. 119–20, 122–23.

[65] On *rathakāra*, see Vivekanand Jha, 'Status of the Rathakāra in Early Indian History'. In the *Kauṭilīya Arthaśāstra* (III.7.35), he is described as a vaiśya. The Veṇas seem to have been a non-Aryan tribe of 'bamboo workers' or basket weavers.

[66] *Ṛgveda*, VIII.5.38 has *carmamna*. Sāyaṇa explains that it refers to armour made of leather.

[67] Suvira Jaiswal, *Caste*, p. 82.

[68] Vivekanand Jha, 'Stages in the History of Untouchables', p. 19.

[69] *Manusmṛti*, IV.218.

[70] Ibid., X.15.49.

[71] Ibid. X.36. Also repeated in *Mahābhārata* (critical edition), XIII.48.26.

[72] R.S. Sharma, *Śūdras in Ancient India*, pp. 330–33.

[73] *Epigraphia Indica*, vol. X, Lüder's List No. 1273.

[74] Patañjali on Pāṇini, II.4.10, *Mahābhāṣya* of Patañjali, p. 475.

[75] See Vivekanand Jha, 'Stages in the History of Untouchables', pp. 21–31.

[76] D.N. Jha, *The Myth of the Holy Cow*, chapter 3.

[77] Ajay Mitra Shastri, *India as Seen in the Bṛhatsaṃhitā of Varāhamihira*, p. 214.

[78] *Manusmṛti*, cited above. It also approves of meat eating by declaring the flesh of an animal killed by a dog, a carnivorous animal and a Caṇḍāla pure. Caṇḍālas, called *dasyu*, in this verse, were apparently hunters selling animal flesh.

[79] *The Parāśarasmṛti* places the women of washermen (*rajakī*), leather workers (*carmakāri*), hunters (*lubdhakī*) and bamboo workers (*venujīvanī*) in the same category, and lays down the rules for purification if a woman of any of these castes stayed even unknowingly in the house of a member of any of the four *varṇas*. *Parāśarasmṛti*, VI.44–45.

[80] The *Vedavyāsasmṛti* (I.13) enumerates Carmakāra, Bhaṭa, Bhilla, Rajaka, Puṣkara, Naṭa, Varaṭa, Meda, Caṇḍāla, Dāsa, Śvapāca and Kolika as *antyajas*, and states that on seeing one of these or any other beef eater (*gavāsanaḥ*) one should wash one's eyes and bathe after speaking to them. *Smṛtīnām Samuccayaḥ*, p. 357. An example of the internalization of this ideology by untouchable groups themselves is provided by K.R. Hanumanthan who notes that according to *Valaṅkai Caritram*, the Pallas as non-beef eaters considered themselves superior to the Paraiyas who ate beef, although both were untouchable castes. K.R. Hanumanthan, 'Evolution of Untouchability in Tamil Nadu, up to 1600 A.D.', p. 64.

[81] Joan P. Mencher, 'The Caste System Upside Down, or the Not So Mysterious East', p. 472. Briggs writes that the Chamar belongs to the great class of unskilled labour: 'He is a grass-cutter, coolie, wood and bundle carrier, drudge, doer of odd jobs, maker and repairer of thatch and of mud walls, field labourer, groom, house servant, peon, brick maker and even a village watchman.' G.W. Briggs, *The Chamars*, p. 56. Dumont has to concede in this case that 'those who are most oppressed materially are at the same time seen as supremely impure'. Louis Dumont, *Homo Hierarchicus*, p. 180.

[82] S.M. Dahiwale, 'The Broken Men Theory of Untouchability'. Dahiwale points out that V.R. Shinde was the first to indicate the Buddhist background of a few of the present-day untouchable castes, such as the Pulayas of Kerala and some outcastes of Orissa. He also quotes from P.C. Alexander's *Buddhism in Kerala*, which shows that the Nambuthiri Brāhmaṇas converted Buddhist *vihāras* into Hindu temples and destroyed the influence of Buddhism by using the weapon of 'social ostracism'. However, K.R. Hanumanthan finds in the Buddhist and Jaina works such as *Maṇimekalai* and *Ācārakovai*, some traces of the concept of pollution and untouchability 'due to puristic and ahiṃsā doctrines of these religions'. K.R. Hanumanthan, 'Evolution of Untouchability in Tamil Nadu', p. 65.

[83] Gail Omvedt, *Buddhism in India*, pp. 149–85.

[84] D.D. Kosambi, 'The Decline of Buddhism in India', pp. 63–66. Also see, D.D. Kosambi, *An Introduction to the Study of Indian History* (first edition), pp. 246–47, 261–63, 291–94.

[85] R.C. Mitra, *The Decline of Buddhism in India*.

[86] It is for this reason that in propounding Navayana Buddhism Ambedkar rejected altogether the doctrine of *karma* and rebirth as, according to him, it was contradictory to the basic Buddhist teaching of *anattā* (non-soul). Gail Omvedt, *Buddhism in India*, pp. 2–6.

Badri Narayan (*Women, Heroes and Dalit Assertion in North India*, p. 34) writes that in the word 'Dalit' itself there is an inherent denial of *karma*, pollution and legitimized caste hierarchy.

[87] Irfan Habib, 'The Peasant in Indian History', p. 17.

[88] Y. Gopala Reddy, 'Socio-Economic Tensions in the Coḷa Period'; R.S. Sharma, *Early Medieval Indian Society*, pp. 214–34; Suvira Jaiswal, 'Social Dimensions of the Cult of Rama'.

[89] For traces of such conflicts in the story of Viṣṇu's Hayagrīva incarnation, see chapter 8 below.

[90] Bageshwar stone inscription of Bhūdeva dated 916 Vikram Samvat. Dabaral, *Uttarākhaṇḍa ke abhilekh evaṃ mudrā*, pp. 68–69, 162.

[91] Ibid., Pāṇḍukeśvara copperplate inscription of Padmaṭadeva, tenth century, p. 71.

[92] D.C. Sircar, *Indian Epigraphical Glossary, s.v. parama-brahmaṇya.*

[93] B.N. Sharma, 'Religious Tolerance and Intolerance in Indian Sculpture'; C.S. Pathak, ed., *Nalanda: Past and Present.* Also see B.N.S. Yadava, *Society and Culture in Northern India*, p. 345, for some instances of the persecution of Buddhists.

[94] K.A. Nilakanta Sastri, *A History of South India*, p. 424; Friedhelm Hardy, *The Religious Culture of India*, p. 51. He cites many examples of religious intolerance and conflict (pp. 105ff.). D.N. Jha, *Rethinking Hindu Identity*; D.N. Jha, *Contesting Symbols and Stereotypes*, chapter 3. The literature of this period also reflects intense sectarian rivalry. Haribhadra Sūri's *Dhūrtākhyāna* is a biting satire on Purāṇic myths.

[95] Padmanabha S. Jaini, 'Jina Ṛṣabha as an avatāra of Viṣṇu'.

[96] *Śaṅkara Prādurbhāva*, quoted in Wendy Doniger O'Flaherty, 'The Images of the Heretic in Gupta Purāṇas', p. 121.

[97] N. Venkataramanayya, in G. Yazdani, ed., *The Early History of the Deccan*, p. 712.

[98] S.R. Sharma, *Jainism and Karnataka Culture*, p. 25; A.D. Pusalker, in R.C. Majumdar, *The Age of Imperial Kanauj*, p. 291.

[99] Gawarwad inscription of 1071 CE, *Epigraphia Indica*, XV, p. 337; K.A. Nilakanta Sastri, in G. Yazdani, ed., *The Early History of the Deccan*, vol. I, part VI, p. 443. Also see the Ablur inscription of the twelfth century in *Epigraphia Indica*, vol. V, no. 25E. R.N. Nandi has shown that Jaina temples had become like landlords and organized charities only for the Jaina followers, excluding non-Jainas. R.N. Nandi, *Religious Institutions and Cults in the Deccan*, p. 76.

[100] Śaṅkaravarman plundered 64 temples to meet, among other things, the expenses of the royal household (*gṛhyakṛtya*). *Rājataraṅgiṇī*, V.167–79, p. 200.

[101] Kṣemendragupta had the Jayendra Vihāra burnt down as his enemy Dāmara Saṃgrāma had taken refuge in it. He also robbed the brass statue of the Buddha and built a shrine of Kṣema Gaurīśvara in Śrīnagara. *Rājatarangiṇī*, VI.171–73, p. 243.

[102] King Kalaśa took away the copper image of the Sun god known as Tāmrasvāmin and also many brass statues from the *vihāras*. *Rājatarangiṇī*, VII.696, p. 319.

[103] *Rājatarangiṇī*, VII, verses 1080–90, pp. 351–52. Harṣa, however, spared the images of Raṇasvāmin and Mārtaṇḍa along with two Buddha images: verses 1096–98. In the *Prabandha Cintāmaṇi* (p. 151), Ācārya Merutuṅga refers to king Ajayadeva's destruction of the temples constructed by his predecessor, presumably by his father Kumārapāla.

[104] According to B.V. Krishna Rao (*A History of the Early Dynasties of Āndhradeśa*, pp. 57–58) and M. Rama Rao (*Ikṣvākus of Vijayapuri*, pp. 35ff.), the Ikṣvāku king Vīrapuruṣadatta had renounced Śaivism and adopted Buddhism. A sculpture at Nāgarjunikoṇḍa depicts him trampling a Śiva *liṅga* under his foot, showing his denunciation of Śaivism.

[105] R.C. Mitra, *The Decline of Buddhism in India*, pp. 38ff., 55ff., 74 and elsewhere; K.A. Nilakanta Sastri, in G. Yazdani, ed., *The Early History of the Deccan*, vol. I, part VI, pp. 438ff.

[106] The Hoysala ruler Ballāladeva is described in his inscriptions as the supporter of all the four *samayas*, Māheśvara, Bauddha, Vaiṣṇava and Arhat. R.C. Mitra, *The Decline of Buddhism in India*, p. 114. Similarly an inscription of 1022 CE from Belur (*Indian Antiquary*, vol. 18, pp. 279–85) informs us that Akkādevi, the elder sister of Jayasimha II of the Cālukyas of Kalyāṇī, performed all the *dharmas* mentioned in the *āgamas* of Jaina, Buddha, Ananta (Viṣṇu) and Rudra.

[107] It is wrong to hold that royal patronage of Buddhism ceased after the seventh century and the Pāla dynasty (750–1161 CE) was the sole exception (Gail Omvedt, *Buddhism in India*, p. 172). In Central India, the Gahaḍavāla ruler Jayacandra of Kanauj was a Buddhist and his preceptor was a Buddhist monk named Śrīmitra. His predecessor Govindacandra, although himself a *paramamāheśvara*, granted villages to Buddhist monks living in the Jetavana *vihāra*.

His two queens Kumāradevī and Vasantadevī were Buddhists and the former had the famous Dharmacakra Jinavihāra constructed at Sarnath. See N.N. Das Gupta, in R.C. Majumdar, ed., *Struggle for the Empire*, pp. 422–23. In Orissa and the Deccan, too, several kings patronized Buddhism in the eleventh–twelfth centuries.

[108] In the *Agañña Suttanta* of the *Dīgha Nikāya*, the Buddha explains to his two young brāhmaṇa disciples the origin of the universe, as well of the *khattiya* and brāhmaṇa *maṇḍalas* (groups), and of the *vessas* and *suddas*. In its origin the division is functional with the *khattiyas* occupying the first place, but later these are assumed to be fixed or hereditary. *Dīgha Nikāya*, vol. 3, eds. Rhys Davis and Carpenter, pp. 93ff., tr. T.W. Rhys Davis (*The Dialogue of the Buddhā*), pp. 88ff.

We do not have Jaina works of a comparable early date, but the *varṇa* divisions are taken for granted in the *Ācārāṅga* and *Uttarādhyayana sūtras*.

[109] N. Wagle, *Society at the Time of the Buddha*, pp. 125ff.

[110] Uma Chakravarti, *Social Dimensions of Early Buddhism*, Appendix C.

[111] A.K. Warder, *Indian Buddhism*, pp. 232–33.

[112] Debiprasad Chattopadhyaya, *Religion and Society*, Lecture VII; Dev Raj Chanana, *Slavery in Ancient India*, pp. 60ff.

[113] *Jātakas*, edited by V. Fausböll, nos 59,179, 309, 497, 498.

[114] P.V. Kane, *History of Dharmaśāstra*, vol. V, part II, pp. 926, 1009–10.

[115] *Viṣṇudharma Purāṇa*, chapter 25, *Bṛhannāradīya Purāṇa*, 14–70, 186, 22.9, quoted in R.C. Hazra, *Studies in the Upapurāṇas*, vol. I, pp. 147–48, 325–27. The *Arthaśāstra* of Kauṭilya (II.4.23) instructs that the dwelling place of the *pāṣaṇḍas* and Caṇḍālas should be on the outskirts of the cremation ground. *Kauṭilīya Arthaśāstra*, vol. I, p. 39.

[116] Nalinaksha Dutt, in R.C. Majumdar, ed., *The Classical Age*, vol. III, p. 386.

[117] *Vajrasūcī* of *Āsvaghoṣa*. The identification of this Āsvaghoṣa with the author of the *Buddhacarita* is, however, doubtful.

[118] *Laṭakamelaka*, Act II, quoted in B.N.S. Yadava, *Society and Culture in Northern India*, p. 8.

[119] *Padma Purāṇa*, part I, chapter 4, verses 86ff., quoted in Ram Bhushan Prasad Singh, *Jainism in Early Medieval Karnataka*, pp. 75–76.

[120] *Ādi Purāṇa*, VIII.64, XV.6–12, quoted in Malini Adiga, *The Making of Southern Karnataka*, p. 259.

[121] U.N. Ghoshal, *A History of Indian Political Ideas*, pp. 457–62.

[122] Malini Adiga, *The Making of Southern Karnataka*.

[123] Jyoti Prasad Jain, *The Jaina Sources of the History of Ancient India*, p. 215.

[124] *Yaśastilaka*, part II, book VIII, quoted in Ram Bhushan Prasad Singh, *Jainism in Early Medieval Karnataka*, p. 73. R.S. Sharma quotes Dharmanand Kosambi (*Bhagavan Buddha*, p. 258) to point out that Jainism forbids the initiation of untouchables (*jumgita*) into monkhood. R.S. Sharma, *Material Culture and Social Formations in Ancient India*, pp. 129–30.

[125] Ram Bhushan Prasad Singh, *Jainism in Early Medieval Karnataka*, pp. 74–82.

[126] D.D. Kosambi, *An Introduction to the Study of Indian History* (first edition), p. 155. According to Sukumar Dutta, Buddhism was instrumental in dealing a death blow to the pretensions of caste superiority of the hereditary aristocracy and the idea of divinity of kingship in Cambodia. Sukumar Dutta, *Transactions of Indian Institute of Advanced Studies*, pp. 179ff.

[127] Suvira Jaiswal, *Caste*, pp. 53–54; Irfan Habib, *Essays in Indian History*, pp. 161–79.

[128] Dev Raj Chanana, *Slavery in Ancient India*, pp. 82–84.

[129] Yi-Jing [I-Tsing], *A Record of the Buddhist Religion as Practised in India and the Malay Archipelago*, p. 62, quoted in Irfan Habib, ed., *Religion in Indian History*, p. xxiii.

[130] Dev Raj Chanana, *Slavery in Ancient India*, p. 83.

[131] *Vinaya Piṭaka*, IV, pp. 300–01, quoted in I.B. Horner, *Women under Primitive Buddhism*, pp. 222, 233–34.

[132] Friedhelm Hardy, *The Religious Culture of India*, p. 451.

[133] Debiprasad Chattopadhyaya, *Religion and Society*.

[134] B.N.S. Yadava, *Society and Culture in Northern India*, p. 380; Nupur Chaudhuri and Rajat Kanta Ray, 'Eros and History', p. 107.

[135] For the shift in emphasis from relative purity of function to relative purity of birth in the *varṇa–jāti* organization, see Suvira Jaiswal, *Caste*, pp. 13–18, 71–77.

[136] Suvira Jaiswal, *The Origin and Development of Vaiṣṇavism*, pp. 123–29.

[137] *Manusmṛti* (translated by Bühler), X.84. Irfan Habib writes that this provided one more argument for treating all peasants as śūdras. Irfan Habib, ed., *Religion in Indian History*, p. xxiii.

[138] *Manusmṛti* (translated by Bühler), III.68–70. On the changing concept of the *pañcamahāyajñas*, see Suvira Jaiswal, *Caste*, p. 121 note 239.

[139] R.S. Sharma, *Perspectives in Social and Economic History of Early India*, pp. 45–48.

[140] C.A.F. Rhys Davids, *Psalms of the Early Buddhists*, vol. II, pp. 15, 25; Uma Chakravarti, *Social Dimensions of Early Buddhism*, p. 34.

[141] *Ṛgveda*, I.28.5.

[142] Ibid., I.92.3. Does this hymn represent some older matriarchal substratum? Verse 3 of this hymn prays for the gift of 'troops of *dāsas*'. D.D. Kosambi, *Myth and Reality*, pp. 68–69.

[143] Suvira Jaiswal, 'Semitising Hinduism'. Reference is to the Brahmanical ideology and not to the particular role of the brāhmaṇa caste. Also see S. Selvam, 'Sociology of India and Hinduism', p. 189.

[144] Richard F. Gombrich, *Buddhist Precept and Practice*, p. 345.

[145] Brajadulal Chattopadhyaya speaks of the shaping of regional societies as essentially a movement from within. He also draws attention to the fact that the horizontal spread of the *varṇa* ideology 'drew widely dispersed and originally outlying groups into a structure which allowed them in a large measure to retain their original character'. B.D. Chattopadhyaya, *The Making of Early Medieval India*, pp. 35, 203. Also see Suvira Jaiswal, *Caste*, pp. 230–31.

[146] Hermann Kulke, *Kings and Cults*, pp. 82–93; Bhairabi Prasad Sahu, 'The Past as a Mirror of the Present'.

[147] S. Nagaraju, 'Emergence of Regional Identity and Beginnings of Vernacular Literature'.

[148] The confusion has been traced to Rāmānujācārya, who in his book *Brahmasūtra-bhāṣya* (II.1.37–42) identifies the Kālāmukhas with Kāpālikas. But in fact these two were quite distinct and the Kālāmukha monks seem to have been in active competition with Jaina monks. Lorenzen is quite positive that there is no reason why the Kālāmukhas should not be regarded as orthodox pundits. David N. Lorenzen, 'The Kālāmukha Background to Vīraśaivism, p. 279. Also see S.C. Nandimath, 'Śaivism', in R.R. Divakar, ed., *Karnataka through the Ages*, pp. 153–54; R.N. Nandi, *Religious Institutions and Cults in the Deccan*, pp. 85–90.

Nagaraju refers to the anti-caste feelings expressed in the poems of Mallikārjuna Paṇḍitārādhya. But he belongs to the twelfth century and was a contemporary of Basava, the founder of the Lingāyata movement, which was strongly anti-Vedic and anti-caste, at least in its origins.

[149] The ninth-century Maruru inscription of Arkalgud taluk records a land grant to a Kālāmukha centre for *vidyā dāna*. B.R. Gopal *et al.*, *Epigraphia Carnatica*, p. 8, Ag 28, quoted in Malini Adiga, *The Making of Southern Karnataka*, p. 308.

[150] Jabalpur stone inscription of Jayasimha, verse 44. V.V. Mirashi, *Corpus Inscriptionum Indicarum*, vol. IV, pl. I no. 64 for text, translation, p. 339.

[151] J.H. Hutton, *Caste in India*, p. 249.

[152] Louis Dumont, *A South Indian Subcaste*.

[153] Ibid., p. 12. For the reinterpretation of the śūdra category in the context of South Indian communities, see Suvira Jaiswal, *Caste*, pp. 70–71.

[154] Nicholas B. Dirks, *Castes of Mind*, pp. 12–60.

[155] Ibid.

[156] J.H. Hutton, *Caste in India*, pp. 178–79, for the eight prohibitions propounded by the Kallars of Ramnad in December 1930. Some of these were that the *ādi draviḍa* (untouchable) women shall not cover the upper portion of their bodies, shall not use flowers or saffron paste, the males shall not wear clothes above their hips or below their knees, and so on. Non-compliance led the Kallars to use violence against the *ādi draviḍas*, whose huts were burnt, granaries and properties destroyed, and livestock looted.

[157] Louis Dumont, *A South Indian Subcaste*, pp. 218–23.

[158] Nicholas B. Dirks, *Castes of Mind*, p. 72.

[159] For example, the assumption of the 'Yādava' title by Gwala, Ahir, Gope, Sargope and Ghasi castes, and the formation of the All-India Yādava Māhasabhā. Not rarely, the drive towards unification remains confined at the political level, social interactions still being regulated by traditional customs.

[160] Nicholas B. Dirks, *Castes of Mind*, pp. 295–96; Kancha Ilaiah, 'BSP and Caste as Ideology'; Kancha Ilaiah, 'Productive Labour, Consciousness, and History'.

[161] B.R. Ambedkar, *Annihilation of Caste*, pp. 81–82.

[162] This entire essay goes against Dirks' assertion (*Castes of Mind*, p. 278) that Ambedkar was convinced that caste (or rather untouchable) identities had to be fostered in order to combat centuries of oppression. Ambedkar was so disillusioned with the caste system that in the end he, along with a large number of his followers, converted to Buddhism.

[163] On the Dalit mentality, see Suvira Jaiswal, '*Dalit asmitā aur agenda jāti vināśa 'kā'*'.

3

Interpreting the Dynamics of Social Differentiations in Early India: R.S. Sharma on Class and Caste

In his seminal work *Material Culture and Social Formations in Ancient India*, R.S. Sharma gives us two epigrams: 'no theory, no history' and 'no production, no history'.[1] These encapsulate beautifully his methodology of historical reconstruction and commitment to Marxism, which are clearly discernible even in his first article, published in 1952, entitled 'Some Economic Aspects of the Caste System in Ancient India'.[2] Through an analysis of the Brahmanical, Buddhist and Jaina accounts of pre-*varṇa* society and the origin of the *varṇas*, he demonstrates how these reflect memories of transition from a food-gathering and hunting stage to a stable agricultural economy resulting in the rise of private property and social differentiation in the form of *varṇas*, perpetuating not merely a socio-economic functional division of labour, but also a mechanism of class exploitation ensuring the rights and privileges of the non-producing upper class–castes. These ideas are fundamental in his delineation of the dynamics of early Indian social formations, and in his later works, he covers the entire range of early Indian history from its remote beginnings to 1200 CE, demolishing many myths held sacrosanct in earlier historiography and buttressing his arguments with the critical use of a variety of hitherto untapped sources.

Although the Indus valley experienced the earliest stratified society with a well-developed urban culture on the Indian subcontinent, its script remains undecipherable. Hence, any assertion regarding the nature of social stratification prevailing therein is mere speculation. Our earliest historical source continues to be the *Ṛgveda*, which, in Sharma's opinion, reflects more than one type of social formation. There are vestiges of the earlier type of organizations, but it primarily mirrors a tribal, pastoral, rather than food-producing society, particularly in its kernel. It also contains traces of the mixing of the Aryan and the non-Aryan, Vedic and non-Vedic tribes.

The view that the early Vedic society as revealed in the *Ṛgveda* was essentially pastoral with agriculture playing only a marginal role in their economy has been vehemently contested, without, however, producing any convincing evidence from Books II–VII of the *Ṛgveda*, which form the basis of Sharma's generalizations. A detailed critique of such criticisms and the unreliability of their readings has been taken up earlier.[3] The issue has an important bearing on the nature of social differentiation among the Vedic tribes and the origin of *varṇa* categories, as Sharma's main concern is to establish the linkage between 'modes of material life' and stages in a social formation.

Sharma characterizes the Ṛgvedic society as largely egalitarian. Ṛgvedic families took to sedentary agriculture through interaction with speakers of the non-Aryan languages whose vocabulary they heavily borrowed, but their wealth consisted primarily of cattle as they were predominantly pastoral and the cultivation of land did not produce enough surplus for sustaining a class of non-producers lording over the actual producers. The tribes supplemented their wealth through capture of booty and hence are depicted as perpetually preoccupied with war.[4] War had 'a logical and economic function' in the tribal society, Sharma writes,[5] and it was the unequal distribution of the spoils of war by the tribal chiefs that began the process of erosion of an egalitarian ethos. But in the absence of surplus, socio-economic disparities between the ordinary tribesmen and their chief, and his entourage of warriors, kinsmen and priests, were not wide enough to give rise to a class–caste structure.[6] Classes in the form of *varṇa* divisions appeared only in later Vedic times when stable agriculture provided enough surplus for a segment of the tribe, comprising the kinsmen of the chief and his associates, to emerge as a distinct group of *rājanyas* ruling and living off the labour of the common tribesmen, who now constituted the *viś* and carried out the work of production through agriculture and cattle-keeping.

The geographical milieu of the Ṛgvedic hymns was mainly eastern Afghanistan and the land of the seven rivers, comprising the Indus basin and Punjab. The later Vedic texts reflect a shift in the locale from north-west to south-east, with the regions of Haryana, Rajasthan and the Ganga–Yamuna *doab* figuring more prominently. Cattle-herding was still a very important occupation but sedentary agriculture had become the mainstay of the later Vedic economy, and a number of crops not known to the Ṛgvedic people were cultivated. Archaeologically, Sharma identifies the later Vedic people with the Painted Grey Ware (PGW) culture, and argues that in their eastward march in the mid-Ganga plains, they came across the chalcolithic peoples of Black and Red Ware (BRW) cultures who also practised agriculture and raised a number of crops. Their encounter led to an ethnic and cultural fusion in which the Vedic tribes had an upper hand owing to their superiority in war and speedy transportation because of their use of horse and spoked wheel,[7] but, in the course of time, the privileged groups from the two cultural streams must have come together and laid the foundations of a hierarchical society.[8] Sharma points out that although both the PGW and

BRW sites have yielded iron artefacts, these are mainly weapons which must have been accessible only to privileged groups, owing to the limited availability of the metals and primitive technology.

Thus Sharma traces the beginnings of social stratification not in the segregation of the Aryan and the non-Aryan or the Vedic and non-Vedic peoples, but in material terms, to the availability of surplus due to a change in the mode of production and the use of force for its appropriation by the tribal chiefs and their clansmen, described in the later Vedic texts as *rājanyas*. This situation led to kin conflicts within the tribal society and ultimately to its decline. However, he is careful to assert that it was not the 'genealogical superiority' of the *rājanyas* which made them claim the surplus as tribute but their muscle power; forcible methods adopted by the descendants of the elected chiefs led to the 'social distancing which was frozen into genealogical ideology at a much later stage', he argues.[9] In this assertion of power, the chief and the 'kin aristocracy' did not hesitate to take support from those who were outside the kin structure.[10]

Thus, alliance, assimilation and integration with non-kin groups mark the decline of tribal structure and the emergence of the *varṇa* order. Sharma points out that the term 'kṣatriya', which came to signify a *varṇa* category, is derived from *kṣatra*, meaning 'power' or 'authority', and in some Vedic passages it is apparently applied to those who were of non-Vedic origin, although at many places 'kṣatriya' and '*rājanya*' are used interchangeably. However, there are also rituals suggesting a hostility between the kṣatriya and the *rājanya*, indicating a conflict between the consecrated non-kin king and the old kin aristocracy over the appropriation of surplus from the *viś* and labour power of śūdras and women slaves. Thus, the kṣatriya *varṇa* was formed by the coming together of powerful groups of Vedic and non-Vedic origins, and later constituting 'a kind of kin-ordered group'.

However, it is the 'non-kin' brāhmaṇa priests who have been attributed a crucial role in the formation of the fourfold *varṇa* order. Sharma states that the 'non-Vedic' brāhmaṇas joined hands with the Vedic *rājanyas* to strengthen the authority of the latter.[11] It is curious that he should use the term 'non-Vedic' in the context of the brāhmaṇas, for, if brāhmaṇa stands here for the priestly class, even the earliest Veda would be largely the handiwork of priests. Perhaps he implies that the brāhmaṇa priesthood originated in a different cultural complex. Earlier, in *Śūdras in Ancient India*, he is more circumspect.[12] He does not dub them as 'non-Vedic' but speaks of some pre-Aryan priests, such as Kaṇva, Dīrghatamas, Divodāsa and black Aṅgiras whose compositions are included in the later books of the *Ṛgveda*, as assimilated in the newly organized, composite Aryan society, which included non-Aryans at various levels. Sharma expresses his agreement with D.D. Kosambi's hypothesis that the priestly class of the 'Aryan conquerors' was largely recruited from the conquered.[13] Elsewhere he speaks of the brāhmaṇa priests initially being one of the seventeen types of priests but eventually overshadowing all the others, which results in 'brāhmaṇa' becoming a generic term for the entire priestly class.[14] In his later works, however, Sharma does not speak of the Aryan invasion but their immigration in several waves in post-Harappan times, and the evolution of a new type of Aryan society with a synthesis of the immigrant Aryan and indigenous elements.[15]

However, the real dynamic of class formation, according to him, derived from a change in the mode of production. In the predominantly tribal society of the early Vedic phase, the production unit broadly coincided with the consumption unit, and the tribal chiefs received voluntary and occasional gifts from their clansmen. In addition, the frequent intra- and inter-tribal wars allowed them to retain a larger share of the captured booty, with which they patronized priests and close kinsmen. Thus, gifts as a form of exchange or redistribution benefited the higher ranks of tribal society, but this cannot be seen as introducing class differentiation in terms of relations of production. Romila Thapar has underlined the significance of gift-giving as a means of exchanging and redistributing economic wealth.[16] Sharma goes further and characterizes the Ṛgvedic economy as a 'gift economy'.[17] It is the changeover to stable agricultural economy in the Indo–Gangetic divide and the upper Gangetic plains – the location of later Vedic tribes – which gave rise to incipient class and state structures.

The later Vedic texts regularly mention the brāhmaṇa, *rājanya*/kṣatriya, vaiśya and śūdra *varṇas* as distinct identities. Were the *varṇas* at this stage classes, castes or status categories? According to Sharma, these were still 'occupational and ritualistic' ranks, with the brāhmaṇa and *rājanya*/kṣatriya combining to establish their authority and control over the vaiśya and śūdra and thus constituting the ruling class, but as they did not have ownership or control of the means of production these cannot be regarded as classes in the Marxist sense of the term. Sharma describes this stage as proto-class and proto-state. It was based on an economy which produced enough surplus for the chiefs to corner the lion's share and indulge in ostentatious consumption or redistribution of wealth in potlatch-like ceremonies such as the *Rājasūya* and *Aśvamedha* sacrifices, mentioned in later Vedic texts and the great epics,[18] but it was not enough to give rise to a full-fledged state and class structure. These developments could take place only around 600 BCE in a flourishing agricultural economy invigorated by the use of iron implements in the middle Gangetic basin.

Sharma argues that migrants from modern-day western Uttar Pradesh and adjacent areas moved eastwards in several waves and played a pioneering role in founding settlements in the middle Gangetic basin. Magadha is associated with Vrātyas, a term referring to Aryan tribal groups who were not yet Brahmanized, and for whose purification/Brahmanization the later Vedic texts recommend the *Vrātyastoma* sacrifice. They represent an earlier wave of migration into this area. The orthodox Brahmanical elements moved in later and established their sway, as indicated by the story of Videgha Māthava and Agni Vaiśvānara related in the *Śatapatha Brāhmaṇa*.[19] The Aryan colonizers encountered the neolithic–chalcolithic peoples of the region and there was social adjustment and accommodation in terms of the *varṇa* hierarchy, the ideology of the dominant social groups developed in later Vedic times.

Thus the śūdra *varṇa*, which came into existence as a class of servile labour, was from the very beginning a heterogeneous category consisting of both the defeated and the dispossessed Aryan tribesmen and pre-Aryans, with the vanquished Śūdra tribe of Aryan affinities forming its nucleus. The Śūdras entered from the north-west in the post-Ṛgvedic phase and their subjugation resulted in their being subjected to a kind of 'generalized slavery'[20] by the Vedic tribes, apparently because the institution of private property, particularly in land, was yet to develop. Like D.D. Kosambi, Sharma too considers the condition of the śūdra *varṇa* analogous to the helots of Sparta, but points to an important difference: whereas in Sparta agricultural work was mainly the function of helots, in India the common tribesmen, the vaiśyas, constituted the peasantry, and the śūdras were forced to work as domestic servants, agricultural labourers and 'in some cases as slaves' of the upper three *varṇas*.[21] Nevertheless, all śūdras were not reduced to slavery, although the slaves or *dāsas* mentioned in the Pali texts of early Buddhism must have by and large belonged to the śūdra *varṇa*. Initially only a small servile class was characterized as śūdra and many of them were 'poor cousins' of the Aryan priests, (brāhmaṇas), princes (*rājanyas*) and peasants (vaiśyas), and their position in Vedic texts is ambiguous. In some instances the śūdras are allowed to participate in Vedic rituals, but elsewhere totally excluded. Apparently the inclusion of such divergent sections as the *rathakāra* (wheelwright) and *takṣaka* (carpenter), and the Niṣāda and Caṇḍāla tribes, within this *varṇa* – as they stood in a relationship of inequality to the upper *varṇas* – could not but have contributed to its fragmentary character; they would have constituted one social class only from the Brahmanical or elitist point of view, a class on whose labour they claimed to have a hereditary right. Does this, then, mean that the śūdra *varṇa* contained within it caste-like structures from the very beginning? It is a complex question that requires investigation into the extent to which tribes had been assimilated in the *varṇa* society and the different labouring groups had acquired distinct graded identities, germs of which process were embedded in the four-*varṇa* caste system as it developed among the late Vedic tribes.

The category of śūdra swelled in post-Vedic times, when new methods of production involving paddy transplantation and the use of iron tools for agriculture demanded greater use of land and labour, and transformed a subsistence economy into a burgeoning surplus-producing economy, providing the material basis for a full-fledged class society to develop in the age of the Buddha. Even at this stage the śūdras worked mainly as agricultural labourers, artisans or domestic servants, and the peasantry was composed of vaiśyas who were the primary producers and principal tax-payers. Sharma names this form of socio-economic organization 'vaiśya–śūdra social formation',[22] which prevailed in mid-India from the sixth century BCE to the fifth century CE, as the creation of social surplus was mainly the function of those two *varṇas*.

Like Kosambi, Sharma is firmly of the view that the mode of production in ancient India was not slave-based, although the relative importance of slavery, wage labour and free peasantry in agricultural production varied in different epochs and regions. The *Ṛgveda* mentions warrior chiefs having large numbers of female slaves, *dāsīs*, i.e. captured women of Dāsa tribes. They constituted items of liberal gifts to priests by their patrons. But male slaves, *dāsas*, are rarely mentioned and there is nothing to suggest their employment in the production processes. Slaves were employed for production in North India when iron technology led to greater productivity in agriculture and crafts, and the enslavement of prisoners in the continuous wars for territorial expansion along with increase in debt slavery facilitated by the use of metallic money led to an increase in slave labour. Slaves, along with hired labour (*dāsa–kammakaras*) working in the fields, are frequently mentioned in the Buddhist Pali sources. They formed an important part of the Mauryan state production. Nonetheless, by and large, the backbone of the peasant economy in the age of the Buddha comprised of affluent *gahapati* landowners and ordinary *karṣakas* (cultivators) belonging to the vaiśya *varṇa*, and although members of the upper *varṇas* too could be reduced to debt slavery, most of the slaves and hired labourers came from the śūdra *varṇa*. This kind of peasant production prevailed from post-Vedic to the beginnings of the feudal phase, and Sharma, wary of using an 'omnibus term' such as 'peasant society',[23] prefers to call this social formation the vaiśya–śūdra formation.

Sharma asserts that in this type of formation it was the vaiśya peasantry and not the śūdras who were the main props of production. Curiously, he does not give much attention to the system prevailing in the *gaṇarājyas* in the time of the Buddha, although the important work of Dev Raj Chanana[24] clearly establishes that in these oligarchies there were mainly two social classes – the landowning kṣatriya nobility, and the slaves and hired labourers – and the membership of both classes was determined by birth. Agriculture was the principal industry and it was entirely dependent on the labour of slaves and servants of the nobility. The employment of slave labour, even in contemporary monarchies, was not negligible. However, there is no doubt that the expansion of the fourfold *varṇa* system and the reduction of the labouring groups to the level of śūdras as a form of 'generalized slavery' obviated the need for large-scale employment of slaves. This trend was further strengthened by the depression of many communities as 'untouchables' in later times. As pointed out by Ambedkar[25] in a very forceful and lucid manner, the caste system provided a much cheaper source of labour in the form of 'untouchables' than slavery as the former did not require any investment or expenses on obligatory maintenance, provision of food, clothes or shelter. Nevertheless, agrestic slavery was well-entrenched in Kerala, tied up as it was with the matrilineal institution of *taravad*,[26] and domestic slavery existed in all regions of India till it was formally abolished by the Government of India Act V of 1843.

However, Sharma's statement[27] that there is hardly any evidence of slaves being employed in production in the post-Mauryan times should be understood in a broad sense. If we accept the testimony of Lama Tārānātha, even in the eighth century Kumārila Bhaṭṭa had received from his patron king 'many rice fields, five hundred male slaves, five hundred women slaves and many hundred men'.[28] The number may be conventional and the last mentioned may be a reference to the subject peasantry as well, but the passage also suggests the use of slaves in paddy fields. A passage of the *Padma Purāṇa* of Raviṣeṇa (seventh century CE) refers to slaves ploughing the field and speaks of them as *sairikaḥ* (ploughmen).[29] A fourteenth-century Tamil inscription from Tiruppalatturai in Tiruchirappalli district records the transfer of two Veḷḷāla and two Pulaiya *adiyans*, i.e. slaves, by a local magnate to a lady and her son along with a piece of land.[30] It is interesting that the Veḷḷālas are a respectable peasant caste but some of them could be reduced to slavery. Slavery was not indispensible to the means of production, but there is merit in Kosambi's assertion that the feudal landlords always retained some land directly cultivated by their slaves and servants so as not to be entirely dependent on the village peasantry, which could offer united resistance or fail to raise a crop in bad weather conditions. He points out that Indian feudalism differed from European feudalism in that it was marked by an increase in slavery, absence of guilds and lack of an organized church.[31] Sale of human beings is mentioned in the tenth chapter of the *Manusmṛti*, which, in Sharma's view, is to be dated to the late Gupta period. It lays down that in times of distress the brāhmaṇas and kṣatriyas may earn their living by taking up professions suitable for vaiśyas, but they must not practise agriculture as it involves injury to other beings and servitude (*hiṃsāprāyāṃ parādhīnāṃ*), or trade in certain items such as the sale of cooked food, sesame, animals or human beings.[32] Thus, agriculture and trading in humans and animals are lowly occupations but not prohibited.

However, Sharma argues that prior to 300 CE, śūdras were numerically not large enough to be considered as the mainstay of the production process. They were 'slaves and subordinates' of the upper three *varṇas*, and subjected to forced labour for construction, porterage and artisanal work. The main producers were the vaiśyas, organized in village communities and paying taxes to the king. The upgrading of śūdras to peasanthood in Gupta and post-Gupta times was the consequence of a serious crisis afflicting the vaiśya–śūdra mode of production in the third–fourth centuries CE when the *varṇa* order was severely threatened; this is reflected in the descriptions of the Kali age in the epics and the Purāṇas. Sharma admits that the time of this upheaval is difficult to determine. In his *Śūdras in Ancient India*, he designates the period roughly extending from 200 BCE to 300 CE as the period of 'Crisis in the Old Order', but in *Early Medieval Indian Society* he is more specific and dates the social crisis to 'the period between the fall of Kuṣāṇa power and the rise of the Gupta empire in North India',[33] with its effect being echoed down to the fifth century or even later. In his view, this is confirmed by the archaeological evidence of the decline of early historic urban settlements. The factors which led to this turmoil may be summarized as follows:

(i) The nature of royalty and nobility changed during this period. Flourishing foreign trade also brought in its wake the demand for luxury goods and a change in the lifestyle of kings and nobles. They began to resort to oppressive taxation. The texts speak of the miseries of the peasants, oppressed by tyrannical taxation in addition to the sufferings caused by famine and droughts, and their migration to other places in search of livelihood.

Moreover, many of the dynasties ruling in this period were of foreign or aboriginal origin. They took time to acquire legitimacy in the Brahmanical social order. Political instability led to greater exploitation and coercion of the producers, which made them revolt. The subjection of the śūdras was at its peak when the majority of them laboured under strict state control. But subsequent centuries record some improvement in their condition. The texts of this period narrate that in the Kali age the śūdras would refuse to provide labour, and the vaiśyas to pay taxes. This upset the vaiśya–śūdra mode of production.

(ii) Growth in the internal and external trade in the early centuries of the Common Era led to an improvement in the material condition of artisans and traders and made them aspire to a better status than what was accorded to them in the Brahmanical scheme. They were given an opportunity to do so by non-Brahmanical Buddhism and heterodox 'liberal' Vaiṣṇavism which favoured the lower *varṇas*. Inspired by these unorthodox, oppositional ideologies, the advanced sections of śūdras and vaiśyas, such as artisans and traders, may have mobilized the exploited sections and created a situation in which the norms and values established under the *varṇa*[34] system were upset for quite some time.

Social turmoil and conflicts generated a number of significant developments, leading to a change in the character of śūdra, vaiśya and kṣatriya communities and in the state structure. Powerful indigenous and foreign lineages managed to gain recognition as kṣatriyas, and new ruling dynasties acquired legitimacy by patronizing brāhmaṇas and Brahmanical institutions. Peasant resistance and difficulties in tax collection were resolved by giving land grants in lieu of salaries or cash gifts for remunerating the services of officials and priests. The practice of granting land to religious beneficiaries is well attested and it is argued that secular services too were rewarded in the same manner. But, unlike religious grants, these rewards were inscribed on perishable materials and hence have not survived. This system ultimately resulted in depression of the peasantry, and transformation of the śūdra slaves and labourers into sharecroppers and agriculturists, recalling the transformation of slaves in Europe into serfs and modifying the vaiśya–śūdra mode of production into the feudal mode of production.

Sharma's thesis has received strong support in the researches of B.N.S. Yadava, in whose view the Kali age narratives symbolize the transition from antiquity to the Middle Ages.[35] He too speaks of the loosening of state control in the Gangetic zone, on the decline of the Mauryan empire resulting in the transformation of śūdra slaves, servants and hired workers into dependent peasants, and points out that although slavery was never a major factor in the system of production in ancient India, it was by no means negligible. There was a gradual weakening of slavery as the economy expanded with the opening up of new land resources and improvement in the means of production. Many of the manumitted slaves became agricultural labourers, sharecroppers or tenant agriculturists with varying degrees of ties of dependence on their masters,[36] and with the degradation of peasantry in the early medieval complex there was a levelling of the śūdras and lower sections of the vaiśyas.

Earlier, in his monograph entitled *Society and Culture in Northern India in the Twelfth Century*, Yadava speaks of the splitting of the 'class' of vaiśyas with bigger merchants joining the ranks of the ruling aristocracy and giving rise to the concept of 'vaiśya–kṣatriya', and of the tendency of contemporary writings to mention only trade and commerce as the distinctive occupations of a vaiśya, implying thereby their disconnection from agriculture.[37]

These formulations, no doubt convincingly argued in their broad essentials, may be applicable to the Gangetic valley, but are not without problems and do not quite explain why communities practising agriculture in the regions of the Deccan, South and East India were assimilated in the *varṇa* system as śūdras and not as vaiśyas, which would have been in consonance with the traditional notion of *varṇa* duties as laid down in earlier Brahmanical texts. Sharma writes that in pre-Manu times, i.e. prior to the fifth century CE, most tribals were accommodated in the second and third *varṇas* as warriors and peasants through means of the *vrātya* theory, from which the fourth *varṇa* was carefully excluded.[38] But this changed after the age of Manu, as trade and commerce declined and land grants created a class of landlords with superior rights in land, downgrading the vaiśya peasants in settled areas of the Ganga basin. On the other hand, slaves, domestic servants and agricultural workers of the śūdra *varṇa* had been turned into farmers in the post-Maurya scenario, and land grants in the peripheral areas led to the recruitment of backward tribes as śūdra peasants cultivating the fields of brāhmaṇa landowners. With the beginning of the Common Era the vaiśyas and the śūdras begin to approximate closely in the Smṛti literature, and by the sixth century CE, the 'vaiśyas practically lose their identity as a peasant caste'.[39]

However, it may be noted that the approximation of vaiśya and śūdra is frequently seen in the early Pali texts, dated several centuries before the beginning of the Common Era, although these same texts speak of the high status of the *gahapatis*, mentioning them along with the brāhmaṇas and the kṣatriyas as an elite category of prosperous landowners and traders who were able to employ slaves and hired labourers to work for them. In *varṇa* terms they are generally seen as coming from the third *varṇa*, since the brāhmaṇas and the kṣatriyas are mentioned separately together with the *gahapatis*. This suggests that whereas the ordinary vaiśya cultivators were considered close to the śūdras, the prosperous, landowning vaiśyas enjoyed high status, and this development must have facilitated the splitting of the vaiśya *varṇa* and crystallization of distinct social and professional groups taking the form of *jātis* on territorial and occupational bases, and their dissociation with the lowly occupation of agriculture that entailed hard physical labour.[40] It has been shown that the *jātis* among the vaiśyas are generally distinguished on the basis of their trade or territorial affiliation.[41] We may also note that the land-based feudal aristocracy of the later centuries looked down on traders as well, but this was not the case in the centuries before and after the beginning of the Common Era, when trade flourished and the peasantry was depressed. It was under these circumstances that trade became the hallmark of the third *varṇa*, which continues to this day, and peasanthood of the fourth, i.e. the śūdra[42] *varṇa*. Although the *varṇas* had a lineage-based origin as they emerged from the declining tribal social formations in the later Vedic times, their specific role in the mode of production gave them an occupational basis and stressed their class character. Hence it became convenient to assimilate or form new communitarian identities within the *varṇa* framework, depending on their occupation and class positions. This does not mean that the *varṇas* no longer had the character of caste, only status implications. If that were so, then the elaborate rules about the share of property to be inherited by the sons of wives belonging to different *varṇas* in the *Arthaśāstra* of Kauṭilya (III.6.17–22) and Smṛti literature would make no sense. Nor would the mention of kṣatriya merchants in the inscriptions, ranging from early centuries of the Common Era to the tenth century,[43] or the mention of vaiśya, brāhmaṇa and kṣatriya kings by the Chinese pilgrim Hsuan-tsang.[44] Nevertheless, these developments also led to a modification of the very definition of the vaiśya and śūdra *varṇas*. The changing relations of production had their impact on the *varṇa* identities in the real social process, and brought about a shift of emphasis on 'purity of birth' rather than on the exclusivity of the *varṇa*-specific traditional functions. Hence, new entrants into the system, particularly the peasant communities of the South, were assimilated as śūdras. The process was greatly facilitated by the emergence of the 'untouchable' groups, as now it was these groups and not the śūdras in general who were subjected to a generalized form of slavery by the imposition of strict pollution rules, and also exploited for cheap agrarian labour.

However, Sharma relates the modifications in the *varṇa* order to measures taken to overcome the social crisis of the early centuries of the Common Era, and argues that whereas the vaiśya peasants were reduced to the position of servile śūdras, the śūdras of the mid-India regions who had earlier worked as slaves and hired labourers on agricultural farms were now transformed into rent-paying peasants.[45] But in the outer backward areas, communities which had been almost-complete masters of their lands were now subservient to religious and secular beneficiaries of extensive land grants and reduced to śūdra status. The process was not smooth. It led to struggles in the areas which were less 'varṇized',[46] such as Maharashtra, Andhra Pradesh and northern Tamil Nadu. A significant piece of evidence is provided by a Sātavāhana record,[47] which states that the brāhmaṇa ruler Gautamīputra Sātakarṇi, ruling over Vidarbha, conciliated the brāhmaṇas and the lower *varṇas*, crushed the pride and conceit of the kṣatriyas, and stopped the confusion among the four *varṇas*. It is plausible that since the inscription clearly speaks of furthering the interest of the twice-borns (i.e. the brāhmaṇas) and *avarakuṭumbas*, i.e. the households of the lower orders, the latter phrase refers to agriculturists and traders later known as *kuṭumbins*.[48] Sharma thinks that the kṣatriyas mentioned in this inscription were rulers of foreign origin who were defeated and the *varṇa* order was restored, and suggests that the foreign rulers, the Śakas and Kuṣāṇas, not being committed to *varṇa* ideology, may have fraternized with the śūdras and fomented discontent among them.

No doubt, it is tempting to interpret the evidence of the Nasik cave inscription of Gautami Balaśrī,[49] cited above, in terms of *varṇa* conflicts, with the brāhmaṇas and low-ranking agriculturist classes allying against the foreign rulers who may have claimed kṣatriya status.[50] The inscription speaks of Gautamīputra Sātakarṇi as an *eka bahmana* (unique brāhmaṇa) who destroyed the Śakas, Yavanas and Pahlavas. There were protracted hostilities between the Sātavahanas and the Scythian *kṣatrapa* houses of Kṣaharāta and Caṣṭāna ruling in Western India. Nevertheless, the assumption that the Śaka and Kuṣāṇa rulers fraternized with the lowly śūdras and undermined the *varṇa* system needs substantiation.[51] Uṣavadāta (Sanskrit, Ṛsabhadatta), son-in-law of *kṣatrapa* Nahapāna (119–124 CE), claims in his inscriptions to have made gifts of 3,00,000 cows and sixteen villages to the brāhmaṇas, and fed a thousand brāhmaṇas the whole year round.[52] Sharma himself points out that Rudradāman (150 CE) of the family of Caṣṭāna proudly claimed to be a supporter of the *varṇa* system.[53] He gave his daughter in marriage to a Sātakarṇi, perhaps Vāsiṣṭhiputra Puḷumāyi, whom he had defeated twice in battle but spared because of the marriage relationship. The adoption of Sanskrit by Rudradāman and his daughter for political and public announcements through their inscriptions symbolized their closeness to the Brahmanical literati, as Sanskrit had become, in Kosambi's words, 'a fresh instrument to mark the unity of new upper classes to emphasize their distance above the rest'.[54] Moreover, as the *varṇa*/caste system was tied up with petty production and provided a useful mechanism for surplus extraction, the ruling class, whether of foreign or indigenous origin, would no doubt be keen to uphold it, particularly as the system was flexible enough to absorb the incoming foreign hordes within its hierarchy. Even the tyrannical Hūṇa king Mihirakula, who is described as the god of destruction by Kalhaṇa and is known as a terrible persecutor of the Buddhists, is said to have gifted one thousand *agrahāras* to the brāhmaṇas and promulgated the 'observance of religious conduct' by settling people from the land of the Āryas.[55] Nonetheless some orthodox brāhmaṇas might have been critical of these developments, looking upon these as confusion of the *varṇas* symptomatic of the Kali age.

However, Sharma argues that the social crisis reflected in the descriptions of the Kali age in the epics and the Purāṇas was as much an outcome of foreign invasions as of internal crisis within the *varṇa* system. And this led to a change in the religious, social and economic conditions of the śūdras.[56] Adding a new dimension to the interpretation of the term *varṇa-saṃkara*, he states that it does not mean merely an unapproved mixing of castes through inter-caste marriages, but also the contamination of *varṇas* owing to non-performance of their traditional duties: the refusal of vaiśyas to pay taxes, of śūdras to provide labour, and the members of different *varṇas* practising occupations prohibited to them.[57]

This interpretation is particularly significant as it links the confusion of *varṇa* duties to changes in the mode of production, and attributes to the resistance of the lower *varṇas* a catalytic role in the transition from the *varṇa*-based to feudal mode of production, by the creation of landed intermediaries for better control, expansion and extraction of surplus from the countryside through the medium of land grants.

The entry of foreign hordes from the north-west in considerable numbers in the early centuries preceding and succeeding the beginning of the Common Era, and the challenge of heterodox sects such as Buddhism and Jainism, had compelled the brāhmaṇa priests and thinkers to devise ways of coping with the changed situation, and ensuring the supremacy and stability of the Brahmanical social hierarchy. I have argued that an important measure towards this end was the Brahmanical infiltration into non-Vedic popular forms of worship, and preaching the sanctity of the *varṇa* system and Brahmanical social ethics through their medium. The *Bhagavadgītā* is a product of this movement.[58] Sharma describes this as a period of crisis in the old order caused by the weakening of Mauryan state control, improved conditions of the śūdra artisans and traders owing to the rise of new arts and crafts, and flourishing internal and external trade and urbanization. Social tensions caused by these material developments found their expression in descriptions of the Kali age and the harsh measures recommended against the śūdras by the *Manusmṛti*. In response to this social crisis, changes took place in the land system in the Gupta and post-Gupta times, which had a significant and far-reaching impact on the *varṇa*/caste system.

Land grants to brāhmaṇas in the aboriginal areas led to an enormous increase in the number of communities ranked as śūdras. Sharma points out that the brāhmaṇas did not cultivate land themselves and employed local tribal labour to cultivate their lands. But they had no administrative apparatus or coercive machinery to enforce compliance; only the strength of refined rituals and the ability to propagate the *varṇa* ideology and convert the people to it.[59] So they converted the aboriginal tribes into śūdra castes and made them subscribe to the values of the *varṇa* system. Was the process of assimilation of the tribals as śūdras really so smooth? Sharma himself points out that in Bengal and peninsular India, brāhmaṇa beneficiaries of land grants had a position similar to Rajputs in the politics and society of northern India.[60] In fact, medieval epigraphs provide ample evidence of brāhmaṇas functioning as generals, ministers, managers of temples, and head priests (*rājaguru*) with wide religious and secular powers. Members of the same brāhmaṇa family could perform both administrative and religious functions. For example, an inscription of king Madhavavarman II of the Talakad branch records the gift of five villages and a tenth share of taxes from Kirumundaniri-Nagara to twenty-two brāhmaṇa families 'employed within the palace enclosure', whose members were adept in counselling, acting as envoys; they were skilled in the protection of the kingdom and in wielding arms, constructing fortresses, governing urban and rural settlements, as well as performing sacrifices to gods, conducting congregational services, uttering sacred formulae, carrying on the study of the Vedas and protecting the *varṇāśramadharma*.[61] Transgression of caste rules was a punishable offence. The inscriptions of the Rāṣṭrakūṭas of the western Deccan, the Pālas of Bengal and the Cālukyas of Gujarat mention the grant to brāhmaṇa donees of the privilege of receiving fines imposed for the ten offences (*daśāparādha*) in the donated villages, and one of these offences was transgression of caste rules (*varṇasaṃkara*).[62] The role of the early medieval state and its alliance with the brāhmaṇa *varṇa* for the establishment and stability of its power structure, through the use of *varṇa–jāti* ideology, cannot be underestimated. The emergence of the *brahma–kṣatra* category symbolizes the closeness of brāhmaṇa–kṣatriya orders in early medieval polity,[63] and in several regions of early medieval India, the rulers regulated and enforced caste rules through the office of *dharmādhikārī* or *varṇādhikārī*.[64] Sharma meticulously cites passages from the *Manusmṛti* and the Śānti parva of the *Mahābhārata* emphasizing the importance of coercive measures for the enforcement of *varṇa* duties and the fixity of the *varṇa* order. He interprets these as responses of orthodox brāhmaṇas to the social crisis of the early centuries of the Common Era. But the collaboration of the priestly class with the ruling lineages and their musclemen is the foundational feature of the *varṇa* system, which aimed at securing the submission of the vaiśyas and śūdras – the producing classes – even in later Vedic times. The hegemony of the Brahmanic *varṇa* ideology was achieved not without the use of coercion for subjugating recalcitrant elements, traces of which are available in some early medieval records.

The Sātavāhana inscription discussed above testifies to the social tension affecting the various *varṇas* in the western Deccan and its successful resolution by Gotamīputra Sātakarṇi. Sharma draws our attention to a Pallava inscription of the fifth century, recording the gift of a village named Neḍḍuṅgarāja in Maṇḍarāṣṭra to a number of brāhmaṇas as *śāraṇika grāma*, meaning 'refugee village', which shows that in the neighbourhood of Nellore district in Andhra Pradesh, the brāhmaṇas were persecuted and had to be given refuge.[65] A similar inference may be drawn from a Vākāṭaka grant of the same period in the Vidarbha region.[66] The overthrow of the Kaḷabhras who had taken away the land granted to brāhmaṇas in the deep southern regions is seen as suppression of the tribal peasantry which revolted against the brāhmaṇas. Similarly, the revolt of the Kaivartas in the eleventh century against Rāmapāla in Varendri (Rajshahi district in modern-day Bangladesh) is seen as an uprising of the tribal peasantry against the oppression of the Pālas, and the brāhmaṇa and Buddhist landed beneficiaries.[67] The protracted struggle had both religious and economic dimensions, and was resolved, according to Sharma, in the twelfth century by Ballālasena who raised them from the *antyaja* (i.e. last-born, 'untouchable') to *sat śūdra* (pure śūdra) category and bestowed feudal titles on their headman. If the tradition recorded in the *Ballālacarita* deserves credence, it would be a unique example of an 'untouchable' group rising to the 'pure' status. But the Kaivartas were a large aboriginal tribe spread over Assam, Bengal and Orissa, practising both fishing and agriculture from ancient times.[68] Hutton notes that although they were divided into two sections occupationally – Jaliya Kaivartas working as fishermen, and Haliya or Chasi Kaivartas living by agriculture – they regarded themselves as a single caste.[69] But in the course of time, Haliya Kaivartas began to consider themselves superior to Jaliya Kaivartas, apparently under the influence of Brahmanic ideology, and inter-marriage was forbidden. The two have now become separate castes.

It is interesting that the instances of resistance or revolt available to us seem to be related to communities which were already settled and practising agriculture. The *Aṅguttara Nikāya* mentions Assaka (Sanskrit, Aśmaka), a *mahājanapada* situated on the banks of the Godavari with its capital at Bodhan in the Nizamabad district of modern-day Telangana. Some accounts by the Greek classical writers describe the Andhras as a powerful race having numerous villages and thirty fortified towns.[70] It is reasonable to assume that these were tribal polities not without some degree of stratification, even before the spread of the Brahmanical *varṇa* system in the areas. The Andhras seem to have been a large Cis-Vindhyan tribe of great antiquity with segments at different stages of development spread over various regions. In the inscriptions of the Gahaḍavālas of Kanauj and Pālas of Bengal, they figure with the Medas and the Caṇḍālas as menial communities. However, the powerful dynasty of the Sātavāhanas is given an Āndhra ethnicity (*Āndhra-jātīya*) in the Purāṇas. Andhra Pradesh had settled peasant communities like Kapus, Teligas and Kammas practising agriculture before the advent of the Sātavāhanas.[71] Further south, we have clear evidence of settled agriculture and plough cultivation going back to the Saṅgam age. It is believed that the agrarian society of Marudam region was hierarchically stratified even in the Saṅgam period, and a poem in the *Puranānūṛu* collection speaks of 'women of the last classes (*kadaisiyar*)' engaged in agricultural operations.[72] It has been suggested that the *kadaisiyars* may be identified with the Pallars, an untouchable caste with a subcaste of this name listed in the Census Report of 1901.[73] Deliège quotes a popular saying that a farm will not prosper unless there is a Pallar to till it.[74] On the other hand, the agricultural community of the Veḷḷālas, mentioned in a late Saṅgam work,[75] figures as dominant landowning peasantry with a number of privileges – such as the monopoly of raising tolls and octroi duties in the villages over which they had tenure (*kāṇi*) – in the Pallava and Coḷa inscriptions.[76] Etymologically, '*veḷḷāla*' is interpreted as 'the owner of the soil' or, alternatively, as 'one who specializes in channelizing flood waters for irrigation'.[77] The author of the *Tolkāppiyam* (fifth century CE) makes a deliberate attempt to foist the fourfold *varṇa* categories on the Tamil society, and places the Veḷḷālas in the śūdra *varṇa* as their sole occupation was cultivation.[78] The Veḷḷālas themselves do not seem to have questioned their ranking as śūdra, although *Eredupadu*, a poem written in praise of the Veḷḷālas in early medieval times, claimed that birth into a Veḷḷāla family was superior to being born as a brāhmaṇa.[79]

Evidently, these śūdra communities of the South cannot be considered as having the same low status as the śūdras of the North (the Āryāvarta of Manu), despite their low rank in the fourfold *varṇa* system. Analysing a seventh-century inscription of Mahārāja Mahāsāmanta Samudrasena granting the village Nirmaṇḍ on the banks of the Sutlej as an *agrahāra* to a body of Atharvan brāhmaṇas, Kosambi points out that the land was granted together with plain, marsh and forest along with its inhabitants, which means that the inhabitants were all śūdras without any proprietary rights and were tied to the soil. The fact that the grant needed the formal sanction of the *rāṣṭra*, presumably an assembly of the upper classes consisting of the three upper *varṇas*, suggests that these śūdra inhabitants were of the older Smṛti type, having 'neither solidarity, nor kinship support outside the village', and were regarded as the property of the Vedic 'Aryan' tribe as a whole. Kosambi adds that these śūdras were different from those of peninsular India, which was divided into two major *varṇas* – the brāhmaṇa and the śūdra – the latter further divided into countless endogamous *jātis* of tribal origin with their own strong caste assemblies who could not have been given away along with a piece of land.[80] It is significant that the evidence of resistance and conflict comes mostly from what are termed as the peripheral areas, namely Vidarbha, Andhra Pradesh, Tamil Nadu and Bengal, from people who were 'non-' or 'less varṇized', and for them it was not so much a matter of learning new methods of cultivation through the agency of the brāhmaṇas, as resistance to the superior position of brāhmaṇa intermediaries with superior land rights over them.[81] Nevertheless, these regions, and the Indian subcontinent as a whole, gradually came to accept *varṇa* categorization,[82] primarily because of its adaptability to the new relations of production in a changed mode of production as long as it rested on class and gender exploitation. Early medieval historical sources clearly establish that the system allowed a great deal of flexibility at the top – the forging of new kinship alliances through marriage, and the assimilation of tribal and foreign power groups as kṣatriyas through invented ritual devices – but rigid at the bottom, distancing the elite from the working populace who were roundly dubbed as śūdra. However, as much of the Deccan and peninsular India at this stage was populated with tribes at various stages of their cultural development, their incorporation into the prevailing mode of production was facilitated by the *varṇa* ideology[83] that justified a hierarchy of socio-economic community identities based on birth in the interest of the dominant classes, but did not interfere with their internal matters, i.e. kinship structure, customs, etc. Manu enjoins that a righteous king should carefully enquire into the customs of each caste (*jāti*), country (*janapada*), guild (*śreṇī*), family (*kula*), and enforce them in accordance with their own traditions.[84] This accounts for the bewildering diversity of personal laws in pre-independence India, and for the fact that the comparatively well-off and numerically dominant peasant communities of the South did not mind becoming part of the *varṇa* order as śūdra; because, in practice they stood only next to the brāhmaṇas, the kṣatriya and vaiśya categories being largely ephemeral.[85] What mattered was the issue of hierarchical stratification to which Brahmanical ideology gave religious sanction by relating it to birth in 'pure' and 'impure' communities correlated with 'pure' and 'impure' occupations. Hence we have in the seventh–eighth centuries, in the Vengi region, tribal chiefs with local roots claiming to belong to the śūdra *varṇa*[86] and extending patronage to the brāhmaṇas. The myth of the śūdra *varṇa* originating from the feet of Viṣṇu bestowed respectability and was proudly mentioned by the Reḍḍi chiefs of Andhra.[87] The panegyrist of Singaya Nayaka's Akkalapuṇḍi grant even goes to the extent of claiming that the śūdra *varṇa* is purer than the other three since it was born from the feet of Viṣṇu along with the river Bhāgīrathī.[88] The Kākatīya ruler Pratāparudra too is described as born in the 'fourth *varṇa*', i.e. śūdra, but he was well versed in Sanskrit and is reputed to be the author of a work on *nītiśāstra* (politics).[89] Apparently restrictions on access to Sanskrit, or what is termed as 'pedagogic violence',[90] were imposed on those who constituted the 'subaltern', socio-economically depressed communities; for them, placement in the hierarchy of 'pure' and 'impure' castes (*jātis*) was now more relevant than contestations in terms of *varṇa*.

It is generally acknowledged that the number of communities dubbed as 'śūdra' proliferated in medieval times. This made the brāhmaṇa priests and learned men to take notice of them and to try to cater to their needs. P.V. Kane, in his *History of Dharmaśāstra*, has enumerated as many as thirty Brahmanical law books dealing with rules of conduct or *dharma* of the śūdras, composed between the fourteenth and seventeenth centuries. Viśveśvara Bhaṭṭa, who wrote his *Smṛti-Kaumudī* in the latter half of the fourteenth century, frankly stated that the earlier law-givers generally dealt with the *dharma* of the upper three *varṇas* and had not paid attention to the *dharma* of the śūdras; hence he proposes to 'clearly expound the *dharma* of the last *varṇa*'.[91] He goes on to meticulously delineate the rights of 'simple (pure) śūdras and śūdras born out of mixed marriages'. The work was written at the behest of king Madanapāla who ruled over a petty kingdom near Delhi.

Irfan Habib has shown that the establishment of the Delhi Sultanate stimulated the process of urbanization, an infusion of technology, and increased the demand for artisanal services.[92] The artisan castes in particular faced socio-economic disparities. Their resentment was voiced by the *nirguṇa bhakti* saints, such as Kabīr, Dadu and Nanak. In my opinion, the brāhmaṇa priests too tried to diffuse social tensions by adopting a flexible and liberal attitude towards the so-called śūdras, and tried to regulate their religion by laying down rituals and ceremonies appropriate for the so-called śūdra communities.

However, the historical situation of the communities loosely constituting the śūdra *varṇa* in different regions of India is not identical. As we have seen, in the southern regions, powerful and dominant landowning communities such as the Reḍḍis and the Veḷḷālas too were dubbed as śūdra, and their documents suggest that they did not resent this categorization. If we want to elicit the 'historical conditions' to which these texts on śūdra *dharma* respond, we have to place them in their historical context. The 'unyielding' 'śūdra archive'[93] will make historical sense only if we look to it as a pointer to the changes in the concept and practice of the śūdra *varṇa*, its proliferation and hierarchization giving rise to numerous legal disputes needing adjudication by brāhmaṇa priests.

Sharma links the modifications in the conceptualization and functioning of the *varṇa* order to feudal developments, arguing that the landed hierarchy need not necessarily correspond to the caste hierarchy.[94] We may add that the integration of tribal chiefs as military officers, landlords and even as independent rulers – in the feudal politico-economic formation – while retaining their śūdra *varṇa* status is indicative not only of their strong kinship ties with the local tribal population, but also of the fact that the Brahmanic conceptualization of communities – born of 'pure' or 'impure' births – facilitated the segregation and exploitation of subjugated communities in the local power hierarchy, giving a ritual basis to relations of servitude and economic dependence. It is worth noting that the *Manusmṛti*, which emphatically asserts that there are only four (primary) *jātis* and no fifth *varṇa*,[95] mentions a number of communities lower than the śūdras and described as *bāhyas* (exteriors), *bāhyātaras* (outside of the outsiders) and *antyas* (lowest).[96] These terms are generally taken to refer to the 'untouchable' groups. Ambedkar poignantly speaks of the unbridgeable cleavage between the *savarṇas*, i.e. those who are born within the four *varṇas*, and those considered outside it, the *varṇa-bāhyas* or *avarṇas*.[97] This sharp divide is the cumulative effect of many kinds of discriminations: ritual, economic and political. Sharma traces the origin of this phenomenon in post-Vedic times to a combination of ritual and material factors, low material culture of the aboriginal tribes, primitive ideas of taboo and impurity of certain materials, and upper-class contempt for manual labour.[98] He points out that the five despised castes (*hīna jātis*) mentioned in the Buddhist and Jaina texts – Caṇḍāla, Niṣāda, Veṇa, Rathakāra and Pukkusa – roughly correspond to 'untouchables' of the Brahmanical society, and were not included in the śūdra *varṇa*. However, it is significant that neither the *Manusmṛti* which speaks of such groups as *bāhyas* nor the earlier Pali texts connect them with agricultural labour. Manu connects the Caṇḍālas, Niṣādas, Medas, etc., with fishing, killing of wild animals, executing criminals condemned to death and other similar activities, and describes them as living near burial grounds, on hills and groves outside the villages, and as often on the move with no role in agricultural production.[99] On the other hand, field work has shown that in contemporary India, the so-called untouchable castes constitute the bulk of the agricultural force, and castes like the Pallars of Tamil Nadu have no other occupation but agricultural labour.[100] This lends credence to the suggestion that the notion of untouchability of some social groups may have emerged in 'the period of Buddhist ascendancy . . . but the systemic founding of outcastes occurred basically after medieval society was in place'.[101] Perhaps the division of the śūdra *varṇa* into *sat* and *asat*, pure and impure categories, had roots in the land system of the early medieval period in which dominant peasant communities received the status of a pure *varṇa*, albeit lower than their brāhmaṇa landlords, and assimilated the Brahmanical notions of *varṇa* hierarchy which reinforced social and economic inequalities. The underpinning economic factors in such a division are indicated by Lakṣmīdhara (twelfth century) who divides the śūdras into two classes: *āśrita* (dependent) and *anāśrita* (independent).[102] As the division of labour in medieval villages was based on caste, the continuity of caste identities was an essential ingredient of the existing mode of production, and, as has been remarked, 'the essence of feudal relationship lay in the capacity to deploy power'.[103] Sharma writes of the existence of several sub-types of social formations within the broad feudal framework, based on varying shades of servility of the subject peasantry, forms of extracting labour and sub-infeudation.[104] Parallel to this, one has to take note of the variations in caste structure within the broad *varṇa* framework as the division of labour was based on caste and the continuity of caste identities, both an essential condition for the prevailing mode of production in medieval India.

Notes

[1] R.S. Sharma, *Material Culture and Social Formations in Ancient India*, pp. 1–11.

[2] Reprinted in R.S. Sharma, *Economic History of Early India*.

[3] See chapter 1, Appendix above.

[4] Sahlins describes the 'segmentary lineage', a constituent of tribal society, as an organization for predatory expansion. Marshall D. Sahlins, 'The Segmentary Lineage'.

[5] R.S. Sharma, *Material Culture and Social Formations in Ancient India*, p. 38.

[6] Sharma (ibid., pp. 50–51) suggests that as Ṛgvedic hymns speak of the tribal chiefs donating a large number of cattle to priests, it is likely that the donors and the donees leased out their cattle to ordinary clansmen on a 'sharing basis', thus creating 'relations of dependence between herdsmen and cattle owners'. Irfan Habib and V.K. Thakur, however, assert that 'oxen from the herds were bartered away for grain from the peasants' and cattle was a form of 'capital' yielding regular income in the Ṛgvedic society (see chapter 1, Appendix above). Nevertheless, Ṛgvedic hymns provide no evidence for it. Even the later Vedic texts, which provide clear evidence of a sedentary agricultural economy, and speak of the gift of cattle, thatched houses and even 'well-prepared cultivated fields' as sacrificial fees to brāhmaṇas, contain no hint of cattle being used as barter for grain! On the other hand, the main function of the *viś* (the clan or tribe) in the Ṛgvedic passages is to raise cattle, while in later Vedic texts it denotes peasantry which also raised cattle.

[7] R.S. Sharma, *The State and Varna Formation in the Mid-Ganga Plains*, pp. 54–63.

[8] Ibid., p. 62.

[9] R.S. Sharma, *Aspects of Political Ideas and Institutions in Ancient India*, p. 179. Cf. Romila Thapar, *From Lineage to State*.

[10] R.S. Sharma, *Aspects of Political Ideas and Institutions in Ancient India*, p. 174.

[11] R.S. Sharma, *Origin of the State in India*, p. 23; R.S. Sharma, *Aspects of Political Ideas and Institutions in Ancient India*, p. 177.

[12] R.S. Sharma, *Śūdras in Ancient India*, pp. 22–23.

[13] For a critique of Kosambi's views on caste, see Suvira Jaiswal, 'Kosambi on Caste'.

[14] R.S. Sharma, *Material Culture and Social Formations in Ancient India*, p. 82.

[15] R.S. Sharma, *Advent of Aryans in India*, pp. 50–52, 84–89, 92–96, 99; R.S. Sharma, *Looking for the Aryans*, pp. 73–74.

[16] Romila Thapar, 'Dāna and Dakṣiṇā as Forms of Exchange'.

[17] R.S. Sharma 'Forms of Property in the Early Portions of *Ṛgveda*'.

[18] R.S. Sharma, *Material Culture and Social Formations in Ancient India*, pp. 39–40, 144, 150; Romila Thapar, *Ancient Indian Social History*, p. 111. The resemblance of these *yagñas* to the potlatch ceremony performed by the Kwakiufla Indians was suggested by Irawati Karve in her work *Yugānta*, p. 172.

[19] R.S. Sharma, *Śūdras in Ancient India*, p. 96; R.S. Sharma, *The State and Varṇa Formation in the Mid-Ganga Plains*, pp. 56–62. Cf. Michael Witzel, 'Early Indian History'.

[20] R.S. Sharma, *Śūdras in Ancient India*, p. 316.

[21] Ibid., p. 87.

[22] R.S. Sharma, *Material Culture and Social Formations in Ancient India*, p. 17; R.S. Sharma, *Perspectives in Social and Economic History of Early India*, pp. 26, 31.

[23] R.S. Sharma, *Material Culture and Social Formations in Ancient India*, p. 304.

[24] Dev Raj Chanana, *Slavery in Ancient India*, chapter 4.

[25] B.R. Ambedkar, 'Slaves and Untouchables'; Dev Raj Chanana, *Slavery in Ancient India*, p. 177. In the nineteenth century, the Cherumans and Pulayans of Kerala were agrarian slaves who could be bought, sold, mortgaged and rented out by their landlords. Oliver Mendelsohn and Marika Vicziany, *The Untouchables*, pp. 32, 85–86.

[26] Padmanabha Menon, *History of Kerala*, II, pp. 272–73, quoted in Sharad Patil, 'Problems of Slavery in Ancient India', p. 40.

[27] R.S. Sharma, *Śūdras in Ancient India*, p. 252.

[28] Dev Raj Chanana, *Slavery in Ancient India*, p. 149 note 40.

[29] *Padma Purāṇa* of Raviṣeṇa, V.125.

[30] *South Indian Inscriptions*, VIII: 590, quoted in Noboru Karashima, 'The Untouchability in Tamil Inscriptions and Other Historical Sources in Tamil Nadu', p. 26.

[31] D.D. Kosambi, *An Introduction to the Study of Indian History* (second edition), pp. 306, 354.

[32] *Manusmṛti*, X.83, 86.

[33] R.S. Sharma, *Early Medieval Indian Society*, pp. 68–69.

[34] Ibid. Sharma even suggests that the rise of the Vaiśya dynasty of the Guptas was a reaction against oppressive taxation; 'some vaiśya families may have mobilised fellow vaiśyas and set up their independent rule' (ibid., p. 68). However, in *Aspects of Political Ideas and Institutions* (p. 250), he characterizes the Gupta state system as 'brāhmaṇa-dominated', presenting a contrast to the 'kṣatriya-dominated centralized Maurya state'. Apart from their surname there is nothing to show that they belonged originally to a family of traders.

[35] B.N.S. Yadava, 'The Accounts of the Kali Age and the Social Transition'; B.N.S. Yadava, 'Problems of the Interaction Between Socio-Economic Classes in the Early Medieval Complex'; B.N.S. Yadava, 'Immobility and Subjection of Indian Peasantry in the Early Medieval Complex'; B.N.S. Yadava, 'Some Aspects of the Changing Order in the Saka–Kuṣāṇa Age', pp. 75–97.

[36] The following statement of Robert Deliège (*The Untouchables of India*, p. 124), translated from the French by Nora Scott, is pertinent in this connection: 'Throughout India slavery has given way to various forms of bonded labour, though in some places the worker has kept his formal freedom. In practice, however, the line between various types of labour was a thin one, for even when he was not legally a slave, the agricultural worker was still bound to the master by customary, moral and even hereditary ties . . . a runaway had few places to hide; the members of his family were reluctant to take him in for fear of repressive measures on the fugitive's family. The distinction between true slave, who could be bought and sold and other workers was therefore tenuous'.

The bracketing of the *dāsas* and *karmakaras* in our texts also shows their close approximation. Patañjali's comment on Pāṇini I.4.54, putting together the *dāsas* and *karmakaras* and separating them from wage-earning artisans, also confirms it. G.K. Rai, *Involuntary Labour in Ancient India*, pp. 119–20.

[37] B.N.S. Yadava, *Society and Culture in Northern India in the Twelfth Century*, p. 13.

[38] R.S. Sharma, *Śūdras in Ancient India*, pp. 338–39.

[39] R.S. Sharma, *Early Medieval Indian Society*, p. 34.

[40] Suvira Jaiswal, 'Caste in the Socio-Economic Framework of Early India', pp. 23–48.

[41] B.N.S. Yadava, *Society and Culture in Northern India in the Twelfth Century*, p. 38. R.S. Sharma (in *Śūdras in Ancient India*, pp. 334–35) points out that the *Manusmṛti*, X.23 speaks of six degraded vaiśya castes, the progeny of the vaiśya *vrātya* men from vaiśya women. These are: (1) *sudhanvā*, (2) *ācārya*, (3) *kāruṣa*, (4) *vijanmā*, (5) *maitra* and (6) *sātvata*. Of these the first were apparently great archers as their name denotes; the second were fallen priests (?). Sharma identifies *kāruṣa*, the third *vrātya* caste, as a tribe inhabiting the jungles of Sasaram and Palamau districts of Bihar; the fourth, *vijanmā*, merely meant 'illegitimate'. Only the fifth and the sixth, Maitras and Sātvatas, are located in western India and associated with cattle-keeping.

[42] Suvira Jaiswal, *Caste*, pp. 71–73.

[43] See K. Gopalachari, *Early History of the Andhra Country* (p. 91) for kṣatriya merchants in the early centuries of the Common Era; Indore inscription of the time of Skandagupta (Fleet, *Corpus Inscriptionum Indicarum*, III, No. 16) for kṣatriya merchants Acalavarnan and Bhūkanṭhasiṃha founding a Sun temple. For reference to a kṣatriya merchant and a kṣatriya *sūtradhāra* in two tenth-century inscriptions from Rajasthan, see B.D. Chattopadhyaya, *The Making of Early Medieval India*, p. 77.

[44] T. Watters, 'On Yuan Chwang's Travels in India', pp. 303, 343.

[45] R.S. Sharma, *Material Culture and Social Formations in Ancient India*, p. 18. Although Sharma has used the term 'caste' for *varṇa* in some of his earlier writings, he generally translates '*varṇa*' as class or order.

[46] R.S. Sharma, *Early Medieval Indian Society*, p. 66.

[47] Nasik cave inscription of Vāsiṣṭhīputra Puḷumāvi, quoted in R.S. Sharma, *Śūdras in Ancient India*, pp. 219, 235.

[48] It is suggested that the category of *kuṭumbins* corresponds to the present-day Kurmi caste of śūdra cultivators in Uttar Pradesh, Bihar and West Bengal, and the Kunbi caste of Maharashtra. Ibid., pp. 258–59.

[49] Nasik cave inscription of the time of Vāsiṣṭhīputra Puḷumāvi. D.C. Sircar, *Select Inscriptions Bearing on Indian History and Civilization*, vol. 1, p. 197.

[50] Some scholars identify the kṣatriyas defeated by Gotamīputra Sātakarṇī not with the kṣatriya *varṇa* but with the *khatriaioi* tribe mentioned by Ptolemy and other classical writers. H.C. Raychaudhuri, *Political History of Ancient India with Commentary*, pp. 365–66 note 4, p. 683 commentary on note 4.

[51] R.S. Sharma, *Śūdras in Ancient India*, pp. 235, 237. Analysing the evidence of the *Manusmṛti*, Sharma remarks, 'the relations between the highest and the lowest *varṇas* were very strained' (ibid., p. 213). But this cannot be inferred from the inscription of Balaśrī.

[52] Nasik cave inscriptions, nos 10 and 12, *Epigraphia Indica*, vol. VIII.

[53] R.S. Sharma, *Śūdras in Ancient India*, pp. 241, 331.

[54] D.D. Kosambi, *An Introduction to the Study of Indian History* (second edition), p. 280. Cf. Sheldon Pollock, *The Language of the Gods in the World of Men*, pp. 72–73.

[55] *Rājataraṅgiṇī*, I.289–329 (R.S. Pandit's translation, pp. 40–43); also see Suvira Jaiswal, *Caste*, pp. 20, 31 note 111.

[56] R.S. Sharma, *Śūdras in Ancient India*, p. 243.

[57] R.S. Sharma, *Early Medieval Indian Society*, pp. 51–52; R.S. Sharma, *Perspectives in Social and Economic History of India*, p. 31.

[58] Suvira Jaiswal, *The Origin and Development of Vaiṣṇavism*, pp. 12–14, 120–23.

[59] R.S. Sharma, *Śūdras in Ancient India*, p. 341.

[60] R.S. Sharma, *Early Medieval Indian Society*, p. 34.

[61] The Keregalur copperplates are discussed in chapter 1 above.

[62] *Śukranītisāra* IV.602–03 (Calcutta edition, IV, 5.83ff.), cited in B.N.S. Yadava, *Society and Culture in Northern India in the Twelfth Century*, pp. 316, 412.

[63] Suvira Jaiswal, *Caste*, pp. 61–65.

[64] Ibid., pp. 99–100; for *varṇādhikārī*, see B.N.S. Yadava, *Society and Culture in Northern India in the Twelfth Century*, p. 5.

[65] R.S. Sharma, *Early Medieval Indian Society*, pp. 67–68.

[66] J.F. Fleet, *Corpus Inscriptionum Indicarum*, vol. III, no. 55.

[67] R.S. Sharma, *Early Medieval Indian Society*, pp. 221–27.

[68] For Assam, see Nayanjot Lahiri, *Pre-Ahom Assam*, pp. 102, 115–16.

[69] J.H. Hutton, *Caste in India*, pp. 4, 181.

[70] R.C. Majumdar, ed., *The Classical Accounts of India*, p. 343. In the *Aitareya Brāhmaṇa* (VII.318), the Andhras are mentioned along with Puṇḍras, Pulindas, Mūtibās and Śabaras as tribes condemned to live on the borders of Aryan settlements. The *Manusmṛti* clubs them with the Medas and Chenchus as mixed castes of very 'low' origin.

[71] P.V. Parabrahma Sastry, 'Society and Economy of the Sātavāhana Age', p. 21.

[72] *Puranāṇūṛu*, 61.1.1, quoted in K.A. Nilakanta Sastri, *The Coḷas*, p. 87.

[73] Vijaya Ramaswamy, 'The Kuḍi in Early Tamiḻaham and the Tamil Women', p. 241.

[74] Robert Deliège, *The Untouchables of India*, p. 64.

[75] *Paripāḍal*, quoted in Vijaya Ramaswamy, 'The Kuḍi in Early Tamiḷaham and the Tamil Women', p. 224.

[76] K.A. Nilakanta Sastri, *The Coḷas*, p. 473.

[77] Vijaya Ramaswamy, 'The Kuḍi in Early Tamiḷaham and the Tamil Women', p. 233.

[78] Suvira Jaiswal, 'Studies in the Social History of the Early Tamils', p. 130.

[79] Nilakanta Sastri suggested that it could have been Kamban. K.A. Nilakanta Sastri, *The Coḷas*, p. 679. Suvira Jaiswal, *Caste*, p. 29 note 93; Gita Dharmapala-Frick, 'Shifting Categories in the Discourse on Caste'.

[80] D.D. Kosambi, 'The Basis of Ancient Indian History'.

[81] R.S. Sharma, *Early Medieval Indian Society*, pp. 67, 106–07; Suvira Jaiswal, 'Studies in the Social Structure of the Early Tamils', pp. 145–47, 151–54. Also see chapter 6, section II, below.

[82] The People of India project data show that more than half of the Indian communities consider themselves as part of the *varṇa* order and recognize their place within it. Kumar Suresh Singh, *People of India*, pp. 78–79.

[83] N.K. Bose, 'The Hindu Method of Tribal Absorption', p. 208.

[84] *Manusmṛti*, VIII.41. Kosambi argues that each group had to be judged by its own particular laws as it was than as a unit of production. D.D. Kosambi, *Combined Methods in Indology*, p. 322. The extra-judicial powers enjoyed by the caste panchayats, such as the *khaps*, over their caste members derive from this policy of feudal times.

[85] This is the genesis of categorization into brāhmaṇa and non-brāhmaṇa castes. Nayanjot Lahiri holds that in the pre-Ahom period Assam too was divided into these two broad categories from the *varṇa* point of view. Nayanjot Lahiri, *Pre-Ahom Assam*, p. 115.

[86] The powerful local lineages mentioned in the inscriptions of the Veṅgi Cālukyas, Durjayas and Koṇḍapadumatis claimed to belong to the fourth (śūdra) *varṇa*. P. Aruna, in B. Rajendra Prasad, *Early Medieval Andhra Pradesh* AD *624–1000*, p. 180.

[87] Madras Museum Plates of Vema AD 1345, *Epigraphia Indica*, vol. VIII, no. 3, lines 2–3.

[88] H.S. Kotiyal, 'Śūdra Rulers and Officials in Early Medieval Times', pp. 80–87.

[89] J. Duncan Derrett, *Religion, Law and the State in India*, p. 173 note 2.

[90] Jayant Lele, *Hindutva*, pp. 83–84.

[91] P.V. Kane, *History of Dharmaśāstra*, vol. I, pp. 383–84.

[92] Irfan Habib, 'Economic History of the Delhi Sultanate'; Irfan Habib, 'Medieval Popular Monotheism and Its Humanism'.

[93] Ananya Vajpeyi, '*Śūdradharma* and Legal Treatments of Caste', p. 159.

[94] R.S. Sharma, *Early Medieval Indian Society*, pp. 212–13, 266.

[95] *Manusmṛti*, X.4.

[96] *Manusmṛti*, X.16, 29–39; V.68.

[97] For example, B.R. Ambedkar, *Dr Babasaheb Ambedkar's Writings and Speeches*, vol. I, pp. 142–48, 285–87; vol. V, pp. 168–69. This sharp divide is often ignored by scholars of ancient India.

[98] R.S. Sharma, *Śūdras in Ancient India*, pp. 138,145–46.

[99] *Manusmṛti*, X.39, 48–56; Vivekanand Jha, *Caste, Untouchability and Social Justice*, p. 11.

[100] Robert Deliège, *The Untouchables of India*, pp. 6–7; Joan P. Mencher, 'The Caste System Upside Down or the Not-So Mysterious East', p. 472.

[101] Osama Konda, in K.N. Panikkar, Terence J. Byres and Utsa Patnaik, eds, *The Making of Indian History*, p. 69.

[102] *Gṛhasthakāṇḍa* of *Kṛtyakalpataru*, p. 380, quoted by B.N.S. Yadava, *Society and Culture in Northern India in the Twelfth Century*, pp. 15, 85 note 160.

[103] Hamza Alavi, quoted in Biplab Dasgupta, 'Mode of Production and the Extent of Peasant Differentiation in Pre-British Bengal', p. 6.

[104] R.S. Sharma, *Material Culture and Social Formations in Ancient India*, p. 18.

PART II

4

The Evolution of Patriarchy in Brahmanism: The Early Phase

Representations of women in Brahmanical literature have not been subjected to critical analysis, thanks to the axiomatic view that Aryans were always patriarchal. It has been assumed, *a priori*, that patriarchy provided cohesive unity to the 'social life' of the Vedic peoples from the earliest times; hence there was no need to investigate the changing gender relations.[1] The writings of Irawati Karve, D.D. Kosambi and R.S. Sharma are some notable exceptions to this axiomatic view, but their pioneering attempts in this field have been often dismissed as deriving from obsolete nineteenth-century anthropological concepts. Nevertheless, in recent decades, the feminist critique of social anthropology has revealed how an overwhelming male orientation and a male bias led to distortions in the representation of women and gender relations in anthropological studies of tribal or traditional societies; consequently, the attribution of universality to sexual asymmetry has been seriously questioned. The debate underscores the need for taking a fresh look on such taken-for-granted images of the Vedic people to re-evaluate, with rigorous analysis, evidence relating to the operation of patriarchy among them.[2]

It is often assumed that biological rather than cultural factors were responsible for the subordination of women universally, and that the role of women in the reproduction process led to the earliest division of labour and to male supremacy. Steven Goldberg in his book *The Inevitability of Patriarchy* (1973) argues that patriarchy results from hormonal differences. Earlier, Evans-Pritchard, in his *Fawcett Lectures* given at the University of London in 1955–56, had also emphasized biological, psychological and sociological factors for the subordination of women, rejecting the arguments of Margaret Mead and Simone de Beauvoir that the temperamental and social differences between men and women were products of cultural conditioning and not biology.

This kind of biological determinism in the analysis of gender relations is closer to the nineteenth-century racial theories which argued that the west triumphed over African and Asian peoples because of the biological superiority of the 'white' race, and the weak intellect of the 'Negro', 'black' and 'yellow' races. Untold harm was done by the 'Aryan race' theory and its so-called superiority which gave rise to Nazism and fascism. Since then, modern anthropology has developed a theoretical perspective which separates biology from culture and history; hardly any responsible academic now would make the mistake of attributing subordination or defeat of a people to racial or biological factors. However, the study of gender continues to be vitiated by such prejudices.

A number of feminist anthropologists, such as Eleanor B. Leacock, Karen Sacks and Gerda Lerner, have convincingly argued that in Palaeolithic times – when humans lived on food-gathering and hunting – gathering and processing of food and small game hunting were carried out by the women of the band. And this provided more than 60 per cent of the economic produce. Men went out in groups for big game hunting. As the decision-making process in the band was collective and women were economically strong, they had a major say in all the vital processes of life. Gender relations at this stage were autonomous and not hierarchical, and the bands could have been matrilineally or patrilineally structured as these traits are culture-specific and not universal.

There has never been a 'matriarchal' society as distinct from matrilineal, in the sense of power being held by women over men comparable to later patriarchies.[3] The emergence of patriarchies is embedded in the development of cattle-breeding and agriculture, when seizure of cattle belonging to other bands and the issue of access to material resources like land and water led to the use of weapons employed earlier against the big game and human enemies, resulting in cattle raids, wars and enslavement of defeated humans. Gerda Lerner makes this point forcefully in her seminal work, *The Creation of Patriarchy*.

Lerner argues that initially, men of the defeated tribes were killed, as their survival would have posed a grave threat to the captors. But their women and children were captured and enslaved. Women of the defeated tribes were exploited sexually as well as physically for their labour; and the existence of female slaves ante-dates the emergence of a subordinate labouring class of men and the invention of 'slavery'. She cites several passages from the *Iliad* in support of this hypothesis and quotes the view of E.A. Thompson on slavery in classical antiquity, that the practice of killing the men and enslaving the women prevailed when agriculture was still rudimentary.[4] At a later stage, when better techniques of agricultural production required more manpower, captured men were not killed but enslaved and made to do heavy work, giving rise to institutionalized forms of slavery.

Lerner, however, suggests that men first experienced the power of domination by subordinating women of their own group, and later women and children of alien tribes. And this experiment helped them in realizing the potential of human beings 'for tolerating enslavement'. It further led to the developing of techniques and forms of enslavement through 'elaboration of symbols of the subordination of women'. Thus, she also explores the conditions which may have contributed to the mental and cultural invention of the power of dominance, coming to the conclusion that the subordination of women ante-dates the rise of private property and class society. It is an interesting hypothesis, which is likely to remain a conjecture. In my view, the important contribution of Lerner's work lies in her underlining the linkage between the creation of patriarchy and a stratified inegalitarian society.

It is worthwhile to keep in mind that anthropological studies provide us with an explanatory framework within which we can try to fit the fragments of information embedded in our meagre historical sources. They also help us to take note of those passages we would have dismissed as having no significance. But models cannot fill the gaps in our knowledge and these have to be constantly buttressed or modified in the light of fresh evidence, for which assiduous research must be undertaken. The concept of patriarchy has two basic components. First, it is based on the notion of subordination of the female sex; second, it presumes the family as an autonomous unit under the control of the father, the patriarch, whose is the primary organizing principle of society. The evidence of patriliny and patrilocality is fairly strong among the Vedic Aryans, and even among the proto-Indo–Europeans as a whole; but if matriliny does not prove the existence of matriarchy, patriliny alone need not indicate patriarchy, although it could be a step in that direction. Eleanor Leacock writes:

> ... such patrilineal elements as might have existed in horticultural societies would be altogether different from patrilineality as it developed in societies with class structures, private property and political organization. In class structured societies, direct power of one individual over another becomes possible in a way that is foreign to collective society. The patriarchal family, in which an individual male could have complete control over the household of wives, children and servants or slaves, who could be virtually isolated from the larger society, has no parallel in the pre-political world.[5]

An important indicator of the autonomy of woman is the freedom to choose her spouse and to be in control of her sexuality. It is held that among the Celtic people, who were of Indo–European origin, women maintained their autonomy much longer than the other Indo–Europeans.[6] Several hymns of the *Ṛgveda* speak of women going to communal festivals (*samana*)[7] well-adorned and smiling (*smāyamānāsaḥ*),[8] to win their mates. According to a verse of the tenth *maṇḍala* (86.10), it was an ancient custom for women to go to communal sacrifices (*samhotra*) and to *samanas*. Sāyaṇa interprets *samana* in this context as 'battle' showing that the institution was long forgotten. According to Karve, Upadhyaya and others, *samanas* were social gatherings where the youth of the tribe met and, in the course of festivities, chose their partners. Hans-Peter Schmidt, however, has strongly questioned any such inference regarding the freedom of choice enjoyed by women, and has remarked that if the *samana* served as a 'marriage market', the maids could not have visited it without chaperones.[9]

Schmidt is of the view that patriarchy was firmly established in Ṛgvedic times. But his translation of the relevant verses is problematic and needs to be re-examined. A verse of the tenth *maṇḍala* (X.27.12), which is generally taken to indicate autonomy of women, runs as follows:

kiyatī yoṣā maryato vadhūyoḥ
paripṛītā panyasā vāryeṇa,
bhadrā vadhūr bhavati yat supeśāḥ
svayaṃ sā mitraṃ vanute jane cit.

Schmidt translates:

> How different a young woman who is being wooed by the praiseworthy gift of a young man eager for a wife! She becomes an auspicious wife beautifully adorned; she wins herself an ally even among the foreign people.

And remarks:

> The inference to be drawn from the last *pada* is not that the woman makes choice independently but rather that she attracts suitors also from foreign places through her beauty. The praiseworthy gift in the second *pada* refers to the bride price or morning gift, and this rather indicates that she goes to the highest bidder.

It seems to me that the interpretation of '*jane*' as 'suitors from foreign places' or 'foreign people' is unwarranted. I have shown elsewhere that the term *jana* has a special significance in the context of marriage alliance.[10] Hence a wife is called *janī* and *janyamitra* is a relative by marriage. *Janya* has the meaning of son-in-law (Monier-Williams, *Sanskrit–English Dictionary*, s.v. *janya*). The companions of the bridegroom are described as *janyāḥ* in the *Atharvaveda* (XI.8.1). A couple (*mithuna*) desirous of cattle and offering sacrifice to Indra are described as *dvā jana*,[11] and Indra, the giver of wives, is called *janidā*.[12] Moreover, there is no suggestion of 'bride price' or the 'bidder' in the hymn under discussion. *Panyasā* derives from *panyas* (= *panīyas*), and merely means 'worthy of great praise' or 'admiration'. The verse may be re-translated as follows:

> Many a woman wooed by a young man eager to have a wife (*maryato vadhūyoḥ*) is pleased (*paripṛītā*) by the excellent (or praiseworthy, *varyena* = *varaṇīya*) admira-

tion (bestowed on her). That beautiful girl (*yat supeśaḥ*) becomes an auspicious (or charming, *bhadrā*) wife, and on her own (*svayam sā*) chooses or wins (*vanute*) an ally (or spouse, *mitraṃ*) from among the *janas*.

It is evident that the verse, far from referring to 'bride price' and the presumed sale or a 'gift' of the girl to the highest 'bidder', clearly speaks of the choice available to a beautiful maiden and of the autonomy of women in general. A similar inference may be drawn from *Ṛgveda* I.23.2, which refers to many suitors seeking the hand of a single maiden (*varā-iva*).

Schmidt traces the institution of *putrikā*, the inheriting daughter, corresponding to the Greek epiclerate, to Ṛgvedic times and argues that *Ṛgveda*, IX.46.2, which speaks of a young woman as *pitryāvatī*, 'in possession of paternal property adorned with ornaments', could only refer to a daughter inheriting her father's property in the absence of a brother. According to him, the term was quite close in meaning and concept to the Greek *patroiokhos*, applied to the inheriting daughter in the law code of Gortyn. However, Schmidt himself has drawn attention to fundamental differences between the institutions of *putrikā* and the epiclerate owing to differences in marriage rules of the two cultures; it is likely that with the growth of individual property and the formulation of the laws of inheritance, terms derived from the same Indo–European roots were coined for concepts which developed much later and independent of each other. It has been argued that *pitṛ* in the *Ṛgveda* stands for the collectivity of ancestors, and terms such as *piṭṛvitta*, meaning paternal wealth,[13] should not be interpreted in the sense of individual inheritance.[14]

A couple of Ṛgvedic verses speak of a brotherless maiden chasing men (I.124.7; IV.5.5) and this, according to Schmidt, is indicative of the predicament of such women. There was a general aversion towards marrying a brotherless woman, for such a woman would become a *putrikā*, her children belonging to her father's lineage and not to her husband's. For this reason even later authorities such as Manu and Yājñavalkya do not recommend it,[15] the Brahmanical law books generally favouring the claims of the joint family over those of the nuclear family. However, the first clear piece of evidence of the institution of *putrikā* comes from Yāska in seventh century BCE, by which time patriarchy was well-established and women reduced to objects serving the interest of one lineage or the other, depending on their situation. Yāska explicates it while commenting on *Ṛgveda*, III.31–32, but the interpretation of these verses is highly controversial and difficult. Scholars have interpreted the verses as reflecting a transition from matriarchy to patriarchy or as a reference to incestuous procreation for purposes of rituals. Geldner, in his translation, rejects the interpretation of Yāska, and, according to Schmidt, 'no really plausible interpretation has been offered so far'.[16] At any rate Irawati Karve has understood the Ṛgvedic passages very differently, referring to brotherless girls looking for mates.[17] She argues that Ṛgvedic kinship terminology is classificatory and that, before the emergence of the custom of clan exogamy, boys and girls married within the clan, classificatory brothers and sisters were the most suitable marriage mates. Only in the absence of such 'brothers' maidens had to look for husbands outside the clan, breaking the ancient rule of the gods Varuṇa and Mitra (*Ṛgveda*, IV.5.4–5). It has been forcefully argued that clan exogamy is a specifically Indian attribute, not practised by any other group of Indo–European speakers, and is not the earliest form of marriage exchange.[18] It seems to have evolved as the nuclear family embedded closely in the clan structure gave way to linear joint families organized on patriarchal principles.[19] The dialogue hymn of Yama–Yamī (*Ṛgveda*, X.10) seems to have been a ritual enactment symbolizing the transitional process of the brother's abandonment of sexual rights over his sister.[20] The social significance of this hymn is denied by some scholars who interpret it as an adelphic creation myth or a rain-making ritual duet with cosmic symbolism;[21] but these interpretations can hardly be sustained in view of the fact that the hymn records not the consummation of the Yama–Yamī union but its total rejection. Yamī's lament (verse 1) – 'What sort of a brother are you when (while you live) I have become *anātha* (without a husband or protector)' – is indicative of the predicament of the brotherless maidens. Yamī pleads for the union, arguing that the creator–god Tvaṣṭrā, whose rules no one violates, made them *dampatīs* (husband and wife) and it is known to sky and earth; Yama retorts, 'who knows of the earliest day of which you speak', meaning thereby that the ancient rule is no longer in vogue. He hails the apparently new law of Varuṇa and Mitra, telling Yamī that the sons, the heroes of mighty Asura (Varuṇa) are everywhere and they see far and wide. It is not without significance that a Ṛgvedic magic spell for driving away the demon causing abortion enumerates the *bhrātā* (brother) along with the *pati* (husband) and *jāra* (lover) to whom the pregnant woman could be sexually accessible.[22]

This is not to deny that there is evidence of polygamy, monogamy as well as fraternal polyandry in the *Ṛgveda*,[23] and that on the whole the text reflects a growing patriarchal trend. My argument is that the composition of Ṛgvedic verses is spread over a vast span of time and shifting spaces, and that the Vedic society was neither static nor monolithic. There are traces of social customs having diverse origins, some going back to earlier times when gender relations were different, and some derived from groups which were part of the mainstream Aryan society and were absorbed into it later.

Such were the Dāsas. Their *viś* (clans or settlements) are mentioned (*Ṛgveda*, II.11.4; IV.28.4; VI.25.2; X.148.2), their chiefs killed by the Aryans and their wealth looted. Two Ṛgvedic verses speak of female fighters of the Dāsa tribe fighting along with their men against the Āryas. The *Ṛgveda* (V.30.8.9) describes Dāsa Namuci as having made women his weapons (*striyo hi dāsaḥ āyudhāni cakre*). This makes Indra exclaim: 'what can his feeble army do to me (*kim-ma-karann abalā asya senāḥ*)? Having discovered the two female breasts of this one, Indra went forth to fight the Dasyu.' Incidentally, taken together these verses also suggest the identity of the Dāsas with Dasyus, and it is rightly held that the categories of 'Dāsa' and 'Dasyu' are not mutually exclusive in the *Ṛgveda*.[24] In another verse (*Ṛgveda*, X.27.10), Indra claims to have brought together the quadrupeds and the bipeds, and divided without fight the riches of his adversary who had come with his women (*strībhiḥ*) to fight against him. Although Indra's enemy here is not named, it may be assumed that it was a Dāsa/Dasyu chief. The mighty patriarchal god of the Aryans often declares to have taken away the 'manliness' (*nṛmṇam*) of the Dasyus (*Ṛgveda*, X.48.2). Some Sanskritists try to explain away these references as cosmic allegories alluding to the fight between the thunder-cloud god Indra and the Sun and his rays.[25] But they ignore the unmistakable evidence[26] of the existence of an ethnic group known as Daha-Dāsa or Dasyu inhabiting regions of West Asia in the second–first millennium BCE. The defeat of the Dāsas and their enslavement in large numbers brought about a semantic change in the word, and whereas some verses of the *Ṛgveda* refer to the rich Dāsa chiefs whose wealth was coveted by the Aryans, in several other verses the term has the meaning of 'slave', buttressing the view that the *Ṛgveda* reflects a long period of historical development.[27]

The hostility and contempt with which the Vedic bards speak of the Dāsas/ Dasyus underline their differences not only in matters of speech and modes of worship, but also social customs. The Dasyus are called *avrata* (without vows), *anyavrata* (having other vows) and *mṛdhravācaḥ* (of alien or corrupt speech).[28] They have women warriors. The *Ṛgveda* names only one woman warrior, Viśpalā, who lost her leg in 'a battle of thousand combats' (*sahasramīḷha*) (I.112.10), elsewhere called Khela's battle (I.116.15). The twin gods Aśvins gave her a metal leg at Agastya's prayer, enabling her to move about again.[29] This event was important enough to be celebrated in a number of hymns. This story, mentioned only in the first and the tenth books of the *Ṛgveda*, seems to have preserved the memory of some remote event. The *Ṛgveda* (I.179.6) speaks of the sage Agastya as having fostered both the *varṇas* (*ubhau varṇau*), which is taken to mean the *ārya* and *dāsa varṇas* by Kosambi, but the meaning is uncertain. However, the gods Aśvins seem to have been connected with the Austric-speaking pre-Aryans of India. Their well-known alternative name, Nāsatya, according to Przyluski, has a non-Aryan radical *sata*, derived from a Munda language.[30] He points out that the word is found in the modern Munda language in the form of *sadam*, meaning 'horse'. Thus, whereas the Indo–Aryan term for horse is *aśva*, the Sanskrit *sadin*, meaning 'rider', is borrowed from Munda sources. If this suggestion is accepted, the fusion of the Aryan and Munda deities must have taken place a long time ago, for the twin deities are mentioned as Nāsatyas in the Hittite inscription of the fourteenth century BCE, discovered at Boghozkoy in Asia Minor.

Although the study of Munda elements in Indian culture is still in its infancy, there is a general consensus that 'Munda speech was well represented in the Ganges valley by the time the Aryans had arrived and, after a considerable period of bilingualism, gradually died out on the plain, surviving only in the central and eastern highlands'.[31] It appears that some breed of horse or pony was known to the Austric-speaking pre-Aryans of India, and the *Mahābhārata* describes the king of Prāgjyotiṣa and other eastern kings bringing some of the finest horses of the world as gifts to Yudhiṣṭhira.[32]

In an illuminating study of the *Apālā-sūkta* (*Ṛgveda*, VIII.91) and its variants in later Vedic texts and their interpretations by later commentators, Schmidt confirms the views of von Schroeder that the Apālā hymn 'is a puberty spell which appropriately ends with a ritual purification of the female body for the sexual, marital union'.[33] Thus the hymn telescopes a girl's 'slow process of incipient pubescence to full maturity', and its last stanza is used during the marriage ritual in the *Atharvaveda* and some Gṛhyasūtras. This, in Schmidt's view, shows its original purpose, for it could not have been an 'independent female puberty-rite' as Indo–Europeans were patrilineal, and pastoral societies 'show little evidence for female puberty rites'. Nevertheless, if we examine the hymn independently, it becomes quite clear that it does not have a pastoral but agricultural context; and that the girl is praying for the fertility of her father's corn-fields and the maturing of her body. Could this be a fertility spell of non-Aryan origin? Schmidt is not able to find a satisfactory etymology of 'Apālā' and takes it to be a phonetic variant of *apārā*, meaning 'boundless', an epithet of Indrāṇī, the wife of Indra, thus identifying Apālā with Indrāṇī. But it is also possible that the name derived from some non-Indo–Aryan source.[34] Later identification of Apālā with Indrāṇī is indicative of the spousing of an independent mother-goddess according to patriarchal norms. The *Ṛgveda* is a compilation of verses made for hieratic purposes and although it is primarily an Aryan document, the interaction of the Aryan tribes with the pre-Aryan settlers during the long span of several centuries covering its composition could not have been limited to hostilities and conflicts only. There must have been also an assimilation and a give-and-take, particularly in the field of agricultural technology and related rituals.[35]

However, the *upanayana* ceremony described in the later Vedic texts seems to have been originally a puberty rite signifying formal entry into adulthood; Kane has put forward cogent arguments in favour of the view that initially it was performed both for boys and girls on reaching adolescence.[36] From the fact that many of the Gṛhyasūtras are entirely silent about the use of the sacred thread in the *upanayana* ceremony and no Vedic *mantra* is prescribed for the act of giving the *yajñopavīta* (sacred thread), Kane concludes that probably, in older times, it was the upper garment which was folded in various positions while performing certain ritual acts during the ceremony. The use of the sacred thread came into vogue later. Whatever the case may be, the *Gobhila* and *Baudhāyana Gṛhyasūtras* mention its use; Kane quotes the *Gobhila Gṛhyasūtra* (II.i) which speaks of the bride as *prāvṛtāṃ yajñopavītinīṃ*, 'wearing the sacred thread'. He cites passages from later Smṛtis to support the view that in earlier times *upanayana* was performed for the women too. Thus Yama (II.i) clearly states that the tying of the girdle of *muñja* (*maunjibandhana*, a synonym for *upanayana*) was approved for the maidens during former ages. They were taught the Vedas and recitation of *Sāvitrī* (*mantra*).[37] Hārīta repeats the same verse with the slight variation of substituting 'women' (*nārīnāṃ*) in place of maidens (*kumārīnāṃ*).[38] He further observes that there are two types of women: *brahmavādinīs* and *sadyovadhūs*. The former go through *upanayana*, keep the (holy) fire, study the Vedas and beg alms in their own homes. In the case of the latter, i.e. *sadyovadhus*, it is said that when the time of marriage draws near, the ceremony of *upanayana* should be performed somehow and marriage celebrated. In the *Kādambarī* of Bāṇabhaṭṭa, the body of Mahāśvetā, who is engaged in practising severe austerities, is described as being rendered pure by the *brahmasūtra* (i.e. the *yajñopavīta*, the sacred thread).[39]

Although the *Ṛgveda* does not mention *upanayana* explicitly, it appears that the rite goes back to the Indo–Iranian phase, as it has a close parallel in the Navjote ceremony performed for boys and girls of the Zoroastrian community to this day. Schmidt rejects this view, arguing that the authority for the initiation of girls in Zoroastrianism is a later interpolation.[40] He also rejects the literal meaning of the phrase *prāvṛtāṃ yajñopavītinīm* in the *Gobhila Gṛhyasūtra*, (which Kane translates as '[the bride] is wrapped in a robe and wears the sacred thread'), and asserts that this ought to be interpreted as referring to the upper garment of the bride arranged in the fashion of *yajñopavīta* as mentioned by the commentator and is no proof of the bride wearing the *yajñopavīta*. The commentary explains *yajñopavītinī* as *yajñopavītavatkṛtottarīyam*, the upper garment arranged in the fashion of the sacred thread. However, it appears more plausible to me that the commentator, writing at a time when *upanayana* for women was no longer performed, explains the phrase *yajñopavītinī* in this manner. The crucial question is, why does a later Smṛti writer admit the prevalence of women's *upanayana* in the past and a literary text of the seventh century mention a woman wearing the sacred thread, unless there was some survival of the ancient practice that was in the process of being discontinued?

Taking an overall view of the construction of gender in the Vedic tradition, the trend is clearly from a relative autonomy of women and their participation in Vedic ritualism, to their increasing subordination and exclusion from activities carrying a high-status value. In later times, recitation of the Vedic *mantras* was prohibited for both women and śūdras.[41] The prejudice of *Manusmṛti*[42] and the early Dharmasūtras against a śūdra listening to recitation of the Vedas[43] is extended to women in the medieval Purāṇas, and the *Bṛhannāradīya Purāṇa* informs us that a man who reads the Vedas in the proximity of women and śūdras goes to hell successively during thousands of crores of *kalpas*.[44] Even Manu lays down (*Manusmṛti*, II.66) that the *saṃskāra* rites for women should be performed without the use of Vedic *mantras*. This is also the view of the *Āśvalāyana Gṛhyasūtra* (I.17.18), which, interestingly, prescribes the offering of water libations to three female sages, Gārgī Vācakanavi, Vadavā-Prātitheyī and Sulabhā-Maitreyī, along with other male sages in the daily (*āhnika*) *ṛṣi-tarpaṇa*.[45] The *Āpastamba Gṛhyasūtra* informs that a *homa*, i.e. offering of oblations into the fire in the Vedic mode, is rejected (*paricakṣate*) if made by a woman or by a man who has not had his initiation (*anupetena*).[46] In the *Mahābhārata*[47] it is stated that women who make offerings to the fire go to hell, as also those for whom these offerings are made. But in Vālmīki's *Rāmāyaṇa*, Kausalyā is described as worshipping Viṣṇu in the Vedic mode, pouring oblation into the holy fire (*agni juhoti*), reciting *mantras* (*mantravat*).[48] The poet of *Ṛgveda*, VII.11.6 finds nothing incongruous in likening the ladle dripping with ghee to a young woman who goes to the sacrificial fire morning and night of her own accord (*sva*), in search of wealth (*vasūyuḥ*). In the second century BCE, Patañjali explained the formation of the term *kāśakṛtsnā* for denoting a brāhmaṇa woman who has studied *Kāśakṛtsnī*, a *mīmāṃsā* work dealing with Vedic sacrifices written by Kāśakṛtsna,[49] and Kauṭilya speaks of female ascetics of the brāhmaṇa caste known as *parivrājikās* who could visit the royal harem and the families of high officials.[50] They are generally widows but the *brāhmaṇī* Sulabhā who argues with king Janaka in the *Mahābhārata*,[51] if identified with Maitreyī, is the wife of sage Yājñavalkya, and the female ascetic Svayamprabhā in the *Rāmāyaṇa* of Vālmīki[52] introduces herself as the daughter of Manu Sāvarṇi. Patañjali speaks of a *parivrājikā* Śaṇkarā,[53] and Paṇḍitā Kauśikī figures in the garb of an ascetic in Kālidāsa's *Mālavikāgnimitra* (I.14). However, later Smṛti writers clearly state that the life of an ascetic is sinful for women and is not approved by the Vedas and the Śāstras.[54]

Altekar suggested that the chanting of the *Soma* hymns was originally the function of the wife of the sacrificer, which was later taken over by the *udgātṛ* priest.[55] Later studies have shown that in systematizing the Vedic rituals in their *śrauta* form the Vedic priesthood suppressed and displaced the role of women, as female sexuality posed both 'physical and metaphysical problems'.[56] The priest designated as Neṣṭṛ functioned as a substitute for the wife of the sacrificer, uttering the words meant for her, thus enacting her role in a number of rites. Commenting on the ritual of '*patnīvata* cup of Soma', S.A. Dange quotes several passages from the *Brāhmaṇas* which identify Agnīdhra priest as man and Neṣṭṛ as woman, commenting that the representation of the wife of the sacrificer by the Neṣṭṛ priest 'was a later phase; or it may be an alternate ritual to the one where the "wife" actually must have figured as in the case of Horse sacrifice'.[57] It seems to me that *Ṛgveda*, VIII.33.19 – which asks a Brahman priest to act like a woman for 'now he has become a woman' – was apparently recited at some such rite. The verse translated by Griffith runs as follows:

> Cast down thine eyes and look not up.
> More closely set thy feet. Let none
> See what thy garment veils for thou, a
> Brahman, hast become a dame.

It is a part of the dialogue added rather arbitrarily to the hymn and has a verse preceding it (no. 17) that speaks of women in derogatory terms:

> Indra himself hath said, the mind of
> Woman brooks no discipline,
> Her intellect hath little weight.

Sāyaṇa explains that stanza 19 is addressed by Indra to Asaṅga, son of Plāyoga, whom the curse of gods had changed into a woman, but this seems to be a late invention at a time when the real purpose of the ritual dialogue was no longer understood.[58]

The suppression of women is reflected at the divine level in the myth of Uṣā and Indra. The *Ṛgveda*[59] speaks of Uṣā as having been superior (*abhūt*) to Indra, full of wealth (*indratamā maghoni*) and the daughter of Heaven (*divaḥ*), the best of the Aṅgirasas (*aṅgirastama*). In a brilliant analysis of the hymns relating to the Dawn-goddess, D.D. Kosambi points out that the aorist past sense (*abhūt*) indicates that Uṣā had been, but is no longer, equal to Indra.[60] Indra hit (or killed) the evil-plotting Uṣas, the daughter of Heaven, destroyed her wagon (*anasaḥ*) on the banks of the Vipāś river, smashing it to bits, and made her flee far away. Kosambi regards Uṣas as a pre-Aryan, Harappan mother-goddess who was vanquished by Indra, typifying the 'Aryan tribal war-chieftain'; but his thesis of the patriarchal Aryans coming into direct conflict with the 'matriarchal' Harappans has won little acceptance as it conflicts with available archaeological evidence.[61] Moreover, 'Uṣas' is Indo–European and cognate with the Greek *Eos*. Although Greece has not preserved traces of her importance in the same fashion as the *Ṛgveda*, her wagon, which is described as *anas*, an ox-cart, testifies to her antiquity.[62]

Thus, it is probable that the Aryan tribes too had more equitable gender relations in the past when social units were differently structured, and mother-goddesses such as Aditi, Uṣā, Sinīvālī and Indrāṇī occupied high positions in the conceptualization of divinities. Sinīvālī (*Ṛgveda*, II.32.7) is described as *viśpatnī*, the protector of the clan or settlement and a sister of the gods, suggesting the importance of the sister in the family, and Indrāṇī (*Ṛgveda*, X.86) is the maker of *ṛta*, the universal law, in some passages.

At the human level, although the wedding hymn (*Ṛgveda*, X.85) speaks of the marriage of Sūryā, the daughter of the Sun god, with the twin gods Aśvins, it may be taken as an adequate representation of the wedding of human couples. It contains a benediction for the bride: may god Pūṣan take her by the hand and conduct her, the two Aśvins carry her in their chariot, and may she go to the houses (*gṛhān*) and become *gṛhapatnī* (mistress of the house) having authority (*vaśinī*) and also speak in the *vidatha* (Vedic tribal assembly).[63] I have argued elsewhere that the Ṛgvedic *gṛhapati* and *gṛhapatnī* are not ordinary householders or a *gṛhastha* couple.[64] The *gṛhapati* was the head of an extended kin group responsible for the group's rituals and material needs. He kept the sacred *gārhapatya* fire (one of the *śrauta* fires, not to be confused with the domestic fire or *gṛhyāgni* of the later Gṛhyasūtras) on behalf of the entire kin group. For this reason, even when the concept of the patriarchal joint family as a single residential unit with its members living under one roof, eating food cooked in one 'hearth', was well-established, the *Gobhila Gṛhyasūtra* (I.4.24–25) seems to have the earlier, close-knit extended kin group (*kula*?) in mind when prescribing that the sacrificial food for the *bali* offerings should come from the kitchen of the *gṛhapati* only. The *Śāṅkhāyana Gṛhyasūtra* (I.2–5) lays down that the eldest son should keep the fire burning of his *gṛhapati* (father) on his death, and in the event of the death of the elder brother the younger brother should do so, apparently succeeding him as *gṛhapati*. Thus the *gṛhapati* is not to be confused with *gṛhastha*. He had a position of power and authority. The nature of the kin unit over which he presided changed with the changes in the social structure.

The wedding hymn exhorts the *gṛhapatnī* to be ever-vigilant in keeping the *gārhapatya* fire burning.[65] Her authority over the families of the junior kin members is suggested by the pronouncement that she may have 'easy control' of the houses (*suyamā-gṛhebhyaḥ*) and extender of houses (*pratāriṇī, gṛhānām*) apparently, of her husband's kin.[66] Her responsibilities are not confined to a single patriarchal household but extend to several *gṛhas*, perhaps nuclear units embedded in the larger clan/*kula* or extended kin unit. No doubt a later verse blesses the bride that she may rule over her father-in-law, mother-in-law, sister-in-law and brother-in-law, painting the picture of a lineal joint family; but this is apparently a later addition couched in a language closer to later Sanskrit rather than the Vedic.[67] It is held that the wedding hymn, which is still recited on the occasion of marriage, has received additions by several hands; hence it has a curious mixture of old and new concepts.[68]

Whatever the case may be, the prayer that the bride may speak in the *vidatha* and may do so till her old age underscores the presence of women in the public sphere.[69] That the ability to speak in the *vidatha* was a matter of prestige or authority is revealed in a verse which states that the god Soma bestows upon his worshipper a milch cow (*go*), a fleet-footed horse (*arvantaṃ-āśuṃ*), and a son (*vīraṃ*) who is skilful (*karmaṇyaṃ*), worthy of the house (*sadanyaṃ*), of the *vidatha* (*vidathyaṃ*), of the *sabhā* (*sabheyaṃ*) and brings glory to his ancestors (*pitṛśravaṇaṃ*).[70] Generally the epithet *vidathya* is applied to gods, but at one place speech is described as worthy of *vidatha* and *sabhā* (*Ṛgveda*, I.167.3). At another place in the same hymn, Rodasī (lightning), the wife of Maruts, is described as a young, devoted woman who is set up on the chariot (*rathaṃ*) and in the *vidathas* by the young men, her husbands (verses 5 and 6). A worshipper who makes offerings to Ādityas is said to gain their everlasting blessings and thus he 'moves about in a chariot', becomes first in rank (*prathama*), wealthy and lauded in the *vidathas*.[71] The *Atharvaveda* (VIII.1.6) expresses the desire for a man of advanced age to speak in the *vidatha*. The nature and composition of the *vidatha* is a controversial issue. Sāyaṇa interprets it as 'sacrifice' in most passages, and as the (three) 'stations' or 'worlds' of gods (the earth of the Vasus, the firmament of the Rudras and the heaven of the Ādityas) in one passage (*Ṛgveda*, VI.51.2). Griffith has translated the term variously as 'assembly', 'gathering' or 'synod', and Geldner as 'wisdom', 'knowledge', 'priestly lore', 'sacrifice' and 'spiritual authority'.[72] However, according to R.S. Sharma, the meaning of 'assembly', 'council' or a 'gathering of the people' suits better the context of the passages.[73] But what was the nature of this assembly?

There is no doubt that the *vidatha* was an ancient institution which became defunct in later times. Its importance may be judged from the fact that a refrain is woven around it in twenty-two hymns of the second book of the *Ṛgveda*, as '*bṛhad vadema vidathe suvīrāḥ*': 'Lord may we speak, with brave sons in assembly.' According to one view,[74] *vidatha* was a 'local assembly' meeting for religious purposes, but Sharma seems to be right in suggesting that it was the assembly of a kin-based community, the 'earliest folk assembly of the Indo–Aryans, attended both by men and women, performing all kinds of functions, economic, military, religious and social'.[75] His study shows that as we proceed along the arrowline of time in Vedic literature, references to such tribal assemblies as *sabhā* and *samiti* increase, but those to *vidatha* decrease. *Vidatha* is hardly mentioned in the post-Vedic literature. The *Nighaṇṭu* explains it as 'sacrifice', and *Nirukta* both as 'sacrifice' and 'assembly'.[76] V.S. Apte lists 'battle' as one of its meanings (*Sanskrit–English Dictionary*, *vidatha*). This may be compared with the semantic change in the meaning of *samana*, which, when the memory of such gatherings had faded, was little understood by later generations and Sāyaṇa explained it as 'battle'.[77] Similarly *samiti*, a tribal assembly in the Vedic period, acquired the meaning of 'battle' (*bhavānbhīṣmaśca karṇaśca kṛpaśca samitiṃjayaḥ*; *Bhagavadgītā*, I.8) or 'sacrifice' in later sources.[78]

Whatever may have been the exact nature of the *vidatha* assembly, its decline underscores the withdrawal of women from public spheres. It has been argued that the 'participatory' role of women in the Vedic period need not necessarily imply that 'participation *per se* is an intrinsic good', and the real question to ask is, 'participation in service of whose goals, in the construction of what kind of gender roles?'[79] Nevertheless, in a society which deemed the right to recite Vedic hymns and participation in Vedic rituals a matter of prestige, power and accessibility to knowledge and learning, exclusion became symbolic of women's subordination and marginalization. Feminist studies have shown that control over language, the instrument for knowledge, is central to the creation and preservation of patriarchy.[80]

It is held that in tribal conflicts, initially, defeated males were killed and their women captured and enslaved, giving rise to a small category of women slaves.[81] It is a plausible hypothesis, although the term *dāsī* in the sense of a female slave appears for the first time only in the *Atharvaveda*.[82] A few verses of the *Ṛgveda* speak of the gift of women apparently captured in battle and awarded as prizes; but they are called *janīs* or *vadhūs*, and not *dāsīs*. Thus Trasadasyu, literally the tormenter of *dasyus*, son of Purukutsa, is said to have given the singer fifty *vadhūs*, i.e. brides, though translated by Griffith as 'female slaves'.[83] The Ṛgvedic poets often pray to the warrior-god Indra to give them cows, horses, food and wives (*janīḥ*), no doubt acquired as booty, and Indra is called *janidā*, giver of wives.[84] Perhaps the 'stately' young woman (*yoṣaṇā*) adorned with gold ornaments being led forth to Vasa, the son of Aśva, mentioned in *Ṛgveda*, VIII.46.33, was some important female personage captured in war and acquired as a *vadhū*. There are references to a common husband of the *janīs*.[85] The tribal chief had more than one wife, a fact given recognition in the later *Ratnahavīṃśi* ceremony of the *Śrautasūtras*.[86]

Altekar thinks that the introduction of a 'non-Aryan wife into the Aryan household' was the key to the general decline in the position of women.[87]

According to him, the 'non-Aryan wife with her ignorance of Sanskrit language and Hindu religion' would have committed mistakes in the performance of rituals, shocking the orthodox priests. But a mighty king, mad in love for his non-Aryan beloved, was not to be dictated to by priests dependent upon him for subsistence. So the priesthood eventually retrieved the situation 'by declaring the whole class of women to be ineligible for Vedic studies and religious duties'. This argument is too naive to deserve serious consideration. Nevertheless, availability of women of defeated tribes – Aryan or non-Aryan – for exploitation of their physical and sexual labour could have led to the erosion of egalitarian gender norms. The Ṛgvedic data do not clearly indicate whether this happened before the enslavement of any category of men, as assumed in Lerner's schema. The term *dāsa* in the sense of 'slave' appears only in the later portions of the *Ṛgveda*,[88] but several hymns club together the 'two-footed humans'[89] and 'four-footed' animals in such a manner as to suggest that the former belonged to the same category as the latter – objects constituting wealth for the singers. At one place the god Savitā is praised for giving wealth (*artha*) in the form of 'bipeds' and 'quadrupeds'.[90] In the wedding hymn, the bride is invoked twice (X.85.43, 44) to come to her husband's house and bring blessings to his house, and to his 'bipeds' and 'quadrupeds'. The god Soma is requested to give healthy food to his worshippers and their 'animals' (*paśave*), the two-footed and four-footed ones (*dvipadecatuṣpadecapaśave*).[91] The inclusion of the 'two-footed' in the category of tethered animals is significant. Émile Benveniste has shown that the notion of 'sale' and 'purchase' appeared among the Indo–Europeans, not in connection with merchandise of goods but in the context of sale by auction of men who were prisoners of war or had lost their liberty in gambling.[92] The number of such slaves would be small but crucial to the erosion of the egalitarian ethos of tribal societies. However, it is difficult to establish on empirical evidence whether the enslavement of women preceded that of defeated men or it was a simultaneous process. A hymn of the first *maṇḍala* (92.8) contains a prayer for the gain of a multitude of slaves (*dāsapravarga*), and in one of the *Vālakhilya* hymns (VII.56.3 in Max Müller's edition), the poet praises his patron for giving him one hundred slaves (*dāsas*) along with a hundred asses and a hundred sheep.

Availability of servile labour would create conditions for the withdrawal of women – at least of the elite groups – from the process of social production and cause a decline in their status, as noticed by Altekar long ago.[93] It could also lead to an overemphasis on their role in reproduction. Exaltation of motherhood would be one aspect of this outlook; the other would be the identification of women with sexuality. It is significant that in several dialogue hymns (*saṃvāda*) between a male and a female which relate to fertility, the woman stands for desire and sexuality and making advances, and the man either resists in the name of upholding a higher moral principle – as in the case of the Yama–Yamī dialogue (X.10) – or gives in reluctantly to have a progeny, like the sage Agastya in the Lopāmudrā hymn (I.179.4), presumably to pay his debt to ancestors, as explained in later sources. The act, however, does no damage to his ascetic powers.[94] The beginnings of the stereotype of the ascetic male who is self-possessed and calm (*dhīra*), and the woman who is just the opposite, *adhīra*, a temptress, may be traced in verse 4 of this hymn.

It can hardly be disputed that the main concern of the Ṛgvedic religion was fertility of humans, cattle and land; hence sexual symbolism constitutes a pronounced ingredient of Vedic ritualism.[95] This necessitated the participation of women and their gradual withdrawal from it with changing social norms and value systems. Sexual imagery is vivid in several hymns with no trace of prudery. Nevertheless, it is strange that the *Ṛgveda*, VII.33 (verses 9–13) make a clearly contrived attempt to deny the involvement of the female body in the birth of the illustrious sages Vasiṣṭha and Agastya. We are told that Vasiṣṭha was a 'mind-born' (*mānasodhijātaḥ*) son of Urvaśī and the gods Varuṇa and Mitra. The two, on seeing the *apsara*, dropped their semen. The All-gods (*viśvedevāḥ*) placed Vasiṣṭha (that is, the semen) into a lotus pond (*puṣkara*), and in this way Vasiṣṭha was born of Urvaśī. Verse 13 further clarifies that Varuṇa and Mitra, urged through prayer, had dropped their semen into a pitcher simultaneously during the performance of a *sattra* sacrifice; from this pitcher issued Agastya, and later Vasiṣṭha was born. Earlier in the same hymn, verse 10 narrates that when the 'one and only birth' of Vasiṣṭha took place, Agastya brought him here from his people (or settlement, *viśaḥ*). Kosambi is right in asserting that both *kumbha* (pot) and *puṣkara* represent the mother-goddess; he sees in these multiple convoluted accounts of the birth of Vasiṣṭha, a transition from matriarchy to patriarchy, elements of the former coming from Harappan culture. There are difficulties in accepting Kosambi's thesis *in toto*, particularly his view that the priestly class of Aryan conquerors was largely recruited from the conquered Harappans, giving rise to a separate endogamous brāhmaṇa caste;[96] we have already seen the concept of matriarchy reduced to matriliny in anthropological investigations. The worship of a mother-goddess or goddesses was widespread in the Neolithic–Chalcolithic period; and even when women had been subordinated in patriarchal societies, goddesses continued to hold their own and were venerated for a long time.[97] Whether the story of Vasiṣṭha's birth symbolized the adoption of Harappan elements into patriarchal Aryan society or not will remain a speculation till such time that more definitive knowledge becomes available about Harappan culture. What is significant from our point of view is the fact that the myth circumvents the role of the female biological process in procreation, and makes Vasiṣṭha a 'mind-born' son of Urvaśī. Later Puranic myths use this device to emphasize the 'purity' of birth of the founder-members of important priestly and ruling lineages. The *Matsya Purāṇa* narrates that the creator–god Brahmā practised severe asceticism and created the Vedas, the *Vedāṅgas* and the *Upāṅgas*.[98] Becoming conscious of his 'supreme potentiality' and through his desire, he then created the ten sages known as his 'mind-born sons' (*mānasa-putras*), namely, Mārīci, Atri, Aṅgirā, Pulastya, Pulāh, Kratu, Pracetā, Bhṛgu, Vasiṣṭha and Nārada. Later, he created from the various limbs of his body another group of ten sages 'who had no mother'. Not only the brāhmaṇa patriarchs but the first ruler of human beings, Virajas, too was born in this manner. The *Mahābhārata* states that the ruler–god Viṣṇu created by fiat of his will the first ruler of mankind; and Virajas was his *mānasaputra*.

The Brahmanical attitude towards procreation increasingly emphasizes two points: the importance of the male seed and the 'impure' nature of the female generative processes. The pure and the best are born uncontaminated. The 'field' which nurtures the seed is in any case secondary and can be dispensed with in case of illustrious birth. The seed constitutes the soul. The *Chāndogya Upaniṣad*,[100] explaining transmigration, states that after exhausting its *karma* the soul returns to earth in the rain and enters a plant. 'Ultimately the plant is eaten by a man or male animal and the soul is transferred to a woman in his semen. Thus it is reborn as a living being.'[101] Later, the idea that a woman was the 'field' or merely a leather bag for holding the male seed is repeatedly expressed in the Dharmaśāstras, and the debate centres on the issue whether the child belongs to the owner of the 'field' or the donor of the seed, with the 'mother' being a passive instrument.

The idea that women as biological creatures are polluting and therefore constitute the condemned lot is clearly articulated in the later Vedic texts. The *Taittirīya Saṃhitā* relates that Indra incurred the sin of Brahmanicide by killing Viśvarūpa and was condemned for this heinous sin.[102] He persuaded the earth, trees and women to take over a third of his guilt and in return granted each of them a boon that the earth when dug would be able to close the cleavage within a year, trees when cut would grow again, and women would enjoy sexual intercourse any time even during pregnancy. The myth is repeated in later sources such as the *Mahābhārata*[103] and the *Bhāgavata Purāṇa*[104] with certain variations regarding the identity of the parties receiving the guilt, but women remain constant recipients in all the lists. As Julia Leslie remarks, 'Menstruation, the sign of a woman's participation in Brāhmin-murder, is thus a mark of both her sexual appetite and her innate impurity.'[105] The *Taittirīya Saṃhitā* makes a woman during menses completely untouchable and unapproachable as 'she keeps emitting the colour of brāhmaṇa murder', and lays down elaborate rules for her to observe during this period, any breach of which was to result in dire consequences.[106] This text speaks of women as weaklings and hence not entitled to a portion of the *soma* drink during the sacrifices. 'Therefore, women are without strength, take no *dāya* (portion) and speak more weakly than even a wretched man.'[107] This may be contrasted with the Ṛgvedic hymn (VIII.91) which speaks of the girl Apālā who, having found *soma* stalk while returning from her bath in a stream, chewed it with her jaws and offered it to Indra. Even if it is assumed that Apālā is a mythic personification, at least at the divine level the *soma* drink is offered not only to the gods but also to goddesses such as Indrāṇī, Varuṇānī, Agnāyī,[108] the goddess Earth and Aditi;[109] its preparation is a household affair.[110] The daughter of Sūrya has the task of purifying it[111] and *nārī*, the woman of the house, is said to be marking and keeping count of the rise and fall of the pestle during its preparation in a hymn,[112] which is apparently a song sung during the preparation of *soma*. Even clearer is the description of the *dampatī*, the husband-and-wife couple, in hymn VIII.31. They wash and press out the *soma* juice and offer the sacrifice together, gaining 'strength' and 'glory'. Interestingly, this hymn speaks of the *dampatī* reaching its full extent of life with 'sons and daughters by their side'[113] without any hint of daughters being less welcome than the sons.

However, growing suspicion and subjection of the female sex becomes quite pronounced in the later Vedic texts. In the *Varuṇapraghāsa* sacrifice, which is one of the four-monthly sacrifices mentioned in the *Śrauta Sūtras*, the sacrificer's wife is made to confess if she has any lovers. If she names one, the *pratiprasthātṛ* priest is to pronounce, 'May Varuṇa seize him'. If, however, the wife does not name the paramour although she has one, 'she will be kept away from her dear kinsmen'. Therefore, she should point to him with the words, 'This is my paramour.' 'By pointing him out she causes him to be seized by means of Varuṇa's fetters.'[114] This is often cited as evidence of sexual laxity or the lenient attitude of the brāhmaṇa ritualists towards an adulterous woman, but is perhaps better understood as a ritual device for securing a wife's faithfulness and monandry. The *Ṛgveda* condemns women who are brotherless and have gone astray, and those who are hostile to their husbands (*patiripaḥ*), are of evil conduct (*durevaḥ*), sinful (*pāpāsaḥ*), false (*anṛta*), and untruthful (*asatya*).[115] They are held as violators of the fixed rules of Mitra and Varuṇa. The wife's confession of guilt, as Gonda remarks,[116] 'approximates to purification' and systematizes conduct 'yielding the possibility of a new mode of life'. The later Vedic texts inculcate the new morality, which sought to rigorously control female sexuality in a situation of increasing male dominance. Any aberration on the woman's part merited serious consequences for her near and dear ones. The *Pāraskara Gṛhyasūtra* provides for the extirpation of the harmful substance latent in a bride with the following *mantra*: 'The evil substance that dwells in you that brings death to your children, death to the cattle, destruction to the house, destruction to fame, that I change into one that brings death to your lover.'[117] Even the wedding hymn visualizes the bride as being possessed by a female demon (*kṛtyā*), which has to be exorcized by giving away the bride's woollen (old? *śāmūlya*) clothes and gifting wealth to priests.[118] She is blessed not to be inauspicious (*adurmaṅgali*), evil-eyed (*aghoracakṣuḥ*) and a killer of her husband (*apatighnī*).[119] Perception of the feminine gender as causing harm through magic may be seen also in a verse of the *Atharvaveda*,[120] which seeks to throw back the evil (*kṛtyā*) on the one engaged in it. It could be a śūdra, a chief (*rājā*), a woman or a brāhmaṇa.

It is repeatedly enjoined that a woman should be a devoted, virtuous wife (*patyuranuvratā*) and never oppose her husband (*patya-avirodhayanti*).[121] The *Bṛhadāraṇyaka Upaniṣad* ordains that a wife not complying with her husband's instructions should be not only 'censured but also compelled to do so by physical force'.[122] However, elsewhere it recommends that a couple wishing to obtain a learned daughter should eat rice cooked with *tila* (sesame) and clarified butter. The *Aitareya Brāhmaṇa* rules out polyandry: 'therefore, one man has many wives, but one wife has not many husbands at the same time'.[123] Such statements do not prove the absence of polyandry among the Indo–Aryans as is assumed sometimes.[124] Prevalence of polyandrous practices is well-attested among other Indo–European groups, such as the Iranian Medes, Bactrians, Sogdians and even among Romans and Britons;[125] the later Dharmaśāstras, while denouncing polyandry, testify nevertheless to the existence of such customs in certain communities.[126] However, polyandry alone, particularly fraternal polyandry, need not imply high status for women or their autonomy. It may as well reflect her equation with an item of property to be shared in common through fraternal polyandry, as is shown in the story of Draupadī in the *Mahābhārata*. The emphasis on monandry may indicate a structural transition from kin dominance to lineal patriarchal families.

Later Vedic sources show an increasing appropriation of women's sexual and reproductive capacities in the interest of developing institutions of private property and the formation of a class society in the shape of a heredity-based *varṇa* system. The practice of *niyoga* or levirate as discussed and debated in the early Dharmasūtras originated in this milieu.[127] Attempts to trace it in the *Ṛgveda* on the basis of doubtful interpretations do not bear scrutiny.[128] Levirate in the Dharmasūtras is a temporary union restricted for the purpose of begetting a son, and as Schmidt remarks, 'chaste' *niyoga* mentioned in these texts must have been 'a frustrating and humiliating experience for both partners'. The Ṛgvedic references seem to suggest a regular conjugal union with the younger brother-in-law.[129] The need for 'brave sons' is articulated so strongly by the Ṛgvedic poets for defending against as well as engaging in cattle raids that, according to Sarva Daman Singh, 'widows of child-bearing age are incompatible with the whole pattern of early Aryan existence'. The same could be said for the practice of *satī*, i.e. burning of the widow on the funeral pyre of her husband, the case for which rests on a forcible emendation of a Ṛgvedic verse.[130] Reference to the widow being raised by hand from the pyre of her dead husband by her suitor (*didhiṣu*)[131] perhaps signifies a ritual breaking of her ties with the dead husband on whom she was bestowed by the gods, according to the wedding hymn, in order to return to the 'world of the living' (*jīvalokam*). It is not necessary to presuppose an 'archaic Satī custom . . . gone out of vogue'.[132] The idea that marriage ties were binding even after death is confirmed by a hymn of the *Atharvaveda*,[133] which prescribes a ritual to secure the union of the remarried woman with her husband in heaven, both going to the same world (*samānaloka bhavati punarbhuvā aparaḥ patiḥ*). The description of the remarried woman as *punarbhuvā* (rejuvenated) later gave rise to the conventional Sanskrit term *punarbhū* for the remarried woman.

It has been argued that *niyoga* originated with the emergence of primogeniture in the archaic joint family: 'the eldest son usurped the right to continue individually the lineage of the family . . . if the first-born died without a son, the junior members were duty-bound to produce one in his name';[134] hence *niyoga* applies only to the elder brother's wife and not to the younger one's. This is a tempting hypothesis, although the *Mahābhārata* records several exceptions to this rule. For example, on the death of Vicitravīrya, Satyavatī, his mother, had first appealed to Bhīṣma, the elder brother, to procreate sons by *niyoga* on the wives of the dead king to continue the lineage of the Kurus, and on his refusal Vyāsa, another elder half-brother of Vicitravīrya, was persuaded to do so. Thus Dhṛtarāṣṭra and Pāṇḍu were obtained by *niyoga* in order to prevent the line of the Kurus becoming extinct. The *Āpastamba Dharmasūtra* mentions the view of those who hold that a woman is given to a family (*kula*) and hence it is appropriate that a near relative or a *sagotra* should beget children by her on the failure of the husband; but Āpastamba himself condemns the practice in no uncertain terms.[135] According to him, transgression of marriage vows would condemn both husband and wife to hell; and the reward gained by observing the 'restrictions' imposed by the rule of marriage is greater than the one obtained by having an offspring from *niyoga*. Similar views are expressed by Gautama, Baudhāyana and other *sūtrakāras*, as well as Manu.[136]

A passage of the *Mahābhārata* ordains that in the absence of her husband, a woman may make her younger brother-in-law her husband.[137] This is a sanction for remarriage different from the classical *niyoga* envisaged as a temporary union for a fixed purpose. *Niyoga* would be quite unnecessary in a joint family structure where the next senior male member would inherit and discharge the religious and economic responsibilities of a sonless patriarch. The concept that a wife is a 'field' (*kṣetra*) belonging to her owner–husband, and as such a son born to her from an 'appointed' male relative would belong to her husband, seems to ensure the succession within the framework of a lineal patriarchal family, rejecting the claims of the collaterals. The same could be said about the appointment of a brotherless daughter as *putrikā*.

Although the existence of the institution of *putrikā* – signifying in its technical sense a brotherless daughter appointed in Ṛgvedic times to inherit and extend her father's lineage – appears doubtful, Schmidt's penetrating study of the 'brotherless maiden' shows that by the time of Yāska the practice was well-established. Initially, the brotherless daughter inherited her father's property in her own right, and discharged all the religious and social obligations expected of a son.[138] She was even offered *piṇḍa*, the funeral cake, on her death in the *śrāddha* ceremony, although as a general rule *piṇḍa-dāna* is not done for female ancestors. However, the later law books lay emphasis on the *putrikā-putra*, the son of the daughter, who is regarded as a substitute for the *aurasa* son (i.e. 'a son begotten on his wedded wife of the same caste'),[139] although, as Sontheimer points out,[140] *putrikā-putra* could also mean a daughter treated as a son, at least in some passages. Schmidt draws attention to the *Vasiṣṭha Dharmasūtra* (XVII.23), which states that if an unmarried daughter bears a son from a man of the same caste (*tulyataḥ*), the maternal grandfather has a son in him.[141] He (i.e. the daughter's son) shall offer *piṇḍa* for his maternal grandfather and inherit his property. According to Schmidt, Yāska's comment on *Ṛgveda*, III.31.1 also seems to refer to a son obtained by the maternal grandfather in this manner through his unmarried daughter. This suggests a gradual evolution of the institution of *putrikā* in conformity with the changing social norms. Whatever the case may be, Schmidt is right in asserting that both levirate (*niyoga*) and epiclerate (*putrikā*) are governed by the laws of property, the woman serving the interests of her legal owner – in the former, the interests of her husband's lineage and in the latter, that of her father.

The consolidation of patriarchy in later Vedic society was intrinsically related to the growth of an inegalitarian class society in the form of *varṇas*. There has been a lot of discussion on whether *varṇa* denotes a class-based caste structure or whether it was merely a status group approximating to 'estate' in medieval European thought.[142] Scholars who view *varṇa* as an artificial category having little empirical value and as superimposed upon a pre-existing *jāti* structure ignore or misinterpret the historical evidence, indicating that the latter-day *jāti* structure was an elaboration of the earlier *varṇa* structure. The development relates to the growth of the small-scale later Vedic communities into a complex society spread over the whole subcontinent, accommodating communities of diverse origins within a loose socio-economic and cultural framework, but the fundamental principles of the earlier *varṇa* organization and later-day *varṇa–jāti* organization were the same. The *varṇas* were not merely hierarchical functional groups, these were also endogamous and hypergamous – endogamy and hypergamy being two sides of the same coin. Although endogamy was the general rule, hypergamous marriages were not uncommon till the ninth–tenth century CE.[143] The *Āpastamba Dharmasūtra*[144] and Manu[145] recommend that one should marry a girl of the same *varṇa* (*savarṇa*), and later authorities such as Śaṅkha and Nārada use the term *sajāti* while making a similar recommendation.[146] In translating *varṇa* as an 'order' or 'estate' or 'status group', as distinct from 'caste', Trautmann[147] has to explain the *savarṇa* rule as 'isogamy', giving it a 'biological' meaning and avoiding the term 'endogamy', which has a sociological significance. Such theoretical devices ill-conceal the historical reality that the control of female sexuality and its subordination was an essential prerequisite for restricting power and privileges to hereditary classes; the ideology sanctioned hypergamy but finally resulted in strengthening endogamous trends.

The *varṇas* emerged on the disintegration of Vedic tribal communities integrating priestly and warrior elite families of different tribes into brāhmaṇa and *rājanya* categories based on hereditary privileges and expertise, and the brāhmaṇa *varṇa* crystallized first. The commoners were the producers, cultivators and cattle herders, and were known as vaiśyas, the settlers, mainly peasants. The small class of specialized artisans, too, was initially within the vaiśya category but later came to be counted among the clean or *sat śūdras*, a concept that seems to have evolved in the early centuries of the Common Era with changes in the meaning and function of the two lower *varṇas*. The category of śūdra, which originated with the degradation of defeated and backward tribes and aborigines, expanded a great deal in the post-Vedic times and was split into *sat śūdra* and *asat śūdra* categories, to account for the wide disparities in the socio-economic and cultural conditions of numerous communities dubbed loosely as śūdras in Gupta and post-Gupta times. The entire process has been discussed in detail in my book titled *Caste*. What is pertinent for our discussion here is the fact that the entire edifice of caste, originating in a fourfold *varṇa* organization and later diversifying into a complex *varṇa–jāti* structure, rests not on an opposition of the 'pure' and the 'impure', a religious principle as assumed by Louis Dumont,[148] or on the incomplete 'fusion of tribal elements into a general society' leading to the fragmentation of society in endogamous units,[149] but upon the patriarchal control of gender which ensured the marking out and continuance of sharp boundaries between the exploited and exploiting classes in a hierarchical manner. Initially hypergamy was sanctioned,[150] but the logical consequence of wife-givers considered to be of lower status would be to confine marriage alliance within one's own caste group, as with the proliferation of *jātis* the hierarchical position of different castes in a particular locality was often a matter of dispute. This is not to say that the incoming tribal groups did not retain their separate identity through endogamy, but the reason for endogamy becoming the most enduring feature of caste organization while its other two main characteristics, the hereditary basis of occupations and notions of hierarchy, weakened under the impact of industrialization, is the fact that in the past, while a few elite lineages of the assimilating tribal group could find a place in the brāhmaṇa and kṣatriya categories and have marriage alliances with them, the majority of the incoming tribal groups would have only limited interaction of a politico-economic nature with the wider community. Its women being dubbed as 'śūdra' would be accessible only for hypergamous exploitation and the group as a whole would acquire the characteristics of a caste-practising endogamy.

Brahmanical theory specializes in sanctifying practices in the interests of a hierarchical *varṇa* order. The Dharmaśāstras develop the notion of *kanyādāna*, which is regarded as a highly meritorious act. Trautmann argues that *kanyādāna* is a religious gift; and in a religious gift, the recipient is always of a superior status with no obvious obligation of reciprocity.[151] Hence, *kanyādāna* perpetuates asymmetry, givers cannot be takers, 'gifts and deference must flow always and only from the bride's people to the groom's'. Defining 'religious gift' in this manner, charity towards the poor, disabled and orphans would obviously be outside the scope of 'religious gift' or *dharma-dāna*, as the recipient could not have been deemed to be of superior status. Trautmann argues that the Dharmaśāstras restructured an ancient or even pre-Vedic morality of reciprocity in terms of the kind of asymmetrical, transcendent reciprocity we find in the doctrine of the gift, 'turning a system of reciprocities into a system of asymmetrical relations with an eye to salvation rather than to manifest social benefit'.[152] Thus, according to him, the Dharmaśāstra theory of gift is not sociology of reciprocity but a soteriology. The argument conceals or at least diverts the attention away from the social perspective of this kind of soteriology that treats women as 'objects' to be gifted in the same way as land (*bhūmi*) or cow (*godāna*). R.S. Sharma has cited a number of passages from the epics and the Purāṇas which make joint references to women and property, thus equating the two.[153] Gifts of material items like land and cattle as well as of a maiden (*kanyā*) ensure similar rewards: a place in heaven in the world of the Vasus or divine progenitors Dakṣas and Aṅgirasas, enjoyment in the world of Indra, and so on.[154] Guaranteeing to protect the life of someone or *abhayadāna* and the gift of learning (*vidyādāna*) are also treated in the same fashion,[155] and it is said that the 'gift' of the Vedas brings the reward of all sacrifices, of *upavedas*, the attainment of the world of Gandharvas and of Vedāṅgas, the world of Indra. Of course, *abhayadāna* and *vidyādāna*, not being tangible items but highly meritorious acts, would be outside the 'theory of gift' as envisaged by Trautmann, for these cannot be said to flow upwards to superior beings. But these form part of the same soteriology. However, the real explanation for the low status of the bride and her natal kinsmen lies not in the soteriological constructions of the Dharmaśāstras, but in the decline of the position of women and the triumph of patriarchy. In the early Vedic times daughters were not unwelcome even if sons were solicited more. Women's position declined in later Vedic times,[156] although, as we have seen, by making specific dietary prescriptions for a couple desiring the birth of a learned daughter, the *Bṛhadāraṇyaka Upaniṣad* suggests that girls had not yet become a burden and could still be wished for. But the Dharmaśāstra ideology of *kanyādāna* is closer in time and spirit to the epic–Purāṇa complex which glorified the ideal of women's total subservience, denying them any individuality. The *Manusmṛti* states that for women there is no separate sacrifice (*yajña*), vow (*vrata*) or fast (*upoṣaṇa*).[157] They attain heaven only by serving the husband. There are repeated assertions that women have no freedom (*svātantryahīna*).[158] It is the duty of men to see to it that women are never independent, day or night;[159] 'a woman is protected by her father in her childhood, by her husband in her youth and by her son in her old age'.[160]

Such emphasis on protection was necessary for guarding the chastity of women, to ensure the purity of the *varṇa*/caste organization and avoid any danger of mixing of castes or *varṇasaṃkara*. The growing rigidity of caste organization has its parallel in the deteriorating position of women, and both trends are represented forcefully in the *Manusmṛti*. The early Gṛhya and Dharmasūtras made it incumbent upon the father to give away his daughter in marriage as soon as she attained puberty. Neglect of this duty amounted to murdering an embryo (*bhrūṇa-hatyā*). It is rightly held that such injunctions aimed at ensuring the young wife a long period of reproductivity and later this ideology contributed to the spread of child marriage. Altekar holds that by about 200 CE, pre-puberty marriage had become the order of the day. Manu recommends that a groom of thirty years should marry a bride of twelve, and one who wishes to marry early, at the age of twenty-four, should wed an eight-year-old girl.[161] Such paedophilic recommendations may have been made in view of the fact that whereas a brāhmaṇa boy spent long years studying the Vedas and ancillary subjects, girls did not have any formal education and it was thought that they should be given away in marriage safely before they developed an independent personality in the comparatively free atmosphere of their natal homes. Whatever be the reason, the Dharmaśāstric evidence belies the communalized popular misconception that child marriages began due to fear of capture of women by Muslim invaders, as the practice came in vogue long before the advent of Islam. Exaggerated emphasis on chastity made women not only vulnerable, but also instruments of exploitation. If, on the one hand, we have stories in the epics and Purāṇas extolling the extraordinary powers of chaste women practising *pātivrata dharma*, we are also told how gods seduced chaste women by guile in order to gain victory over their husbands. For example, the *Skanda Purāṇa* (II.4) narrates that the god Viṣṇu could defeat the demon king Jālandhara only after he was able to seduce Tulasī-Vṛndā, his chaste wife, through deceit. (Raping or violating women of the lower castes or minority communities by way of punishing them or teaching them a lesson is an extension of the same ideology.)

The trend of identifying women with 'untruth', 'sin' and 'evil' noticed in some later Vedic texts becomes very pronounced in the *Mahābhārata*, *Manusmṛti* and other texts composed in the early centuries of the Common Era,[162] provoking Varāhamihira to offer a spirited defence of women; but, as Kane remarks, his was a 'solitary voice'.[163] The predominant Śāstric perception, repeated down to modern times by old men as recorded by P.V. Kane, is that 'falsehood, thoughtless action, trickery, folly, great greed, impurity, and cruelty – these are natural faults of women'.[164]

Women also came to be clubbed with the śūdras. The *Baudhāyana Dharmasūtra* prescribes the same penance for killing a woman as for killing a śūdra.[165] Similar prescriptions are made by the *Parāśarasmṛti*,[166] a work from about the eighth century CE, and the *Agni Purāṇa*.[167] It is generally believed that the growth of the *bhakti* movement in Brahmanism marks an improvement in the position of women and śūdras as they were given the religious rights denied to them in the Vedic tradition, since now they could strive for their spiritual upliftment by worshipping their chosen god with devotion.[168] But a passage of the *Viṣṇu Purāṇa* clearly states, in the words of sage Vyāsa, that in the Kali age women attain heaven by serving their husbands in utter devotion with their body, mind and speech, and the śūdras by serving the twice-born similarly.[169] The verses are repeated in the *Brahma Purāṇa* and some other works.[170] Lumping together of women and śūdras is found in the later Vedic texts as well as in the Smṛtis and Purāṇas, and R.S. Sharma has drawn our attention to their analogous position in civic, social, religious and economic matters.[171] However, it needs to be added that although, in material terms, a woman's actual position would have been mediated by the fact of her birth in a particular *varṇa* and her sexual ties to the man of a particular *varṇa*, the inferiority of her gender made her, in certain perceptions, even lower than the lowliest of the male. Thus the *Viṣṇudharma*, a text known to Alberuni and written earlier than the *Viṣṇudharmottara*, which claims to be its sequel, extols *yoga*, particularly *kriyā-yoga*, for attaining emancipation and severing the bonds of *karma* (deeds). In this context, it states that anyone, without any distinction of caste and sex, can obtain the benefit of *yoga*; and by practising *yoga*, one passes successively through different states of existence, from womanhood to śūdra and so on, until one becomes a brāhmaṇa and attains final liberation. Thus, women as beings were inferior to even the śūdras. The text was very popular in Bengal.[172]

Attempts at contesting the gender and caste biases within Brahmanical society were made in various *bhakti* movements of the medieval period, but the elements of protest seem to have been soon overwhelmed by the processes of Brahmanization. There is need to study the social content and context of each of these movements, their impact and limitations.[173] The history of early medieval Deccan offers rich scope for an exploration of this kind. In this area, particularly in the regions of Andhra Pradesh and Karnataka, there has been a rich debate on the issue of a woman's capability to attain salvation (*strīmokṣa*) outside the Brahmanical circle among the Jainas, particularly the Yāpanīyas, from roughly the second century down to the eighteenth century.[174] Scholars have also noted that despite the decline in the status of women, there was improvement in their proprietary rights over landed property in early medieval times.[175] Strong kinship and familial loyalties in the prevailing feudal ethos sometimes necessitated subversion of patriarchal norms, giving greater scope to women for assuming familial or public responsibilities. Nevertheless, it is the strong clutch of patriarchal prejudices that made the royal scribes of Rudramā Devī, the grandmother of Pratāparudra of the Kākatīya dynasty, give her an androgynous personality and address her as Mahārāja Rudradeva while referring to her acts of governing the kingdom of Gaṇapati, a political role restricted to men in the dominant patriarchal perspective.[176]

Notes

[1] V.M. Apte, 'Religion and Philosophy', p. 387.

[2] Suvira Jaiswal, 'Women in Early India', pp. 54–60.

[3] David M. Schneider and Kathleen Gough, eds, *Matrilineal Kinship*.

[4] Gerda Lerner, *The Creation of Patriarchy*, p. 86.

[5] Eleanor Leacock, 'Introduction to Engels, *The Origin of the Family, Private Property and the State*', pp. ii, xvi.

[6] Bernard Sergent, 'Three Notes on the Trifunctional Indo–European Marriage'; Hans-Peter Schmidt, *Some Women's Rights and Rights in the Veda*, p. 103.

[7] *Ṛgveda*, I.124.8, VII.2.5, VIII.51.9.

[8] Ibid., IV.58.8.

[9] Hans-Peter Schmidt, *Some Women's Rights and Rights in the Veda*, p. 77.

[10] Suvira Jaiswal, *Caste*, p. 11.

[11] *Ṛgveda*, I.131.3.

[12] Ibid., IV.17.16.

[13] Ibid., I.73.1.9.

[14] Suvira Jaiswal, *Caste*, pp. 166–67, 197.

[15] P.V. Kane, *History of Dharmaśāstra*, vol. II, part I, pp. 435–36.

[16] Hans-Peter Schmidt, *Some Women's Rights and Rights in the Veda*, p. 54 note 5.

[17] Irawati Karve, 'Kinship Terminology and Kinship Usages in *Ṛgveda* and *Atharvaveda*', pp. 109–44, 213–14.

[18] G.S. Ghurye, *Two Brahmanical Institutions*.

[19] Suvira Jaiswal, *Caste*, pp. 163–69.

[20] For the prevalence of brother–sister and father–daughter incest in ancient Iran, see J.S. Slotkin, 'On a Possible Lack of Incest Regulations in Old Iran', pp. 612–15; Sarva Daman Singh, *Polyandry in Ancient India*, pp. 19, 43.

[21] S.A. Dange, *Vedic Concept of Field and the Divine Fructification*, pp. 117–40.

[22] 'He who sleeps with you becoming your brother, husband or lover and who kills your progeny, him I destroy', *Ṛgveda*, X.162.5. A reason for the strained relationship with the son-in-law, as indicated by *Ṛgveda*, V.28.3, could be the fact that later he came from a different lineage and as such was a 'stranger' (*ari*).

[23] Sarva Daman Singh, *Polyandry in Ancient India*, chapter II; D.D. Kosambi, *An Introduction to the Study of Indian History* (first edition), pp. 66–67; Hans-Peter Schmidt, *Some Women's Rights and Rights in the Veda*, pp. 67–68. Also see, *Ṛgveda*, X.85.37, 38, 40.

[24] Wash Edward Hale, *Asura in Early Vedic Religion*, p. 159.

[25] On Max Müller's approach, see D.D. Kosambi, *Myth and Reality*, pp. 44–45. This is not, however, to deny that there are a few hymns, such as *Ṛgveda*, I.164, which mystify cosmic phenomena.

[26] H.W. Bailey, 'Iranian Arya and Daha', pp. 109ff.; Asko Parpola, 'The Coming of the Aryans to Iran and India and the Cultural and Ethnic Identity of the Dāsas'.

[27] *Ṛgveda*, VII.86.7, X.62.10. For *dāsapravarga* (troops of slaves), see *Ṛgveda*, I.92.8. Cf. a similar change of meaning in the term *ārya/orja* (Jaiswal, *Caste*, p. 198). A branch of the Aryans went towards Finland, and was defeated and enslaved, giving the word *orja* the meaning of 'slave' in Finnish. *Orja* is a cognate of *ārya*: Asko Parpola, 'The Coming of the Aryans to Iran and India and the Cultural and Ethnic Identity of the Dāsas', p. 123 note 203; R.S. Sharma, *Perspectives in Social and Economic History of Early India*, p. 4.

[28] Suvira Jaiswal, *Caste*, pp. 144–46.

[29] The technical expertise of attaching severed legs with metal screws was apparently known to the ancient world. A news item published in *Times of India*, Sunday, 11 February 1966 reports that researchers at the Brigham Young University (BYU) X-rayed six mummies at the Rosicrucian Egyptian Museum. On examining the mummy of the Egyptian priest named Usermontu they discovered that the thigh and calf bones of the priest had been re-attached with a 9-inch (13 cm) metal screw, and it was cemented into place with resin. Julie Scott, the director of the museum, expressed the view that the recipient was probably dead at the time of re-attachment. It may have been done to make the body suitable for the afterlife. According to Bruce Miff, a BYU researcher, 'they went to a lot of trouble to put this leg back together again and make it look normal'. The mummy is reported to be 2,600 years old. The story of Viśpalā, if not to be taken literally, may have been inspired by the tales brought from West Asia. D.D. Kosambi (*An Introduction to the Study of Indian History*, first edition, pp. 53–58) has argued on the basis of metrology and glyptic motifs that a substratum of culture and technique was common to the Indus and Mesopotamian river-valley civilizations. Some of the myths of the *Ṛgveda* derive from non-Aryan sources.

[30] J. Przyluski, 'Satvant, Sātvata and Nāsatya', pp. 88–91.

[31] Thomas Trautmann, *Dravidian Kinship*, pp. 9–10; Sarva Daman Singh, *Polyandry in Ancient India*, pp. 46–48.

[32] U.N. Ghoshal, quoting *Mahābhārata*, II.15.34, in K.A. Nilakanta Sastri, *Comprehensive History of India* (p. 432), expresses the view that an important local breed of horse was raised in eastern India in post-Mauryan times. Also see, S.K. Chatterji, 'Race-Movements and Prehistoric Culture', p. 152. Horse remains found at Mahagara in the neolithic layers and dated between 5000 BCE and 1500 BCE seem to have been of a different breed not associated with the Aryans. G.R. Sharma, V.D. Misra, D. Mandal, B.B. Misra and J.N. Pal, *Beginnings of Agriculture* (1980), quoted in R.S. Sharma, 'Material Background of the Genesis of the State and Complex Society in the Middle Gangetic Plains', p. 23.

[33] Hans-Peter Schmidt, *Some Women's Rights and Rights in the Veda*, pp. 1–29.

[34] Another legend of Austro–Asiatic origin is the Boar myth found in the same *maṇḍala* (*Ṛgveda*, VIII.66.77), as is shown by F.B.J. Küiper, 'An Austro–Asiatic Myth in the *Ṛgveda*'. Interestingly, this hymn speaks of *odanaṃ* (cooked rice) and *kṣīrapaka odanaṃ* (rice cooked in milk) at two places (verses 6 and 10). Cultivation of rice was known to neolithic people of the middle Gangetic plains, but not to the Harappans. Küiper has shown that there are at least 300 non-Indo–European words in the *Ṛgveda*. Many of these are connected with agriculture. Thus, *ulūkhala* (mortar) in *Ṛgveda*, I.28.6 is a borrowing from a Dravidian language, but *lāṅgala* (plough) is a proto-Munda loan word. For the absorption of the pre-Aryan priesthood in Vedic society, see Suvira Jaiswal, *Caste*, pp. 154–60.

[35] Field study of the types of ploughs and husking implements used in India by Jaya Datta Gupta and B.N. Saraswati suggests that the 'ploughs of India are likely to line up with east and south-east Asia in historical relationship'. Jaya Datta Gupta and B.N. Saraswati, 'Ploughs and Husking Implements', pp. 25–34.

[36] P.V. Kane, *History of Dharmaśāstra*, vol. II, part I, pp. 291–96.

[37] Ibid., p. 294.

[38] Jogiraj Basu, *India of the Age of the Brāhmaṇas*, p. 214.

[39] *Kādambarī* of Bāṇabhaṭṭa, Purvārdha, para. 133, quoted in P.V. Kane, *History of Dharmaśāstra*, p. 295.

[40] Hans-Peter Schmidt, *Some Women's Rights and Rights in the Veda*, p. 26 note 7.

[41] For example, *Viṣṇudharmottara Purāṇa*, I.155.27–28, I.157.16–17; I.163.8–11.

[42] *Manusmṛti*, IV.99–108.

[43] R.S. Sharma, *Śūdras in Ancient India*, p. 133.

[44] *Bṛhannāradīya Purāṇa*, XIV.144, quoted in R.C. Hazra, *Studies in the Upapurāṇas*, vol. I, p. 325.

[45] P.V. Kane, *History of Dharmaśāstra*, vol. II, part I, pp. 366, 690–91; vol. III, p. 4.

[46] *Āpastamba Gṛhyasūtra*, II.8.3.

[47] *Mahābhārata* (critical edition), XII.159, 19–20.

[48] *Śrīmadvālmīkīya Rāmāyaṇa* (Gita Press edition), II.20–25.

[49] *Mahābhāṣya* of Patañjali, vol. II, p. 206; P.V. Kane, *History of Dharmaśāstra*, vol. II, part I, p. 366.

[50] *Kauṭilīya Arthaśāstra*, I.12.4.

[51] *Mahābhārata*, XII. 308.

[52] *Śrīmadvālmīkīya Rāmāyaṇa* (Gita Press edition), Kiṣkindhā kāṇḍa, 50–52.

[53] P.V. Kane, *History of Dharmaśāstra*, vol. II, part I, p. 945.

[54] *Atri Saṃhitā*, in *Smṛtīnāṃ Samuccayaḥ*, I.36–37; P.V. Kane, *History of Dharmaśāstra*, vol. II, part II, p. 945.

[55] A.S. Altekar, *The Position of Women in Hindu Civilization*, p. 197.

[56] Fredrick M. Smith, 'Indra's Curse, Varuṇa's Noose and the Suppression of Women in Vedic *Śrauta* Ritual'.

[57] S.A. Dange, *Sexual Symbolism from the Vedic Ritual*, pp. 73–74.

[58] According to D.D. Kosambi, this Ṛgvedic verse 'shows the absorption of a pre-Aryan stream

of culture, which goes into the very source and origin of Brahminism'. D.D. Kosambi, *Myth and Reality*, p. 77.

[59] *Ṛgveda*, VII.79.3.

[60] D.D. Kosambi, *Myth and Reality*, pp. 61–67.

[61] Suvira Jaiswal, *Caste*, pp. 154–58.

[62] For 'common' or 'clan-wives' in a system of fraternal polyandry of the nomadic Aryans who travelled riding bullock carts (*Ṛgveda*, I.126.5), see D.D. Kosambi, *Myth and Reality*, p. 67.

[63] *Ṛgveda*, X.85.26–27.

[64] Suvira Jaiswal, *Caste*, pp. 206–23.

[65] *Ṛgveda*, X.85.27.

[66] *Atharvaveda*, XIV.1.121; *Ṛgveda*, X.85. 26.

[67] Ibid., verse 46.

[68] Shakuntala Rao Shastri, *Women in the Vedic Age*, pp. 13–18; Suvira Jaiswal, *Caste*, pp. 163–67.

[69] *Ṛgveda*, X.85.26, 27.

[70] Ibid., I.91.20.

[71] Ibid., II.27.12.

[72] J.P. Sharma, *Republics in Ancient India*, p. 68.

[73] R.S. Sharma, *Aspects of Political Ideas and Institutions in Ancient India*, pp. 87ff.

[74] J.P. Sharma, *Republics in Ancient India*, pp. 62–80.

[75] R.S. Sharma, *Aspects of Political Ideas and Institutions in Ancient India*, p. 103.

[76] Ibid., p. 104.

[77] Commenting on *Ṛgveda*, VI.75.3.

[78] Yaska, quoted in R.S. Sharma, *Aspects of Political Ideas and Institutions in Ancient India*, p. 94.

[79] Laurie L. Patton, 'The Fate of the Female *Ṛṣi*', pp. 21–37.

[80] Sally J. Sutherland Goldman, 'Speaking Gender', pp. 57–83.

[81] R.S. Sharma, *Śūdras in Ancient India*, pp. 24, 50.

[82] *Atharvaveda*, V.13.8; Wash Edward Hale, *Asura in Early Vedic Religion*, pp. 168–69; Suvira Jaiswal, *Caste*, p. 48.

[83] *Ṛgveda*, VIII.19.36.

[84] Ibid., IV.17.16; V.31.2; VIII.2.42.

[85] Ibid., VII.26.3; X.101–11.

[86] *Rājevahijanibhiḥ*, *Ṛgveda*, VII.18.2.

[87] A.S. Altekar, *The Position of Women in Hindu Civilization*, pp. 345–46.

[88] See endnote 27 above.

[89] Macdonell and Keith clearly state that the term 'two-footed' denotes 'man', as opposed to 'quadruped' from the *Ṛgveda* onwards. A.A. Macdonell and A.B. Keith, *Vedic Index*, *s.v. dvipada*.

[90] *Ṛgveda*, I.124.1.

[91] Ibid., III.62.14.

[92] Émile Benveniste, *Indo–European Language and Society*, pp. 105–12; Suvira Jaiswal, *Caste*, pp. 137–38, 172–73.

[93] A.S. Altekar, *The Position of Women in Hindu Civilization*, p. 342.

[94] Laurie L. Patton, 'The Fate of the Female *Ṛṣi*', p. 34.

[95] Although S.A. Dange often ignores the historical processes in myth-making and his interpretations are often far-fetched, he has nevertheless successfully drawn attention to pervasive sexual imagery in the Vedic texts.

[96] Suvira Jaiswal, *Caste*, pp. 154–60; Suvira Jaiswal, 'Kosambi on Caste', pp. 134–54 for a detailed discussion.

[97] Gerda Lerner, *The Creation of Patriarchy*, pp. 141–60.

[98] *Matsya Purāṇa, addhyāya* 3, verses 2–12.
[99] *Mahābhārata*, XII.59.117–18.
[100] *Chāndogya Upaniṣad*, V.10.6.
[101] A.L. Basham, *The Origin and Development of Classical Hinduism*, p. 47.
[102] *Taittirīya Saṃhitā*, II.5.1ff.
[103] *Mahābhārata*, V.10–13, XII.329.28–41.
[104] *Bhāgavata Purāṇa*, VI.9.6–10.
[105] Julia I. Leslie, *The Perfect Wife*, p. 251.
[106] P.V. Kane, *History of Dharmaśāstra*, vol. II, part II, pp. 802ff.
[107] *Taittirīya Saṃhitā*, VI.5.8.2; P.V. Kane, *History of Dharmaśāstra*, vol. II, part I, p. 576.
[108] *Ṛgveda*, I.22.9–12.
[109] Ibid., IX.8.1–5.
[110] Ibid., VIII.2.7.
[111] Ibid., IX.1–6.
[112] Ibid., I.28.3.
[113] Ralph T.H. Griffith, *The Hymns of the Ṛgveda*, p. 420.
[114] *Śrautakośa*, pp. 682–83, 702–03.
[115] *Ṛgveda*, IV.5.4–5.
[116] Jan Gonda, *Change and Continuity in Indian Religion*, pp. 399–400.
[117] *Pāraskara Gṛhyasūtra*, I.11.2.
[118] *Ṛgveda*, X.85.28–31; *Atharvaveda*, XV.1.25.
[119] *Ṛgveda*, X.85.43–44.
[120] *Atharvaveda*, X.1.3.
[121] *Atharvaveda*, XIV.1.42; II.36.4.
[122] *Bṛhadāraṇyaka Upaniṣad*, I.4.17; IV.42; VI.4.17.
[123] *Aitareya Brāhmaṇa*, XII.11.
[124] P.V. Kane, *History of Dharmaśāstra*, vol. II, part I, pp. 550–51.
[125] Sarva Daman Singh, *Polyandry in Ancient India*, pp. 70–75; Hans-Peter Schmidt, *Some Women's Rights and Rights in the Veda*, pp. 67–68.
[126] Gunther-Dietz Sontheimer, *The Joint Hindu Family*, pp. 13–14.
[127] P.V. Kane, *History of Dharmaśāstra*, vol. II, part I, pp. 599–607.
[128] Sarva Daman Singh, *Polyandry in Ancient India*, pp. 53–55; Hans-Peter Schmidt, *Some Women's Rights and Rights in the Veda*, pp. 64–65.
[129] *Ṛgveda*, X.18.8, 40.2.
[130] *Ṛgveda*, X.18.7; M. Srimannarayana Murti, 'Sati in the *Ṛgveda*'.
[131] *Ṛgveda*, X.18.7.
[132] A.S. Altekar, *The Position of Women in Hindu Civilization*, p. 150.
[133] *Atharvaveda*, X.5.27–28.
[134] Hans-Peter Schmidt, *Some Women's Rights and Rights in the Veda*, p. 73.
[135] *Āpastamba Dharmasūtra*, II.10.27, 2–7.
[136] *Manusmṛti*, IX.64–68.
[137] *Mahābhārata*, XIII.12.19.
[138] A.S. Altekar, *The Position of Women in Hindu Civilization*, p. 235; Hans-Peter Schmidt, *Some Women's Rights and Rights in the Veda*, pp. 38ff.
[139] P.V. Kane, *History of Dharmaśāstra*, vol. III, p. 647.
[140] Gunther-Dietz Sontheimer, *The Joint Hindu Family*, p. 54 note 1.
[141] Hans-Peter Schmidt, *Some Women's Rights and Rights in the Veda*, p. 37.
[142] Thomas Trautmann, 'On the Translation of the term *varṇa*'; Suvira Jaiswal, 'Caste in the Socio–Economic Framework of Early India', pp. 23–48.
[143] P.V. Kane, *History of Dharmaśāstra*, vol. II, part I, pp. 449–50.

144 *Āpastamba Dharmasūtra*, II.6.13.
145 *Manusmṛti*, III.12.
146 Quoted in P.V. Kane, *History of Dharmaśāstra*, vol. II, part II, p. 448.
147 Thomas Trautmann, *Dravidian Kinship*, pp. 271–74.
148 See Suvira Jaiswal, 'Caste: Ideology and Context'.
149 Irfan Habib, *Essays in Indian History*, p. 165.
150 A.S. Altekar, *The Position of Women in Hindu Civilization*, pp. 75–77; Thomas Trautmann, *Dravidian Kinship*, pp. 274–75.
151 Thomas Trautmann, *Dravidian Kinship*, pp. 25–27, 277–94.
152 Ibid., pp. 282, 294.
153 R.S. Sharma, *Perspectives in Social and Economic History of Early India*, pp. 39–48.
154 *Viṣṇudharmottara Purāṇa*, III.303–06.
155 Ibid., III.30.1, 30.2.
156 V.M. Apte, 'Social and Economic Conditions', pp. 424, 458.
157 *Manusmṛti*, V.155.
158 *Viṣṇudharmottara Purāṇa*, III.322–24.
159 *Manusmṛti*, IX.2.
160 *Manusmṛti*, IX.3; *Mahābhārata*, XII.46.3, 21.19.
161 *Manusmṛti*, IX.94.
162 *Maitrāyaṇī Saṃhitā*, III.6.3; *Śatapatha Brāhmaṇa*, XIV.1.1.31.
163 P.V. Kane, *History of Dharmaśāstra*, vol. II, part I, p. 580.
164 Ibid., p. 578.
165 *Baudhāyana Dharmasūtra*, II.1.11–13.
166 *Parāśarasmṛti*, VI.16.
167 *Agni Purāṇa*, 173.13.
168 *Bhagavadgītā*, IX.32.
169 *Viṣṇu Purāṇa*, VI.2.23–26.
170 P.V. Kane, *History of Dharmaśāstra*, vol. V, p. 929.
171 R.S. Sharma, *Perspectives in Social and Economic History of Early India*, pp. 45–46.
172 *Viṣṇudharma Purāṇa*, chapter 98, quoted in R.C. Hazra, *Studies in the Upapurāṇas*, pp. 136, 153.
173 See Vijaya Ramaswamy, 'Anklets on the Feet'; Vijaya Ramaswamy, 'Women in the Warkari Panth'.
174 Padmanabh S. Jaini, *Gender and Salvation*.
175 A.S. Altekar, *The Position of Women in Hindu Civilization*, pp. 224–28; Suvira Jaiswal, *Caste*, pp. 93–94.
176 Cynthia Talbot, 'Rudramā Devi, the Female King'.

5

Female Images in the *Arthaśāstra* of Kauṭilya

The *Arthaśāstra* of Kauṭilya is a work on politics or statecraft, a field of activity that was regarded as almost exclusively a male prerogative. This notion is implicit in the way '*arthaśāstra*' is defined in this text. *Artha* is wealth or livelihood of men; hence, land inhabited by men and providing them their livelihood is also *artha*, and science which deals with the acquisition and protection of the realm is '*arthaśāstra*' (*Arthaśāstra*, XV.1.1–2). The acquisition and protection of a realm involved the promulgation and enforcement of law and criminal justice, and wisely using resources for further aggrandizement. Hence women figure in this work primarily as objects and instruments for furthering the aims of the state. However, since the work deals with practical concerns, in spite of its recommendatory patriarchal and Brahmanical framework, it gives us a better idea of the visibility of women in public spaces than the Dharmaśāstra literature which is mainly focused on the Brahmanical norms in the domestic and public contexts.

The *Arthaśāstra* contains interesting data on women of diverse backgrounds obliged to earn their living. It speaks of women skilled in handicrafts (*śilpavatī*) who could be employed for spying, living inside the house of the enemy (I.12.21). But there were also those women who did not stir out of their homes (*aniṣkāsinī*) and supported themselves by spinning yarn. Apparently, such women belonged to the upper castes. The superintendent of yarns and textiles was to give them work by sending his female slaves (*dāsīs*) to their homes rather than asking them to come to him; if they came on their own to the yarn house, the interchange of goods and wages had to be done in the dim light of early dawn. Any attempt at looking at the face of such a woman was a punishable offence. These were women who had been marginalized due to circumstances: widows (*vidhavā*), maidens or unmarried spinsters (*kanyakā*), women with some physical defect (or disgraced, *nyaṅgāḥ*) and *proṣitās*, i.e. women who had left home and were living separately (II.23.11–14). It is noteworthy that Kauṭilya allowed divorce by mutual consent if both husband and wife were disaffected with each other. However, further on he asserts by way of explanation that there could be no divorce in pious marriages, i.e. in the approved forms of marriages (III.3.16–17). Hence, *proṣitas* were apparently not divorced women, but deserted or disaffected wives of upper-caste men living on their own.

Spinning yarn could provide livelihood even to such helpless women as old female slaves of the royalty (*vṛddha-rājadāsībhiḥ*), *devadāsis* (female slaves of the temple) whose services to the gods were no longer required, and mothers or matrons (*mātṛkā*) of prostitutes (*rūpājīvā*). Women who had committed some offence could pay off the fine in the form of personal labour by spinning yarn (II.23.2). Thus spinning was a major industry providing livelihood to needy women.

References to women of the lower orders are frequent in Kauṭilya's *Arthaśāstra* as they could be easily pressed into the service of the state for spying and doing menial work. Moreover, as they constituted a significant part of the labour force, Kauṭilya had to provide rules concerning them. Kauṭilya seems to be the only author who speaks of *ardhasītikās*, or women tenants tilling for half the produce (III.13.9). It is well known that even today, the largest section of rural women are directly involved in field agriculture, animal husbandry, forestry, etc. Since they belong to landless rural households, they are hardly visible in either ancient sources or in present-day census reports, and are seldom taken into consideration by our social and economic historians. However, field studies have shown that these women are primarily responsible for their families' subsistence and survival, and it is for this reason that Kauṭilya lays down (III.11.23–24) that normally a wife shall not be liable for the debt incurred by her husband, unless she had given assent to it. But in the case of cowherds (*gopāla*) and cultivators tilling for half the produce (*ardhasītikas*), this rule does not apply; their wives are held responsible for the debt incurred by the husbands, whether it was with their assent or not. In my view, this evidence should be interpreted not in terms of greater subordination of these women but with reference to their economic role.

Kauṭilya informs us that women of such low status as wandering minstrels (*cāraṇa*), dancers (*tālavacara*), fishermen (*matsya-bandhaka*), hunters (*lubdhaka*), cowherds (*gopālaka*) and the sellers of women are 'uncontrolled' (*prasṛṣṭa*). Their accompanying a man, apparently with carnal intentions, is not an offence unless specifically prohibited. If this were so, a fine amounting to half of that stipulated in the case of an upper-caste woman is to be imposed on the parties concerned (III.4.22–23). The occupation of all these communities required greater freedom of movement for their women, for apart from performing other chores, the women of fisherfolk, cowherds and hunters have to carry their products to market or door to door for sale. They are the counterparts of the *aniṣkāsinī* women mentioned earlier; Kauṭilya exhibits a typically gendered upper-caste view of these communities. As for the women from backgrounds such as actors (*naṭas*), dancers (*nartakas*), singers, musicians (*gāyana-vādaka*), storytellers (*vāgjīvana*), bards (*kuśīlavas*), rope dancers (*plavaka*), showmen (*saubhika*) and wandering minstrels (*cāraṇas*), Kauṭilya lays down that they be subject to the same rules as the *gaṇikas* with regard to dues and state supervision (II.27.25).

Kauṭilya looks upon prostitution as an occupation and mentions several categories of prostitutes: *gaṇikā, pratigaṇikā, rūpājīvā, puṃścali, bandhakī*, etc. He devotes a chapter in Book II to discuss the duties of the *gaṇikādhyakṣa*, the superintendent of courtesans, and rules regarding women following this profession. The *gaṇikā* was no ordinary prostitute but had a state-appointed, institutionalized position. She was to receive a salary of one thousand *paṇas* for her family-establishment (*kuṭumba*). In case she ran away or died, her mother had to provide a temporary courtesan or *pratigaṇikā* who was to receive only half the family-establishment, perhaps till such time a new *gaṇikā* was appointed. A *gaṇikā* could come from a family of *gaṇikās* or from some other family, but she had to possess beauty, youth and expertise in the arts. It is held that she was appointed primarily for attending on the king, fanning him or carrying the water jug for him, holding the umbrella over his head and accompanying him on processions (II.27.1–4), although she was also obliged to entertain men at the command of the king; a refusal could entail 'one thousand strokes with the whip, or a fine of five thousand paṇas' (II.27.19).[1] Thus, although a *gaṇikā* had access to arts and wealth, she was not free to follow her own inclinations and her dealings were strictly regulated. Still, violence against her was severely punishable. It was decreed (II.27.14ff.) that if a man kept her under restraint when she was unwilling, or helped her to run away, or spoilt her beauty by inflicting a wound, he was to be fined one thousand *paṇas*, which could be increased to double the amount of a *gaṇikā*'s ransom, i.e. 48,000 *paṇas* (the ransom price of a *gaṇikā* was fixed at 24,000 *paṇas*; II.27.6). Causing the death of a *gaṇikā* who had obtained all the rights of the office (*prāptādhikāraṃ*) invited the penalty of a fine three times the ransom amount, i.e. 72,000 *paṇas*. Apparently she was an important treasure of the state, and the safety of her mother (*mātṛkā*), daughter (*duhitṛkā*) and female slave or attendant (*rūpādāsī*) was of great importance as killing any of these women led to punishment involving the highest fine for such violence (II.27.17).

In the male-dominated patriarchal society of the *Arthaśāstra*, prostitution was a socially sanctioned profession. It uses the terms *rūpājīvā* (one who makes a living out of her beauty: I.20.20, II.4.11, II.23.2 and elsewhere), *puṃścali* (III.13.37) and *veśyā* (II.6.2) for a common prostitute, and she does not seem to have lived in a segregated area. The text stipulates that grain dealers of the city (*nagaradhānyavyavahārika*), 'factory officers' (*karmāntika*) and army officers (*balādhyakṣa*), dealers in cooked food, wine and meat, prostitutes (*rūpājīvā*), dancers (*tālavacaras*) and (persons of) vaiśya *varṇa* should be located in the southern quarter of the fort (II.4.11). Moreover, a part of the income of the prostitute was collected in the form of tax every month and constituted a source of revenue under the heading 'fort' (II.6.2; II.27.27). On the other hand, Kauṭilya also lays down that the person who gives training in music, dancing and the other arts to the *gaṇikās* and female slaves making a living by performing on the stage (*dāsī raṅgopajīviniśca*) should get maintenance from the king's treasury (II.27.28). Thus, although the prostitute had a low status, her profession received state protection and patronage. This was not simply because she could be used for spying on and ensnaring the enemy (for example, XI.1.34–39), but because she was considered necessary for the fulfilment of male desire and provision had to be made for the accommodation of *rūpājīvās* along with traders on the main highways in a military camp (X.1.10) when the army was on the march. Kauṭilya stipulates that a man forcing himself on a *rūpājīvā* against her will for enjoyment shall be fined twelve *paṇas*, and when several men do so, each will be fined twenty-four *paṇas* (IV.13.38). However, many *rūpājīvās* were employed in the royal harem attending on the queens (I.20.20). Those who were to attend on the person of the king, giving him a bath, shampoo, preparing his bed and laundering his clothes are described as *dāsīs* (female slaves) (I.21.13). This may be compared with the statement of Megasthenes that 'the care of the king's person is committed to women, who also are purchased from their fathers'.[2] Kauṭilya does not hesitate in making them a means for replenishing the royal treasure. He recommends that the *bandhakīpoṣakas*, keepers of harlots, should replenish the treasury through female servants (*preṇyābhiḥ*) of the king, who may be endowed with great beauty and youth (V.2.28).

Bandhakīs too were harlots and part of a brothel maintained by brothel-keepers (*bandhakīpoṣakas*). As such, they may have been under greater constraint than the ordinary *rūpājīvās*. At the same time, they may have had some security as well. Kauṭilya makes a distinction between the two as he remarks that in order to replenish an empty treasury the *bandhakīpoṣakas* will pay a tax of ten *paṇas* (V.2.21) and the *rūpājīvās* half their wage (V.2.23). Perhaps the latter were the *svairiṇī* women operating on their own or at the behest of their parents or guardians, and the *bandhakīs* were pledged women bound to an establishment. There is only one reference to female slaves dedicated to gods as *devadāsīs*, a euphemism for temple prostitution, in the *Arthaśāstra*. Kauṭilya instructs that the superintendent of yarns should have the yarn from wool, bark fibres, cotton, etc., spun by widows, *nyaṅgas*, maidens, women living independently as recluses (*pravrajitā*), those who have to pay off a fine by personal labour (*daṇḍapratikāriṇī*) and the mothers of *rūpājīvās*, old female slaves of the king (*vṛddharājadasī*) and those *devadāsīs* who are no longer in the service of the gods (II.23.2). Apparently *devadāsīs,* being notionally dedicated to gods, could not have served the state through their earnings or employment in some politically useful role, unlike *rūpājīvās* and *rājadāsīs*, and hence are less visible in the text. Inscriptional evidence does testify to the existence of the *devadāsī* institution in the third century BCE (Lüder's List, No. 921). However, all these exploited women, including the female slaves of the king, faced penury and insecurity in old age and had to fend for themselves by spinning yarn.

Megasthenes is reported to have observed that female bodyguards protected the Mauryan king, and when he went out to hunt, women hunters accompanied him riding on chariots, horses and elephants equipped with weapons.[3] This is confirmed in the injunction of Kauṭilya that on rising from his bed, the king should be surrounded by a troupe of women archers (*strīgaṇairdhenvibhiḥ*: I.21.1). Our sources are, however, tantalizingly silent regarding the social background of these armed women. Hunting, training in archery and use of other weapons is generally considered a masculine activity. How were these women recruited and trained? It is pointed out that one of the Bharhut sculptures depicts the figure of a woman riding a horse fully caparisoned and carrying a standard.[4] We may add that the image of a woman hunter (*śvaghnī*) cutting flying birds into pieces is as old as the *Ṛgveda* (I.92.10), and a twelfth-century sculpture from the Varāha-Shyāma Mandir, Bhinmal, Rajasthan, shows a woman hunter carrying a stick on her shoulders with animals hanging from each side of the ends and a man standing on the left handing her arrows.[5] She could be a woman from a Bhīla or Kirāta tribe, and it is likely that the female bodyguards of Candragupta Maurya too were recruited from the *āṭavika* or forest tribes, who are described by Kauṭilya as brave (*vikrānta*), fighting in the open and many in number (VIII.4.43). The *āṭavikas* had compelled Aśoka to follow a policy of conciliation as well as punishment.[6] It is a moot point whether religious images of Hindu goddesses wielding numerous weapons and killing thereomorphic demons go back to the early tribal milieu, or are projections of male fantasies serving 'to mask widespread masculine violence' against women.

In any case, Kauṭilya permits physical violence against a wife whose offence against her husband is well known (III.3.7–11). The passage here does not specify clearly the nature of her offence, but a little later it is said that a wife going on a pleasure trip or to a show without the permission of her husband, or leaving home when the husband is asleep or intoxicated, or one who does not open the door for her husband merited fines of various amounts up to 24 *paṇas* (III.3.21–24). Kauṭilya recommends that the wife should be verbally told to behave submissively or modestly without the use of abusive language; alternatively, she could be thrashed three times with a split bamboo cane or rope or the hand. A woman must not leave the husband's house except in case of ill-treatment, and anyone giving her shelter without her having been ill-treated was liable to be punished. However, women of the lower orders, such as wet nurses (*dhātrī*: III.13.9 and 11), *paricārikās* or female attendants, and *upacārikās*, personal female attendants and prostitutes, were more endangered by male violence, and Kauṭilya's prescriptions for punishing such crimes are mediated by considerations of caste, class and proprietary claims. For example, city guards misbehaving with a woman who was a slave (*dāsī*) were to pay the lowest fine for violence (*sāhasadaṇḍa*) but with one who was not a slave the middle fine, and with a woman who was in the exclusive keeping of a man (*kṛtāvarodhaṃ*) the highest fine (II.36.41), apparently because in the last case it was an encroachment on someone else's proprietary rights. Misbehaving with a woman of a respectable family was to be punished with the death penalty. A similar approach is exhibited in the section dealing with punishment for transgressions (IV.13) and elsewhere. For violating an unprotected brāhmaṇa woman a kṣatriya had to pay the highest fine, the vaiśya had to face the confiscation of his entire property and the śūdra burnt alive in a fire of straw (IV.13.32).

One need not dilate on the obvious – the entire discourse is characterized by patriarchal and Brahmanical prejudices. The *Arthaśāstra* repeats the well-known Dharmaśāstric view that a wife is only a leather bag for holding the male seed, an object for procuring a male issue (III.7.1–2). Hierarchical difference between the sexes is reiterated through the dictum that a woman should be married at the age of twelve and a man at the age of sixteen, any delay would lead to penalization with fines (III.2.1–2). Early marriage allows maximum chances of reproduction and greater parental control over girls, ensuring pre-marital virginity. The *Arthaśāstra* reflects the high value placed on virginity in traditional culture (IV.12.15–19), and terms coined to indicate a fortunate or unfortunate woman – *subhagā* or *durbhagā* – refer to her reproductive power. This attribute could also bring her freedom and empowerment. If a female slave gave birth to her master's child, not only she along with her child would become free, but also her brother and sister (III.13.23–24). Women of the lower orders were pledged to serve their masters. However, Kauṭilya takes a humane view of them and ordains that if a *dhātrī* (wet nurse), *paricārikā* (female attendant), *upacārikā* (personal maid) or *ardhasītikā* (woman tenant tilling for half the produce) was made to give a bath to a naked person, or corporally punished or dishonoured, it would result in her gaining freedom and loss of capital for the master (III.13.9). However, the asymmetry in gender relations is reflected in the rule that a husband, if unwilling, may not approach a wife who suffers from leprosy or is insane, but a woman must approach a husband even if he were of this type for bearing a son (III.2.46–47). In other words, the marital right of a husband remains intact even if he is a leper or insane.

Rigorous patriarchal norms and the absence of family support must have compelled many women to leave society and the *Arthaśāstra* provides ample evidence of the existence of female renouncers. Later Smṛtis assert that the Vedas and the Dharmaśāstras have not ordained for a woman the life of an ascetic. The proper *dharma* for a woman was looking after her progeny born of a male of her own *varṇa*,[7] but there are glimpses of female ascetics in the epics and other early Sanskrit texts – e.g., the female ascetic Svayamprabhā in the *Rāmāyaṇa* of Vālmīki, and Brāhmaṇī Sulabhā in the Śānti parva, chapter 208, of the *Mahābhārata*. Parivrājikā Śaṅkarā is mentioned in the *Mahābhāṣya* of Patañjali, and Paṇḍitā Kauśikī figures in the garb of an ascetic in the *Mālavikāgnimitra* (1.14) of Kālidāsa. The *Arthaśāstra* speaks of two types of female ascetics: *parivrājikās*, who seem to have been brāhmaṇa women and *bhikṣukīs*, also described as *muṇḍas* (head-shaved), and *vṛṣalīs* (heretical), who were apparently followers of non-Brahmanical sects such as Jainism and Buddhism. In the eyes of Kauṭilya, these women constituted a significant resource for recruitment as secret agents or spies. He recommends that a *parivrājikā* brāhmaṇī, who is a poor widow, bold and desirous of earning a livelihood and treated with respect by the inmates of the palace, be employed as a spy and visit the families of the *mahāmātras*, high officials of the state (I.12.4). The *muṇḍa* and *vṛṣalī* wandering nuns too may be employed in similar fashion (I.12).

One may speculate that to some extent the adopting of the lifestyle of a wandering nun was an attempt to resist as well as subvert the existential inferiority of the female gender, but the lack of data does not allow us to form an adequate picture of women's subjective ideas and experiences. A recent analysis of the *Sulabhā-Janaka Saṃvāda*, in the Śānti parva of the *Mahābhārata*, shows how the female ascetic uses the arguments of *Sāṃkhya* philosophy to challenge the hierarchical differentiation of individuals in terms of gender and social class.[8] Whatever the case may be, the *Arthaśāstra*'s evidence projects these female ascetics as a significant element in female sociability, providing support to women at crucial moments. Thus an ill-treated woman could take shelter with a female mendicant (*bhikṣukī*) or her kinsmen without fear of punishment (III.4.9). However, inducing a woman to renounce her home and adopt the lifestyle of an ascetic (*pravrajyā*) was a punishable crime (II.1.29).

As for women's property rights, Kauṭilya allows daughters to inherit their father's estate if they are born of pious marriages and there was no son (III.5.9–10). But no such right is accorded to the widow. The property could go to the brothers or other heirs of the deceased's agnatic family. On the other hand, it is expressly stated that the king should take the property of those who leave no heirs, with the exception of the property of a brāhmaṇa, which is to be distributed among learned brāhmaṇas, and the wives be entitled only to maintenance (III.5.28–29). Nevertheless, at several places the text speaks of rich widows and specifically refers to their contestation for a *dāya* or inheritance at one place (XI.1.42). At another place there is a suggestion that female spies posing as rich widows should tempt enemy chiefs with their *dāya*. In view of the fact that Kauṭilya clearly distinguishes between *strīdhana* – the wealth gifted to a woman at the time of marriage and other occasions – and *dāya*, the inheritance, his evidence on the property rights of women is clearly contradictory. He even suggests to a prince who has fallen into disfavour to revive his fallen fortunes by robbing the wealth of *pāṣaṇḍa-saṃghas* (perhaps Buddhist monasteries), the wealth of temples, or of a rich widow after gaining her confidence (I.18.9). The text ordains a fine of one hundred *paṇas* on one who molests a widow living 'according to her will', i.e. independently.[9]

In conclusion, it may be said that despite its typically patriarchal cultural representations, the *Arthaśāstra* of Kauṭilya gives some inkling of the variety of female experiences and scope for independent activities, notwithstanding gender discrimination and a large section of women suffering from the disadvantages of poverty and caste exploitation.

Notes

[1] *Kauṭilīya Arthaśāstra*, part II, p. 164.

[2] R.C. Majumdar, ed., *The Classical Accounts of India*, p. 271.

[3] Ibid.

[4] Radha Kumud Mookerji, 'Candragupta and the Maurya Empire', in R.C. Majumdar and A.D. Pusalker, eds, *The Age of the Imperial Unity: The History and Culture of the Indian People*, vol. II, p. 66.

[5] *Catalogue of the Kala Sarvekṣaṇa Purātatva Saṅgrahālaya*, no. 40.

[6] Rock Edict XIII, in Sircar, *Inscriptions of Asoka,* p. 43.

[7] *Smṛticandrikā and Other Texts*, quoted in P.V. Kane, *History of Dharmaśāstra*, vol. II, part II, pp. 945–46.

[8] Nicholas Sutton, 'An Exposition of Early Sāmkhya, A Projection of the Bhagavad-Gītā and a Critique of the Role of Women in Hindu Society'.

[9] *Chandavāsini Vidhavā*, III.20.16; *Kauṭilīya Arthaśāstra*, part III, p. 153.

PART III

6

Viṣṇu's Incarnations: Strategies of Cultural Hegemony

The doctrine of incarnation as adumbrated in the *Bhagavadgītā* provided Brahmanism with an extremely useful device for establishing its cultural hegemony. An oft-quoted verse of the *Gītā* makes the godhead proclaim:

> O descendant of Bharata! Whenever *dharma* declines and *adharma* is on the rise, I create myself. I am born age after age for protection of the good and destruction of the evil-doers and for the establishment of *dharma*. (*Bhagavadgītā*, IV.7–8)

The term '*dharma*' occurring in this verse has been variously explained. The two great *ācāryas* Śaṅkarācārya and Rāmānujācārya, in their commentaries, take it to mean *varṇāśramadharma*.[1] Some others interpret it in the sense of 'righteousness'. In any case, the clearly stated purpose of an incarnation is to uphold the Brahmanical view of socio-political and moral values; and as such divine forms (*divya vibhūtis*) were limitless.[2] The doctrine provided a potent tool for the capacious accommodation of numerous aboriginal, local cults and religious legends within the mainstream Brahmanical culture through processes of acculturation, retaining, modifying or expanding them in accordance with the Brahmanical norm.

It has been convincingly argued that the early centuries of the Common Era witnessed profound changes in the economic and political scenario, which gave a fillip to processes of interaction between the mainstream society and tribal people living on its margins.[3] The entry of foreign powers from the north-west, such as Greeks, Scythians, Kuṣāṇas and Parthians, and the establishment of their rule on the settled regions of North India forced the native rulers and chiefs to carve out new kingdoms in tribal spaces, accelerating the processes of state formation and social restructuring in those areas. The period was also marked by a flourishing trade and commerce, particularly in the western Deccan, generating an increase in demand for many agricultural products. All this resulted in a growing pressure on agricultural land, and motivated ruling chiefs to make land grants to brāhmaṇas and monastic organizations in peripheral tribal territories in order to bring virgin and waste land under cultivation and expand plough agriculture. This development had important consequences in terms of social and cultural restructuring. The donees needed labour to work on their lands, the aborigines supplied labour power. Economic interdependence was conducive to some accommodation at the social and cultural levels too. The tribals were recognized as 'castes' in conformity with the *varṇa* model, and their cultural traditions were appropriated, modified or reinvented by the brāhmaṇa ideologues, many of whom acted as priests and minstrels of tribal chiefs. Vijay Nath attributes the composition of the Purāṇas to these 'semi-literate' priests in Gupta and post-Gupta times. The Purāṇas appeared as a new genre of Brahmanical literature created as instruments of acculturation and dissemination of the Brahmanic ideology, written in a dialogue form of storytelling and claiming to be 'ancient sacred lore'; but unlike the sacred Vedic texts, these were open to all irrespective of caste and sex, and were meant for public recital and collective listening. Earlier, R.S. Sharma had put forward a similar hypothesis connecting the origin of Tantrism and Tantric literature to Brahmanical colonization of the tribal areas through land grants.[4] He observes that large-scale land grants were made to brāhmaṇas from the fifth to seventh centuries in peripheral areas such as Assam, Bengal, Orissa, Central and South India; and a little later Nepal and the Himalayan regions too were opened to brāhmaṇas in similar fashion. It is not without significance that almost all Tantric texts were composed in the outlying tribal areas and the initial reaction of the orthodox brāhmaṇas was to condemn Tantrism as non-Vedic. Nevertheless, the decline of towns in the early medieval centuries and the pressure on land made the brāhmaṇas migrate to the countryside, to new areas and tribal spaces. Long-term continuous contact with the aboriginal population resulted in acculturation and adjustments in the socio-economic sphere, and whereas dependent tribal labourers, artisans and peasants were assimilated as low-ranking śūdra castes, cultural interactions helped in the growth of *bhakti* cults and the emergence of Tantrism.[5]

Thus the emergence and growth of Purāṇic and Tantric literatures are attributed to the material conditions of the Gupta and post-Gupta times, when land grants to religious beneficiaries in tribal zones made it economically expedient to acculturate indigenous groups through 'peaceful and sustained religious indoctrination' in order to overcome their hostility. However, acculturation was not a one-way process. Many of the tribal cultures and practices found their way into mainstream religions – Buddhism, Jainism and Brahmanism – with suitable texts composed to provide them legitimacy. But their mainstream version was a reinterpreted, sanskritized version, making them suitable vehicles for the dissemination of mainstream religious ideologies. In this endeavour, Brahmanism has been most successful.

Nevertheless, I would like to point out that the process of drawing the cults of non-Vedic/tribal deities within the vortex of Brāhmanism began much earlier, in the centuries immediately preceding and following the Common Era when Brahmanical social and religious structures faced grave threat from multiple sources. This was a period when trade, particularly foreign trade and commerce, flourished, giving rise to new arts and crafts, and a growing demand for various types of agricultural products acted as a strong incentive for the expansion of agriculture. Consequently, people engaged in these activities – traders, artisans, peasant cultivators – were able to improve their economic position. But they had a low social status, of the vaiśya and śūdra *varṇas*, in the Brahmanical social ranking. Vedic priesthood had ignored the religious requirements of these categories as emerging from tribal antecedents, it was orientated mainly towards the needs of the ruling elites, the kṣatriyas, for whose benefit it had evolved elaborate animal sacrifices. However, with the transition from a pastoral to a stable agricultural economy these had become too expensive and redundant, and were strongly denounced by post-Vedic religious movements such as Buddhism, Jainism, the Ājīvikas and similar other heterodoxies which were gaining popularity. Added to this was the entry of a large number of foreign hordes from the north-west, the Śakas, Yavanas and Kuṣāṇas (and later Hūṇas), who could only be condemned as 'śūdra' or '*mleccha*' by the Vedic orthodoxy but could hardly be ignored because they were able to establish their political control over a large part of North India. The new rulers too began to patronize Buddhism on a large scale. With the demand for Vedic sacrifices which had been a lucrative source of income for Vedic ritual specialists much reduced, the brāhmaṇa priesthood had to look for or invent alternative forms of religiosity to which they could offer their priestly services. This was done by penetrating into the popular tribal cults, giving them a Brahmanical orientation and making them suitable vehicles for the propagation of Brahmanical social and ethical values, thus widening the social base of a refashioned neo-Brahmanism. The orthodox Vedic tradition had become too rigid and sanctimoniously inviolable to allow access to or accommodate non-Vedic tribals, foreigners and aspiring groups engaged in trading and artisanal activities. But the worship of tribal popular deities, who were identified or linked with the deities of the Vedic pantheon to give them sanction, was open to all and suitably modified to adjust to contemporary needs and the environment. The integration of the non-Vedic deities with Vedic ones ultimately led to the conceptualization of the doctrine of incarnation, a cardinal principle of Vaiṣṇavism as adumbrated in the *Bhagavadgītā* and embedded in the great epic, the *Mahābhārata*.

It is known that the *Mahābhārata* has gone through several stages of growth, its nucleus consisting of a heroic poem narrating events leading to the disastrous battle at Kurukṣetra between the Kauravas and the Pāṇḍavas. Originally, it consisted of 8,800 verses and was called *Jaya* or *Itihāsa*.[6] Later, it was expanded to 24,000 verses, the figure mentioned in the *Āśvalāyana Gṛhyasūtra*, and came to be known as the *Bhārata*.[7] However, the transformation of the *Bhārata* into *Mahābhārata* with the addition of many didactic portions and *upākhyānas* (episodes), and raising it to the status of a Dharmaśāstra, is said to have been the work of Bhṛguide brāhmaṇas;[8] they were largely responsible for making it an important vehicle for the propagation of a new set of religious ideologies which upheld Brahmanical social and moral values while synthesizing Vedic and non-Vedic divinities and their forms of worship.[9] The remodelled version of the *Bhārata* epic forcefully propounded the idea that the popular god Vāsudeva–Kṛṣṇa of non-Vedic origins was none other than the Vedic god Nārāyaṇa–Viṣṇu. The *Bhagavadgītā* formed the keystone of this reconstructed version, and it gained so much authority and prestige that in course of time it was called the fifth Veda.[10] It continued to receive interpolations till it expanded to the traditional number of one hundred thousand verses. It is difficult to date an epic of this character and magnitude. Nevertheless, scholarly opinion dates its earliest stratum to roughly 400 BCE and the latest accretions to around fourth–fifth centuries CE. The process of its transformation into a religious text of neo-Brahmanism seems to have begun a few centuries before the Common Era in the circumstances described above. The doctrine of incarnation enunciated in this text proved to be a powerful instrument of integration and acculturation of marginal peoples. In the following pages, I have tried to trace the origin and evolution of the concept of three major incarnations of Viṣṇu: Rāma, Narasiṃha and Hayagrīva.

From Human Hero to God Incarnate: Evolution of the Rāma Legend

There is a general consensus among scholars that the envisioning of Rāma, son of Daśaratha, as an incarnation of Viṣṇu is a later feature of the *Rāmakathā*, which had its beginnings in the ballads or tales of heroism and self-sacrifice of a human hero narrated by bards before audiences in the post-Vedic times. Some have even assumed the historicity of its nucleus, particularly of the events narrated in the Ayodhyā kāṇḍa of Vālmīki's *Rāmāyaṇa*.[11] Perhaps the earliest attempt to historicize the Rāma story was made in a nineteenth-century textbook written by an Indian academic in response to the colonial criticism that Indians had no sense of history.[12] Much work has been done since these early probings. Yet critical scholarship has not been able to go beyond asserting that although the names Rāma, Daśaratha, Sītā, Janaka, Vasiṣṭha and Viśvāmitra are found in various strata of the Vedic literature, there is not a shred of evidence other than the idealized, exaggerated and clearly largely imaginary account of Vālmīki that the events recounted in the Ayodhyā kāṇḍa have any historical basis.[13] Nilakanta Sastri, the doyen among historians of the South, had asserted that the *Rāmāyaṇa* 'altogether lacks a historical basis'.[14] All this has not deterred the communally partisan archaeologist–historians to dig up several sites in Ayodhyā in a futile attempt to establish the historicity of Rāma and the antiquity of Ayodhyā going back to 2000 BCE, the presumed date of Rāma Dāśarathi.[15] From the point of view of a devout Hindu, the question of historicity may be meaningless; the stories narrated in the epics and the Purāṇas are to be understood as symbolizing 'eternal verities in an allegorical fashion'. But authoritative Indian scholarship has been fully aware of the fact that religious beliefs and practices are not static, even if there are contestations regarding the nature and dynamics of change.[16] Accordingly, I study in the following two sections the evolution of the Rāma legends and the growth of a cult of personal devotion centering around him.

The ancient Indian tradition has preserved at least three main versions of the Rāma story – the Brahmanical, the Buddhist and the Jaina – with each of these streams having their own variations. No doubt, the beautiful poem of Vālmīki, who is regarded as the *ādikavi*, 'the first author of ornate poetry', played a key role in stereotyping the framework of the Rāma narrative; nevertheless, this does not mean that Vālmīki's *Rāmāyaṇa* constitutes the original Ur text and that the other versions are merely borrowings or subversive modifications of the same. That there were many tellings of the Rāma story is ingeniously acknowledged in the *Adhyātma Rāmāyaṇa* where Sītā, pleading with Rāma, remarks: 'I have heard many *Rāmāyaṇas* from many *dvijas* (twice born), but tell me, did anywhere Rāma go to the forest without Sītā?'[17] As A.K. Ramanujan convincingly demonstrated, even when the Rāma story is the same in the two tellings, the 'discourse' and therefore the 'import' could be vastly different.[18]

However, variations in the tellings of the three principal religious streams documented in our earliest available sources are very significant, and strongly suggest that the Rāma saga was popular in folklore, from which each of these streams borrowed freely and adapted it to suit their own purposes. The variations are not 'distortions', 'rationalizations' or 'deliberate falsifications' of the Brahmanical version, although in some instances that may be so, but they originated in a different milieu. The most controversial in this context is the *Daśaratha Jātaka*. Father Camille Bulcke regards it as merely a distorted version of the Brahmanical *Rāmakathā*.[19] His painstaking study of the numerous tellings of the Rāma story spread over a vast time and space is unique in its empathetic treatment and meticulous research. Hence, his view deserves serious consideration. He concedes that the *gāthā* (verse) portions of the Jātakas relating to the *Rāmakathā* found embedded in the Buddhist religious text *Tripiṭaka* are pre-Vālmīki, and states that the poets of the *gāthā* as well as Vālmīki borrowed from the legendary ballad-narratives independent of each other; the *gāthās* of the *Daśaratha Jātaka* too are not borrowed from Vālmīki, although some of them (*gāthās* 1, 5, 13) resemble closely the verses in the *Rāmāyaṇa*. But as the *Jātakaṭṭhavaṇṇanā*, containing the *Daśaratha Jātaka*, was translated from Sinhalese into Pali in the fifth century CE, Bulcke argues that by this time Vālmīki's *Rāmāyaṇa* was already well known and that the story of the *Daśaratha Jātaka* narrated in prose is based on Vālmīki's narrative, albeit distorting it in the process.[20] However, I shall show presently that certain elements of this *Jātaka* story are indicative of its greater antiquity. The story, in brief, is as follows.

In ancient times, king Daśaratha was the ruler of Vārāṇasī. He had two sons, Rāma–Paṇḍita and Lakkhana, and a daughter, Sītā Devī, born to him by his eldest queen. On the death of this queen, the king appointed a younger queen as his chief consert (*agga-mahasī*). A son was born to her too, and was named Bharata Kumāra. The king granted her a boon on the occasion. When Bharata was seven years old, the queen began to insist that her son should be made the heir-apparent. Fearing a palace intrigue against his elder two sons, Daśaratha asked them to go into exile for twelve years and come back on his death to claim the throne, as soothsayers had predicted that he would die after twelve years. Sītā Devī insisted on joining her brothers in exile and they all went to the Himalayas. However, Daśaratha died after nine years. Bharata refused to be crowned as king and, along with *amātyas* (counsellors) and the army, set out to find Rāma and persuade him to return. He reached Rāma's hermitage and gave the news of their father's death. Lakkhana and Sītā fainted with grief and had to be revived, but Rāma–Paṇḍita showed perfect equanimity and preached on the impermanence of life, the inevitability of death and the utter futility of sorrow in a few *gāthās* (verses). He refused to go back to Vārāṇasī, saying that he had promised his father to return only after twelve years. Lakkhana and Sītā went back with Bharata; Rāma gave his sandals to Bharata, telling him that these would rule the kingdom during his absence. After twelve years, Rāma returned to Vārāṇasī, married his sister Sītā and ruled righteously for sixteen thousand years (this is again stated in verse). As the Jātakas are stories of the Buddha's former births which occurred in the distant past and were narrated by the Buddha himself on specific occasions, these end with the Buddha identifying different characters of the past with their present incarnations. In this case the Buddha informs that the king Daśaratha was born as Śuddhodana, Rāma's mother as Mahāmāyā (the mother of the Buddha), Sītā Devī as Yaśodharā (the wife of the Buddha and mother of Rāhula), and the Buddha himself was Rāma–Paṇḍita.

Bulcke thinks that the change of the capital city from Ayodhyā to Vārāṇasī and of the place of exile from Daṇḍakāraṇya to the Himalayan forests was made to suit the Buddhist milieu as these occur frequently in the Buddhist narratives and the Buddhist audiences were familiar with them. However, he concedes that ballads regarding a heroic king Rāma, the descendant of the legendary king Ikṣvāku, were current in post-Vedic times, and the poet of the *Rāmāyaṇa* as well as the compilers of the *Tripiṭaka* drew upon these independently of each other, with Vālmīki shaping them to produce the first epic in Sanskrit and the Buddhists using them to expound their own doctrine. If so, it is not clear why the Buddhist telling should be regarded as a change or distortion of the Brahmanical version. The antiquity and strength of the Jātaka version is shown by its persistence in a Jaina *Rāmāyaṇa*, embedded in the *Uttara Purāṇa* of Guṇabhadra (ninth century CE). This text makes Daśaratha a king of Vārāṇasī who later changed his capital to Ayodhyā. After the marriage of Rāma and Sītā, Daśaratha makes Rāma his crown prince and sends him to Vārāṇasī to look after his subjects there. In this way, both the versions are synthesized. We may note that several kṣatriya tribes in the age of the Buddha, such as the Śākyas and the Mallas,[21] claimed descent from the legendary king Ikṣvāku; it is very likely that the Rāma ballads were popular in their circles. The location of the events in Vārāṇasī (Kāśī), a well-known city in the age of the Buddha, and the Himalayan forests is quite natural as these tribes were located in the Himalayan region.

Early references to Ayodhyā are mythical, suggesting its origin in the sacred imagination.[22] Kosala and Magadha figure in the well-known list of the sixteen *mahājanapadas* in the Pali texts, but the capital of Kosala in the age of the Buddha was Śrāvasti, not Ayodhyā. The kingdom had another great city, Sāketa, described as a *mahānagara* in early Buddhist and Jaina texts. The city is also mentioned by Pāṇini and Patañjali, and the *Yuga Purāṇa*. It is located on the river Sarayu and there is no mention of Ayodhyā in these sources.[23] The surmise[24] that with the deification of the hero of the *Rāmāyaṇa* epic the mythical city of Ayodhyā came to be identified with Sāketa in order to give the god, who had come down to earth, a real historical location, has a great deal of plausibility. It is interesting to note that the *Rāmāyaṇa* of Vālmīki makes no mention of Sāketa, though it is mentioned in the *Yuga Purāṇa* (300 CE) as an important regional centre conquered by the Yavanas (identified as Kuṣāṇas) along with the city of Pāṭaliputra.[25] It is only in the Brahmanical sources of the Gupta period, such as the *Raghuvaṃśa* of Kālidāsa and the *Brahmāṇḍa Purāṇa*, that Sāketa and Ayodhyā become synonymous.[26] Later the name Ayodhyā becomes more popular, apparently owing to its growing religious significance.

Archaeological excavations have shown that human habitation at the site of present-day Ayodhyā began some time in the seventh century BCE,[27] although some date it still later. People lived in houses made of wattle-and-daub or mud during this phase of occupation. Houses of kiln-burnt brick, terracotta ring-wells, etc., which indicate urban settlement, appear only in the next phase of occupation, dated between the third century BCE and first century CE. The presence of sherds of rouletted ware in levels assignable to the first–second centuries CE indicate its emergence as an important trade and regional centre during this period, confirming the evidence derived from the textual sources. We may point out that this was also the period when the epic hero Rāma was gaining recognition as an incarnation of Nārāyaṇa–Viṣṇu, and the mythical city of Ayodhyā was getting identified with the well-known city Sāketa of Kosala Janapada.

Analysing the material culture as reflected in the text of the critical edition[28] of the *Rāmāyaṇa*, H.D. Sankalia convincingly demonstrates that it cannot be dated earlier than the fifth century CE.[29] However, the critical edition, despite having eliminated 'full twenty-five percent of the vulgate',[30] can lay no claim to the original (Ur) reconstruction of Vālmīki's poem, as it includes the first and the last, Bāla and Uttara kāṇḍas, which are generally accepted to be later additions to Vālmīki's *Rāmāyaṇa*. The length of the critical edition approximates to the traditional belief that the 'seer recited twenty-four thousand *ślokas* in five hundred *sargas* making up six kāṇḍas plus the Uttara'.[31] However, scholarly opinion holds that Vālmīki's poem originally had only 6,000 verses, which increased to 12,000 by the third century CE, as this is the number given in the Buddhist text *Abhidharmavibhāṣā* written about that time.[32] The *Kalpanāmaṇḍatikā*, a text of the same period,[33] speaks of its public recital. Another Buddhist text, the *Daśaratha Kathānam*, translated into Chinese in 472 CE, shows the influence of Vālmīki's narrative, as it locates king Daśaratha in Ayodhyā and describes Rāma as having the valour and prowess of Na-ra-yen (Sanskrit: Nārāyaṇa).[34] Perhaps it reflects an early stage of his identification with Nārāyaṇa–Viṣṇu. In subsequent centuries. the Buddhists in India stopped using the Rāma story for their own purposes owing to the fact that by the fifth century CE Rāma had become a well-known incarnation of Viṣṇu.[35]

However, the Buddhist and Jaina streams of the Rāma saga stress his human character, a model of virtuous conduct according to their own canons. The earliest of these, the *Daśaratha Jātaka*, contains some very primitive features.[36] It makes Sītā both the sister as well as the wife of Rāma. Bulcke dismisses it as Buddhist influence and quotes the *Vessantara Jātaka* (*gāthā* 541), where the wife of prince Vessantara says that she is as devoted to her husband as Sītā was to Rāma, to support his contention that Sītā was known as the wife and not sister of Rāma.[37] But he ignores the clear description of Sītā in the same *Jātaka* as Rāma's younger sister (*kaniṭṭha-bhaginī*) as well as chief queen (*agga-mahisī*) in another verse.[38] Sibling marriage was an important symbolism to preserve the purity of descent of the non-monarchical kṣatriya clans, which demanded purity of descent on both sides. Buddhist sources contrast the kṣatriya practice of insisting on purity of birth up to seven generations on the side of both parents, with the contemporary practice of brāhmaṇas who accepted sons born of partial non-brāhmaṇa origin on either side and allowed them to participate in their rituals.[39] In fact, purity of lineage was of vital concern to the ruling class of the *gaṇa-rājyas* of the age of the Buddha because access to political power depended upon it. Moreover, both the Brahmanical and the Buddhist streams were inheritors of the oral tradition about the legendary king Ikṣvāku in equal measure as the kṣatriya clans, the Śākyas, the Koliyas and the Licchavis who traced their origin to king Ikṣvāku (Pali: Okkāka), were located in the regions adjoining Ayodhyā and Videha where the Brahmanical sources situate the Ikṣvākus of the solar race.

Was the motif of sibling marriage in the *Daśaratha Jātaka* merely due to its Buddhist orientation, or is there a substratum of such myths which finds its resonance in the Buddhist version? Elsewhere I have discussed the traces of the cult of a black mother-goddess flanked by two associate gods, one of whom later becomes her husband, in the worship of goddess Ekānaṃśā (also described as Ekādaśā) together with Baladeva and Kṛṣṇa, the Vṛṣṇi brothers.[40] She was the guardian deity of the Vṛṣṇis; and early sculptures of the second century CE in Mathura art show her standing in the middle with images of Baladeva and Kṛṣṇa on either side.[41] She is equated with Bhadrā or Subhadrā in the Āryāstava of the *Harivaṃśa*, and the triad of deities enshrined in the Jagannātha temple at Puri in Orissa are identified as Jagannātha (Vāsudeva), Subhadrā and Balarāma. The sixteenth-century poet Balarāma Dāsa, in his *Rāmāyaṇa*, stresses the oneness of Rāma, Sītā and Lakṣmaṇa with Jagannātha, Subhadrā and Balarāma at two places,[42] and it is held that the popularity of the Puri triad in the region must have led to this equation, ignoring the inherent ambiguity that whereas Rāma and Sītā constituted a husband–wife couple, Ekanaṃśā/Subhadrā was the sister of Jagannathā (also known as Vāsudeva–Kṛṣṇa and Puruṣottama). However, a passage in the Utkala khaṇḍa of the *Skanda Purāṇa* clearly states that Subhadrā, who is worshipped with Baladeva and Vāsudeva at Jagannātha Purī, is both the sister and wife of Vāsudeva, and embodies his energy.[43] Divine symbolisms may not be exact replicas of accepted societal norms, but it is possible to see in them a long process of development.[44] The honorific 'Devī' given to Sītā in the *Daśaratha* and *Vessantara Jātakas* may not be sufficient proof of her divine nature, although her association with Rāma and Lakṣmaṇa as their sister in the *Daśaratha Jātaka* has a parallel in the story of Añjanā Devī, the black goddess, mentioned along with her two younger brothers Baladeva and Vāsudeva in the *Ghaṭa Jātaka* (no. 454). However, the intent of the *Daśaratha Jātaka* is to exalt the figure of Rāma–Paṇḍita as a Bodhisattva possessing an exemplary calm and self-control in difficult situations. Lakṣmaṇa and Sītā play a subordinate role, and the latter is married to Rāma after his return from exile. There is strength in Weber's argument[45] that the fact that the children of Rāma and Sītā are born only when they return to Ayodhyā, and not during the long years of being together in exile, shows that the tale[46] influenced the plot in Vālmīki's original version.

Whatever the case may be, the conception of a mythical trio, Puruṣottama, Subhadrā and Balarāma (or Añjanā Devī with her two younger brothers), or Rāma, Sītā and Lakṣmaṇa, seems to reflect an archetype of a female deity flanked by two associate male gods, originally her brothers, assisting her in cosmic roles. The eulogy for the great mother-goddess called Āryā Devī in the *Harivaṃśa*, extolling her as the sister of the gods Mahendra and Viṣṇu, suggests the same thing. Later, in accordance with patriarchal mentalities, the role of the goddess is subordinated and one of her associates becomes her husband. A substratum of such myths could underlie the concept of Sītā having a dual relationship with Rāma, both as his wife and sister in the *Daśaratha Jātaka*, particularly as she is called 'Devī' in this case.

In the Bāla kāṇḍa of Vālmīki's *Rāmāyaṇa*, Sītā is described as *ayonijā* (not born of the womb).[47] King Janaka found her while ploughing the field and named her Sītā, meaning 'furrow'; she does not die but goes into the receiving arms of mother-earth. A goddess Sītā personifying the furrow is invoked in a late sūkta[48] of the *Ṛgveda*. The Gṛhyasūtras prescribe her worship at the start of ploughing operations (*halābhiyoga*). She is possessed of radiant beauty and black eyes, and is sometimes mentioned as the wife of Indra and Parjanya.[49] It is likely that the similarity of names led to the identification of the daughter of Janaka with this goddess at some stage of development of the Rāma story. Rāma too is identified with Indra in a verse of the Yuddha kāṇḍa.[50] But this does not seem to be of any particular significance as it forms part of the eulogy uttered by Brahmā to make Rāma aware of his true divine nature, identifying him as the great god Nārāyaṇa, supreme Puruṣa, Viṣṇu, Kṛṣṇa, the slayer of Madhu, the soul of the Veda and so on. The passage is evidently a late insertion proclaiming Rāma as an incarnation of Viṣṇu, but is included in the critical edition and belongs to the final stages of the epic's redaction. Sītā too is identified as Lakṣmī in this passage, but with the exception of this late passage, there is hardly any trace of her divinity in Vālmīki's *Rāmāyaṇa* despite the story of her miraculous origin.

The composition of two major epics propagating the ideals of Brahmanical social ethics and norms of piety around the same time was not, as I have argued, a fortuitous phenomenon, but the response of the Brahmanical literati to the situation of crisis outlined above. Textual analysis has established that Books II to VI of Vālmīki's *Rāmāyaṇa*, with the exclusion of a few late interpolations, reflect a unity of composition and are the work of a single author. The poem is certainly post-Buddhist and most likely post-Aśokan. Thus, the time of its composition roughly coincides with or may be a little earlier than the promulgation of the *Bhārata* as *Mahābhārata*. Vālmīki composed his *kāvya* in the face of the rising tide of Buddhism. As opposed to the ideals of celibacy and monkhood preached by the heterodox religious movements, he presented the Brahmanical ideal of virtue exalting the *gṛhasthāśrāma*, the householder's stage of life. His epic provided a role model for all kinds of human relationships: father, son, mother, wife, friend and others. Weaving together legendary tales centering on Ayodhyā, Kiṣkindhā and Laṅkā, he created a fascinating saga in which values of patriarchal, *varṇa*-based society were upheld by various characters at a great deal of personal cost and dramatic appeal. The story was so captivating that it spread far in the ancient world. It was taken to South-East Asia, China, Japan and Central Asia, dramatized and presented at royal courts, portrayed in sculptures and paintings. In the process, it went through many variations and local adaptations. The diversity of its multiple tellings and retellings and their use and 'abuse' in political and socio-cultural discourse are truly astounding, and have been brought out vividly by A.K. Ramanujan's famous article, 'Three Hundred Rāmāyaṇas', and two books edited by Paula Richman.[51] For a proper understanding of the social and cultural history of early India, a contextual study of the various narratives of the Rāma saga are quite enlightening.

It is a measure of the popularity of the Rāma story that the Jainas too have made full use of it for the propagation of their own doctrines and value system, and produced many Rāmāyaṇas of their own. Jaina works were composed and recited in constant competition and confrontation with the custodians of the Brahmanical religious tradition, and an element of counter-culture is conspicuous among them. Several of their works are known as *prati-purāṇas*, i.e. counter-*purāṇas* which mock and parody Purāṇic stories. Nevertheless, the story of Rāma occupies an important place in their religious tradition; the Jaina *Rāmāyaṇa* written by Raviṣeṇa (678 CE) in Sanskrit and titled as the *Padma Purāṇa* or *Padma Carita* is esteemed by the Jainas in the same fashion as the Hindus esteem the *Rāmacaritamānasa* of Tulasī. A copy of its Hindi translation is to be found in all the Jaina temples of North India.[52]

However, Raviṣeṇa's *Padma Carita* is a Sanskrit rendering of the earliest Jaina *Rāmāyaṇa* written by Vimalasūri (*c*. 473 CE) in Mahārāṣṭrī Prakrit.[53] Vimalasūri named his poem *Paumacariyam* and called Rāma, the son of Daśaratha, Padma, perhaps to distinguish him from Balarāma, the elder brother of Kṛṣṇa, who also figures prominently in the Jaina legends. Nevertheless, he also calls him Rāma and Rāghava, and shows full awareness of the *Rāmāyaṇa* of Vālmīki.[54] In fact his work is clearly written to contest and reject the Brahmanical appropriation of the Rāma saga; hence his style, message and characterization of the various characters constitute a complete antithesis of the Brahmanical version. The Jainas resented Brahmanical dominance and adopted a rational, commonsensical approach mocking Brahmanic mythic constructions.[55] The *Paumacariyam* opens with king Seṇiya (Śreṇika) asking the ascetic Goyama (Gautama), the disciple of Mahāvīra, how it was possible for the monkeys to defeat the mighty Rāvaṇa and how Rāvaṇa, a devout Jaina, could be a flesh-eating demon drinking blood, or for Kumbhakarṇa to sleep for six months without waking up even when boiling oil was poured into his ears and for him to be trampled upon by elephants. The king expresses grave doubts about the authenticity of such accounts which appear to him fanciful and irrational. He wants to know the authentic version. In response, Gautama refutes the characterization of Rāvaṇa as a demon. He was a devout Jaina and a great king. He is one of the *mahāpuruṣas* of the Jaina canon. Sage Gautama retells the Rāma story beginning with an account of the creation and then proceeds to give the genealogies of the *Rākṣasa-vaṃśa* and *Vānara-vaṃśa*, and a list of the 63 *mahāpuruṣas*. After all this he comes to the genealogies of king Janaka and Daśaratha, and gives the Jaina version of the Rāma story. The very beginning shows the reversal of the Brahmanical version, for it gives precedence to the genealogy of Rāvaṇa over Rāma. The Rākṣasas and Vānaras were not demons and monkeys but two branches of Vidyādharas, humans endowed with extraordinary knowledge (*vidyā*). Rāvaṇa is the real hero of the story; he is learned and noble, and even takes a vow not to force himself on another's wife.[56] His only weakness is his passion for Sītā. Even then, during the course of the war against Rāma and his army, when Rāvaṇa visits Sītā and finds her fainting with grief, he repents and resolves to return Sītā to Rāma after defeating him, but is killed by Lakṣmaṇa.[57]

Although Rāma, Lakṣmaṇa and Rāvaṇa are at par in the Jaina tradition – all three being counted among the 63 *mahāpuruṣas* – it is Lakṣmaṇa who does all the killings while Rāma is a non-violent follower of the teaching of Mahāvīra. Both Rāma and Sītā are said to have taken Jaina *dīkṣā* (initiation) in the end and attained *nirvāṇa* (liberation).

However, the important point is that neither the Brahmanical nor the Jaina religious texts present a uniform, unchanging version of the Rāma story, even if these adhere broadly to the basic plot framed by Vālmīki. This is quite in contrast with the Hindu Right's aggressive negation of the plurality of the *Rāmāyaṇa* tradition by forcing the withdrawal of Ramanujan's 'Three Hundred Rāmāyaṇas' from the syllabus of the University of Delhi, or closing down the Sahmat exhibition for the same reason. Thus, for example, in most of the Brahmanical *Rāmāyaṇas*, beginning with Vālmīki to Tulasīdāsa's *Rāmacaritamānasa*, the act of mutilating the nose of Śūrpaṇakhā is attributed to Lakṣmaṇa on the orders of Rāma but Rāma himself does not do so. In the *Irāmāvatāram* of Kamban, Lakṣmaṇa cuts off not only Śūrpaṇakhā's nose but also her nipples and ears. But the *Bhāgavata Purāṇa*, no less a revered text of the Bhāgavatas/Vaiṣṇavas, describes Rāma himself as cutting off the nose of Śūrpaṇakhā in its two passages.[58] Apparently, the audience which heard the Purāṇic stories regarded the mutilation as just punishment for a shameless, infatuated woman;[59] so the author of the *Bhāgavata Purāṇa* preferred to attribute this exploit to Rāma himself. This feat of Rāma is mentioned in the *Garuḍa*, *Padma* and *Devī-Bhāgavata Purāṇas* too.[60] Later commentators have tried hard to explain away this unsavoury deed of the *maryādā puruṣottama* Rāma by offering various apologetics.[61] Tulasīdāsa uses this episode to expatiate on the frailty and evil nature of women, but it finds no mention in the Jaina *Rāmāyaṇas*. Vimalsūri names Śūrpaṇakhā as Candranakhā who has a son named Śambūka. He is killed by Lakṣmaṇa while practising severe asceticism to gain a divine sword. The incident leads to the kidnapping of Sītā, culminating in the battle between Rāma and Rāvaṇa. In the Brahmanical versions, however, Śambūka is a śūdra ascetic who is killed by Rāma for practising asceticism and thus committing the sin of breaking the rules of *varṇa-dharma*. The transgression causes the death of the son of a brāhmaṇa.

Similarly, there are multiple versions of the birth of Sītā. In a number of Jaina and Brahmanical texts, such as *Vasudeva-Hiṇḍi* of Saṅghadāsa (609 CE), *Uttara Purāṇa* of Guṇabhadra (ninth century CE) and *Mahābhāgavata Purāṇa* (tenth–eleventh centuries), Sītā is said to be the daughter of Rāvaṇa and Mandodarī. The *Adbhuta Rāmāyaṇa*, written in Kashmir, narrates that Mandodarī drank the blood of ascetics collected by Rāvaṇa in a pot thinking that it was poison in order to commit suicide, as she was piqued by her husband. Instead she became pregnant and buried the foetus in a field. When king Janaka began ploughing this field for the performance of a sacrifice, he found a beautiful girl born of this foetus. He adopts her and names her Sītā. Later Rāvaṇa falls in love with his own daughter. Some other narratives, such as the *Paumacariya* of Vimalasūri and the *Padma Purāṇa* of Raviṣeṇa, follow Vālmīki more closely and make Janaka the real father of Sītā, transferring the incestuous motif to her long-lost twin brother Bhāmaṇḍala, who, at the instigation of sage Nārada, turns up at her *svayaṃvara* as a suitor! The mystery surrounding the birth of Sītā and the introduction of the 'incest' motif in various forms reflect an assimilation of legends relating to a female divinity with the story of Sītā depicted by Vālmīki as a devoted wife in a patriarchal set-up. Later, as in the *Adhyātma Rāmāyaṇa* (fourteenth–fifteenth centuries CE), Rāma is raised to the level of the highest god transcending all others; Sītā is given the attributes of the supreme goddess Mahākālī in the *Adbhuta Rāmāyaṇa*. According to this text, Rāma is killed by

Sahasraskandha Rāvaṇa, ruler of Puṣkara, in a duel. Enraged, Sītā assumes the terrible Ghorakālī form, cuts off the head of Rāvaṇa and his warriors, and begins to dance, which threatens the entire world. In the end Brahmā revives Rāma who recites an eulogy in praise of the goddess. Sītā is pacified and returns to her normal form.[62]

However, there is a gap of several centuries in the identification of Rāma as an incarnation of Viṣṇu and the emergence of a cult centred on his worship. The point will be dealt with in detail in the next section. Here we may note the stages in the evolution of the concept of *Rāmāvatāra*. Internal evidence of the present critical edition of the *Rāmāyaṇa* too indicates a gradual growth of the concept. Thus, in the Bāla kāṇḍa of the *Rāmāyaṇa*, the gods request Viṣṇu to divide himself into four parts and be born as the sons of Daśaratha from his three wives in order to kill Rāvaṇa.[63] Next we are told that Kausalyā gave birth to Rāma who was one-half Viṣṇu; Kaikeyī bore Bharata who was a quarter of the incarnate Viṣṇu; and Sumitrā gave birth to two sons, Lakṣmaṇa and Śatrughna, imbued with the remaining portions of Viṣṇu.[64] Thus Rāma was only a partial incarnation of Viṣṇu. This idea is repeated in the *Raghuvaṃśa* of Kālidāsa.[65] However, in the *Rāmāyaṇa* there are also passages eulogizing Rāma as the 'Primordial creator of three worlds, imperishable *Brahman* . . . transcending the worlds . . . the soul of the Vedas . . . the syllable Om . . . the entire universe comprising his body', and so on.[66] Interestingly, the passage also describes him as Nārāyaṇa, the wielder of a discus, and twice as Kṛṣṇa, ignoring the fact that traditionally the Kṛṣṇa incarnation is supposed to have taken place much later, after a whole *yuga*. Some scholars regard the entire passage as a late interpolation. Nevertheless it is included in the critical edition. This development is similar to the gradual recognition of Vāsudeva–Kṛṣṇa as the incarnation of Nārāyaṇa–Viṣṇu. In the *Mahābārata* Vāsudeva is described as the incarnation of only a fraction of the supreme god Nārāyaṇa, impersonating only his one black hair. Later he is said to represent an eighth portion of the same god whose eighth part comprises the whole world. Finally, in the *Bhāgavata Purāṇa* Kṛṣṇa gains recognition as Viṣṇu incarnate in all his potency, the supreme Godhead.[67]

However, despite the growing religious significance of Rāma in the Brahmanical stream, his tale was not considered so sacrosanct that poets and dramatists could not twist or remodel it to suit their own vision or requirements. The Rāma theme has inspired a large number of classical literary writings and continues to attract creative writers to this day. Certain developments in the Rāma story had taken place under sectarian inspiration in the medieval times. We have already noticed the composition of the *Adbhuta Rāmāyaṇa* (*c.* fifteenth century) which betrays a strong Tantric influence. The work was popular in Bengal where a number of other *Rāmāyaṇas*, borrowing incidents from this work, were composed in the seventeenth century.[68] On the other hand, the *Yoga Vāsiṣṭha Rāmāyaṇa*,[69] written in Kashmir in the twelfth contury CE, approaches the Rāma story in a totally different perspective. It has a long section (*vairāgya prakaraṇa*) in which Vasiṣṭha, on the advice of Viśvāmitra, expounds to Rāma the philosophy of *jñana-karma-samuccaya*, that is, combining true knowledge with unattached action to achieve salvation. It has been argued that the author of *Yoga Vāsiṣṭha Rāmāyaṇa* was reacting against the ideal of *sanyāsa* or renunciation upheld by Buddhism as well as the Vedānta philosophy of Śaṅkarācārya.[70] So he gave a new interpretation to Vedānta, which inculcated a positive attitude towards life, advocating the performance of 'action' not in the form of rituals or ascetic practices, but 'action' in search of truth and spiritual experience while leading the life of a householder and thus becoming *jīvanamukta*, the Liberated Human. Rāma figures in this text as *jīvanamukta*, presenting an oppositional model to the renouncer's way of life.

The choice of the Rāma incarnation of Viṣṇu as an example of *jīvanamukta* was quite in harmony with his general characterization. It has been pointed out that in the character of Rāma sexuality appears to be completely suppressed.[71] Nonetheless, it did not impede his being made the cult object of a highly emotional and erotic form of devotional theism, popularized by adherents of the Rasika *sampradāya* in the medieval centuries.[72] The *Rasika Prakāśa Bhaktamāla*, written by Jīvarāma, traces the origin of this sect to Rāmānanda; the majority of the temples in Ayodhyā are controlled by this sect. The Rasikas, also known as Bhāvikas, envisioned an eternal world of Sāketa (*Sāketa-loka*), a vast magnificent city with luxurious gardens, streets and houses studded with gold and gems. In the middle of the city is located Kanaka Bhavana, house of gold, in which the divine couple reside engaged in eternal sport (*līlā*). They are attended by a large retinue of servants and friends (*sakhās/sakhīs*). The initiates of the *sakhī* branch of the Rasikas identified themselves mentally with one of these *sakhās* or *sakhīs*, and worshipped Sītā and Rāma with the devotional attitude of *mādhurya* (ecstatic, erotic love). But other kinds of relationships with the divine dyad could also be imagined. Some worship them with parental love (*vātsalya*), others visualize other kinds of personal relationships.[73] However, the emphasis is on *mānasa-pūjā* (mental worship), and the daily worship in the Rasika temples follows the ritual of *aṣṭayāma*, dividing the day into eight periods beginning with the awakening of the divine pair in the morning till their retirement to their bedchamber at night. The famous Kanaka Bhavan temple at Ayodhyā is supposed to be an earthly representation of the divine Kanaka Bhavana of Sāketa.

The emergence of erotic devotionalism in mainstream religious traditions is ascribed to the interaction of the mainstream peoples with the marginal, aboriginal population, as land grants to monks and monasteries, priests and temples in tribal areas unleashed processes of acculturation and absorption of the tribal erotic fertility rituals into the mainstream religions. This took the form of Tantricism, which affected all the major religious traditions – Jainism, Buddhism and Brahmanism – in varying degrees and forms. The process started in the early medieval centuries. In Buddhism it manifested itself as Sahajayāna; in Śaivism through the worship of Śiva and Śakti, the male and the female principles in their eternal union; and in Vaiṣṇavism through the worship of Lakṣmī or Rādhā as the consort of Viṣṇu or Kṛṣṇa. In the cult of Rāma the Rasika *sampradāya* gained popularity around the sixteenth century, which peaked in the eighteenth–nineteenth centuries. It appears to have been deeply influenced by the Kṛṣṇaite theology and mystical practices of the Vrindavan Gosvamis. Rajasthan seems to have been the chief centre of its activity, with its main seat located at Galata near Jaipur. The Rasikas produced copious literature, most of which is still unpublished. It is interesting that most of them had an upper-caste background, mainly brāhmaṇas. They were also adept in classical music and composed their songs in the vernacular. The rulers of Amer were great patrons of the Rasika saints and it is believed that Rājā Mānsingh had become the disciple of the Rasika saint Agradāsa who lived in the later half of the sixteenth century. In later centuries, the Rasikas received liberal patronage from the rulers of Banaras, Rewa, Tikamgarh and Dumrao, and also from the eclectic Nawabs of Avadh who ruled Ayodhyā till 1765.

Thus, the variegated theological developments of the Rāma story defy any attempt at a monolithic construction of his cult.

Cultic Worship of Rāma Dāśarathī

I

Although, according to Purāṇic accounts, Viṣṇu's *Rāmāvatāra* preceded his incarnation as Vāsudeva–Kṛṣṇa, there is consensus among scholars that the cultic worship of Rāma began much later than Kṛṣṇa's. One of the early pioneers in the field, R.G. Bhandarkar, was of the view that the cult of Rāma came into existence as late as the eleventh century CE.[74] The popularity of the Rāma story led to the carving of episodes from the *Rāmāyaṇa* on the panels of Vaiṣṇava as well as Śaiva temples. A number of such panels from the fifth–sixth centuries onwards are found at various places, such as Bhitargaon near Kanpur (fifth century CE), Deogarh (Jhansi district, sixth century CE), Paunar (near Wardha, sixth century CE), rock-cut caves of Undavalli (Vijayawada, seventh century CE), Cālukyan temples at Paṭṭadakal (seventh century CE). But these cannot be taken as indicative of Rāma's cultic worship. However, claims have been made of the existence of Rāma temples in the Gupta period, and these need to be examined carefully.

Claims for the existence of Rāma temples in the Gupta period are based on two inscriptions: the Bhitari stone inscription of Skandagupta, and the Rithpur copperplate inscription of the Vākāṭaka queen Prabhāvatīguptā, daughter of Candragupta II. The Bhitari stone inscription of Skandagupta speaks of the installation of an image of god Śārṅgin, the bearer of the bow Śārṅga, by the Gupta king, and on this basis it is argued that as among the incarnations of Viṣṇu only Rāma Dāśarathī's characteristic weapon is the bow, the inscription proves the installation of an image of Rāma for the purposes of worship and there existed a temple of Rāma in the Ghazipur district of present-day Uttar Pradesh in the Gupta age.[75] But historians of mythology know that epithets and attributes of a particular deity are often transferred to another, particularly when the cult of the latter is becoming popular. For example, Macdonell shows that many of the appellations originally applied to Indra or Prajāpati were later transferred to Viṣṇu.[76] So, in order to ascertain the identity of the god mentioned in the Bhitari inscription, we have to examine which god was known as Śārṅgin in the Gupta period.

The poet Kālidāsa, who is generally regarded to have lived at the court of a Gupta king, uses the term 'Śārṅgin' at three places in the *Raghuvaṃśa*. At one place, the bridge constructed by the monkeys over the ocean is said to have risen like the snake Śeṣa for Śārṅgin to sleep on.[77] Evidently, it is the god Viṣṇu–Nārāyaṇa who lies on the serpent bed and not Rāma Dāśarathī. The second reference is even more pertinent.[78] Here, the way Rāma receives Śatrughna on his return after killing the demon Lavaṇa is compared with Indra's joyous welcome of Viṣṇu on killing the demon Kālanemī. In this context, the poet uses the term *agraja*, 'elder brother', to denote Rāma and names Viṣṇu as Śārṅgin. A third verse almost using the same language as the *Bhagavadgītā* speaks of Rāma ('the descendant of Kakutstha') as Śārṅgin, who has come down to the earth for protection of the righteous.[79] Here, the poet imagines Rāma as an incarnation of Viṣṇu–Śārṅgin, but for him Rāma is a partial incarnation embodying only a quarter portion of the great god. He is the first among the equally endowed four brothers, Viṣṇu having divided himself equally in 'four forms'.[80] Thus, a close study of these passages reveals that for Kālidāsa 'Śārṅgin' was an epithet for Viṣṇu, and the evidence of Kālidāsa cited above clearly contradicts any assumption that the Śārṅgin of the Bhitari inscription must be taken as a reference to Rāma Dāśarathī.

We may further add that in the *Dhanurveda*,[81] the Śārṅga bow is specifically described as Viṣṇu's bow. Just as Śiva's bow was known as Pināka and Śiva was called Pinākin, similarly Viṣṇu's bow was Śārṅga and the god was called

Śārṅgin. The god Viśvakarmā made two powerful bows, giving one to Śiva and the other to Viṣṇu, but in the fight between the two gods Viṣṇu's bow proved to be the superior one.[82] What is more, in several stories Rāma is said to have received Viṣṇu's bow from the sages.[83] Thus, there is no doubt that Viṣṇu was the original Śārṅgin, the wielder of the Śārṅga bow.[84]

The other piece of evidence cited in this connection relates to the Rithpur copperplate inscription of the Vākāṭaka queen Prabhāvatīguptā, daughter of Candragupta II. The inscription records an order issued by the queen from the 'foot of Rāmagirisvāmin (*Rāmagirisvāmin pādamūlāt*).[85] As Kālidāsa too pays homage to the hills of Rāmagiri (modern Ramtek, near Nagpur) in the *Meghadūta* and describes them as marked by the footprints of Raghupati,[86] it has been argued that this clearly shows the prevalence of the Rāma cult in the fifth century.[87] But it is more likely that some natural crevice or a spot on the hill was supposed to have been marked by Rāma's footprints during his southern wanderings and was worshipped as such. The worship seems to have been confined to the sacred spot and was local. It need not be interpreted as indicative of a widespread cult of Rāma. Many such sacred spots, worshipped initially by local aboriginal tribes, are known to have been absorbed in Śaiva and Vaiṣṇava systems of worship.[88] Exploration of the site of Ramtek has revealed as many as five structures of Vaiṣṇava affiliation going back to the Vākāṭaka times, but none of these shows any trace of the Rāma cult.[89] These were dedicated to the Man–Lion and the Boar forms of Viṣṇu, the two most popular incarnations of the Gupta age. The worship of Rāma, Lakṣmaṇa and Sītā at Ramtek at present in modern structures is no proof of its existence in the Vākāṭaka period.[90] According to a local legend, the site derives its sanctity from the fact that Rāma had killed the śūdra ascetic Śambūka engaged in austerities on this hill.[91] With the growing popularity of *Rāmāyaṇa* and *Mahābhārata* stories, many places in India came to be associated with various incidents connected with the characters of these epics, and are now part of the folklore narrated by tourist guides. However, for the origin of the Rāma cult we shall have to look for more reliable evidence.

II

There is a well-known couplet in Hindi which says that *bhakti* (devotion to the deity) originated in the Draviḍa country, and Rāmānanda brought it to the North, and Kabīr spread it to seven islands and nine divisions.[92] Perhaps it is inspired by the story given in the *Bhāgavata Purāṇa-Māhātmya* which allegorizes the sacred geography of the *bhakti* movement.[93] Personifying *bhakti* as a female, the *Māhātmya* narrates that Bhakti was born in the Draviḍa country, grew up in Karnataka, was honoured at a few places in Maharashtra, but when she reached Gujarat she became old along with her two sons Jñāna and Vairāgya. Now she has come to Vṛndāvana where she has again become young and youthful. Apparently, the story attributes the origin of *bhakti* to the Āḷvār saints of the Draviḍa country whose period of activity extends from the sixth to the tenth century CE. It is said to have been nurtured in Karnataka, no doubt with the Vaiṣṇava *ācāryas* who, beginning with Rāmānuja in the eleventh century to Nimbārka and Madhvācārya in the thirteenth century, expounded the doctrine of *bhakti*, modifying the doctrine of non-duality (*advaitavāda*) and cosmic illusion (*māyā*) of Śaṅkara. In Gujarat, the most notable Vaiṣṇava poet Narsi Mehta lived in the fifteenth century, and is said to have been deeply influenced by the teachings of the Maharashtrian *nirguṇī* saints Jñāneśvara and Nāmadeva. Moreover, Jainism had a strong hold on medieval Gujarat and its influence is seen on the Vaiṣṇava poets too. So the narrative relates that although Bhakti lived here and there, at a few places in Maharashtra, when she reached Gujarat, she became old along with her two sons and her body was mutilated. In the first half of the sixteenth century the region of Mathurā–Vṛndāvana had become an important seat of the followers of Vallabhācārya and Caitanya, whose worship of Rādhā and Kṛṣṇa was imbued with ceremonials and emotional mysticism bordering on the erotic. Hence, according to the composer of the *Bhāgavata-Māhātmya*, Bhakti was rejuvenated in Vṛndāvana. It seems that he wrote some time in the sixteenth century CE. But the significant question is: why does he trace the origin of *bhakti* to the Draviḍa country and not Kurukṣetra where Kṛṣṇa himself taught *bhakti* through the *Bhagavadgītā*, the original source of Vaiṣṇava *bhakti*? Does this mean that recognition of the *Bhagavadgītā* as the Hindu text par excellence was a gift of British Orientalism readily adopted by the Hindu elite, beginning from Rammohan Roy to Mahatma Gandhi, although the earlier indigenous tradition traced the roots of *bhakti* idealogy and practice to the Āḷvārs?[94]

This brings us to the question, what were the distinctive features of Āḷvār *bhakti* which became the distinguishing characteristic of Vaiṣṇava *bhakti* in later times and which can hardly be traced to the *Bhagavadgītā*? It is well known that the activities of the Āḷvārs gave impetus to temple worship; they sang in praise of many temples and cult-spots as haunts of their favourite deities. Worshipping images in temples and elaborate ceremonials constitute an important feature of the *saguṇa* stream of *bhakti*.[95] But it is hardly traceable to the *Bhagavadgītā* which countenances image worship; nevertheless, unlike the Vedic *yajña* ritual whose performance it approves, it makes no mention of temple ceremonials.[96] No doubt the god of the *Gītā* declares that even those who worship other gods with faith are in fact worshipping him, albeit not in the proper mode;[97] and he enjoys whatever the pious-minded offer with devotion, leaf, flower, fruit or water.[98] But this is a reference to the cults of folk divinities worshipped in images, trees and sacred spots. As I have shown elsewhere,[99] the *Bhagavadgītā* and the remodelled version of the *Bhārata* epic were parts of a project which tried to infuse new life into the crisis-ridden Brahmanical order by appropriating idolatrous folk cults and making them a medium of disseminating the Brahmanical value system. The development would ultimately encourage the building of magnificent temples as expressions of *bhakti*, but the *Gītā* pre-dates this phenomenon.

However, a more important reason for the apparent disregard of the *Bhagavadgītā* as the fountainhead of *bhakti* by the *Bhāgavata-Māhātmya*, is the fact that the character of medieval *bhakti*, beginning with the Āḷvārs down to Caitanya, was highly emotional, ecstatic, sensual and often erotic, a feature that cannot be traced to the *Bhagavadgītā*.[100] The tone of the *Gītā* is of calm intellectual contemplation, quite devoid of emotionalism. It teaches love of the Supreme Being who has a terrifying, all-encompassing (*viśvarūpa*) form but condescends to resume the more bearable four-armed human appearance at the request of his overwhelmed, frightened devotee. A.L. Basham rightly likened the divine grace in the *Gītā* to 'the condescension of a mighty potentate stern and functional'.[101] In fact, in this text 'devotion or loyalty'[102] to god is inextricably linked with the doctrine of *niṣkāma karma*, doing one's duty without any desire for returns. The doctrine, variously interpreted by modern intellectuals like Tilak and Gandhi, is a major contribution of the *Gītā*, expounded apparently for the first time. But in the *Gītā*, it invariably means performance of one's *varṇa* duties, non-performance of which could lead to fearful consequences.[103] Moreover, it is repeatedly stressed that the *varṇa* duties are determined by birth,[104] that these are in accordance with inborn (*svabhāvajam*) qualities and the consequence of past deeds (i.e. deeds performed in previous births). Thus, going beyond the Vedic rituals of *yajña*, which were performed for the fulfilment of various desires, the *Gītā* teaches that whatever one's station in life, one should go on performing one's duties in consonance with it without any desire for reward. And the God of the *Gītā* is the syncretic deity Nārāyaṇa–Kṛṣṇa–Vāsudeva, not Rāma Dāśarathī,[105] whose cultic worship evolved, as we shall see presently, in the ambience of the South Indian *bhakti* movement.

III

The earliest expression of an exclusivist devotion to Rāma is found in a hymn of Namma Āḷvār (ninth century),[106] wherein he asserts that he takes refuge in the son of Daśaratha alone and none other.[107] Although the cowherd god Kṛṣṇa–Viṣṇu as Māyōn – already celebrated in the classical Caṅkam (Saṅgam) works – was the favourite deity of the Āḷvārs, they have also sung hymns in praise of Rāma. A number of hymns extolling the achievements of Rāma, composed by the early Āḷvārs, Poykai, Pūtattu and Pēy who are generally placed in the sixth century CE, are collected in the *Nālāyira Divyaprabandham* compiled by Ācārya Nāthamuni in the tenth century CE.[108] However, the sentiment of *Rāmabhakti* is most pronounced in the poems of Kulaśekhara Āḷvār who lived in the first half of the ninth century and ruled over parts of Kerala. In his *Perumāl Tirumoḷi* he narrates the entire story of Rāma in eleven decads, using every situation to express a deeply personalized and loving relationship with the deity. The last two decads of this poem express the god's deep concern for the welfare and protection of his devotees, and it is concluded that one can attain union with the Supreme Being through an intense, passionate love.[109] Kamil Zvelebil speaks of Kulaśekhara Āḷvār as the founder of the cult of Rāma in the Tamil country.[110]

Weighty arguments have been put forward to assert that the Āḷvār poets had inherited the traditions of the classical Caṅkam poetry, particularly the *akam* genre depicting tender human love and its intimacies.[111] Zvelebil speaks of 'a direct connection between the idealized and typified love of the *akam* genre . . . and the ecstasies of the eternal love between the soul and the Lord' expressed in the poems of the Śaiva Nayanār and Vaiṣṇava Āḷvār saints.[112] Hardy has shown that 'anthropocentrism' constituted a significant feature of ancient Tamil culture and had led to the visualization of the transcendental Kṛṣṇa–Viṣṇu of the *Bhagavadgītā* as Māyōn, the god who was the ideal 'full man', the *cānror*, excelling both in war and love sport.[113] Hardy writes that Jainism and Buddhism, which had became dominant in the period between the Caṅkam age and the rise of the *bhakti* movement, had aimed precisely at this anthropocentrism, and the Āḷvārs were reacting against the life-denying negative values of those religions. Their positive anthropocentric concept of the deity, which was life-affirming and in tune with the Tamil cultural milieu, appears to have provided the right stimulus for the growth of the cult of Rāma.

Opinions differ regarding the nature of the *bhakti* movement in the South. S. Vaiyapuri Pillai characterized it as a popular movement of protest in religious garb against the growing social inequalities, feudal oppression and exploitation of the masses due to perpetual strife among the southern states. In his view, it was a 'bloodless revolution' which took place in the Tamil country between the seventh–tenth centuries CE.[114] Nilakanta Sastri, on the other hand, views it as a purely religious movement aiming at 'Hindu religious revival', directed against the heretical faiths.[115] He describes the age of the Āḷvārs and the Nāyanārs as the 'golden age of Tamil Hinduism'. A third view regards it as a by-product of the Aryanizing or Sanskritizing trends which were given a major fillip by the Pallava rulers and later by all the major dynasties of Tamilakam, the Coḷas, Pāṇḍyas and Ceras.[116] The movement centred on the temples, which played an important role in disseminating Brahmanical propaganda. It also legitimized the feudal order and had a pronounced feudal-agrarian bias, but did not have much influence among merchants and artisans who were partial to Jainism and Buddhism. It is further argued that the movement had some element of dissent and anti-ritual and anti-caste attitudes in the beginning, but this was soon dissipated. There was a return to orthodoxy by the tenth century.

Zvelebil and Hardy have strongly disputed the view that the *bhakti* movement of the Āḷvārs had a popular 'mass base', and was anti-caste or anti-feudal, even in its initial stages. Analysing the 'class origin' of the poet-saints, Zvelebil shows that the majority of them were of brāhmaṇa and kṣatriya origin, and almost twenty per cent belonged to the Veḷḷāḷa caste which, although dubbed as 'śūdra', was in fact a landowning caste.[117] Among the twelve Āḷvārs, only Tiruppan, who belonged to the Pānar (bard) caste, may be said to have a low-caste origin; even this is contested by Hardy.[118] Pānars are shown in the Caṅkam literature as mixing freely with the warrior-chieftains, eating and drinking in their company. According to Hardy, the hagiographical accounts which look upon Tiruppan as a low-caste devotee whose entry into the Śrīrangam temple needed divine intervention reflect the social attitudes of the late tenth–eleventh centuries when these texts were written. By this time the *varṇa* system had consolidated in the South, the indigenous minstrels had been reduced to a low-caste status and increasing Brahmanization of the *bhakti* stream had taken place.[119] Hardy is of the view that even the language of at least the first three Āḷvārs is 'classical Tamil' (*centamil*) and not the 'spoken dialect' (*kotuntamil*). They composed in the language of the *cānron*, the refined elite.

Both Zvelebil and Hardy look upon the *bhakti* movement as primarily directed against Jainism and Buddhism, re-awakening the Tamil spirit of this-worldly humanism. Zvelebil speaks of the growth of a 'strong Tamil nationalist feeling' in the sixth century CE, which found its political expression in the rise of the Pallavas, and religious and literary expression in the poems of the Āḷvārs. In his view, Jainism and Buddhism were perceived as 'alien', connected with foreign non-Tamil powers, chiefly the Cālukyas, and hence 'inimical' to the 'national self-identification of the Tamil'. Hence, the Pallava and Pāṇḍya kings rejected Jainism and patronized Śaivism.[120]

This thesis of Zvelebil is acceptable only partially. There is hardly any evidence to show that the Cālukyas posed a threat to the Tamil powers in the period preceding the advent of the Āḷvārs, for a reaction to set in. The rise of the Cālukyas of Bādāmī, the Pallavas of Kāñcī (of Sanskrit charters) and the Pāṇḍyas of Madurai took place at about the same time in the sixth century CE. The denunciation of Jainism and Buddhism by Śaiva and Vaiṣṇava *bhakti* poets cannot be explained as an assertion of Tamil national pride, and as forming a subtext of the conflict among the Cālukya, Pallava and Pāṇḍya rulers, for the simple reason that although Jainism had a considerable presence in the Cālukyan kingdom, members of the Cālukyan royal family were generally worshippers of Śiva and Viṣṇu. They built some of the most magnificent temples of the time in honour of these gods at Bādāmī, Paṭṭadakal and elsewhere.[121] Nor would it be proper to interpret the movement with reference to North–South, Aryan–Dravidian tensions and antagonisms, for the *bhakti* imagery was thoroughly imbued with northern and Aryan symbolisms. S.K. Aiyangar was of the view that even the first three Āḻvārs were fully acquainted with Vedic, Purāṇic and other Sanskrit texts.[122] According to Hardy, too, the early Āḻvārs had direct knowledge of the *Bhagavadgītā* and their main thrust was against the ideologies of Jainism and Buddhism, which was accomplished through 'the conscious revival of Caṅkam tradition'.[123] He calls it a 'Tamil renaissance'[124] as well as a strong 'Hindu revival',[125] and suggests that the collapse of the Gupta empire may have resulted in the immigration of large groups of northern intellectuals and religious leaders to the South, accelerating brāhmaṇa–Tamil interaction and providing an incentive to the *bhakti* movement. Nilakanta Sastri too describes the Kaḷabhra interregnum from the close of the Caṅkam age to the rise of the Āḻvārs (250–550 CE) as a 'long historical night'.[126]

However, from the point of view of Tamil literature, the period pre-dating the Āḻvārs can hardly be described as a dark period. Not only were a number of works included in the collection titled 'The Eighteen Minor Works' (*Patinenkīḻkaṇakku*) written during this period, but also the two classic epics, the *Cilappatikāram* and *Maṇimekalai*, composed by a Jaina and a Buddhist poet respectively, as well as the *Peruṅkatai*, the Tamil version of the Sanskrit *Bṛhatkathā*, also authored by a Jaina. It is generally acknowledged that the earlier Tamil literary conventions continue in these works. Zvelebil writes that the *Cilappatikāram* celebrates both love and war 'in the tradition of classical Tamil poetry',[127] and the work mitigates the tragic end of the heroine Kannakī in the typical Indian fashion by her deification and final union with the hero in a divine chariot.[128] So, if one speaks of a 'Tamil renaissance', it would basically be the revival of the anthropocentric spirit of Tamil culture which was celebratory and life-affirming, as opposed to the self-denying world-views of Jainism and Buddhism.

It seems to me that just as a section of the liberal Brahmanical intellectuals, in the centuries preceding and succeeding the Christian era, played a key role in the evolution and consolidation of the Vaiṣṇava *bhakti* movement in the North to meet the challenge of heterodoxy and resolve the crisis faced by the Brahmanical value system by incorporating the worship of folk divinities within a Vedic framework,[129] similarly, the *bhakti* movement of the South spearheaded by the Tamil poet-saints with an elite background successfully integrated local folk cults within a Vaiṣṇava (or Śaiva)[130] framework in order to combat the dominance of Jainism and Buddhism. It is likely that many of the temple deities in whose honour the Āḷvārs composed their songs had folk origins, including the deity of Veṅkaṭam (Tirupati).[131] The difference in the internal structure of *bhakti* as expounded in the *Bhagavadgītā* and that of the Āḷvār poets is indicative of the different cultural background of the leaders of the two movements, but their outlook had a unity which made the two movements part of the same tradition and later allowed its takeover by the brāhmaṇa *ācāryas*. Not much is known of the Kaḷabhras who are described in a Pāṇḍyan inscription as a tribe of evil rulers.[132] They had uprooted many rulers (*adhirājas*) and revoked the land grants to brāhmaṇas (*brahmadeyas*). A Tamil literary tradition speaks of them as having kept the kings of the Cera, Coḷa and Pāṇḍya dynasties in confinement. A Kaḷabhra ruler named Accyuta Vikrānta was a patron of Buddhists and another, a Jaina, had occupied Madurai.[133] According to R.S. Sharma,[134] Kaḷabhras were tribal peasants who had risen in revolt against the Tamil landed powers, and the anti-Brahmanical religions must have played a significant role in polarizing peasants against their oppressors. Their decline would thus mean a revival of the patronage of brāhmaṇas and Brahmanical institutions. Sharma also draws attention to a Pallava grant of the fifth century made by Yuvamahārāja Viṣṇugopa. It records that the prince made the gift of a village named Neḍḍuṅgarāja in the Maṇḍarāṣṭra region, identified with a place in Nellore district of Andhra Pradesh, to a number of brāhmaṇas as a *śāraṇika grāma*, i.e. a refugee settlement.[135] Apparently, these brāhmaṇas must have faced persecution at the hands of the local non-brāhmaṇa population. The fact that the presence of brāhmaṇas and ascendancy of Brahmanism in the Deccan and the South were not entirely through peaceful processes is also shown by a fifth-century inscription of the Vākāṭaka king Pravarasena II. It records the grant of a village named Carmāṅka (near Illichpur in the Vidarbha region) to a thousand brāhmaṇas on the condition that they would not resort to arms, harm other villages or commit treason against the kingdom. If they acted otherwise or assented to such acts, the king would commit no theft in taking away the land.[136] The implied aggressive attitude of the brāhmaṇas who were being pacified in this fashion is all the more significant as the Vākāṭaka kingdom was founded in the third century CE by Vindhyaśakti, a brāhmaṇa of Viṣṇuvṛddha *gotra*, in western Madhya Pradesh or Berar. We may also refer to a sixth-century inscription of Nandivarman Pallavamalla granting two villages named Kumāramangalam and Vennatturaikoṭṭa free of tax to 108 brāhmaṇas.[137] We are told that the grant was made after removing from these villages 'all those whose deeds are offensive to religion'. The editor of the inscription sees in this phrase a reference to the Jainas, but it could have been the aboriginal local population as well. In any case, the practice of dispossessing earlier settlers and giving villages to brāhmaṇas as *vidyābhogam* had become quite common under the Pallavas, whose kingdom was the scene of activity of the early Āḷvārs.[138] The social underpinnings of Vaiṣṇava *bhakti* in the South were clearly Brahmanical, which as a trend becomes even more pronounced with the growth of the Rāma cult.

IV

It is possible to trace the gradual emergence of a full-fledged Rāma cult in the Draviḍa country. As we have remarked earlier, the Āḷvārs sang in praise of local cult-spots sanctified by the presence of their favourite deities. This gave scope for the identification of various places as scenes of events associated with the characters of the *Rāmāyaṇa* and the celebration of existing temples as enshrining the images of Rāma Dāśarathi. For example, Tirumaṅgai and Kulaśekhara Āḷvārs describe the deity installed in the Govindarāja temple within the Naṭarāja temple complex at Chidambaram as lord Rāma being present there along with his devotee Hanumān, and speak of the temple as Citrakūṭa. On the basis of these utterances, R. Nagaswamy concludes that although the Govindarāja temple at Chidambaram at present enshrines an image of Nārāyaṇa in his *śayana* (lying posture) form, at the time of the Āḷvārs it had an image of Rāma Dāśarathī.[139] But it may be pointed out that the Śaiva saint Māṇikkavācagar, who lived in the ninth century and was perhaps a contemporary of Kulaśekhara Āḷvār, has left us a vivid description of the iconography of the famous Naṭarāja and Govindarāja images at Chidambaram. A verse of his well-known poem *Tirukkōvaiyār* describes the Govindarāja image as Nārāyaṇa lying in front of Naṭarāja, absorbed in the contemplation of the foot of Naṭarāja lifted in dance and entreating the latter to grant him the view of his other foot as well.[140] Evidently, even at the time of the Āḷvārs the image in the Govindarāja temple was that of Nārāyaṇa–Viṣṇu in a lying posture, but they visualized it as Rāma attended by Hanumān and described the location figuratively as Citrakūṭa. Such devotional impulses may be seen operating in Central India too, at places such as Rajim[141] and Khajuraho,[142] confirming the hypothesis that with the growing popularity of the Rāma incarnation, certain pre-existing Viṣṇu temples came to be celebrated as Rāma temples.

Clear evidence of the erection of shrines for the Rāma incarnation of Viṣṇu is available from the tenth century CE onwards in the Coḷa and Pāṇḍya kingdoms, which had been the locale of Āḷvār activities. Several inscriptions of the time of the Coḷa king Parāntaka I (907–955 CE) indicate the existence of Rāma temples in his kingdom. The earliest of these, dated in the seventh year of his reign, records a gift of land to the 'Lord of Ayodhyā' (*tiruvāyottiperumāḷ*) of the Kodaṇḍarāma temple in Madurāntakam (present-day Chingleput district).[143] A fifteenth-year inscription of the same king gifts land to the 'Lord of Ayodhyā' situated in Uttaramerur Caturvedimaṅgalam village.[144] A third record issued in the thirty-fourth year of his reign speaks of a gift of ten *kaḷañjus* of gold by the queen Seyyabuvana Sundara-maniyār for the purpose of burning a perpetual lamp in the temple of Śrī-Rāghavadeva, who is said 'to have been pleased to take his stand at Tiruvāyodhi (sacred Ayodhyā) temple at Palavelur in Eyirkoṭṭam'.[145] Another reference to a temple of Rāma as 'sacred Ayodhyā' (*tiruvāyottiyai*) occurs in an inscription of Villavan Mahādevī, the queen of Pārthivendrādhi-pati-varman. She had an image of Rāma set up in the Uttaramerur temple but the inscription is found on the north wall of the Vaikuṇṭha Perumāḷ temple at Uttarāmallur (present-day Chingleput district).[146] A record of the ninth year of the reign of Rājarāja I (922–93 CE) too mentions the reconstruction of a shrine Tiruvaiyotti for the god Rāmadeva-perumāḷ and the consecration of his image.[147]

It is interesting that the Rāma temples are called 'sacred Ayodhyā', lending credence to the view that the concept of Ayodhyā of Rāma was originally mythical, having little to do with modern Ayodhyā in the Faizabad district of Uttar Pradesh. It reminds one of the famous saying of Tulasīdāsa, '*avadha tahān jahan Rāma nivāsū*', 'wherever Rāma resides, that is Ayodhyā'.[148] However, in the beginning it seems that separate subsidiary shrines for Rāma were built within larger Vaiṣṇava temple complexes. The inscriptions of the Coḷa king Rājendra I in the Narasiṃha temple at Ennayiram (South Arcot district) contain numerous references to Rāma or Rāghava, the 'universal king' (*Rāghavacakravartikaḷ*).[149] An interesting record of the twenty-fifth regnal year (1037 CE) of the same king from the Ādikeśava temple at Vadamadurai (present-day Dindigul district) refers to the marriage of goddess Sītā (Nambirāttiyār) with the 'Cakravarti king of the sacred Ayodhyā'. An areca garden was gifted to the goddess as dowry on this occasion.[150] A Rāmasvāmin temple of roughly the same date is also reported to have existed at Sermādevi in Tirunelveli district.[151] In the twelfth century CE a temple of Rāma was built by Malayasiṃha, a feudatory of the Kaḷacuris of Tripurī.[152] However, most of the independent Rāma temples seem to have been constructed in the late medieval period.

V

The inscriptional evidence cited above is substantial enough to dismiss the attempt to link the rise of the Rāma cult to 'Muslim' invasion of India in the twelfth–thirteenth centuries and interpret it as a deliberate design fostered by the 'Hindu' communal consciousness, which divinized the Hindu ruler by identifying him with the Viṣṇu incarnation and demonized the Muslim as the 'other'.[153] Such anachronistic reconstructions are part of a trend in contemporary western scholarship that seeks to sidestep the role of colonial politics in the creation of two homogenized and antagonistic 'Hindu' and 'Muslim' identities, projecting the roots of the battle-cry for 'Hindutva' raised by the Sangh Parivar on to medieval Indian history. However, a repeated mention of the deity as Cakravartī, the universal monarch or the lord of Ayodhyā, no doubt underscores his connection with kingship. Although the Coḷa kings were worshippers of Śiva and constructed magnificent temples in honour of their favourite deity, several of them assumed titles suggestive of their identification with Rāma. Āditya Coḷa (871–907 CE), who claimed to have built several Śiva temples on the banks of the Kaveri, assumed the title 'Kodaṇḍarāma' (bow-wielding Rāma). His son Parāntaka I called himself Sangrāma-Rāghava, i.e. Rāma in battle. He also built a sepulchral temple on the remains of his father at the site of his death at Tondainad near Kalahasti (Chittoor district, Andhra Pradesh) and named it Kodaṇḍarāmeśvara, using his father's title and integrating it with his Śaiva faith.[154] The eldest son of Parāntaka, Rājāditya, too had assumed the title of Kodaṇḍarāma like his grandfather.

Using religious myths and symbols as a device for the glorification of contemporary rulers has had a long history in the Brahmanical tradition, and is not exclusive to Ramology. Ideas regarding the divinity of the king and the divine origin of kingship are traceable to the later Vedic literature.[155] The *Mahābhārata* and the Purāṇas repeatedly state that kings are partial incarnations of Viṣṇu.[156] The notion had become so deeply ingrained in traditional thinking that the *Caitanyacaritāmṛtam* of Kṛṣṇadāsa Kavirāja, a famous work of Bengal Vaiṣṇavism in the early seventeenth century, depicts a Hindu officer of the Muslim court addressing quite naturally his master as 'an unconsecrated *yavana*', a part of Viṣṇu.[157] Clearly, Muslim rulers were not regarded as 'outsiders' but constituted a section of the indigenous ruling class.'[158] However, whereas one cannot push back the Hindu–Muslim divisive ideology to medieval times, there is also no denying that it is wrong to foist a secularist discourse – implying the separation of religion and politics – upon ancient and medieval history, as protection of *dharma* was, in the Brahmanical theory, an important duty of the king,[159] and meant in general the protection of the Brahmanical social order (*varṇāśramadharma*) sanctioned by orthodoxy. The cult of Rāma has played a significant role both in the exaltation of royalty and its legitimization through linkages with the divine ruler Rāma,[160] as well as in the propagation of an elite-oriented Brahmanical ideology.

D.D. Kosambi writes that *bhakti* was the 'basic need in feudal ideology' as society was held together through ties of personal faith, 'even though the object of devotion may have clearly visible flaws'.[161] But all sections of society did not benefit from this ideology and hence protest movements oriented towards Kṛṣṇa-worship grew in Maharashtra. Kosambi cites the examples of the Mahānubhāva and Varkarī sects having a popular base. However, it should be noted that there is one basic difference in the way the cults of Kṛṣṇa and Rāma, the two most popular incarnations of Viṣṇu today, evolved in the Brahmanic tradition. Kṛṣṇa-worship originated from multiple sources; a number of folk divinities were synthesized and identified with the Vedic Viṣṇu to create the personality of the god celebrated in the *Mahābhārata* and the Purāṇas. Hence, representations of Kṛṣṇa were not unilinear but varied, providing ample scope for non-conformist, deviant modes. But the worship of Rāma did not originate in a folk milieu. Vālmīki had created the character of Rāma in the form of an ideal hero who provided a role model for the *varṇa*-based patriarchal society, upholding its norms through a great deal of personal sacrifice; the popularity of the Rāma saga had led to his recognition as an incarnation of Viṣṇu and later to the growth of a cult around him. Hence his worship was closely linked with royalty and the Brahmanical social order.

Both these aspects characterize the narration of the *Rāmāyaṇa* by Kampan, whose epic composition became popular not only in Tamil Nadu, but also in Karnataka and Kerala.[162] He stresses in particular the royal nature of the Rāma incarnation,[163] suggesting a correspondence between the god–king and the earthly ruler, and referring to the reigning Coḷa king indirectly. What is even more pronounced in his work is its Brahmanical orientation. Kampan is said to have belonged to the Uvacca community, a caste of temple priests who are regarded as low-ranking brāhmaṇas in the Dharmaśāstras.[164] But the *Irāmāvatāram* of Kampan reflects a typically Brahmanical world-view, referring with deep reverence at several places to the law code of Manu.[165] The message of devotion to Rāma is closely linked with the authority of the Vedas, the efficacy of Vedic sacrifices and the veneration of brāhmaṇas. We are told that countless gods suffered for having incurred the wrath of the brāhmaṇas and an equal number of gods attained greatness on receiving their compassion. Rāma worships the brāhmaṇas and does their bidding. The brāhmaṇas are superior to the trinity of Brahmā, Viṣṇu and Śiva, and the Five Buddhas. Even fate awaits the command of the brāhmaṇas, so one should always extol them in this birth as well as in the next.[166] It is not surprising that the *Kampa Rāmāyaṇa* was attacked by the protagonists of the Dravidian movement in the early twentieth century.

VI

The Brahmanical appropriation of the fascinating *Rāmāyaṇa* saga did cause some reaction in non-Brahmanical circles. The Buddhists stopped using the Rāma legends in their discourse once Vālmīki's *Rāmāyaṇa* gained wide popularity and Rāma was integrated in the Brahmanical pantheon.[167] But the Jaina response was more combative. The Jaina poets wrote a number of Jaina *Rāmāyaṇas*, broadly retaining the framework of Vālmīki but modifying it in accordance with their own ethical notions. The divine and supernatural elements of the story are largely eliminated, making it more credible. However, these represent the reactive efforts of the literate, rationalist Jaina intelligentsia, and were limited in their impact. Within the Brahmanical fold, the cult of Rāma made major strides. If the late hagiographical Śrivaiṣṇava traditions are to be believed, Raṅganātha Muni, the first of the Śrivaiṣṇava *ācāryas* who collected and canonized the poems of the Āḷvārs, and Rāmānujācārya were great devotees of Rāma, the former composing a *stotra* in honour of the deity and the latter establishing his temple at Tirupati.[168] Medieval Rāmaite literature elevates Rāma to the level of supreme principle, the highest god, a position already accorded to him by the *Kampa Rāmāyaṇa*. Three sectarian Upaniṣads[169] of uncertain date attempt to provide antiquity to his cult and a connection with the ancient Vedic tradition, and the philosophical work *Yoga-vāsiṣṭha* makes use of the character of Rāma to present the model of *jīvana mukta*.[170] The work is also known as *Vasiṣṭha Rāmāyaṇa* although it is a dialogue between the family priest Vasiṣṭha and Rāma, and not a narration of the life-story of the Rāma incarnation.[171]

A thorough weaving of the Brahmanical philosophy and social ethics into the story of Rāma is to be found in the *Adhyātma Rāmāyaṇa*, a work assigned to the fourteenth or early fifteenth century.[172] The text begins with Viṣṇu's decision to incarnate himself as Rāma for killing the demon Rāvaṇa and ends with his return to heaven. Rāma is the same as Viṣṇu, the highest god, worshipped by Śiva and other deities. He is the *brahman* of the Vedas and is all-encompassing as well as unmanifest and without attributes. Almost every character in the story is aware of this fact and each incident provides the author with an occasion to expatiate on Rāma *bhakti*. The Vaiṣṇava tradition regards it as a part of the *Brahmāṇḍa Purāṇa*, but it seems to be an independent treatise incorporating within it several other compositions such as the *Rāmahṛdaya* and the *Rāmagītā*, the latter evidently inspired by the more famous *Bhagavadgītā*.

According to the *Adhyātma Rāmāyaṇa*, the path of Rāma *bhakti* is open to all. Rāma himself teaches the nine modes of *bhakti* to the low-caste female ascetic Śabarī.[173] But for acquiring *bhakti* or the knowledge of liberation, proper performance of one's caste duties is an essential prerequisite. Heedlessness in this regard turned king Nṛga into a chameleon,[174] and Rāma has no hesitation in beheading the śūdra Śambūka for practising austerities, transgressing his *varṇa-dharma*.[175]

The close connection of the cult of Rāma with the Brahmanical social order and its implications are often underplayed by stressing its so-called liberating potential, as it opens the path of *bhakti* to all irrespective of caste and sex. But the entire range of religious literature on Rāma *bhakti* in the *saguṇa* stream has a clear social message. God is universally accessible and grants salvation to all those who worship him with devotion, but he does not allow violation of caste rules and disrespect to brāhmaṇas, regardless of their qualifications. Concern about the religious needs of the śūdra and depressed castes in Ramology figures in the texts written after the thirteenth century, when certain historical factors had made it necessary for the Brahmanical orthodoxy to take note of the so-called śūdra communities and prepare works like *Śūdrācāra Śiromaṇi, Śūdrakṛtyatattva* and *Śūdra Kamalākara* for the benefit of the śūdras, in the tradition of the Smṛtis. It was in this period also that the low-ranking artisanal and trading castes in the North Indian urban centres were in a state of ferment, and drawn into the *nirguṇa bhakti* movement.[176] The impact of these factors made the Brahmanical custodians of Rāma *bhakti* emphasize that the śūdras too could attain final liberation merely by chanting the name of Rāma.[177] An analysis of the subtle variations in the telling of the Śambūka episode in the texts of different periods throws interesting light on the changing Brahmanical attitudes towards the śūdras.

The Uttara kāṇḍa of Vālmīki's *Rāmāyaṇa*, which narrates the killing of Śambūka, is no doubt a later addition to the original epic, but the story was known in the early centuries of the Common Era and is mentioned in the *Raghuvaṃśa* of Kālidāsa. In the Uttara kāṇḍa, we are told that when Rāma was ruling over Ayodhyā, a young son of an aged brāhmaṇa died an untimely death.[178] Sage Nārada explained to Rāma that the death was caused by the action of some evil-minded śūdra practising asceticism in violation of the *dharma* rules; the low-born śūdras had no right to perform ascetic rites (*tapaścaryā*). Rāma searched in all directions and finally located the śūdra Śambūka in the south, on the Śaivāla mountain, engaged in severe austerities with the object of attaining godhood and entering heaven with his physical body (*saśarīra*). Rāma promptly cut off his head, for which act the gods praised him and granted him the boon that he could bring back to life the dead son of the brāhmaṇa. However, a later verse tells us that the child revived on account of Rāma acting upon his *dharma*.[179] The purpose of the story is to show Rāma as the ideal ruler committed to the maintenance of *varṇa-dharma*. It provides a concrete example of what the *Bhagavadgītā* repeatedly emphasizes, that the consequence of performing the *dharma* of some other *varṇa* is frightening even if it is done in a better fashion. No concern is shown for the śūdra. He deserves the extreme punishment for his presumptuous ambition and Rāma is praised as śūdra-*ghātin*, killer of the śūdra.

However, on the fate of the śūdra, Kālidāsa[180] gives us additional information. We are told that Śambūka went to heaven, for 'the śūdra by the punishment inflicted upon him by the king himself obtained the position of the virtuous, a position which he could not secure even by his severe austerity, being as it was in violation of the rules of caste'.[181] It is in fact a reiteration of Manu's view that those killed by the king himself are absolved of all sin and go to heaven, and is aimed at the exaltation of kingship.[182] One cannot interpret it in terms of divine grace; the possibility of a śūdra obtaining heaven through *tapas* is clearly ruled out.

The Brahmanical version of the Śambūka incident was not acceptable to the Jaina narrators and the *Paumacariyam*, the earliest of the Jaina *Rāmāyaṇas*, makes Śambūka a *vidyādhara* and son of Candranakhā (Śūrpaṇakhā of the Brahmanical versions), the sister of Rāvaṇa.[183] He is killed by Lakṣmaṇa and not Rāma, who is portrayed as a strict practitioner of the Jaina doctrine of non-violence. But Bhavabhūti in his *Uttararāmacarita* broadly follows Kālidāsa, albeit dramatizing the incident by making the murdered Śambūka reappear in the form of a heavenly person (*divya puruṣa*) singing Rāma's praises for having inflicted on him the punishment which brought glory to him, for 'even death arising from the contact of the good brings salvation'.[184] The śūdra expresses his devotion to Rāma and says that he is greatly indebted to the act of performing austerities as it was this that made Rāma seek him out, a wretched śūdra. Rāma sends him to the Vairāja heaven. Thus, while the socio-religious disabilities of the śūdra are recognized, Rāma is depicted as a compassionate god in human form. Despite carrying out his kingly duty of killing the offending śūdra, his attitude towards Śambūka is humane. This seems to mark the middle stage in the growing popularity of the Rāma incarnation.

The *Adhyātma Rāmāyaṇa* makes a brief reference to the killing of Śambūka, but it is in the *Ānanda Rāmāyaṇa* (fifteenth century) that a significant change in the attitude towards śūdras is noticeable in the way the Śambūka episode is narrated. By this time the intensity of the brāhmaṇa–śūdra antagonism, which is witnessed in the early phases of Brahmanization in the South, is much reduced; in the changed socio-economic environment, with the broad category of śūdra subsuming a number of the so-called clean (*sat*-śūdra) and unclean (*asat*-śūdra) castes, a story which was apparently invented to emphasize the exclusion of the śūdra from what was conceived as the privilege of the upper *varṇas* is reinvented in such a way that its central message becomes incorporative.[185] In Vālmīki's *Rāmāyaṇa*, Nārada explains at length that in the Kṛta age only the brāhmaṇas could practise asceticism, but in the Tretā age even the kṣatriyas did so and in *Dvāpara* the vaiśyas too were allowed to perform *tapa*. But the śūdras have never been allowed to do so; and even in the Kali *yuga*, a śūdra practising *tapa* would be an unforgivable violation of *dharma*. Hence, Rāma is exhorted to seek out the evildoer and punish him for the advancement of his *dharma* and the revival of a brāhmaṇa boy. The theme is further developed in the *Ānanda Rāmāyaṇa*, which tells us that the transgression of the *varṇa-dharma* by the śūdra ascetic caused the death of not only the five-year-old son of the brāhmaṇa couple of

Ayodhyā but of six others as well.[186] These were: the husband of a brāhmaṇa woman from Śriṅgaverapura, a kṣatriya, a vaiśya, an oil presser, the daughter-in-law of a blacksmith and the daughter of a leather-worker (*carmakāra*). The killing of Śambūka revived them all. And before cutting off Śambūka's head, Rāma tells him to ask for a boon. The śūdra wants liberation (*mokṣa*) for not only his own self, but for his entire community. Rāma tells him that the śūdras may achieve salvation merely by reciting his name (*japa*) and chanting it collectively (*kīrtana*). But Śambūka points out that in the Kali *yuga* śūdras will be too ignorant and engrossed in agricultural work and other occupations in order to earn a living, to find time for *japa* or *kīrtana*. Rāma then tells him that in the Kali age the śūdras would attain heaven simply by saying '*Rāma Rāma*' while greeting each other, and Śambūka will go to heaven because he is killed by the god himself. Thus, the hostile attitude towards śūdras reflected in the earlier versions is subdued in the *Ānanda Rāmāyaṇa*, a text which was freely used for popular religious discourses and recitals at *kīrtans* and *kathā* performances.[187]

However, the merit of chanting the Rāma name is emphasized in the *Adhyātma Rāmāyaṇa* too, a work undoubtedly earlier than the *Ānanda Rāmāyaṇa*. It relates that Vālmīki was originally an evil brāhmaṇa keeping the company of Kirātas and thieves, and behaving like a śūdra. But he was transformed into a great sage and poet, the composer of the *Rāmāyaṇa*, by reciting the name of Rāma backwards as '*marā-marā*' for thousands of years, on the advice of the seven sages. It was apparently in reaction to such assertions that Kabīr said, 'the *paṇḍita* is preaching a false doctrine. If people could attain salvation merely by uttering Rāma, one would taste sugar merely by saying "sugar".'[188]

Kabīr is often, quite wrongly, regarded as a *bhakta*-saint of the Vaiṣṇava stream. This is apparently for two reasons. Legend makes him a disciple of Rāmānanda, and he often speaks of god as 'Rāma', although he has said very clearly that his god is not the son of Daśaratha but formless and without attributes.[189] He refutes that god had ever incarnated himself as the son of Daśaratha and killed the king of Laṅkā.[190] The historicity of the story that he was trampled on by Rāmānanda who gave him the *Rāma-mantra* on the steps of the bathing ghat in Vārāṇasī is doubtful.[191] Whereas Rāmānanda belonged to the fourteenth century, Kabīr is generally placed in the fifteenth century.[192] It seems that the former, the founder of the Rāmānandī sect, had become so famous as a radical social reformer that later hagiographers invented this story to give a greater legitimacy and respectability to Kabīr and his followers. But the fundamental principle of Vaiṣṇavism is the doctrine of incarnation in which the central place is occupied by the deity of one's sectarian choice, such as by Nārāyaṇa for the Vaiṣṇava followers of Rāmānuja and by Rāma for the Rāmānandīs. This doctrine is firmly rejected by Kabīr. And Kabīr does not use only the word 'Rāma' for his god but all the words current in his time – Allah, Khuda, Karim, Kṛṣṇa, Govinda, Nirañjana, Nātha and so on – but he uses them in a strictly monotheistic sense.

The earliest use of 'Rāma' for god in a monotheistic sense may be traced to the Tamil Siddhas. In the tenth century, Śivavākkiyar uses both 'Rāma' and 'Śiva' to refer to the eternal, omnipresent god, who is described almost exclusively in negative terms.[193] Revolting against Brahmanical orthodoxy, he condems image worship, repudiates the authority of the Vedas, and rejects the caste system and the theory of transmigration. The usage of 'Rāma' as a general word for god seems to have been facilitated by the fact that in contemporary Brahmanical literature, like the *Kampa Rāmāyaṇa* and the sectarian Upaniṣads, Rāma is no longer looked upon as a partial incarnation of Viṣṇu but described as *parama-brahma*, who is beyond activity, immanent as well as transcendent, and beyond the reach of human experience. The *Bhāgavata Purāṇa* tried to synthesize the emotional *bhakti* of Kṛṣṇa with the *advaita* of Śaṅkara. Similar attempts were made by the Brahmanical preachers of Rāma *bhakti* in the *Yoga-vāsiṣṭha*, the *Adhyātma Rāmāyaṇa* and similar other texts. It was this growing religious significance of the term 'Rāma' that led to its general use to refer to god.

There is a tradition that the *Adhyātma Rāmāyaṇa* and the *Agastya Saṃhitā* (a text apparently written for the use of *pujārīs*, priests, of Rāma temples) were brought to the North by Rāmānanda, who came from South India. However, internal evidence of the two texts goes against this supposition.[194] It has been suggested that the *Adhyātma Rāmāyaṇa* was an independent treatise and was adopted by the Rāmānandīs, as its 'scripture' based on *advaita* philosophy is a later attempt to give their sect Brahmanical legitimacy.[195] This seems quite plausible. The *Bhaktamāla* of Nābhādāsa makes Rāmānanda a disciple of the Śrīvaiṣṇava teacher Rāghavānanda, who came to Vārāṇasī from the South and initiated Rāmānanda into Rāma *bhakti*. However, Rāmānanda did not strictly adhere to Śrī Vaiṣṇavism and is reputed to have been a radical reformer who did not differentiate between his brāhmaṇa and non-brāhmaṇa followers, and made them dine together, breaking the taboo on commensality.[196] He also used the vernacular language to propagate his creed among the masses. Although he has been attributed the authorship of a number of Sanskrit works, two of his poems included in the *Guru-grantha-saheb* are in Hindi.[197]

VII

There was a strong resistence to the use of vernacular languages for religious narratives in orthodox Brahmanical circles, and a verse of uncertain authorship commonly cited in this connection asserts, 'whoever listens to the eighteen Purāṇas and the story of Rāma in the vernacular language, would be condemned to Raurava hell'.[198] Even the *Ānanda Rāmāyaṇa*, apparently composed for popular recitation, was written in Sanskrit. No wonder that Tulasīdāsa had to face stiff opposition from the orthodox *paṇḍits* of Vārāṇasī for writing his narrative in the vernacular. Nevertheless, the period from the fourteenth to the sixteenth century saw the flowering of *Rāmāyaṇas* in almost all the major regional languages. Some of these seem to have been inspired by the human drama inherent in the Rāma story, but most were deeply coloured with the sentiment of *bhakti* as well, indicating the growing popularity of the Rāma cult among the common people.[199] Tulasīdāsa was not the first to write a *Rāmāyaṇa* in Hindi. Before him, some time in the fifteenth century, Viṣṇudāsa had rendered a translation of Vālmīki's *Rāmāyaṇa* in Hindi using the *caupāyī* metre that was later adopted so successfully by Tulasī in his *Rāmacaritamānasa*. However, in terms of poetic genius, lyrical quality and impact, the *Rāmāyaṇa* of Tulasī is unparalleled. In order to bring out the social significance of its immense popularity, one will have to examine the value-structure it reflected and which it also helped shape.

It is often said that Tulasīdāsa was not a social reformer but a poet, a saint and devotee of Rāma par excellence. Nevertheless, he did not write only for self-satisfaction or the liberation of his own soul. His societal concerns find a clear expression in his writings. He begins the *Rāmacaritamānasa* with a prayer to Śiva and Pārvatī so that his poetic composition in the varnacular language would have the effect of making all those who listen or recite it devotees of Rāma, devoid of the sins of the Kali age, and transform them into 'blessed beings'.[200] Along with the message of Rāma-*bhakti* there runs the message of an unquestioning acceptance of the hierarchies of caste and the patriarchal family. The *Rāmacaritamānasa* conveys an explicit subtext of belief in the natural, inborn superiority of the *dvijas* (meaning the brāhmaṇas), and the innate and intrinsic inferiority of those who are born as śūdras or women. Tulasīdāsa repeatedly vents his anger against those who are *vipra-drohī*, or hostile to brāhmaṇas. The fire provoked by the hostility to brāhmaṇas is even more destructive than the *vajra* weapon of Indra, the trident of Śaṅkara, the rod of Yama and the discus of Hari.[201] A person who reviles a brāhmaṇa is condemned to many hells and is finally born as a crow.[202] Rāma himself preaches to all his subjects including Vasiṣṭha and other sages, in the Rāmagītā section, that there is nothing so meritorious in this world as worshipping the feet of brāhmaṇas with complete dedication of mind, action and speech.[203] The Uttara kāṇḍa of Tulasi's *Rāmacaritamānasa* is quite different from Vālmīki's Uttara kāṇḍa. It does not speak of the killing of Śambūka and the banishment of Sītā, but mentions the birth of Lava and Kuśa briefly and presents a blissful picture of Rāma's kingdom and his family life. The story ends here; what follows is a clear exposition of the poet's social outlook and purpose, a lengthy description of the Kali age when religion and sacred texts disappear, and arrogant persons bring into existence numerous sects having no scriptural sanction and prompted by their own imagination.[204]

Hazari Prasad Dwivedi has convincingly argued that Tulasīdāsa is not only aware of Kabīr and his teachings, but has repudiated him strongly in vitriolic language.[205] In an obvious reference to Kabīr's assertion that the god Rāma was not the son of Daśaratha and had never incarnated himself, Tulasī remarks that it is only ignorant, blind, crooked, lascivious and hypocrite persons who say that the Supreme God Rāma is different from the son of Daśaratha.[206] The attributeless (*nirguṇa*) Rāma was born as the son of Daśaratha in the family of Raghu for the love of his devotees, for the well-being of the brāhmaṇas, cows and gods, and for the destruction of the wicked and protection of the Vedic religion.[207] For Tulasīdāsa, there is no difference between *nirguṇa* and *saguṇa* Rāma, it is one and the same Supreme Being, who is celebrated in the Vedas and pervades the entire universe.

However, Tulasī's ire against Kabīr is not merely over differences in the conceptualization of god. It stems from their divergent social perspectives and their different locations. Kabīr came from a depressed weaver caste, and must have had personal experience of the demeaning exploitative caste system and religious establishments – Hindu as well as Muslim. He is critical of both. Tulasī, on the other hand, was a pious brāhmaṇa who had to suffer persecution at the hands of the orthodox paṇḍits of Vārāṇasī, jealous of his popularity and fame. His outburst against his persecutors shows that even in his pique his reference points were the caste system and the Brahmanical order.

> Some call me a cheat, some others an *avadhūta* (an ascetic who has renounced all worldly attachments and norms), some say I am a Rajput and some others call me a Jolāhā (a low Muslim weaver caste). My name is Tulasī and I am a slave of Rāma. Let anyone say what he feels like. I am not asking anyone to give his daughter in marriage to my son! I am not ruining anybody's caste! I shall beg for my food and sleep in a mosque but shall have nothing to do with such people.[208]

Respect for the caste hierarchy and its rules despite the irrelevance of caste status in the pursuit of liberation has been the essential feature of Vaiṣṇavism from its first exposition in the *Bhagavadgītā*, and Tulasī had thoroughly imbibed this upper-caste attitude. No doubt the main message of the *Rāmacaritamānasa* is complete devotion and surrender to God, but along with this is conveyed a moral code of conduct which is Brahmanical and patriarchal; and the *Rāmāyaṇa* story provides examples for every situation in life, conforming to these norms. Celebration of the patriarchal joint family had a strong appeal to all classes in medieval times, whether they were peasants, artisans or belonged to the upper castes or nobility, as there was nothing in the material milieu which could have encouraged subversion of the long-established subordination of the female sex.

Caste identities depended on it. The image of Rāma as an ideal family man (*gṛhastha*) was further buttressed by the *Rāmacaritamānasa*, although it seems that even earlier Rāma was never worshipped singly and was always accompanied by at least Lakṣmaṇa and Sītā.[209] The *mūla mantra* for worshipping Rāma, as given in the *Agastya Saṃhitā*, visualizes Rāma in the company of Sītā,[210] and the *Adhyātma Rāmāyaṇa* advises the devotee to complete his worship of Rāma by giving offerings to his companions.[211] The *Vaikhānasāgama* instructs that Rāma should be shown along with Sītā, Lakṣmaṇa and Hanumān.[212] Rāma temples of the early Vijayanagara phase had images of Rāma together with Lakṣmaṇa and Sītā installed in the *sanctum sanctorum* (*garbhagṛha*).[213] The inscriptions of Vijayanagara rulers mention the installation of the image of Rāma along with his family (*saparivārakam*).[214] But the term *parivāra* is used here in the sense of the 'circle' (*āvaraṇa*) of attendants, and not in the sense of a patriarchal household. Rāma is envisioned as a divine king surrounded by his retinue, consisting of his brothers and Sugrīva, Hanuman, Vibhīṣaṇa, Aṅgada and Jāmbavant. Such representations suggest a homology between the divine ruler and the earthly ruler. However, the celebration of the *gṛhastha* (householder) Rāma in folk songs and popular narrations mentioned by Tulasī[215] is accomplished at a different level. Tulasīdāsa also wrote *Rāmalalā Nahachū* (the ceremonial paring of Rāma's nails) and *Jānakī Maṅgala* (the marriage of Jānakī) in the style of folk songs sung on such occasions. This aspect of the Rāma story added colour to the life of the common people and was an important factor contributing to the popularization of the Rāma cult, which, through the *Rāmacaritamānasa*, spread social values essential for the stability of a caste society based on the subordination of women. It is said that already in the lifetime of Tulasīdāsa his work had acquired a sacred character and its recitation was deemed holy. It encouraged the construction of *Thākurbāḍī* (literally, the house of god) shrines containing images of Rāma and his family, often including his favourite attendant and devotee Hanumān as well, attached to the residences of the rich and well-to-do people. But this aspect of the cult of Rāma needs further investigation.

Notes

1 *Bhagavadgītā* (tr. Hill), p. 138.
2 *Bhagavadgītā* (ed. and tr. S. Radhakrishnan), X.40.
3 Vijay Nath, *Purāṇas and Acculturation*, chapters 1 and 2.
4 R.S. Sharma, 'Material Milieu of Tantricism'; R.S. Sharma, 'Economic and Social Basis of Tantrism', in *Early Medieval Indian Society*, chapter 8.
5 R.S. Sharma, 'Economic and Social Basis of Tantrism', p. 264.
6 An attempt to reconstruct the *Jaya Saṃhitā* or the Ur *Mahābhārata* has been made by Keshavram K. Shastri in *Jaya Saṃhitā*.

[7] *Āśvalāyana Gṛhyasūtra*, III.4.4.

[8] V.S. Sukthankar, 'The Bhṛgus and the Bhārata'; V.S. Sukthankar, *On the Meaning of the Mahābhārata*. According to several Purāṇic accounts, the god Viṣṇu had to descend on earth taking the form of an *avatāra* due to a curse of the sage Bhṛgu. See Camille Bulcke, *Rāmakathā*, p. 264. Also see Pradeep Kant Choudhary, *Rāma with an Axe*, pp. 167–68, 176 note 115.

Choudhary contests Sukthankar's thesis that the Bhārgava clan played a specific role in the remodelling of the *Bhārata*, and quotes N.J. Shende's article, 'The Authorship of the Mahābhārata', to assert that statistically the *Mahābhārata* contains more references to the members of the clans of Aṅgirasas and Vāsiṣṭhas than of Bhṛgus, and the text could not have been the property of one clan (ibid., pp. 115ff.). However, giving the Bhārgavas a seminal role in its remodelling does not mean excluding other Brahmanical myths, reworkings and interpolations. It is worth noting that the *Manusmṛti*, an authoritative text of post-Vedic neo-Brahmanism, is also known as the *Bhṛgu Saṃhitā*. The composite group of Bhṛgu–Āṅgirasas is specially linked with the development of the *itihāsa–purāṇa* tradition. See V.S. Pathak, *Ancient Historians of India*, p. 12.

[9] Recently, James Hegarty has analysed the *saṃvādas* embedded in a few episodic narratives of the *Mahābhārata*, such as the Nakula–Yudhiṣṭhira *saṃvāda* in the Āśvamedhika parva and the *saṃvāda* between the Sādhyas and the Swan in the Udyoga parva, repeated again in the Śānti parva. He writes that these texts mobilize 'the Vedic past in order to contextualize, and lend a certain authority to, a rather new set of religious ideas', at the same time achieving 'the conservative goal of protecting and underscoring, the status of the Veda (and by extension the brāhmaṇas)'. James Hegarty, 'The Plurality of the Sanskrit Mahābhārata and of the Mahābhārata Story'.

[10] For the dates of the *Bhagavadgītā* and the Nārāyaṇīya, a section of the *Mahābhārata*, see Suvira Jaiswal, *The Origin and Development of Vaiṣṇavism*, pp. 13–16.

[11] To cite a few, H. Jacobi, *Das Rāmāyaṇa*; *Uttararāmacarita* (ed. S.K. Belvalkar); and Camille Bulcke, *Rāmakathā*, pp. 87ff.

[12] Partha Chatterjee, 'Claims on the Past: The Genealogy of Modern Historiography in Bengal'. Chatterjee refers to Tarinicharan Chattopadhyaya's *Bhāratavarṣer Itihāsa*, first published in 1858, which describes how the South was covered with forests and inhabited by uncivilized tribes in the time of Rāma Candra, who was the first to hoist the Hindu flag in that part of India.

[13] Robert P. Goldman, *The Rāmāyaṇa of Vālmīki*, p. 28.

[14] K.A. Nilakanta Sastri, *Development of Religion in South India*, p. 12.

[15] R.S. Sharma, *Communal History and Rāma's Ayodhyā*, p. 21.

[16] Radhakrishnan wrote: 'It is forgotten that religion as it is today, is itself the product of ages of changes and there is no reason why its forms should not undergo fresh changes so long the spirit demands it.' S. Radhakrishnan, *Indian Philosophy*, p. 777. However, in my view, significant changes are rooted in their social context.

[17] *Adhyātma Rāmāyaṇa* (critical edition), II.4.76. The verse is also found in the *Uttararāghava* (sarga V.48) of the fourteenth century CE, quoted in Camille Bulcke, *Rāmakathā*, p. 153.

[18] A.K. Ramanujan, 'Three Hundred Rāmāyaṇas', p. 25.

[19] Camille Bulcke, *Rāmakathā*, p. 69.

[20] Ibid., pp. 72, 77.

[21] H.C. Raychaudhuri, *Political History of Ancient India*, pp. 114, 170.

[22] In the *Atharvaveda*, X.2.31–33, it is called a *pura* of the gods with eight circles and nine gates and enclosed all around by light. The verse is repeated in the *Taittirīya Āraṇyaka*, I.27.2–3. The *Saṃyukta Nikāya* (III.140 and IV.179, quoted in K.T.S. Sarao, *Urban Centres and Urbanization as Reflected in the Pāli and Sutta Piṭakas*, pp. 92, 121) tells us that the Buddha visited

the city twice, but locates it at the sacred river Gangā and not Sarayū (ibid., p. 92). The early Jaina canonical literature mentions frequently the city of Sāketa in realistic terms, but speaks of Aojjha (Ayodhyā) only once when it is said to be the capital of the north-western district Gandhilavati of the mythological country of Mahāvideha (Hans Bakker, *Ayodhya*, p. 3). Bakker's meticulous study of this city has convincingly established its origin as a mythological place which was later, perhaps some time in the Gupta period or a littler earlier, identified with the historical city of Sāketa; the process was simultaneous with the deification of the hero of the *Rāmāyaṇa*.

[23] K.T.S. Sarao, *Urban Centres and Urbanization as Reflected in the Pāli and Sutta Piṭakas*, p. 92.

[24] Hans Bakker, *Ayodhya*, p. 10.

[25] *Yuga Purāṇa*, verses 47–48, 58–59.

[26] *Raghuvaṃśa*, 5.31, 13.79, 14.13, and *Brahmāṇḍa Purāṇa*, 3.54, quoted in Hans Bakker, *Ayodhya*, p. 12 note 2.

[27] B.B. Lal, *Indian Archaeology 1976–77*, pp. 52–53; B.B. Lal, *Indian Archaeology 1979–80*, pp. 76–77; A. Ghosh, ed., *An Encyclopaedia of Indian Archaeology*, vol. II, pp. 31–32.

[28] *The Vālmīki-Rāmāyaṇa* (critical edition), ed. Bhatt and Shah.

[29] H.D. Sankalia, *Rāmāyaṇa: Myth or Reality*? Although critical of Sankalia's view, D.C. Sircar remarks that in the primitive conditions described in the *Rāmāyaṇa*, it would have been utterly impossible for a party of three persons travelling to Śri Laṅkā (Ceylon) from Faizabad district in Uttar Pradesh to come back to the place alive. D.C. Sircar, '*Rāmāyaṇa* in Inscriptions'. Also see D.P. Mishra, *The Search for Laṅkā*. Mishra locates Lanka somewhere in the Godavari delta.

[30] Sheldon Pollock, 'The Rāmāyaṇa Text and Critical Edition', pp. 91–92.

[31] *Srimadvalmīkīya Rāmāyaṇa* (Gītā Press edition), I.4.2; Robert P. Goldman, *The Rāmāyaṇa of Vālmīki*, p. 285 note.

[32] Camille Bulcke, *Rāmakathā*, p. 71. J.L. Brockington (*Righteous Rāma: The Evolution of an Epic*) is of the view that the *Rāmāyaṇa* arrived in its present form through five stages of evolution. The core consisted of the Ayodhyā and Yuddha kāṇḍas, which constitute a fairly homogeneous composition.

[33] Bulcke dates it towards the end of the third century CE, but V. Raghavan ('The Ramayana in Sanskrit Literature', p. 5) and H.B. Sarkar ('The Migration of the Rāmāyaṇa Story to Indonesia and Some Problems Connected with the Structure and Contents of the Old Javanese Rāmāyaṇa', pp. 103–04) date it a century earlier.

[34] Raghu Vira and Chikyu Yamamoto, *Rāmāyaṇa in China*, p. 27.

[35] Suvira Jaiswal, *The Origin and Development of Vaiṣṇavism*, p. 141.

[36] Many scholars hold this view. See, for example, Dineshchandra Sen, *The Bengali Rāmāyaṇas*; M.A. Mehendale, 'Language and Literature', p. 254; H.B. Sarkar, 'The Migration of the Ramayana Story to Indonesia and Some Problems Connected with the Structure and Contents of the Old Javanese Ramayana', pp. 162–63; Romila Thapar, *Exile and the Kingdom*, pp. 7ff.

[37] Camille Bulcke, *Rāmakathā*, pp. 72–73.

[38] *Jātakas*, edited by V. Fausböll, vol. VI, p. 558.

[39] Buddha's dialogue with the brāhmaṇa Ambaṭṭha, *Dīgha Nikāya*, vol. II, pp. 92–97. For more details, see chapter 2 above, endnote 44.

[40] Suvira Jaiswal, The *Origin and Development of Vaiṣṇavism*, pp. 68–70, 141–43.

[41] Ibid., p. 69. Kulke *et al.* point out that a relief of the Kuṣāṇa period showing Ekanaṃśā standing in the middle with Kṛṣṇa and Balarāma on either side is preserved in the Karachi Museum, Pakistan. Anncharlott Eschmann, Hermann Kulke and Gaya Charan Tripathi, eds, *The Cult of Jagannath and Regional Tradition of Orissa*, p. 180. The deity is apparently mentioned as Añjanā-devī, the black goddess, elder sister of Baladeva and Vasudeva, in the *Ghaṭa Jātaka* (*Jātakas*, no. 454).

[42] Camille Bulcke, *Rāmakatha*, pp. 259–60.

[43] *Skanda Purāṇa*, Utkala khaṇḍa, chapter 19, verse 117.

[44] Sarva Daman Singh quotes a number of examples of brother–sister marriage from Jaina canonical literature to argue that the practice was quite common at one point of time. Sarva Daman Singh, *Polyandry in Ancient India*, p. 145 note 2.

[45] Albrecht Weber, *On the Rāmāyaṇa*.

[46] Sītā remained in captivity of Rāvaṇa for twelve months. *The Vālmīki-Rāmāyaṇa* (critical edition), III.46; *Srimadvalmīkīya Rāmāyaṇa* (Gita Press edition), III.56.24–25. Several scholars, such as Jacobi, Winternitz and Bulcke, are of the view that in the original composition of Vālmīki, Lakṣmaṇa was not married. Camille Bulcke, *Rāmakathā*, pp. 97, 177. Rāma describes him as *akṛtadāra*, 'not married' to Śūrpanakhā (III.17.3).

[47] *The Vālmīki-Rāmāyaṇa* (critical edition), I.65.27.

[48] *Ṛgveda*, IV.57.6–7. See Appendix to chapter 1 above.

[49] For more details, see Camille Bulcke, *Rāmakathā*, pp. 2–18.

[50] *The Vālmīki-Rāmāyaṇa* (critical edition), VI.05.16. For a comparison of Rāma with Indra, see Frank Whaling, *The Rise of the Religious Significance of Rāma*, chaper 8.

[51] A.K. Ramanujan, 'Three Hundred Rāmāyaṇas, Five Examples and Three Thoughts on Translation'; Paula Richman, *Many Rāmāyaṇas*. Also see, Paula Richman, *Questioning Rāmāyaṇas*.

[52] Rama Kant Shukla, *Jainācārya Raviṣeṇa Kṛta Padma-Purāṇa*, p. 32.

[53] A verse in the Jacobi edition claims it is composed in the first century CE, but it is evidently spurious. Suvira Jaiswal, *The Origin and Development of Vaiṣṇavism*, pp. 23–24. For recent views, see K.R. Chandra, *A Critical Study of Paumacariyam*.

[54] Camille Bulcke, *Rāmakathā*, p. 53.

[55] For example, see *Dhūrtākhyāna* written by Haribhadra Śūri (eighth century) in Rajasthan. It is a biting satire on Purāṇic myths.

[56] Camille Bulcke, *Rāmakathā*, pp. 54, 360.

[57] *Paumacariyam*, parva 69; Camille Bulcke, *Rāmakathā*, p. 57.

[58] *Bhāgavata Purāṇa* (Gītā Press edition), X.10.4 and X.10.9.

[59] Kathleen M. Erndl notes that in many North Indian *Rām Līlā* performances, 'The Śūrpaṇakhā episode is a kind of burlesque, to which the (predominantly male) audience responds with ribald jokes and laughter, perhaps again betraying a certain male anxiety about female sexuality.' Kathleen M. Erndl, 'The Mutilation of Śūrpaṇakhā', p. 82.

[60] *Garuḍa Purāṇa*, adhyāya 143, *Padma Purāṇa*, Pātāla khaṇḍa, adhyāya 36, Uttara khaṇḍa, adhyāya 269, quoted in Camille Bulcke, *Rāmakathā*, p. 334.

[61] For an excellent analysis of these, see Kathleen M. Erndl, 'The Mutilation of Śūrpanakhā'.

[62] Camille Bulcke, *Rāmakathā*, pp. 289–302.

[63] *The Vālmīki-Rāmāyaṇa* (critical edition), I.14.18.

[64] Ibid., I.17.6–9.

[65] References are from *The Raghuvaṃśa of Kālidāsa* (ed. and tr. Gopal Raghunath Nandargikar), X.54–56.

[66] Ibid., 105.5–28.

[67] Suvira Jaiswal, *The Origin and Development of Vaiṣṇavism*, p. 77.

[68] Camille Bulcke, *Rāmakathā*, pp. 191–92.

[69] *Śrīyogavāsiṣtharāmāyaṇa*.

[70] T.G. Mainkar, *The Vāsiṣtha Rāmāyaṇa*, p. 246.

[71] Kathleen M. Erndl, 'The Mutilation of Śūrpaṇakhā', p. 82.

[72] For Rasika *sampradāya*, see Bhagavati Prasad Singh, *Rāmabhakti me Rasika Sampradāya*; Bhagavati Prasad Singh, *Rāma Kāvya Dhārā: Anusandhāna Aivam Anucintana*; Philip Lutgendorf, 'The Secret Life of Rāmacandra of Ayodhyā'.

[73] Lutgendorf refers to a Rasika saint Surkisor (*c.* 1600) from the Jaipur region who thought of himself as a brother of king Janaka and of Rāma as his son-in law. Ibid., p. 226.
[74] R.G. Bhandarkar, *Vaiṣṇavism, Śaivism and Minor Religious Systems*, pp. 46ff.
[75] J.F. Fleet, *Corpus Inscriptionum Indicarum*, vol. III, inscription no. 13, lines 17–19.
[76] A.A. Macdonell, *Vedic Mythology*.
[77] *The Raghuvaṃśa of Kālidāsa* (ed. and tr. Gopal Raghunath Nandargikar), XII.70.
[78] Ibid., XV.40.
[79] Ibid., XV.4.
[80] Ibid., X.65, 73.
[81] Quoted in V.S. Apte, *Sanskrit–English Dictionary*, vol. III, *s.v.* Śārṅga.
[82] *Śrīmadvālmīkīya Rāmāyaṇa* (Gita Press edition), I.75.11–20.
[83] Ibid., III.12, 32–36. Also see Camille Bulcke, *Rāmakathā*, pp. 248–329.
[84] The Mandasor inscription of the time of Bandhuvarman dated to 473 CE speaks of Śārṅgin as one whose chest is adorned with the jewel *kaustubha* and who wears a garland of full-blown water lillies. D.C. Sircar, *Select Inscriptions*, vol. I, p. 296, lines 22–23 of the inscription. The description fits Viṣṇu more than Rāma. The stone pillar inscription of Yaśodharman too mentions Śārṅgapāṇi, apparently Viṣṇu, although it is a Śaiva record. J.F. Fleet, *Corpus Inscriptionum Indicarum*, vol. III, inscription no. 33, line 2.
[85] D.C. Sircar, *Select Inscriptions*, vol. I, p. 415, line 1 of the inscription.
[86] *Meghadūta*, pūrva 2, in *Kālidāsa Granthavali.*
[87] Ajay Mitra Shastri, *India as Seen in the Bṛhatsaṃhitā of Varāhamihira*, pp. 131–32.
[88] For the appropriation of some aboriginal cult-spots situated on the hills into Vaiṣṇavism, see chapters 7 and 8 below.
[89] Henry Cousens, *List of Antiquarian Remains in the Central Provinces and Berar*; A.P. Jamkhedkar, 'Ancient Strucures'; Hans Bakker, 'Antiquities of Ramtek Hill, Maharashtra', quoted in Sheldon Pollock, 'Rāmāyaṇa and Political Imagination in India'.
[90] D.C. Sircar, in *The Classical Age*, p. 422.
[91] Quoted by Sheldon Pollock, 'Rāmāyaṇa and Political Imagination in India', p. 266.
[92] *Bhaktī drāviḍa ūpajī, lāye Rāmānanda. Paragat kiyo kabīr ne, sāta dvīpa nau khaṇḍa.*
[93] *Śrīmadbhāgavata-Mahāpurāṇa* (Gita Press edition), Māhātmya, I.38–50.
[94] Rosane Rocher, 'British Orientalism in the Eighteenth Century'.
[95] 'With attributes', i.e. worship of the god in a personified form.
[96] This text supports the performance of Vedic *yajñas* (*Bhagavadgītā*, ed. and tr. S. Radhakrishnan, III.9–15, IV.31–32; IX.16–17), but points out that once the merit earned through the performance of *yajñas* is exhausted in heaven, one has to return to earth and be born again as a mortal; those who worship the Godhead with exclusive devotion are freed forever from the cycle of rebirth (ibid., VIII.16; IX.20–22, 24).
[97] Ibid., IX.23.
[98] Ibid., V.26.
[99] Suvira Jaiswal, *The Origin and Development of Vaiṣṇavism*, pp. 167ff.
[100] Ibid., pp. 116–21.
[101] Quoted in ibid., p. 120.
[102] For the use of '*bhakti*' in the sense of 'loyal' or 'devoted', see R.C. Zaehner, *The Bhagavadgītā*, p. 181, quoted in Friedhelm Hardy, *Viraha-Bhakti*, p. 26.
[103] *Bhagavadgītā* (ed. and tr. S. Radhakrishnan), III.35, XVIII, 47.
[104] Often attempts are made to deny the hereditary nature of *varṇas* in the *Bhagavadgītā* by citing *Bhagavadgītā* (ed. and tr. S. Radhakrishnan), IV.13, which says that the Godhead created the four *varṇas* dividing them on the basis of *guṇa-karma* and it is claimed that the basis of *varṇa* division was *guṇa*, i.e. 'quality' or 'merit' and not birth. But the verse should be interpreted in the light of XVIII.41, which clearly says that the duties (*karmāṇi*) of the four *varṇas* are

divided on the basis of their *guṇas* which originate in their innate nature (*svabhāva-prabhavair-guṇaiḥ*). The following three verses enumerate the inborn (*svabhāvajam*) qualities of the four *varṇas* after which we are told that men achieve final emancipation by performing their own (*varṇa*) duties (verse 45). Also, V.14 tells us that the universe is produced not by the agency of a Supreme Being but because of its 'inherent nature' (*svabhāvastu*). The fact that in the very first chapter of the *Bhagavadgītā* (I.41) evil women (*strīṣu duṣṭāsu*) are held responsible for giving birth to *varṇasaṃkara* children, thus polluting and condemning to hell the entire family, shows the hereditary nature of *varṇa* categories.

105 *Bhagavadgītā* (ed. and tr. S. Radhakrishnan), X.31, while recounting the *divya vibhūtis*, the divine power of the Godhead imbued in each category of objects, declares among the wielders of the weapons (*śastrabhṛtam*), 'I am Rāma'. Some scholars assume (e.g., Camille Bulcke, *Rāmakathā*, p. 511) that it is a reference to Rāma Dāśarathī. But this by no means is certain. The standard list of the ten main incarnations of Viṣṇu mentions three Rāmas – Bhārgava Rāma, Balarāma and Rāma Dāśarathī – all of whom are extolled as great warriors and have their distinctive weapons, namely axe (*paraśu*), ploughshare (*hala*) and pestle (*musala*), and bow and arrow. Considering the role of the Bhārgavas in the redaction of the *Bhārata* epic with the *Gītā* forming its central composition, it is more likely that Rāma in this verse refers to Paraśurāma.

106 I have followed the dates given by K.A. Nilakanta Sastri, *A History of South India*, pp. 426–27.

107 *Tiruvāyamoḷi*, III.68.

108 R. Champakalakshmi, *Vaiṣṇava Iconography in the Tamil Country*, pp. 119, 154, notes 165–67.

109 K.C. Varadachari, *The Āḷvārs of South India*, pp. 76–80; Frank Whaling, *The Rise of the Religious Significance of Rāma*, pp. 98–99.

110 Kamil Zvelebil, *Tamil Literature*, p. 102, quoted in Sheldon Pollock, 'Rāmāyaṇa and Political Imagination in India'.

111 Kamil Zvelebil, *The Smile of Murugan*, pp. 197–98; A.K. Ramanujan and Norman Cutler, 'From Classicism to Bhakti'; Friedhelm Hardy, *Viraha-bhakti*, pp. 241ff., 276, 308.

112 There is a great deal of common ground in the Āḷvār and the Nāyanār world-views, but as the theme of this chapter is confined to Rāma *bhakti*, I focus only on the Āḷvārs.

113 Friedhelm Hardy, *Viraha-bhakti*, pp. 149ff., 233ff., 308.

114 S. Vaiyapuri Pillai, *History of Tamil Language and Literature*, p. 100, quoted in Kamil Zvelebil, *The Smile of Murugan*, pp. 190–91.

115 K.A. Nilakanta Sastri, *A History of South India*, pp. 368–69.

116 M.G.S. Narayanan and Kesavan Veluthat, 'Bhakti Movement in South India'.

117 In the regional social structure, the Veḷḷālas were a peasant community standing only next to the brāhmaṇas. For low-ranking communities it was a matter of status to be recognized as a Veḷḷāla. For changes in the status situation of the so-called śūdra communities in early medieval times, see Suvira Jaiswal, *Caste*, pp. 17–18, 29, 93, 67–70. M.N. Srinivas has shown that although the Okkaligas of Karnataka were a peasant community traditionally ranked as śūdras, in Rampura village they were only next to the brāhmaṇas and highly respected by them. The Okkaligas constituted the dominant community and were strongly opposed to the emancipation of the untouchables. M.N. Srinivas, 'The Dominant Caste in Rampura'.

118 Friedhelm Hardy, *Viraha-bhakti*, pp. 477–78.

119 Refuting Hardy's view, it has been suggested that the brāhmaṇa and upper-caste hagiographers made a 'conscious attempt' to provide a low-caste background to certain Āḷvārs, such as Namma (Veḷḷāla) and Tiruppan (Pāṇar), in order to extend the social base of the *bhakti* movement. R. Champakalakshmi, 'From Devotion and Dissent to Dominance', p. 146. The argument is not only far-fetched, it goes against the well-documented historical trends. The low-caste achievers have been attributed very often a miraculous birth and upper-caste con-

nections for various motives. Suvira Jaiswal, 'Change and Continuity in Brahmanical Religion with Particular Reference to Vaiṣṇava Bhakti', pp. 17–18.

120 Kamil Zvelebil, *The Smile of Murugan*, pp. 196–97.

121 K.A. Nilakanta Sastri, 'The Cālukyas of Bādāmi', pp. 243–44.

122 S.K. Aiyangar, *A History of Tirupati*, vol. I, pp. 133ff.

123 Friedhelm Hardy, *Viraha-bhakti*, p. 300.

124 Ibid., p. 228.

125 Nilakanta Sastri dates the Caṅkam age from *c.* 100 to 250 CE. See K.A. Nilakanta Sastri, *A History of South India*, p. 117.

126 Friedhelm Hardy, *Viraha-bhakti*, pp. 123, 434ff.

127 Kamil Zvelebil, *The Smile of Murugan*, p. 176.

128 This is reminiscent of the *Uttara-Rāmacarita* of Bhavabhūti in which the tragic story of Rāma and Sītā is turned into a happy ending by reuniting them in the last scene.

129 Suvira Jaiswal, *The Origin and Development of Vaiṣṇavism*.

130 For obvious reasons this chapter concentrates on Vaiṣṇavism, but a similar study could be made of Śaivism as well.

131 S.K. Aiyangar refers to a tradition recorded in the Purāṇas that the image of the Tirupati god had been discovered by a śūdra under a tamarind tree. It was a 'self-born' (*svayambhū*) image, not created by human hands. S.K. Aiyangar, *A History of Tirupati*, pp. 295, 375.

132 The Velvikudi grant, quoted in K.A. Nilakanta Sastri, *The Colas*, pp. 101–12.

133 K.R. Venkataraman, 'A Note on the Kaḷabhras'. According to Venkataraman, the Kaḷabhra tribe had come from the Karnataka region. Later, one of the Kaḷabhra chiefs ruling over Toṇḍaināḍu and designated as 'king of Kalandai' was canonized as Kuṟṟuva Nāyanār and included among the 63 Śaiva saints (ibid., p. 99).

134 R.S. Sharma, *Early Medieval Indian Society*, pp. 221–22, 225.

135 Ibid., pp. 67–68.

136 J.F. Fleet, *Corpus Inscriptionum Indicarum*, vol. III, inscription no. 55.

137 Thomas Faulkes, 'A Grant of Nandivarman-Pallavamalla'.

138 T.V. Mahalingam, *Inscriptions of the Pallavas*, pp. 454–59. *Vidyābhogam* was the land assigned as a reward for learning. D.C. Sircar, *Indian Epigraphic Glossary*, *s.v. Vidyābhoga*.

139 R. Nagaswamy, 'Śri Rāmāyaṇa in Tamilnadu in Art, Thought and Literature', pp. 414–15.

140 K.A. Nilakanta Sastri, *The Colas*, p. 643.

141 The Rājīvalocana temple at Rajim (Raipur district, Madhya Pradesh) is today a famous place of pilgrimage for the devotees of Rāma who believe that an idol of Rāma is enshrined there. But A. Cunningham reported that the figure was in fact one of the common four-armed representations of Viṣṇu himself. It held in its hands his typical symbols: the club, the discus, the shell and the lotus. A. Cunningham, *Archaeological Survey of India: A Report*, vol. XVII, p. 322, quoted in Hans Bakker, *Ayodhyā*, p. 64 note 6. The temple has two inscriptions on the left wall of the *maṇḍapa*, one paleographically roughly of the eighth century CE and the other bearing a date corresponding to 3 January 1145. From these we learn that originally a king of the Nala dynasty built a temple of Viṣṇu in the eighth century. Later it was rebuilt in the twelfth century by Jagapāla (also called Jagatsiṃha), a minister of the Kaḷacuri king Pṛthivīdeva of Ratanpura. The twelfth-century inscription speaks of the temple as 'manifesting the splendour of Rāma', and Jagapāla is described as one who read the *Rāmāyaṇa* and listened to the recitation of the Purāṇas, Āgamas, the *Bhārata*, etc. V.V. Mirashi, *Corpus Inscriptionum Indicarum*, vol. IV, part II, pp. 450–57.

142 The so-called Lakṣmaṇa temple at Khajuraho built in 954 CE is in fact a temple of Viṣṇu in his Vaikuṇṭha form. The principal image is a composite of Viṣṇu, Varāha and Narasiṃha. Cf. Devangana Desai, *Erotic Sculptures of India*, p. 49.

The eleventh-century Rāmacandra temple at Khajuraho, also known as the Caturbhuja temple, shows the four-armed male deity holding the female deity in embrace and touching the left part of her breast. The depiction closely resembles the Lakṣmī–Nārāyaṇa images popular in early medieval times. See R. Awasthi, *Khajuraho ki Deva Pratimāyen*, p. 111, plate 36; Kalpana Desai, *Iconography of Viṣṇu*, pp. 31–36. Krishna Deva (*Temples of Khujuraho*, pp. 230ff.) identifies the central image as that of Caturbhuja Viṣṇu in the *lalitāsana* pose. Obviously the imposition of 'Lakṣmaṇa' and 'Rāmacandra' designations on these temples is a later development.

143 *Annual Report of South Indian Epigraphy*, 1896, no. 126; *South Indian Inscriptions* (hereafter *SII*) vol. V, no. 991, quoted in R. Champakalakshmi, *Vaiṣṇava Iconography in the Tamil Country*, p. 122.

144 *SII*, vol. VI, no. 297, quoted in P. Banerjee, *Rāma in Indian Literature, Art and Thought*, p. 215.

145 The inscription is found in the shrine of Kāmākṣī Amman in the Kailāśanātha temple complex. *Annual Report of South Indian Epigraphy*, 1922–23, no. 46, quoted in P. Banerjee, *Rāma in Indian Literature, Art and Thought*.

146 *Annual Report of South Indian Epigraphy*, year 32 of 1898; *SII*, vol. III, no. 193, quoted in R. Champakalakshmi, *Vaiṣṇava Iconography in the Tamil Country*. Pārthivendrādhipativarman is identified with Āditya II who ruled from 955–69 CE.

147 *SII*, vol. XIII, no. 203, in P. Banerjee, *Rāma in Indian Literature, Art and Thought*. Another inscription dated in the thirteenth regnal year of Rājarāja I speaks of a temple of Rāghavadeva situated at Ukkal in Chingleput district, Tamil Nadu; R. Champakalakshmi, *Vaiṣṇava Iconography in the Tamil Country*.

148 *Rāmacaritamānasa* (Gītā Press edition), II.73.2, p. 388. The commentator has rightly interpreted *Avadha* in this verse as Ayodhyā, as is indicated by the context.

149 R. Champakalakshmi, *Vaiṣṇava Iconography in the Tamil Country*, p. 100.

150 *Annual Report of South Indian Epigraphy*, year 1952–53, no. 262. R. Champakalakshmi, *Vaiṣṇava Iconography in the Tamil Country*.

151 Ibid.

152 V.V. Mirashi, *Corpus Inscriptionum Indicarum*, vol. IV, part I, p. 347; P. Banerjee, *Rāma in Indian Literature, Art and Thought*, pp. 189–210ff.

153 Sheldon Pollock, 'Rāmāyaṇa and Political Imagination in India'. According to Pollock, a temple-centred cult of Rāma evolved as a result of Hindu reaction to the 'transformative encounter' with the Ghaznavids, Ghorids, Khaljis and 'perhaps even earlier with the Arabs'; in other words, with Muslims. For a point-by-point demolition of Pollock's thesis, see B.D. Chattopadhyaya, *Representing the Other*, pp. 98–115. Also see, Suvira Jaiswal, 'Rāma-Bhakti', pp. 121–37.

154 K.A. Nilakanta Sastri, *The Coḷas*, pp. 115, 453.

155 U.N. Ghoshal, *A History of Indian Political Ideas*, pp. 25ff.

156 For a detailed discussion of the epic and Purāṇic evidence and also for the claims of the Gupta rulers, see Suvira Jaiswal, *The Origin and Development of Vaiṣṇavism*, pp. 174ff.

157 U.N. Ghoshal, 'Hindu Theories of the Origin of Kingship and Mr. K.P. Jayaswal', p. 384; Suvira Jaiswal, *The Origin and Development of Vaiṣṇavism*, p. 183. Davis points out that the idea that a successful hero was an incarnation of Viṣṇu was so common that even the low-caste Telugu warrior Prolaya with no previous connections to royalty claimed in his inscriptions to be a 'partial incarnation' of Viṣṇu, and the poets made these assertions 'not as metaphors but as facts of identity'. Richard H. Davis, *Lives of Indian Images*, p. 120.

158 Suvira Jaiswal, *Caste*, p. 55. For an interesting account of how officials of the East India Company adopted the traditional role of Indian rulers in the construction of their political authority by 'interacting' or extending patronage to Hindu temples, deities and their custodians, see Richard H. Davis, *Lives of Indian Images*, pp. 203ff.

[159] Ibid., p. 18.

[160] Peter van der Veer speaks of the investment in the pageantry of *Rāma-līlā* by the Bhumihar rājās of Banaras 'as an important aspect of their legitimacy', and points to the linkage between Rāma's divine kingship and Hindu kingship. Peter van der Veer, 'The Politics of Devotion to Rāma', p. 302. For an interesting study of what I view as the use of religious symbols and sacred images for securing and legitimizing political authority in medieval times, see Richard H. Davis, *Lives of Indian Images*, chapter 4.

[161] D.D. Kosambi, *Myth and Reality*, pp. 31–33.

[162] Suvira Jaiswal, 'Rāma-Bhakti', pp. 124–25.

[163] A.G. Menon and G.H. Schokker, 'The Conception of Rāma Rājya in South and North Indian Literature', pp. 611ff.

[164] Suvira Jaiswal, *Caste*, pp. 56–57.

[165] *Kamba-Rāmāyaṇam*, Balā kāṇḍam, chapters 5 and 10, pp. 27, 57 and elsewhere.

[166] Ibid., Ayodhyā kāṇḍam, chapter 2; A.G. Menon and G.H. Schokker, 'The Conception of Rāma Rājya in South and North Indian Literature', pp. 616–17.

[167] Suvira Jaiswal, *The Origin and Development of Vaiṣṇavism*, p. 140.

[168] Bhagwati Prasad Singh, *Rāma Kāvya Dhārā: Anusandhāna Aivam Anucintana*, p. 15; N. Ramesan, *The Tirumala Temple*, pp. 125–26.

[169] *Rāmapūrvatāpanīya, Rāmottaratāpaniya* and *Rāmarahasya Upaniṣads*; Camille Bulcke, *Rāmakathā*, p. 119; Suvira Jaiswal, 'Rāma-Bhakti', pp. 127ff.

[170] V.S. Apte explains it as 'a man who, being purified by a true knowledge of the Supreme Spirit is freed from the future birth and all ceremonial rites while yet living'; *Sanskrit–English Dictionary*, vol. II, *s.v. jīvat*.

[171] The date of the work is uncertain. It is placed between the eighth and twelfth centuries.

[172] The Marathi poet-saint Ekanātha who lived in the sixteenth century refers to the *Adhyātma Rāmāyaṇa* as a modern work; R.G. Bhandarkar, *Vaiṣṇavism, Śaivism and Minor Religious Systems*, p. 48. Camille Bulcke (*Rāmakathā*, p. 132) places it in the fourteenth/fifteenth century.

[173] *Adhyātma Rāmāyaṇa* (critical edition), III.10.1–26.

[174] Ibid, VII.5.2–7.

[175] Ibid., VII.4.22–23.

[176] Irfan Habib, 'Medieval Popular Monotheism and its Humanism'.

[177] P.V. Kane, *History of Dharmaśāstra*, vol. II, part I , p. 158.

[178] *Śrīmadvālmīkīya Rāmāyaṇa* (Gita Press edition), VII.73–76.

[179] Ibid., VII.76.27.

[180] *The Raghuvaṃśa of Kālidāsa* (ed. and tr. Gopal Raghunath Nandargikar), XV.42–57.

[181] Ibid., p. 478; also see note 53 on the same page.

[182] *Manusmṛti*, VIII.318. A slightly changed version of this verse is found in *The Vālmīki-Rāmāyaṇa* (critical edition), IV.18.31. This is, however, considered to be an interpolation. Camille Bulcke, *Rāmakathā*, p. 493 note 1.

[183] *Paumacariyam of Vimalasūri*, parva 43.

[184] *Uttararāmacarita of Bhavabhūti*, Act II.

[185] Suvira Jaiswal, *Caste*, pp. 68–88.

[186] *Ānanda Rāmāyaṇa*, VII.10.50–122.

[187] V. Raghavan, 'The Rāmāyaṇa in Sanskrit Literature', p. 18.

[188] *Paṇḍita bāda badante jhūṭhā. Rāma kahyān duniyā gati pāve khāṇḍa kahyān mukha mīṭhā. Kabīr Vāṇī*, No. 153. Hazari Prasad Dwivedi, *Kabīr*, p. 243.

[189] *Daśaratha suta tinhu loka bakhānā. Rāma-nāma kā maram haī ānā*. Ibid., p. 98.

[190] *Nā Daśaratha ghari autara āvā. Nā laṅkā kā rao satāvā*. Ibid., p. 100 note 1.

[191] Charlotte Vaudeville, *Kabīr*, vol. I, pp. 46ff.; Irfan Habib, 'Medieval Popular Monotheism and its Humanism', p. 84.

[192] Suvira Jaiswal, 'Rāma-bhakti', pp. 127–28.

[193] Kamil Zvelebil, *The Smile of Murugan*, pp. 221–32.

[194] J.N. Farquhar, *Outline of the Religious Literature of India*, pp. 323ff.; Hazari Prasad Dwivedi, *Kabīr*, p. 85.

[195] Frank Whaling, *The Rise of the Religious Significance of Rāma*, pp. 112–13.

[196] An oft-quoted couplet in Hindi attributed to him states, 'Do not enquire to which caste or community one belongs, whoever worships Hari, he belongs to Hari'. It is inscribed over the gateway of the Hanumān Garhi temple at Ayodhyā. Philip Lutgendorf, 'Interpreting Rāmrāj', p. 284 note 18.

[197] Rāmānanda is attributed the authorship of *Ānanda-bhāṣya*, a commentary on the *Brahma-sūtra*, *Śrīmadbhagavadgītā-bhāṣya*, *Vaiṣṇava-matāntara-Bhāskara*, *Śri-Rāmārcanāpaddhati* and several other Sanskrit works. Hazari Prasad Dwivedi, *Kabīr*, p. 83. Nagari Pracharini Sabha, Kashi, has published *Rāmānanda kī Hindī Kavitāyen*. Rajadeva Singh, *Nirguṇa Rāmabhakti aur Dalita Jātiyān*, p. 157.

[198] *Aṣṭādaśa purāṇāni Rāmasya Caritānica. Bhāṣāyām mānavaḥ śrutvā rauravaṃ narakaṃ vrajet.* Quoted in Bhabatosh Datta, 'The Rāmāyaṇa in Bengal', p. 548.

[199] Biswanarayan Shastri notes that the Assamese poet Mādhava Kandali, who wrote the Assamese *Rāmāyaṇa* in the fourteenth century, claimed that he had avoided interpolations and taken only the substance of Vālmīki. Unlike Tulasīdāsa and Kṛttivāsa, he had not imposed 'supreme divinity' on Rāma. Biswanarayan Shastrī, 'Rāmāyaṇa in Assamese Literature', pp. 584–86.

[200] *Rāmacaritamānasa of Tulasīdāsa* (Gita Press edition), I.15.5–6.

[201] Ibid., VII.108.7.

[202] Ibid., 120.12.

[203] Ibid., 44.4.

[204] Ibid., 97ka.

[205] Hazari Prasad Dwivedi, *Kabīr*, pp. 98–101.

[206] *Rāmacaritamānasa of Tulasīdāsa* (Gita Press edition), I.114ff.

[207] Ibid., V.38.1.

[208] *Kavitāvali*, VII.106–07, quoted in Bhagwati Prasad Singh, *Rāma Kāvya Dhārā: Anusandhāna Aivam Anucintana*, p. 237.

[209] G.S. Ghurye, *Gods and Men*, p. 193.

[210] *Agastya Saṃhitā*, 25.19, quoted in Hans Bakker, *Ayodhyā*, part I, p. 6.

[211] *Adhyātma Rāmāyaṇa* (critical edition), IV.4.32–33, p. 99.

[212] Quoted in Sheo Bahadur Singh, *Brahmanical Icons in Northern India*, pp. 83–84.

[213] For example, the Penukoṇḍa temple of Anantapur district, Andhra Pradesh. P. Banerjee, *Rāma in Indian Literature, Art and Thought*, p. 212.

[214] Mangalagiri pillar inscription of Kṛṣṇadevarāya, verses 31–32, 47. P. Banerjee, *Rāma in Indian Literature, Art and Thought*, pp. 210–11.

[215] *Rāmacaritamānasa of Tulasīdāsa* (Gita Press edition), I.10ka mentions the celebration of Rāma and Sītā in the language of the rustics sung and listened to with great attention by the good and the wise.

7

Evolution of the Narasiṃha Legend and Its Possible Sources*

Vedic literature contains no reference to a deity having the form of a lion, or of half-man and half-lion. The solitary exception, the last book of the *Taittirīya Āraṇyaka*, is evidently a later composition, written some time in the early centuries of the Common Era long after the close of the Vedic period.[1] The passage does not show clearly if the god is considered identical with Viṣṇu, but the juxtaposition of the invocation addressed to Narasiṃha with that of Vāsudeva–Viṣṇu is certainly suggestive of an intimate alliance, if not complete identification of the two cults. The *Mahābhārata* speaks of him as an incarnation of Viṣṇu at several places but an exposition of the exploits of this incarnation is given for the first time in the *Harivaṃśa Purāṇa*, which is a supplement to the *Mahābhārata* and is generally placed around 400 CE.[2]

The accounts given in the *Harivaṃśa*,[3] and the *Matsya*[4] and *Padma*[5] *Purāṇas* are almost identical in language and content, and evidently derive from the same source. It is narrated that the demon-king Hiraṇyakaśipu practised severe austerities for 11,000 years and obtained a boon from Brahmā that he would not be vulnerable to men or beasts, not be killed by any weapon, nor would he die during the day or night. Armed with this boon he began to harass the Devas and deprived them of their share in the sacrificial offerings. The Devas prayed to Nārāyaṇa–Viṣṇu who promised them to kill the demon; accordingly he assumed the half-man–half-lion form of Narasiṃha and took the personified Oṃkāra as his assistant. With his assistance Viṣṇu went to the beautiful assembly hall (*sabhā*) of Hiraṇyakaśipu. He saw the demon-king waited upon by thousands of celestial nymphs and the Daityas, such as Bali, Narakāsura and Prahlāda. When Prahlāda noticed the deity, owing to his supernatural vision, he immediately realized that it was not a lion but the supreme deity who had the entire universe within him, and that he had come to annihilate the Daityas.

* Originally presented as a paper at the thirty-fourth session of the Indian History Congress held at Chandigarh, and published in the *Proceedings* volume (1973), pp. 140–51.

Prahlāda expressed this opinion to his father. But Hiraṇyakaśipu, on hearing Prahlāda's words, ordered the Dānavas to capture the lion and, in case of any difficulty, to kill it outright. Thereupon, a terrible fight ensued between the demons and Narasiṃha. Finally, Narasiṃha, supported by Oṃkāra, killed the demon Hiraṇyakaśipu with his nails. The Devas and sages praised him for the feat and Brahmā recited an eulogy in his honour. Afterwards, Viṣṇu went to the northern coast of the Kṣīrābdi ocean, established his Narasiṃha form there and returned to his residence in his original form.

It is significant that in this narrative there is no mention of Narasiṃha emerging out of a pillar; he enters the assembly hall assisted by Oṃkāra in full view of all the demons, including Prahlāda and Hiraṇyakaśipu, and although Prahlāda recognizes Viṣṇu 'hidden within Narasiṃha' and as one who has the three worlds within him, there is no specific mention of his devotion to the deity. Like other demons of Hiraṇyakaśipu's court, he too is surprised and expresses to his father the foreboding that this strange form has come to destroy the Daityas. There is no suggestion of Prahlāda being threatened by Hiraṇyakaśipu or Narasiṃha coming to his rescue.

The *Kūrma Purāṇa* version[6] of the account substantially differs in detail from the one mentioned above. The *Purāṇa* also does not speak of Narasiṃha's appearance from a pillar. According to this account, Viṣṇu at first creates a Puruṣa and sends him to kill Hiraṇyakaśipu; but Prahlāda along with Hiraṇyakaśipu fights against this Puruṣa who is defeated and goes back to Viṣṇu. Viṣṇu assumes the Narasiṃha form and appears suddenly in Hiraṇyakaśipu's city.[7] At first Prahlāda fights him in obedience to his father's command, but later he is defeated and accepts the eternity and universality of Vāsudeva (Viṣṇu). Subsequently, Prahlāda eulogizes him and tries to dissuade Hiraṇyakaśipu, his brother Hiraṇyākṣa and other demons from fighting against Viṣṇu. But Hiraṇyakaśipu does not heed him and is killed by Narasiṃha. Anuhlāda and other sons of Hiraṇyakaśipu are killed by the lions born of the body of Narasiṃha.[8] It is interesting that the *Kūrma Purāṇa* places the Varāha incarnation of Viṣṇu (assumed for the purpose of killing Hiraṇyākṣa) later in time than Narasiṃha, although the Purāṇic tradition in general gives priority to it. It is possible that the account in this *Purāṇa* is prior to the schematization of Viṣṇu's incarnations.

It seems that Prahlāda's devotion to Viṣṇu and the consequent incarnation of Narasiṃha for saving him from the anger of his father is a theme developed much later in the saga of Narasiṃha. It finds its full exposition in the *Bhāgavata Purāṇa*[9] which is the exponent par excellence of the doctrine of *bhakti* (devotion). This *Purāṇa* tells us that while Hiraṇyakaśipu was engaged in practising severe penance, the Devas invaded his palace and captured his queen who had Prahlāda in her womb. Nārada intervened, secured her release and took her to his hermitage, where she stayed till the return of Hiraṇyakaśipu listening to the preachings of Nārada on *Bhāgavata dharma*. Being merely a woman, she forgot all about it, but Prahlāda imbibed it and retained it forever in his memory.[10] From his very childhood Prahlāda turned out to be a great devotee of Viṣṇu, and although Hiraṇyakaśipu tried various methods to kill him, he could not harm him. Ultimately, he got so exasperated with his son that he decided to kill him with his own hands. He taunted Prahlāda that if his god was everywhere, he should reveal himself in the pillar of the hall. Hiraṇyakaśipu then hit hard with his fist against the pillar. The pillar immediately burst asunder with a loud noise and Viṣṇu issued forth in the Narasiṃha form. He tore open the heart of the demon, and was so angry that no one, not even the gods and the goddess Lakṣmī, dared to approach him. Only Prahlāda was able to do so; he pacified the deity with a long eulogy. Later, Brahmā also worshipped him.

The *Viṣṇu Purāṇa* makes only a brief reference to the story of Prahlāda.[11] It states that due to his devotion to Viṣṇu, Prahlāda was thrown into the sea at his father's orders. But later Hiraṇyakaśipu relented and a reconciliation took place between father and son. The son began to serve his father with diligence. At this point the account relates, rather abruptly, that after Hiraṇyakaśipu was put to death by Narasiṃha, Prahlāda became the sovereign of the Daityas. It would seem that although the story of Prahlāda's devotion to Viṣṇu is well-developed in the *Viṣṇu Purāṇa*, it is also aware of some popular version of the myth in which Hiraṇyakaśipu and Prahlāda were not always opposed to each other as depicted in the *Bhāgavata Purāṇa*. The *Mahābhārata* refers to the enmity between Prahlāda and Indra. At one place,[12] Indra claims to have slain in battle Prahlāda and other famous sons of Diti, and, in this way, secured the lordship of the celestials. At another place it is narrated that Prahlāda became the ruler of the three worlds owing to the merit accruing from his virtuous behaviour.[13] Having lost his sovereignty Indra went to Prahlāda in the guise of a brāhmaṇa and begged to be given instruction in true knowledge and righteous behaviour. Prahlāda did so at length and even gifted away his 'meritorious behaviour' to Indra. Consequently he became deprived of Righteousness, Truth, Might and Prosperity. It is curious that in the lengthy discourse given by Prahlāda, there is no mention of his devotion to Viṣṇu.[14]

On the basis of some iconographic texts, T.A. Gopinatha Rao informs us that there are two varieties of Narasiṃha images: Girija–Narasiṃha and Sthauṇa–Narasiṃha.[15] The conception underlying the first is that the deity comes out of a mountain cave; in the second case the deity is supposed to have emerged from a pillar. The two iconographic concepts clearly point to the prevalence of two divergent traditions regarding Narasiṃha; although of these the latter had a greater hold on popular imagination and almost ousted the former, the first one seems to have been earlier in point of time. It seems that Narasiṃha was originally a lion deity.[16] This is also indicated by such Purāṇic statements which tell us that in the battle against Hiraṇyakaśipu, lions born out of the body of Narasiṃha devoured the Dānavas. This view is further confirmed by the evidence of a sculptured panel discovered at Koṇḍamotu on the outskirts of Piduguralla village in Guntur district of Andhra Pradesh.[17] The panel shows in bas-relief six standing figures that have been identified with a good deal of justification as Pradyumna, Viṣṇu, Narasiṃha, Kṛṣṇa, Saṃkarṣaṇa and Aniruddha. It is suggested that the seventh figure, which is almost totally missing, might have been that of Sāmba.[18] Narasiṃha is depicted as a couchant lion with the only difference that two hands are added to his figure at the neck level with which he holds the *gadā* and *cakra*, the two typically Vaiṣṇavite attributes. He also has the Śrīvatsa mark on his chest. On stylistic grounds, the sculpture is dated to the late third or early fourth century CE, and it is the earliest iconographic representation of Narasiṃha. Considering that this unusual theriomorphic portrayal of Narasiṃha is not mentioned in any iconographic text, Abdul Wahid Khan remarks that it is very likely that in the early fourth century CE the anthropomorphic representation is an exception rather than the rule. The codification of the rules of iconography from the fourth century onwards accentuated the tendency to represent deities in human forms. We may point out that the addition of extra hands is merely an indication of the figure's divinity in Indian iconography and need not be assumed to reflect the composite nature of the deity, as is required in the story of Hiraṇyakaśipu. This is proved by the convention of giving extra hands to such purely animal deities as Garuḍa, Matsya and Kūrma. It is only in the later Gupta sculptures of the North, and at Bādāmī and Ellora in the Deccan, that the deity is shown with a lion's head and a human body. According to a recent iconographical study,[19] the demon Hiraṇyakaśipu is remarkably absent in early Narasiṃha sculptures, although in the post-Gupta period Narasiṃha is almost invariably represented as killing the demon.

The Koṇḍamotu sculpture is of great significance for the history of Vaiṣṇavism. It represents a stage when the cults of Viṣṇu, Narasiṃha and the Pañcavīras of the Viṣṇis are in the process of coalescing. Viṣṇu is shown simply as a two-armed god with the right hand in the *abhaya* pose and the left holding a conch-shell, and he stands second from the left. There is no indication in the sculptured panel that Viṣṇu enjoyed the central position in this synthesized worship. However, its discovery in coastal Andhra may suggest that this area was the crucial scene of the evolution of Purāṇic Brahmanism in the post-Ikṣvāku times when a number of Brahmanical dynasties, such as the Bṛhatphalāyanas, Ānandas, Śālaṅkāyanas and Viṣṇukuṇḍins, were exercising their political dominance.[20]

Nevertheless, the concept of a deity with a lion's face and human body is fully developed in Gupta iconography, and references to the killing of Hiraṇyakaśipu in the Śānti parva of the *Mahābhārata* evince that this exploit of Narasiṃha must have been well known in the Gupta period.[21] But, as shown earlier, the same cannot be said about the motif of Prahlāda's devotion to Viṣṇu and Viṣṇu's appearance from a pillar to save his devotee. The question arises: when was the pillar motif added to the Narasiṃha legend and what was its original significance?

A recent study has suggested that the entire region extending from Śabarīnārāyaṇa in Dakṣiṇa Kosala to Mahendragiri in Kaliṅga was inhabited by the Śabara tribes in the early centuries of the Common Era, and they worshipped deities in the form of wooden pillars.[22] With the rise of Brahmanical dynasties in this region tribal deities became Brahmanized; nevertheless, the famous Puri triad consisting of three small, pillar-like wooden images of Jagannātha, Subhadrā and Balabhadra show unmistakable traces of Śabara origins.[23] The aboriginal hill tribes of coastal Andhra and Kaliṅga still worship their gods in the form of wooden pillars, and the practice can be traced back to earlier times.[24] In the fifth–sixth centuries there were rulers in the eastern Deccan who described themselves as worshippers of the goddess Stambheśvarī, i.e. pillar-goddess.[25] Later the Śulkis, who claimed control over the whole of Gondrama, regarded goddess Stambheśvarī as their family deity. Since inscriptions contain reference to eighteen Gondramas, the term has been interpreted in the sense of Gond tribes, although some scholars are of the opinion that it denotes territory.[26] Whatever the case may be, the tribes of Gonds and Konds (also spelt as 'Khonds' and considered to be a branch of Gonds) inhabited and still inhabit large parts of Central India, hilly tracts of Orissa and eastern Deccan, and are more numerous than the Śabaras.[27] In the first century CE Brahmanism began to penetrate these regions, assimilating, transforming and even supplanting tribal cults. In my opinion, the story of Narasiṃha's emergence from a pillar reflects the supersession of an aboriginal worship of a pillar deity by Vaiṣṇavism through the cult of Narasiṃha. This hypothesis receives some support from the history of the Narasiṃha temple at Simhachalam.

The Simhachalam temple is situated on a hill 800 feet above sea level, at a distance of 10 miles to the north of Vishakhapatnam. The small hill range on which the temple is located forms a part of the Eastern Ghats and is known as Kailāśa. It has a number of perennial springs. Of these the most important one is known as Gangādhara, and pilgrims flock to it for its purported medicinal properties. It also fertilizes the pineapple fields and numerous flower and fruit gardens belonging to the temple, which happens to be one of the richest in Andhra Pradesh. However, our chief interest lies in the strange nature of its principal icon. It is installed in the manner of a Śiva *liṅga*, on a pedestal with a water chute in the centre of the *garbhagṛha*, and with the exception of one day every year, it remains covered with the unguent of sandalwood paste that is applied in such large quantities that it acquires the shape of a big sandalwood *liṅga*.[28] The real form of the deity, the *nijasvarūpa*, is open to view only on Akṣaya Tritīyā day, i.e. the third day of the month of Vaiśākha, when the *candanayātrā* festival is celebrated. The sandalwood paste is removed in the early hours of the morning and is applied again at dusk, leaving the *nijasvarūpa* exposed to devotees for twelve hours. Of the total twelve mounds of sandalwood paste covering the image of the deity, four mounds are applied on this day, and the rest in three instalments: on the fourteenth day of the bright half of the month of Vaiśākha, the full moon day in the month of Jyeṣṭha, and the full moon day in the month of Āṣāḍha. The paste is applied on a layer of silk cloth, which comes out in shreds when it is removed. It is curious that no offering is made to the *nijasvarūpa* of the deity; even the daily offering is postponed temporarily till the god gains back the shape of a *liṅga* by nightfall.

According to local tradition,[29] Simhachalam was a centre of Śaivism at first, but Rāmānuja, who visited the place in the course of his travels, defeated the priests of the temple in a religious disputation and won them over to Vaiṣṇavism. He then ordered the masons of the temple to convert the *liṅga* into an image of Varāha–Narasiṃha, but the icon began to bleed before the work was complete. Thinking that the deity was annoyed at this attempt at transformation, the head priest began to apply the sandalwood paste to give it its former shape. This stopped the flow of blood. Since then the idol has remained in the form of a *liṅga* coated with sandalwood paste, appearing in its original form only on the Akṣaya Tritīyā day when the paste is applied afresh. The legend is generally dismissed as a product of sectarian rancour, and it is pointed out that the inscriptional evidence at Simhachalam clearly attests to the fact that the temple was already a Vaiṣṇavite centre in the last quarter of the eleventh century CE – the generally accepted date of Rāmānuja.[30] Similar tales regarding the conversion of Śaiva shrines into Vaiṣṇava ones by Rāmānuja are also current about the Śrīkūrmeśvara temple at Śrī Kūrmam and the Śrī Veṇkaṭeśvara temple at Tirupati.

Nevertheless, there are strong grounds to believe that at one point Simhachalam was a centre of Śaiva worship. Not only that, the principal deity receives worship in the form of a *liṅga* only, the hill range on which the temple is situated is known as Kailāśa and its largest spring is known as Gangādhara. The two gates at the foot of the hill are named Bhairavadvāra and Mādhavadvāra. All these terms indicate a Śaiva influence. Further, the temple celebrates the festival of *Kāmadahana*, which would be quite incongruous for a Vaiṣṇava shrine, for in Vaiṣṇavism the god Kāma, being identical with Pradyumna, is one of the *vyūha* forms of Viṣṇu; on the other hand, the burning of Kāma is an important deed of Śiva. The festival is obviously of Śaiva origin. Finally, the deity is given *vibhūti*, pulses and rice by the devotees, and these objects are generally offered to Śiva and not to Viṣṇu.

The *Viṣṇudharmottara Purāṇa* gives a curious account of Viṣṇu bursting forth from a *liṅga*.[31] It narrates the story of a brāhmaṇa named Viśvaksena, belonging to the family of Gautama. He was a Sātvata, completely devoted only to Viṣṇu (*ekāntabhāvopagatāḥ*) and an adept in the *pañcakāla* worship, in accordance with the rules of the *Pañcarātra*. He wandered all over the earth in order to worship Kṛṣṇa. Once, he arrived at a big mountain where all the people were devotees of Śiva (*Māheśvaraḥ*). He bathed in a nearby spring and worshipped Keśava. On the *vedi* (altar) constructed for the purpose, he offered whatever *bhoga* was available in the locality. By chance, a man accompanied by a number of people armed with swords and bows in their hands arrived there. The man was the son of the local chieftain (*grāmasvāmīkumāra*) and he saw Viśvaksena worshipping Janārdana. He approached the brāhmaṇa and told him that he had a severe pain in his head, and was therefore unable to take his bath and perform worship. Hence, the brāhmaṇa should go to the temple and offer worship on his behalf to the god Śaṅkara, established there in the form of a *liṅga*. The brāhmaṇa replied to him: 'We are well known for worshipping Viṣṇu in his four manifestations or in one of his incarnations. I do not worship any other god. Therefore please go away.' Immediately the Kumāra drew out his sword and told the brāhmaṇa, 'I shall kill you without doubt if you do not go to the temple and worship the *liṅga*. Wicked man, is there a god higher than Śaṅkara?' Having been spoken to thus, the brāhmaṇa went with the Kumāra to the temple in order to save his life. Seeing the *liṅga* there, he thought to himself:

> Viṣṇu is immanent everywhere and Mahādeva is endowed with Viṣṇu's anger. Lord Narasiṃha also is the personification of the same anger. Therefore I shall worship in this *liṅga* the god having the form of Narasiṃha. In this way I shall perform the daily worship to the god and save my life.

He meditated upon Viṣṇu having the form of Narasiṃha in the *liṅga* in his mind, and performed the worship by saying 'I bow unto Narasiṃha' with folded hands. Hearing these words, the Kumāra immediately pulled out his sword to attack the brāhmaṇa. At once, the god in the form of Narasiṃha appeared, breaking open the *liṅga*, and he burnt the son of the local chieftain and his followers with the fire of his eyes. He also blessed the brāhmaṇa, the chief among the Sātvatas, with divine vision, and the brāhmaṇa praised the deity with a *stotra*.

Although this account does not give the name of the place where the incident is supposed to have taken place, there is no doubt that the author of the *Purāṇa* had Simhachalam in mind. It is noteworthy that the brāhmaṇa Viśvaksena is said to have bathed not in a river but in a spring, and Simhachalam is famous for its springs. At the present stage of our knowledge, it is not possible to ascertain whether the brāhmaṇa Viśvaksena is a reference to Rāmānujācārya, the great teacher of Pañcarātra Vaiṣṇavism, but there need not be any hesitation in concluding that the Vaiṣṇavization of the Simhachalam temple was accomplished rather arbitrarily, through some trick in collusion with the priests of the temple, at a time when Śaiva–Vaiṣṇava rivalry was at its height. According to R.C. Hazra, the *Viṣṇudharmottara Purāṇa* was either compiled in southern Kashmir or in the northern parts of Punjab.[32] Earlier, Bühler and Winternitz also had expressed the same view.[33] If this is accepted, it would appear that the events at Simhachalam must have been sensational enough to reach the ears of the compiler of the *Purāṇa* in Kashmir. Hazra thinks that the *Viṣṇudharmottara Purāṇa* cannot be later than 600 CE, although it is now generally dated to two or three centuries later.[34]

We should note that the episode of the bursting asunder of the *liṅga* (*liṅga-sphoṭa-Narasiṃha-darśana*) is narrated in the last two chapters of the *Viṣṇudharmottara Purāṇa*, so it is possible that it is a later addition to the main body of the text. We have been able to trace some additional literary references to Simhachalam, but none of these helps us in dating the temple earlier than the eleventh century. The *Bṛhaspati Sūtra* mentions Simhachalam among the eight important sacred places of the Vaiṣṇavas,[35] but, as F.W. Thomas points out, the text cannot be earlier than the twelfth century CE as it apparently refers to the Yādavas of Devagiri.[36] The *Matsya Purāṇa* mentions Śrīśaila, Narasiṃha, Mahendra and Śriraṅgam as places fit for the performance of *śrāddha*.[37] The sequence of narration suggests that Narasiṃha is to be identified with Simhachalam; this is also mentioned in the *Skanda Purāṇa*.[38] All such references show that Simhachalam was a famous centre of Vaiṣṇavism in the medieval times and corroborate epigraphic evidence from the temple, but they do not throw any light on the origin of the shrine.

K. Sundaram is of the opinion that the Simhachalam temple must have begun as a forest shrine several hundred years before the eleventh century, but its real history started from the time of Kulottuṅga Coḷa.[39] According to him, Simhachalam assumed strategic importance at the time of the Cālukya–Coḷas, and the officers of Kulottuṅga, who renamed Viśakhāpaṭṭana as Kulottuṅga Coḷa-paṭṭana, 'must have activized the life of the temple'. He points out that although Kulottuṅga was a Śaiva, some of his officers were Vaiṣṇavas. Early inscriptions of Simhachalam clearly show a Tamil influence. The conduct of the rituals at the temple was also governed by the Draviḍa tradition of the Śrīvaiṣṇava priests.

Notwithstanding late references to the Simhachalam temple, Sundaram is quite right in postulating the early origins of the shrine. According to some scholars, Simhachalam was at first a Buddhist centre, similar to the Buddhist sanctuaries at Sankaram (Saṅghārāmam) and Rāmatīrtham, situated, respectively, thirty miles south and forty miles north of Simhachalam. But this evidence is not conclusive. It is curious that most of the temples dedicated to Narasiṃha in the Deccan are situated on hilltops and the aboriginal tribes of these areas are known to worship mountain deities.[40] The hill tribe of the Chenchus worships the god Narasiṃhasvāmī enshrined at Ahobilam in the Nandiyal taluk of Kurnool district, and calls him 'Obalesudu'. These tribals believe that this god had married a Chenchu girl and given them the bamboo forest as the bride-price.[41] For this reason, they claim to have an exclusive right to cut and sell the bamboos from the forest.[42] They also put the vertical caste mark on their forehead like the Vaiṣṇavas. The Chenchus of the Nallamalai hills look upon the god Mallikārjuna (Śiva) of Śrīśailam (Nandikotkur taluk of Kurnool district, Andhra Pradesh) as their relative and call him 'Chenchu-Mallaya'. The *liṅga* at Mallikārjuna, worshipped on the hill, is considered one of the *svayambhū* or self-emanated *liṅgas*. It appears that the Chenchus, Yanadis and Śabaras are descended from the same stock. Thurston informs us that the Bonthuk Śabaras who, unlike the Telugu-speaking Chenchus, speak corrupt Oriya are called 'Chenchu *vandhu*' and, like the Telugu Chenchus, they claim relationship with the god Narasiṃha of Ahobilam.[43] It seems that most of these hill shrines began as aboriginal cult-spots and were later appropriated by Buddhism, Śaivism or Vaiṣṇavism, as their respective influences advanced in the region. At Simhachalam the transition to Vaiṣṇavism has been through Śaivism, but the local aboriginal belief in the efficacy of the pillar deities survives in the worship of one of the pillars of the *mukha-maṇḍapa* of the Simhachalam temple, known as '*Kappas Śtambham*', which, according to popular belief, has the power of curing cattle disease and barrenness in women.[44] The choice of the Narasiṃha incarnation of Viṣṇu for his identification with the aboriginal cult-objects may indicate either the popularity of a lion deity in this region or, as is more likely, the fact that Narasiṃha symbolized the wrathful aspect of Viṣṇu, famous for killing those who opposed him, and as such was more suited for sectarian purposes. It is noteworthy that the Śaivite sectarian response to the challenge of Narasiṃha created the concept of the *Śarabheśa* or *Siṃhāghna-mūrti* in which Śiva is shown as trampling upon Narasiṃha. In later tradition, Hiraṇyakaśipu is sometimes represented as a devotee of Śiva. However, the late development of the pillar motif in the Narasiṃha legend and its first occurrence in the *Bhāgavata Purāṇa* suggest that Narasiṃha appropriated the cult of some aboriginal pillar deity, of which a historical example is provided by the temple of Simhachalam. It is interesting to note that Narasiṃha is the presiding deity of the Jagannātha temple of Puri, and in all its ceremonies 'beginning from pūjā to cooking', offerings are first made to Narasiṃha.[45] The wooden pillar deities of Puri, although claimed by Buddhism, Śaivism and Vaiṣṇavism at different stages of their history, are undoubtedly of Śabara origin.[46]

Notes

1 Suvira Jaiswal, *The Origin and Development of Vaiṣṇavism*, pp. 78–79.

2 *Mahābhārata* (critical edition), III.100.19; XII.326.72ff., XII.337.86.

3 *Harivaṃśa* (Gita Press edition), III.41–47. P.L. Vaidya, the editor of the critical edition of the *Harivaṃśa*, regards the entire episode to be a later addition to the original text. He has marked it as *prathama pariśiṣta* no. 42A. However, this does not affect the basic argument presented here as Vaidya too acknowledges that the *Bhāgavata Purāṇa* narrative is much later than that of the *Harivaṃśa* (vol. I, p. xxix).

4 *Matsya Purāṇa*, chapters 161–63.

5 *Padma Purāṇa* (Anandasrama edition), Sṛṣṭi khaṇḍa, chapter 42; T.A. Gopinatha Rao, *Elements of Hindu Iconography*, vol. I, part 1, p. 148.

6 *Kūrma Purāṇa*, 1.15.18ff.

7 Ibid., verses 49–50.

8 Ibid., verse 70.

9 *Bhāgavata Purāṇa*, VII.1–10.

10 Ibid., VII.7–16.

11 *Viṣṇu Purāṇa* (Gita Press edition), I.16ff.; *Viṣṇu Purāṇa,* tr. H.H. Wilson, pp. 118ff.

12 *Mahābhārata* (critical edition), XII.99.49.

13 Ibid., XII.124.19ff.

14 Ibid.; also see XII.215.3ff.

15 T.A. Gopinatha Rao, *Elements of Hindu Iconography*, p. 149 note.

16 Hermann Goetz suggests that Narasiṃha was probably a Scythian or Gurjara god, or 'at least came in fashion because of similar Hūṇa or Scythian gods. The royal animal of south-western Asia had been the emblem of the western kṣatrapas.' Hermann Goetz, *Early Wooden Temples of Chamba*, p. 85 note 34.

17 Abdul Waheed Khan, *An Early Sculpture of Narasiṃha.*

18 Ibid., pp. 3–4.

19 Kalpana Desai, *Iconography of Viṣṇu*, p. 88.

20 It is curious that the Viṣṇukuṇḍins, who had the representation of a lion on their seals, claimed to be devotees of the god Śrī Parvata-Svāmin. He is generally identified with Śiva–Mallikārjuna of the Śriśaila mountain but this is by no means certain. Is it possible to identify the god as the lion-deity, a prototype of Narasiṃha, who is associated with the mountains as indicated by the concept of Girija–Narasiṃha? For more details, see Suvira Jaiswal, *The Origin and Development of Vaiṣṇavism*, pp. 134–35.

21 Kalpana Desai, *Iconography of Viṣṇu*, pp. 86ff.

22 K.C. Misra, *The Cult of Jagannatha.*

23 Ibid., pp. 93ff.

24 S.N. Rajaguru, quoted in ibid., p. 14; B.C. Mazumdar, *Orissa in the Making*, pp. 107ff.; D.C. Sircar, *Epigraphia Indica*, vol. XXVIII, inscription no. 20, p. 112.

25 See the Kalahandi plates of Mahārāja Tuṣṭikara; S.N. Rajaguru, 'The Kalahandi Copperplate of Tuṣṭikara', re-edited by Sircar in *Epigraphia Indica*, vol. XXV, pp. 274ff.

26 R.C. Majumdar, 'Eastern India During the Pāla Period', p. 78.

[27] J.H. Hutton, *Caste in India*, p. 23.
[28] K. Sundaram, *The Simhachalam Temple*, p. 67.
[29] Ibid., p. 67.
[30] Ibid., p. 71.
[31] *Viṣṇudharmottara Purāṇa*, III.354.
[32] R.C. Hazra, *Studies in the Upapurāṇas*, vol. I, p. 580.
[33] Georg Bühler, 'Review of Alberuni's *India*', p. 383; M. Winternitz, *History of Indian Literature*, vol. I, p. 580.
[34] R.C. Hazra, *Studies in the Upapurāṇas*, pp. 209ff.
[35] *Bārhaspatya Sūtram*, III.120.
[36] Ibid., p. 17.
[37] *Matsya Purāṇa*, I.22.27–48.
[38] *Skanda Purāṇa*, Prabhaśa khaṇḍa, chapter 35, verses 16–20.
[39] K. Sundaram, *The Simhachalam Temple*, p. 75.
[40] For example, Yādavādri (Yadugiri) in Karnataka and Vadādri in West Godavari district, Andhra Pradesh.
[41] R. Subba Rao, 'Scope of Anthropological Research in the Agency Division', p. 153.
[42] Rama Rao, 'The Temples of Śriśailam'.
[43] Edgar Thurston and K. Rangachari, *Castes and Tribes of Southern India*, *q.v.* Chenchu.
[44] N. Ramesan, *Temples and Legends of Andhra Pradesh*, pp. 136ff.
[45] K.C. Misra, *The Cult of Jagannātha*, p. 153.
[46] Ibid., pp. 16, 33, 158. In an important article (chapter 4 of *The Cult of Jagannath and the Regional Tradition of Orissa*, eds Anncharlott Eschmann, Hermann Kulke and Gaya Charan Tripathi), Anncharlott Eschmann delineates the gradual evolution of tribal iconological symbols into theriomorphic–anthropomorphic deities in the process of their 'Hinduization'. This would have contributed to the exaltation of cult-spots, growth of temples and processes of state formation in early medieval India, exemplified by Hermann Kulke in the case of the Jagannath cult (ibid., chapter 7).

8

The Demon and the Deity: Conflict Syndrome in the Hayagrīva Legend*

Lack of information on the material circumstances in which a myth is embedded often leads to the supposition that developments in mythological sphere arise spontaneously and directly out of older elements through a process of homogenesis. This has been particularly the case with Purāṇic mythology which is often seen merely as an elaboration of what is available in the Vedic sources in seed form. Learned disquisitions have been written to prove that the worship of Purāṇic deities, such as Brahmā, Śiva, Skanda, Gaṇeśa, Śakti is based on certain Vedic metaphysical–cosmological concepts which were recast in the form of Purāṇic legends.[1] However, the key to a myth often lies with archaeology, history and comparative religion, as has been demonstrated in the case of Greek mythology;[2] this could be equally true of Purāṇic legends which are neither casual priestly elaborations of Vedic symbolism, nor dreamlike 'reflections of the unconscious' psyche. The fact that a myth has several versions or has undergone several alterations shows that its creative process has a social import, the shift indicative of some change in the life of a tribe, community or region. The myth is aimed at making the past intelligible and explicable to the present. It would be naive to look upon it simply as a story 'meant for the entertainment of common people', serving in the past the same purpose as 'detective stories and crime club fiction' in the present.[3] If an attempt is made to assemble the scattered elements of a myth and its variants, it may be possible to determine its meaning and arrive at answers which have an anthropological–historical significance.

The *Mahābhārata* and the Purāṇas contain several references to a Hayaśirśa or Hayagrīva, a horse-headed hybrid form which lacks consistent portrayal. In the *Ādi Parva*, a horse-headed demon is born to sage Kaśyapa and his wife

* Originally published in *Studies in History*, vol. 1, no. 1, n.s. (1985), pp. 1–13.

Danu.[4] In the *Udyoga Parva*, Hayagrīva is a demon who is killed by Viṣṇu in one of his births.[5] He is also described as a wicked king of Videha who was killed by his kinsmen.[6] But in the *Śānti Parva*, Hayagrīva is the name of a king who performed many sacrifices, fought many glorious battles, and was slain on the battlefield when deserted by his followers. He is said to reside now in the region of the gods.[7] However, the *Śānti Parva* also gives the story of the Hayagrīva incarnation of Viṣṇu. It narrates that two demons, Madhu and Kaiṭabha, stole the Vedas from Brahmā and took them to hell with them beneath the great ocean. Brahmā told Viṣṇu what had happened, and Viṣṇu assuming the Hayagrīva form killed the demons and returned the Vedas to Brahmā; later he threw the horse-head into the eastern ocean (*udakpūrve*) and resumed his own form.[8] Nevertheless, in this very *Parva* elsewhere the Hayaśīrśa form of Viṣṇu is placed in the north-western ocean, and the godhead is made to claim that in the north-western ocean he, assuming the horse-head form drinks up the sacrificial oblations, offered to him properly and with faith.[9]

Thus the epic references speak of both a demoniacal and a divine Hayagrīva but the two are not connected. This double identity continues in the Purāṇic tradition untill the paradox is sought to be resolved in the final versions of the myth. The *Harivaṃśa*, which is regarded both as an appendage to the *Mahābhārata* as well as a Purāṇa and undoubtedly one of the earliest specimens of this genre, speaks of an Asura Hayagrīva, who is the doorkeeper of the demon–king Narakāsura of the Bhauma dynasty of Prāgjyotiṣapura. He is killed by Kṛṣṇa at a place situated near Audaka in the middle of the Lohitagaṅgā.[10] The story is repeated in the *Narasiṃha Purāṇa*.[11] We are told that Kṛṣṇa, who was an embodiment of the dark energy (*Kṛṣṇa-Śakti*) of god Narasiṃha, killed Naraka, Hayagrīva and other Daityas of Prāgjyotiṣa. However, the *Harivaṃśa* also knows the divine Hayaśira, the horse-headed incarnation of Viṣṇu, who killed the demon Madhu, as the latter fought against Brahmā and other gods for precedence in performing a sacrifice.[12] In another version of the same story we are told that the demons Madhu and Kaiṭabha, full of false pride in their prowess, challenged Brahmā, when he was engaged in the act of creation, on the order of Puruṣa–Nārāyaṇa, and the latter killed the two demons after a fierce fight.[13] But no mention is made of Viṣṇu–Hayagrīva in this context. A variant of this motif may be seen in the *Bhāgavata*[14] and the *Agni Purāṇas* which introduce the demon Hayagrīva in place of Madhu and Kaiīabha.[15] We are told that the demon Hayagrīva had stolen the Vedas from Brahmā, who had fallen asleep at the dissolution of the universe at the end of the past *kalpa*, and had hidden them under the ocean. To recover the Vedas, Viṣṇu incarnated himself as Matsya (fish) and slayed the horse-headed demon. However, later, evidently in an attempt to explain the contradiction inherent in the same form having been attributed a divine as well as demoniac character, the myth of Viṣṇu appearing in an identical horse-headed incarnation for the specific purpose of killing the demon Hayagrīva was invented. The story is found in its fully developed version in the *Devī Bhāgavata Purāṇa*,[16] which explains that Viṣṇu's original head was cut off accidentally by the chord of his own bow due to the curse of his wife, the goddess Mahālakṣmī. Viśvakarmā took the head of one of the horses of the Sun's chariot and attached it to Viṣṇu's trunk, giving him a horse-headed form which alone could annihilate the demon Hayagrīva.

The roots of the Hayagrīva incarnation of Viṣṇu have been traced to certain Vedic myths and concepts. Bosch connects it with the Vedic sage Dadhyañc, the son of Atharvan, who is asked by the twin-gods Aśvins to teach them *madhu-vidyā* that was taught to him by Indra.[17] To counter Indra's threat to behead him for divulging the secret, the Aśvins give him a horse head, which is to be replaced by his original head after Indra carries out his threat. It is said that the Vedic horse-headed seer is the alter-ego of Puruṣa–Nārāyaṇa of the *Mahābhārata*;[18] the latter in his horse-headed form preached the sacred wisdom of the Vedas and is a fierce demon-destroyer and behaved like a 'true Dadhyañc.[19] The symbolism of the horse is by no means rare in Vedic concepts, nor is it exclusive to the Vaiṣṇava mythology.[20] However, we may note that Viṣṇu's role as the protector or upholder of the Vedas should be traced to his identification with Yajña or sacrifice in the later Vedic literature. In the *Pañcaviṃśa Brāhmaṇa* it is Yajña whose head is cut off by the string of his bow, when termites, on being promised a share in the sacrificial offerings by the gods, bite off the string of his bow.[21] The gods then get the Aśvins to give Yajña a horse's head. The identification of Yajña with Viṣṇu naturally means the transference of the horse-headed form to Viṣṇu and in the *Nārāyaṇīya* section of the *Śānti Parva*, Viṣṇu is eulogized not only as Yajña but also as Hayaśira.[22] Further, in Vedic literature the sun and its rays symbolize knowledge; and the celestial horse Dadhikra, itself a form of the Sun, is equated with Viṣṇu.[23] In later Vaiṣṇava texts, Hayagrīva is regarded as the god of learning and the *Hayaśīrṣa Pañcarātra* credits him with expounding *pañcarātra vidyā*. The *Viṣṇudharmottara Purāṇa* speaks of him as a form of Saṅkarṣaṇa, who is also associated with knowledge;[24] especially the *pañcarātra* knowledge.[25] Hayagrīva's iconographic representations clearly show him holding a book along with other emblems. The *Viṣṇudharmottara* lays down that the eight-handed image of Hayagrīva should depict him holding a conch, wheel, mace and lotus in his four right hands and his four left hands placed on the personified forms of the four Vedas.[26] All this may lend credence to the view that the seeds of the horse-headed incarnation of Viṣṇu were present in later Vedic mythology and that these came to fruition in the Purāṇic tales and that even the *Devī Bhāgavata* story is a Purāṇic rehash of the material found in the *Pañcaviṃśa Brāhmaṇa*. However, this line of argument does not explain the conceptualization of a demon Hayagrīva, his anti-Vedic activities and his fight against Viṣṇu. These are distinctly Purāṇic developments and need further explanation.

It is a significant feature of the Hayagrīva legend that although the deity Viṣṇu–Hayagrīva is associated both with the eastern and western oceans and sometimes even with the Pāñcāla country, the demon Hayagrīva is consistently placed in the region of Prāgjyotiṣapura.[27] The *Kālikā Purāṇa* narrates that Viṣṇu–Hayagrīva killed the fever-demon (Jvarāsura) and took up his abode on the Maṇikūṭa hill; and between the hills of Maṇikūṭa and Gandhamādana flowed the river Lauhitya.[28] Gandhamādana is identified with modern Gandhamau, and both the hills may be located in the village Hajo, fifteen miles north-west of Guwahati.[29] A temple of Hayagrīva–Viṣṇu, also locally known as Mādhava, still exists on the Maṇikūṭa hill and is a living cult. The eighteenth-century Assamese poet Śrī Rāmacandradāsa, referring to this shrine, specifically states that the horse-headed demon (Hayāsura), who lived on the Maṇikūṭa hill and was killed by Viṣṇu for the good of the world,[30] prayed to the deity at the time of his death that the god should make the hill his permanent abode, and assume the same form as that of the demon. Viṣṇu readily acceded to his request. It is not surprising that in the process Viṣṇu–Hayagrīva took on the traits of the demon and came to be known as the Hindu god of fever.[31] In a plate found at Vikrampur, in the Dacca district, Hayagrīva appears in the company of goddess Parṇeśvarī and Śītalā, the goddess of small pox.[32]

It is a well-known anthropological fact that aboriginal India conceived of deities in various theriomorphic forms, such as lions, cats and horses, residing on hills or crevices and the cult symbols were often iconic stones or wooden objects, sometimes arbitrarily given a nose, mouth or eyes by the insertion of beads and other means. Thus Koḍā-pen the horse–god of the Gonds is a shapeless stone, and so too is the tiger–god of the Waralis.[33] It is difficult to ascertain the true iconographic form of images which are still worshipped, but Dalton thinks that the image of Hayagrīva–Mādhava at Hajo is a mutilated Buddha image and to conceal its mutilation its modern votaries have given it 'a pair of silver goggle-eyes, a hooked, gilt or silvered nose', the rest of the form being concealed with clothes and flowers.[34] Dalton is evidently led to this inference by the fact that the locality has retained many a Buddhist association. It has been argued that the term 'Maṇi' in Maṇikūṭa indicates Buddhist influence. Although the temple is at present in the hands of the Brahmanical priests, hundreds of Buddhist pilgrims from Bhutan, Tibet, Ladakh and south-western China visit it to pay their homage to the deity, who is known to them as Mahāmuni. These Buddhists consider Hajo as the place where the Buddha attained the Final

Extinction or *parinirvāṇa*. The tradition is evidently false, for it is well established that the Buddha died at Kuśīnagara, the capital of the northern Mallas near Gorakhpur in Uttar Pradesh. Nevertheless, these Buddhists even point to a rock on the hill where, according to them, the cremation of the Buddha is said to have taken place. The rock has a figure of the four-armed Viṣṇu, but it also has some roughly carved inscriptions in old Tibetan characters bearing the Buddhist mystical formulae *oṃ maṇi padme huṃ, oṃ aḥ huṃ*, etc. The minor stone images in the temple, identified as various forms of Viṣṇu by the Vaiṣṇava priests, are regarded as Buddhist deities by the lama-pilgrims. In fact, every Brahmanical spot in the locality also bears a Buddhist name and interpretation. The present temple is built on the ruins of an older shrine; the Buddhists claim that the earlier shrine was a great *caitya* erected over the cremated relics of the Buddha. It is pointed out that many Buddhist images in Assam are now being worshipped as Viṣṇu images.[35]

Thus, available evidence strongly suggests that the sacred temple at the Maṇikūṭa hill has a Buddhist past which was evidently prior to its Vaiṣṇavization. However, in my opinion, there is no doubt that it was supposed to be originally the abode of some aboriginal deity worshipped by the local tribes. It is possible that the sacred rock, on which the cremation of the Buddha is presumed to have taken place and the scrapings of which are taken away by Buddhists for making amulets to ward off evil, was itself the object of worship by the aborigines. The practice may have been taken over by the Buddhists who associated it with the cremation of the Buddha. According to P.C. Chaudhury, the term 'Hayagrīva' is derived from the Austric *haya*, which means 'red'; and in Khasi, *haim-haim* means 'very red', 'Hayagrīva', therefore, means 'having a red neck'.[36] If we accept this view, it would seem that in the context of Maṇikūṭa, Hayagrīva represents the sanskritization of a phonetically similar term used by the aborigines to denote their red-necked or red-complexioned deity. It is curious that Chaudhury does not use his own linguistic interpretation of the term 'Hayagrīva' to establish the tribal antecedents of the temple at Hajo, but traces the worship of Hayagrīva at Hajo and Kāmākhyā to the Vedic worship of Agni in the form of a horse.[37]

However, even if the Austric derivation of the term is found unacceptable and the deity of Maṇikūṭa is supposed to have been conceived from the very beginning as 'horse-headed' instead of 'red necked', its tribal origins can hardly be denied. It seems that although horses of the best breed were imported from the north-west, eastern India also produced an important local breed,[38] and in the *Sabhā Parva* of the *Mahābhārata*, Bhagadatta, the *mleccha* king of Prāgjyotiṣa is said to have brought as gifts some of the finest horses of the world.[39] The importance of the horse may have been reflected in the conceptualization of a horse–deity in the region. On the other hand, we may also note that, in

Buddhist iconographic texts, Hayagrīva is described as a ferocious deity with a red complexion, three eyes and a protruding belly.[40] J.N. Banerjea writes that the conception of Hayagrīva as a divinity possessing terrific features is a specific contribution of Mahāyāna Buddhism (*sic*), which adopted the Brahmanical Viṣṇu–Hayagrīva but made him Vidyārāja, the king of Vidyādharas, the custodians of magical knowledge,[41] and for this reason Viṣṇu–Hayagrīva came to be invoked chiefly for *abhicāra* purposes. But, in my view, the fierce aspect of Hayagrīva has to be traced to the absorption of an aboriginal deity of the Maṇikūṭa region in the personality of this incarnation of Viṣṇu, through a process that was indirect. It took place through the mediation of Buddhism.

Hayagrīva occupies a very important place in the pantheon of Mantrayāna Buddhism; he figures both as a minor god accompanying other more important deities as well as a major god in his own right.[42] He is connected with Avalokiteśvara and is regarded especially as the god of learning. It is generally assumed that this is a borrowing from Brahmanical mythology which conceives of Viṣṇu–Hayagrīva as the protector of the Vedas. However, in Mantrayāna literature, *Vidyā* refers to the knowledge of spells and occult practices, and *Vidyās* are forms of Śakti or personifications of power. *Hayagrīva Vidyā* is mentioned as an incantation for protection against enemies.[43] It is well known that the worship of aboriginal deities involves magical rites and incantations which are primitive methods of fighting diseases and calamities. So one ought to trace the tantric aspects of Hayagrīva to their aboriginal roots. Some Bhutanese lamas even burn a finger or a thumb of their hand as an offering to the deity. The practice is symbolic of self-immolation in Tantricism and may be a remnant of primitive tribal customs. We may also note that the Pañcarātra Vaiṣṇavism, with which Hayagrīva is generally associated, is often denounced as tantric in the Purāṇas. It is argued that land grants to Buddhist monks and *brāhmaṇas* in peripheral areas adjoining the Madhyadeśa led to the assimilation of tribal cults in Buddhism and the emergence of Tantricism in these regions.[44] It appears very likely that the animistic cult of a theriomorphic deity at Hajo first became a part of Mantrayāna Buddhism and was later appropriated by Vaiṣṇavism. The Buddhist worship of Vidyārāja–Hayagrīva reveals its connections with the eastern regions, and the spread of this cult to Tibet, China, Mongolia, Japan and other countries of South-East Asia.[45] It is quite plausible that a local tribal cult of Assam became universalized upon its assimilation into Tantric Buddhism and extended its area of influence in the eastern countries.[46]

The *Yogini Tantra*, written around the tenth century, refers to the worship of Hayagrīva–Mādhava at Maṇikūṭa hill and recommends that the deity should be offered cow's milk, fish, deer, goat and certain varieties of birds, but never the buffalo meat or its milk. So, even in the early medieval period, the worship of this deity was predominantly tantric. The earliest sculptural representation of the Hayagrīva incarnation of Viṣṇu is found on a small architectural fragment preserved at the Bharat Kala Bhavan, Varanasi. It seems to have been a part of a *vedikā stambha* and has been placed in the third century CE on stylistic grounds.[47] It shows a horse-headed figure wearing a *vanamālā* and holding a mace and a discus in the upper right and left hands, respectively. The normal right hand does not hold anything and is shown resting on the belly, while the normal left hand holds an elongated object, which, according to N.P. Joshi, could be the so-called *jala pātra*, i.e. water vessel, or a manuscript symbolizing the Vedas. The latter suggestion would confirm the linking of Viṣṇu–Hayagrīva with the Vedas. However, many of the earliest extant Vaiṣṇava images of Vāsudeva–Viṣṇu show him holding a vessel in addition to the usual Vaiṣṇava emblems. It is generally believed that this was because these images were modelled after the images of the Buddhist god Maitreya, who is shown holding an *amṛta ghaṭa*. But we have pointed out elsewhere that *amṛta* represents wine in the Buddhist Mantrayāna ritual and the cults of some of the Vaiṣṇavite deities in their early phases were associated with the use of wine and other so-called tantric practices.[48] Is it possible to postulate that tantric features were present in the conception of Hayagrīva even in the third century?

The evidence is no doubt meagre for such an early association of Hayagrīva with tantric practices, especially in the Madhyadeśa. However, attention has been drawn to the fact that Hayagrīva worship at Hajo shows a number of similarities to the cult of Jagannatha at Puri.[49] The *Yoginī Tantra* gives an account of the origin of the stone image of Hayagrīva–Mādhava which greatly resembles the story of the origin of the image of Jagannātha at Puri as given in the *Brahma Purāṇa*. We are told that following the instructions given to him in his dream, King Indradyumna recovered a floating tree from the seashore and cut it into several pieces. Two of these pieces were taken to Puri for fashioning the images of Jagannātha and Balabhadra and one was carried to Maṇikūṭa to make the image of Hayagrīva–Mādhava. Thus a close affinity between the cult of Jagannātha at Puri and that of Hayagrīva at Maṇikūṭa is established. It is interesting to learn that the custom of caning the visitors at the entrance to the temple prevails both at the Hayagrīva temple of Maṇikūṭa and the temple of Jagannātha in Puri.[50] Further, just as the ritual offering of food or *mahāprasāda* is first made to god Narasiṃha at Puri even before it is offered to Jagannātha, similarly at Maṇikūṭa the *mahāprasāda* is first offered to the image of Narasiṃha carved on the stone wall of the temple, and the god is worshipped daily. The tribal roots of the cult of Jagannātha have been generally acknowledged. In my view, the deity of the Maṇikūṭa hill also belonged to a similar tribal complex to be appropriated first by Buddhism and later by Vaiṣṇavism.

It has been suggested that the theriomorphic iconography of the boar and the man–lion incarnations of Viṣṇu facilitated their identification with the aniconcial sacred symbols of tribal India and of the two concepts the latter, the Narasiṃha incarnation of Viṣṇu, proved to be the ideal agent of Hinduization.[51] We may add that this role was not limited to Varāha and Narasiṃha only, other theriomorphic forms of Viṣṇu also served the purpose. Most of the hill shrines found in the Deccan, Orissa and Assam were originally aboriginal cult spots and were later absorbed in to Buddhism, Śaivism or Vaiṣṇavism, depending upon the nature of mainstream institutions penetrating the tribal areas.[52] The process of acculturation had a humanizing effect upon the cult object and its cult and smoothened the process of assimilation of its worshippers in the wider society. Although certain primitive forms of outlandish practices or myths servived, the deity received a respectable place in the Brahmanical, Buddhist and Jaina pantheons as may have been the specific case.

Nonetheless, a curious feature of the Hayagrīva legend is that the godhead is pitted against its exact double, and that he takes on the physical appearance of his adversary on a permanent basis and is worshipped as such. It seems to me that the myth obviously refers to a clash between two cults, each of which had appropriated the worship of the particular epiphany to suit its own purpose. The Purāṇic myth tries to transform what was 'alien' into something 'proper', but in doing so it not only provides a simple justification for the continuation of the worship of the deity of Maṇikūṭa; it also combats the worship of this divinity by a rival faith and records its overthrow; hence the device of two contradictory forms of the epiphany, one demoniacal and the other godly. The killing of the demon Hayagrīva by Hayagrīva–Viṣṇu symbolizes the ousting of the Buddhist hold over his cult by Vaiṣṇavism. Such a conceptualization may have been facilitated by the fact that the Buddhists themselves regarded the site as the place where the earthly life of the Buddha came to an end. It may not be without significance that the *Vṛddha-hārīti-smṛti*, a text of the early medieval period, substitutes Ḥayagrīva in place of the Buddha in its list of the ten incarnations of Viṣṇu and forbids expressly the worship of the Buddha.[53]

A parallel myth to that of Hayagrīva may be seen in the story of Vāsudeva Paunḍraka who is defeated and killed by the true Vāsudeva, an incarnation of Viṣṇu. We have argued elsewhere that the myth symbolizes a conflict between the rival claimants to the worship of Vāsudeva, a popular deity who was acknowledged and venerated both by the Jainas and the Vaiṣṇavas and was given the position of the supreme godhead by the latter.[54] D.D. Kosambi has shown how the clash of the cult of a buffalo deity with that of the mother–goddess had led to the development of two parallel myths.[55] In one of them the buffalo is regarded as the demon Mahiṣāsura and is killed by the goddess

Durgā or Kālī; in the other he is represented as Mahsobā, a form of Śiva, and becomes the husband of the same goddess. Traces of social tensions and sectarian conflicts and their resolution are to be found not only in myths, but also in the rites and observances of the various regional cults. In the previous chapter we have seen how rituals connected with the worship of the principal deity, enshrined at Simhachalam temple in Andhra Pradesh, clearly reveal that although the deity is at present famous as Narasiṃha or Varāha–Narasiṃha, as a synthesized form of Viṣṇu, it was identified as a Śivaliṅga at an earlier stage. The superimposition of Vaiṣṇavism on an earlier Śaiva site is confirmed by the fact of a continuing celebration of the festival of *Kāma dahana* (the burning of Kāmadeva, the god of love by Śiva), quite incongruous in a Vaiṣṇava temple; for Viṣṇu as Pradyumna is regarded as identical with Kāmadeva. Moreover, the deity is still offered *vibhūti* (sacred ashes) typical of Śiva. A study of this site clearly shows that Simhachalam was earlier a Śaiva stronghold and perhaps still earlier an aboriginal cult-spot.[56] The triumph of Vaiṣṇavism changed the designation of the deity but could not uproot the local custom of *liṅga* worship.

A frustrating lack of contextual details does not allow us to work out the material background of such conflicts with any certainty, but the fact of conflicts can be hardly denied. Traces of it may be found in iconological and archaeological evidence too. When Benoytosh Bhattacharya came across iconographic concepts in the *Sādhanamālā* where Buddhist deities were conceived as trampling upon Brahmanical gods,[57] these were dismissed as 'wishful thinking' and purely imaginary.[58] But a number of such sculptures have been discovered in Orissa and Bihar,[59] which shows that religious clashes were not purely academic as has been generally assumed. They involved larger groups of followers of the respective religions. Otherwise, such blatantly sectarian sculptures could not have been placed at places of worship. However, the popular stereotype that early Indian history has been remarkably devoid of religious or sectarian conflicts and that the process of syncretism in Brahmanism and other Indian religions has been free of social tensions has become so axiomatic, that even when the evidence is clear and unmistakable, it is simply overlooked.

Nevertheless, it is a well-known fact that whereas Hinduism allows a great deal of freedom and flexibility in matters of belief and doctrines, it is extremely rigid on questions of religious and social observance; any deviation from the traditionally accepted pattern leads to a fission giving rise to a new or separate sect, caste, or community. Thus, it is difficult to accept the view that clashes were only on an intellectual or academic level and did not involve the masses; for matters of social and religious conduct concern people in general and are not limited to either the renouncer or the literati. It is curious that Śaṅkarācārya, who tradition describes as an inveterate crusader against Buddhism, was himself deeply influenced by Buddhist philosophy, a fact which earned him the dubious distinction of being called a *pracchanna Bauddha*, a disguised Buddhist. Śaṅkara's thesis regarding the *jīvanamuktas*, as great men who postpone their liberation intentionally and who voluntarily continue to live (*cirañjīvī*) or even choose successive rebirths in order to help others attain liberation, comes very close to the Buddhist concept of Bodhisattva.[60] Nevertheless, he travelled throughout the length and breadth of India disputing with the Buddhists and organizing an order of *sanyāsins* (monks) to revive Brahmanism to carry on his crusade against Buddhism. Apparently, his ire was directed towards the institutional form of Buddhism which was no longer in touch with the common people and depended upon the generous support of the upper classes. Buddhist monasticism had degenerated into Lamaism with monks making a career of 'theological games'.[61] Hence, whereas Brahmanical 'inclusivism' succeeded through the cult of Viṣṇu to assimilate the popular worship of Buddha by recognizing him as an incarnation of Viṣṇu, similar attempts by Buddhists did not help it much in its struggle for survival. In a Vajrayāna text, *Ekallavīra Caṇḍa Mahorasana Tantra*, Buddha, like *bhagavat Nārāyaṇa* of the *Bhagavadgītā*,[62] declares that whichever form of the divine the people worship he resides in that very form for the good of all sentient beings.[63] Brahmanical deities were included in the Mahāyāna and the Vajrayāna pantheon albeit in a subordinate position, an assimilative device which was used by Brahmanical cults with equal vigour. If Brahmanism gained in strength while Buddhism declined, the underlying causes were social, and not theological or philosophical.

The existing temple of Hayagrīva–Mādhava at Hajo was built by the Koch king Raghudeva Nārāyaṇa (1583 CE) on the ruins of an older shrine which the king had found completely deserted in the midst of a thick jungle. However, this only means that for some time the temple lacked patrons and had become dilapidated, but its Vaiṣṇavization must have taken place long before the sixteenth century. It is an accomplished fact in the *Kālikā Purāṇa*. The Buddhist stage must have existed still earlier. Buddhist ruins around Guwahati are ascribed to the sixth–seventh centuries CE; hence Buddhist adaptation of the aboriginal cult also must roughly belong to the same time. The origin of Mantrayāna Buddhism also is assigned to the same period. Mantrayāna glorified primitive tribal rituals involving meaningless utterances of certain sounds (*mantras*), symbols or gestures (*mudrās*), and diagrams (*maṇḍalas*), often formed by living groups of participants, and reinterpreted these as 'mystical representations' of the Buddhist doctrine. The emergence of Mahāyāna Buddhism, with its hierarchical pantheon and temple ritual, is seen as an adaptation of Buddhism to the growing feudal trends in the early centuries of the Common Era.[64] The development made it easier for the Buddhist monks living in monastic seclusion in the midst of tribal peoples in marginal areas to interact with and assimilate the popular tribal beliefs. The glorification of the horse-headed deity in Mantrayāna was apparently a product of such interaction and is found in the Buddhist texts of the seventh–eighth centuries.

However, the early medieval period, especially from the seventh century onwards, seems to have been characterized by intense rivalry between Buddhism and Brahmanism. It is wrong to hold that Jainism and Buddhism had ceased to offer a serious challenge to Brahmanism during this period.[65] The composition of a vast body of Buddhist literature from the eighth to the twelfth century in India shows that it was very much a living religion and the literary evidence is confirmed by the archaeological remains. Brahmanical works of this period make scoffing attacks on the Buddhists and works like *Bauddha-dhikkāra* of Udayana were written. To subvert the influence of heterodox religions, the central figures of Buddhism and Jainism were taken over as incarnations of Viṣṇu, though their teachings were denounced vehemently.[66] In the battle between Brahmanism and Buddhism the former ultimately won the day, evidently because, as Kosambi remarks, the large monasteries were 'too expensive and progressively unnecessary for the growing number of self-contained villages'[67] held by petty landowners and feudal intermediaries. The work of acculturation of tribal areas could be done more successfully and cheaply by the brāhmaṇa donees. The decline of Buddhism in India need not be attributed solely to Turkish attacks on Buddhist institutions. Many of the important Brahmanical temples show that they had had a Buddhist past.[68]

We have examined in some detail the conflict syndrome in one specific case, the manner in which a horse-headed anti-Vedic epiphany, originally dubbed as a demon in the earlier Purāṇic legends, was transformed into a restorer and protector of the Vedas and its anti-Vedic past was conveniently explained away as belonging to a demon of the same form. Social and sectarian conflicts have often provided rich material for mythologizing in the epics and the Purāṇas. No doubt one can find many instances of tolerance and syncretism, but in a general atmosphere characterized by fragmentation of sects and sectarian rivalries these may have been attempts at reconciling and resolving conflicts. The nature and extent of such conflicts needs further investigation, but scholars have generally shied away from this aspect of social history presumably because the notion of tension and conflict in ancient India fits ill with the concept of a golden age.

Notes

1 For example, see V.S. Agrawala, 'The Purāṇas and the Hindu Religion'. For Hayagrīva, see J.N. Banerjea, 'Vyūhas and Vibhavas of Viṣṇu'; T.V. Mahalingam, 'Hayagrīva, the Concept and the Cult'.

[2] G.S. Kirk, *The Nature of Greek Myths*. In this, as well as in his earlier work, *Myths: Its Meaning and Functions in Ancient and Other Cultures*, Geoffrey Kirk provides a scholarly critique of different approaches in the interpretation of myths. He successfully shows that no single paradigm can be applied to all types of myths. Myths perform a multiplicity of functions and differ enormously in their morphology as well as social functions depending upon their cultural context.

[3] P.V. Kane, *History of Dharmaśāstra*, vol. IV, pp. 622–23.

[4] *Mahābhārata* (critical edition), I.65.24.

[5] Ibid., V.128.49.

[6] Ibid., V.72.15.

[7] Ibid., XII.25.23–31.

[8] Ibid., 335.54.

[9] Ibid., 326.56.

[10] *Harivaṃśa Purāṇa* (Gita Press edition), II.62.18.

[11] Quoted in R.C. Hazra, *Studies in the Upapurāṇas*, vol. I, p. 233.

[12] *Harivaṃśa Purāṇa* (Gita Press edition), III.26.49.

[13] Ibid., III.13.

[14] *Bhāgavata Purāṇa* (Gita Press edition), vol. I, VIII.24.8–9.

[15] Quoted in T.A. Gopinatha Rao, *Elements of Hindu Iconography*, vol. I, pp.125–26.

[16] Ibid., p. 261; Vettam Mani, *Purāṇic Encyclopedia* (*s.v.* Hayagrīva). Also see *Skanda Purāṇa,* Dharmāraṇya kāṇḍa, chapters 14–15.

[17] F.D.K. Bosch, 'The God with the Horse's Head'.

[18] Ibid., p. 141.

[19] Ibid., p. 143.

[20] For the symbolism of the horse in the mythology of Śiva, see Wendy Doniger O'Flaherty, 'The Submarine Mare in the Mythology of Śiva'.

[21] *Pañcaviṃśa Brāhmaṇa*, VII.5.6. Also see *Taittirīya Saṃhitā*, 4–9.1; *Taittirīya Āraṇyaka*, V.1.

[22] *Mahābhārata*, XII.325.3.

[23] *Śatapatha Brāhmaṇa*, VI.31.29; J.N. Banerjea 'Vyūhas and Vibhavas of Viṣṇu', p. 57.

[24] *Viṣṇudharmottara Purāṇa*, III.7.

[25] Suvira Jaiswal, *The Origin and Development of Vaiṣṇavism*, p. 55.

[26] Quoted in T.A. Gopinatha Rao, *Elements of Hindu Iconography*.

[27] N.P. Joshi, 'Early Brahmanical Sculptures in Bharat Kala Bhavan'.

[28] *Kālikā Purāṇa*, chapter 78, verses 74–81.

[29] Maheswar Neog, 'Hayagrīva Worship in Assam', p. 31.

[30] Ibid., pp. 32–33.

[31] B. Bhattacharya, *Indian Buddhist Iconography*, p. 110.

[32] Ibid.

[33] W. Thomas Northcote, 'Animals', p. 519.

[34] E.T. Dalton, 'Notes on Assam Temple Ruins', pp. 8ff.

[35] Sarat Chandra Goswami, *Introducing Assam Vaiṣṇavism*, pp. 10–11. Also see Maheswar Neog, 'Buddhism in Kamarupa'.

[36] P.C. Choudhury, *The History of Civilisation of the People of Assam to the Twelfth Century AD*, p. 332.

[37] Ibid., pp. 438–39.

[38] U.N. Ghoshal, in K.A. Nilakanta Sastri, ed., *A Comprehensive History of India*, vol. II, p. 432.

[39] *Mahābhārata*, II.47.12–14.

[40] B. Bhattacharya, *Indian Buddhist Iconography*, p. 54.

[41] J.N. Banerjea, 'Vyūhas and Vibhavas of Viṣṇu', pp. 57–58.

[42] B. Bhattacharya, *Indian Buddhist Iconography*, pp. 36ff., 53–54, 68.
[43] A.K. Warder, *Indian Buddhism*, p. 483.
[44] R.S. Sharma, 'Material Milieu of Tantricism'.
[45] R.H. Van Gulik, *Hayagrīva*.
[46] Tantric texts divide the tantric world into three *krāntās* or regions, Aśvakrāntā, Rathakrāntā and Viṣṇukrāntā. This division is also mentioned in some Purāṇas. See, for example, *Matsya Purāṇa*, 102.10. The Aśvakrāntā region is said to extend from the Vindhyas to Mahācīna including Nepal (Avalon, *Principles of the Tantras*, vol. II, quoted in P.C. Bagchi, *Studies in the Tantras*, pp. 46–47). Could it be a reference to the tantric worship of a horse-headed deity in this region? An Aśvakrāntā temple exists near Guwahati. For the legend, see Subhendugopal Bagchi, *Eminent Śākta Centres in Eastern India*, pp. 152–53. Also see, D.B. Chhatry, *The Centres of India*, p. 5.
[47] N.P. Joshi, 'Early Brahmanical Sculptures in Bharat Kala Bhavan', pp. 178–80.
[48] Suvira Jaiswal, *The Origin and Development of Vaiṣṇavism*, pp. 151ff.
[49] Maheswar Neog, 'Hayagrīva Worship in Assam', p. 39.
[50] Ibid.
[51] Anncharlott Eschmann, 'The Vaiṣṇava Typology of Hinduization and the Origin of Jagannātha', pp. 102ff.
[52] See chapter 7 above.
[53] *Vṛddha-hārīta-smṛti*, X.145–46.
[54] Suvira Jaiswal, *The Origin and Development of Vaiṣṇavism*, pp. 90–91.
[55] D.D. Kosambi, *Myth and Reality*, pp. 2–3, 90–91, 122–23.
[56] A local legend at Simhachalam credits Rāmānuja with converting the temple from a Śaiva into a Vaiṣṇava centre of worship. It is said that Rāmānuja won over the local priests in a religious disputation and ordered the masons of the temple to convert the *liṅga* image into an image of Varāha–Narasiṃha. But before this could be achieved, the deity began to bleed profusely. The head priest realized that the deity was against this transformation, and he began to apply sandalwood paste to stop the flow of blood and restore the earlier shape of the image. Shulman has argued that in many temples of the South the shedding of blood by the deity plays an important role in origin myths and is to be linked to an underlying concept of sacrifice. David Dean Shulman, 'Tamil Mythology: An Interpretation of a Regional Hindu Tradition', PhD thesis, School of Oriental and African Studies, University of London, 1976, quoted in George L. Hart, 'The Nature of Tamil Devotion', p. 16.
[57] B. Bhattacharya, *Indian Buddhist Iconography*, pp. 146ff.
[58] R.C. Mitra, *The Decline of Buddhism in India*, p. 138.
[59] B.N. Sharma, 'Religious Tolerance and Intolerance in Indian Sculpture', pp. 657–68.
[60] *Brahmasūtra-bhāṣya*, III.3.32. Also see *Śrimadbhagavadgītā bhāṣya of Śri Śaṅkarācārya*, chapter 2.
[61] D.D. Kosambi, *An Introduction to the Study of Indian History* (first edition), p. 293.
[62] For the identity of the *bhagavat* of the *Bhagavadgītā*, see Suvira Jaiswal, *The Origin and Development of Vaiṣṇavism*, p. 37.
[63] Haraprasad Shastri, *A Descriptive Catalogue of Manuscripts*, vol. I, pp. 134–36, quoted in Pratapaditya Pal, *Vaiṣṇava Iconology in Nepal*, p. 108. Cf. *Bhagavadgītā*, VII.21: 'Whatever form any worshipper wishes to worship with faith, to that form I make his faith steady'; and *Bhagavadgītā*, IX.23: 'Even those who worship other deities with devotion, they too are worshipping me only albeit not in the proper manner (*avidhipūrvakam*).' In the *Lalitavistara*, a Buddhist text written in the Purāṇic style, the Buddha is repeatedly described as Nārāyaṇa, Mahānārāyaṇa or having the strength of Nārāyaṇa. See Suvira Jaiswal, *The Origin and Development of Vaiṣṇavism*, p. 146.
[64] A.K. Warder, 'Feudalism and Mahāyāna Buddhism'.

[65] R.S. Sharma, 'Material Milieu of Tantricism', p. 176; B.N.S. Yadava, *Society and Culture in Northern India in the Twelfth Century*, p. 345.

[66] For Jina Ṛṣabha, see Padmanabha S. Jaini, 'Jina Ṛṣabha as an Avatāra of Viṣṇu'.

[67] D.D. Kosambi, *An Introduction to the Study of Indian History* (first edition), p. 294.

[68] For example, both Jagannātha of Puri and Venkaṭeśvara of Tirupati seem to have been associated with Buddhism at an earlier stage. *The Cult of Jagannāth and Regional Tradition of Orissa* (eds Anncharlott Eschmann, Hermann Kulke and Gaya Charan Tripathi), although a commendable work, does not give due attention to this aspect of the history of Jagannātha. For examples of the persecution of the Buddhists by Brahmanical kings, see B.N.S. Yadava, *Society and Culture in Northern India in the Twelfth Century*, pp. 346–47. He draws attention to the report of A. Führer in the *Archaeological Survey, Lists, N.W. Provinces and Oudh* that there were about forty-seven *kheras* or deserted sites of fortified towns in the Sultanpur district of Uttar Pradesh which were 'ruins of Buddhist cities destroyed by fire when Brahmanism won its final victory over Buddhism'. For the causes of the decline of Buddhism in India, see chapter 2 above.

Bibliography

Primary Sources, Texts and Translations

Adhyātma Rāmāyaṇa (critical edition), edited by Nagendranath Siddhartharatna, Calcutta: Metropolitan Printing and Publishing House, 1935; translated by Rai Bahadur Lala Baij Nath, Varanasi: Bharatiya Publishing House, 1979.

Agni Purāṇa, edited by J.L. Shastri, translated by N. Gangadharan, Ancient Indian Tradition and Mythology (AITM), vols 27–30, Delhi: Motilal Banarsidass, 1987.

Aitareya Brāhmaṇa (with the commentary of Sāyaṇa), edited by T. Weber, Bonn, 1879; translated by A.B. Keith, Harvard Oriental Series (HOS), XXV, Cambridge, Mass.: Harvard University Press, 1920.

Ānanda Rāmāyaṇa, Bombay: Gopal Narayan and Co., second edition, 1926.

Āpastamba Dharmasūtra, translated by G. Buhler, Sacred Books of the East (SBE), 2, Oxford: Oxford University Press,1879.

Āpastamba Gṛhyasūtra (with the commentary of Sudarśanācārya), Varanasi: Chaukhamba Sanskrit Series Office, 1971.

Aśvalāyana Gṛhyasūtra, edited by V.G. Apte, Poona, Anandasrama Press, 1937.

Atharvaveda (Śaunaka), edited by Vishva Bandhu, 5 vols, Hoshiarpur: Vishveshvar-anand Vedic Research Institute, 1960–64.

Atharva-veda-saṃhitā, translated by W.D. Whitney, Harvard Oriental Series (HOS), vols 7–8, Cambridge, Mass.: Harvard University Press, 1905.

Atri Saṃhitā, in *Smṛtīnāṃ Samuccayaḥ*, edited by Hari Narayana Apte, Pune: Ānand-āśrama Sanskrit Granthāvali, no. 48, 1929.

Bārhaspatya Sūtra, edited by F.W. Thomas, Punjab Sanskrit Series, Lahore, 1922.

Baudhāyana Dharmasūtra, edited by E. Hultzsch, Leipzig, 1884; translated by G. Bühler, Sacred Books of the East (SBE), 14, Oxford: Oxford University Press, 1882.

Baudhāyana Gṛhyasūtra, edited by R. Shamasastry, Oriental Library Publications, Mysore: University of Mysore, 1920.

Bhagavadgītā, translated by W.D.P. Hill, London: H. Milford, 1928.

Bhagavadgītā, edited and translated by S. Radhakrishnan, London: G. Allen and Unwin, 1949.

Bhagavadgītā, published by Motilal Jalan, Gorakhpur: Gita Press, Samvat 2019.

Bṛhadāraṇyaka Upaniṣad, edited and translated by S.C. Vasu, Allahabad: Pāṇini Office, 1933.

Chāndogya Upaniṣad, in *The Thirteen Principal Upaniṣads*, translated by R.E. Hume, Madras: Oxford University Press, second edition, 1968.

Dhūrtākhyāna, or Tale of Rogues, edited by Śri-Jinavijaya-Muni, Bombay: Bharatiya Vidya Bhavan, 1944.

Dīgha Nikāya, edited by T.W. Rhys Davids and J.E. Carpenter, 3 vols, London: Pali Text Society, 1890–1911; translated by T.W. Rhys Davis, *The Dialogue of the Buddhā*, *Sacred Books of the Buddhists*, vol. 3, London: Pali Text Society, 1899–1921.

Harivaṃśa (critical edition), edited by P.L. Vaidya, vols I–II, Poona: Bhandarkar Oriental Research Institute, 1969, 1971.

Harivaṃśa Purāṇa, Gorakhpur: Gita Press, second edition, 1966.

The Hymns of the Ṛgveda, translated with a popular commentary by Ralph T.H. Griffith, Delhi: Motilal Banarsidass, reprint, 1986.

Jacobi, H., *Das Rāmāyaṇa*, Bonn, 1893; *The Rāmāyaṇa* (English translation), Baroda: Oriental Institute, 1960.

Jātakas, edited by V. Fausböll, 7 vols with index, London, 1877–97; edited by E.B. Cowell, translated by various hands, 7 vols with index, Cambridge: Cambridge University Press, 1895–1907.

Jaya Saṃhitā, vols I and II, edited by K. Keshavram Shastri, Ahmedabad: Gujarat Research Society, 1977.

Kālikā Purāṇa, Varanasi: Chowkhamba Sanskrit Series, 1972.

Kamba Rāmāyaṇam, translated by H.V. Hande, Mumbai: Bharatiya Vidya Bhavan, 1996.

Kane, P.V., *History of Dharmaśāstra*, vols I–V, first edition, Pune: Bhandarkar Oriental Institute, 1930–62.

Kauṭilīya Arthaśāstra, The, edited and translated by R.P. Kangle, vols I–III, Bombay: University of Bombay, 1970; second edition, 1972.

Khan, Abdul Waheed, *An Early Sculpture of Narasiṃha*, Andhra Pradesh Government Archaeological Series No. 16, Hyderabad, 1964.

Kūrma Purāṇa, edited by Nilamani Mukhopadhyaya, Calcutta: Bibliotheca Indica, 1913.

Lal, B.B., ed., *Indian Archaeology 1976–77: A Review*, New Delhi: Archaeological Survey of India, 1977.

——, *Indian Archaeology 1979–80: A Review*, New Delhi: Archaeological Survey of India, 1980.

Madras Museum Plates of Vema, AD 1345, *Epigraphia Indica*, vol. VIII, 1905–06.

Mahābhārata (critical edition), edited by various hands, Poona: Bhandarkar Oriental Institute, 1927–66. (Unless otherwise stated, all references in the book are to this edition of the *Mahābhārata*.)

Mahābhāṣya of Patañjali, edited by F. Kielhorn, 3 vols, Mumbai, 1892–1909.

Maitrāyaṇī Saṃhitā, edited by Leopold von Schroder, Leipzig: Otto Harrassowitz, 1923.

Manusmṛti, edited by Pandit Gopalashastri Nene, Varanasi: Chowkhambha Sanskrit Sansthan, Vikram Samrat 2054; translated by G. Bühler, Sacred Books of the East (SBE), 33, Oxford: Oxford University Press, 1886.

Matsya Purāṇa, edited by H.N. Apte, Anandasrama Sanskrit Series, No. 54, Poona, 1907; translated by Ram Pratap Tripathi Shastri, Prayag (Allahabad): Hindi Sahitya Sammelan, Samvat 2003.

Meghadūta, in *Kālidāsa Granthavali*, edited and translated by Sitaram Chaturvedi, Varanasi, Vikram Samvat 2007.

Padma Purāṇa, 4 vols, Anandasrama Sanskrit Series, Poona, 1893–94.

Padma Purāṇa of Raviṣeṇācārya (with Hindi translation), edited and translated by Pannalal Jain, Kashi: Bhāratīya Jñānapīṭha, 1958.

Pañcaviṃśa Brāhmaṇa, translated by W. Caland, Calcutta: Bibliotheca Indica, 1931.

Pāṇini-Sūtra-Pāṭha and *Pariśiṣta* (with Word Index), compiled by S. Pathak and S. Chitrao, Poona: Bhandarkar Oriental Research Institute, 1935.

Parāśarasmṛti (with the *Subodhinī* Hindi commentary), edited by Daivajñavācaspati Śri Vāsudeva, Varanasi: Chowkhamba Sanskrit Series, 1968.

Pāraskara Gṛhyasūtra, edited by M.G. Bakre, Bombay: The Gujarati Priniting Press, 1917.

Paumacariyaṃ of Vimalasūri (with Hindi translation), edited by H. Jacobi, second revised edition by Punyavijayaji, translated by Shantilal M. Vora, 2 vols, Prakrit Text Society Series Nos 6, 12, Varanasi, 1962.

Raghuvaṃśa of Kālidāsa, The, edited and translated by Gopal Raghunath Nandargikar, Delhi: Motilal Banarsidass, 1971.

Rājataraṅgiṇī, translated by R.S. Pandit, New Delhi: Sahitya Akademi, reprint, 1990.

Rāmacaritamānasa of Tulasīdāsa (with commentary by Hanuman Prasad Poddar), Gorakhpur: Gita Press, Vikram Samvat 2050 (thick print).

Ṛgveda Saṃhitā (with the commentary of Sāyaṇa), 5 vols, Pune: Vaidika Saṃśodhana Maṇḍala, 1933–51.

Ṛgveda Saṃhitā (Hindi translation), edited by Pandit Ramgovind Trivedi, 9 vols, Varanasi: Chowkhamba Vidya Bhavan, 1991.

Rhys Davids, C.A.F., *Psalms of the Early Buddhists*, vol. II, London: Pali Text Society, 1948.

Śatapatha Brāhmaṇa, edited by Ganga Prasad Upadhyaya, New Delhi: The Research Institute of Ancient Scientific Studies, 1970; translated by J. Eggling, Sacred Books of the East (SBE), vols 12, 26, 41, 43, 44, Delhi: Motilal Banarsidass, reprint, 1988.

Skanda Purāṇa, 7 vols, Bombay: Venkateswara Press, 1909–11.

Smṛtīnām Samuccayaḥ, Ānandāśrama-Sanskrit-Granthāvali, no. 48, second edition, 1929.

Śrautakośa, edited by C.G. Koshikar, R.N. Dandekar *et al.*, vol. I, parts I and II, vol. II, parts I and II, Pune: Vaidika Samśodhana Maṇḍala, 1962, 1973.

Śrīmadbhagavadgītā Bhāṣya of Śrī Śaṅkarācārya, edited by A.G. Krishna Warrier, Madras: Sri Ramakrishnamatha, n.d.

Śrīmadbhāgavata-Mahāpurāṇa, translated by various hands, Gorakhpur: Gita Press, sixth edition, Samvat 2010.

Śrīmadvālmīkīya Rāmāyaṇa, edited and translated by Janakinath Sharma, first edition, Gorakhpur: Gita Press, Samvat 2017.

Śrīyogavāṣiṣtharāmāyaṇa, edited with Hindi Preface by Rai Bahadur Lala Baij Nath, Hindi translation by Thakur Prasad, Bombay: Jñanasāgara Press, 2006; first edition, 1903.

Taittirīya Āraṇyaka of the Black Yajurveda (with commentary of Sāyaṇācārya), edited by R.L. Mitra, Calcutta: Bibliotheca Indica, 1872.

Taittirīya Brāhamaṇa, edited by A.N. Apte, Anandasrama Sanskrit Series No. 37, Bombay, 1989.

Taittirīya Saṃhitā, edited by T.N. Dharmadhikari, 2 vols, Poona: Vaidika Samsodhana

Maṇḍala, 1981; translated by A.B. Keith, 2 vols, Cambridge, Mass.: Harvard University Press, 1969.

Tiruvāyamoḷi, edited and translated by S. Satyamurthi Ayyangar, Bombay: Ananthacharya Indological Research Institute, 1981.

Uttararāmacarita, edited by S.K. Belvalkar, Harvard Oriental Series (HOS), vol. 21, Cambridge, Mass.: Harvard University Press, 1915.

Uttararāmacarita of Bhavabhūti, edited by P.V. Kane, translated by C.N. Joshi, Delhi: Motilal Banarsidass, fourth revised edition, 1962.

Vālmīki-Rāmāyaṇa, The (critical edition), 7 vols, G.H. Bhatt and U.P. Shah (General Editors), Baroda: Oriental Institute, 1960–75.

Varṇaratnākara of Jyotireśvara Kaviśekharācārya, edited by S.K. Chatterji and B. Misra, Calcutta: Asiatic Society of Bengal, 1940.

Vedavyāsasmṛti, in *Smṛtīnāṃ Samuccayaḥ*, Ānandāśrama Sanskrit Granthāvali, No. 48, second edition, 1929.

Viṣṇu Purāṇa, edited and translated by Munilal Gupta, Gorakhpur: Gita Press, Samvat 2014; translated by H.H. Wilson, 5 vols, London, 1864–70, second edition, Calcutta, 1961.

Viṣṇudharmottara Purāṇa, Bombay: Venkateswara Press, Samvat 1969.

Vṛddha-hārīta-smṛti, in *Smṛtīnāṃ Samuccayaḥ*, Ānandāśrama Sanskrit Series, No. 48, Bombay, 1905.

Yuga Purāṇa, edited by Dr. Vishvanath Pandey, Hindi translation by Shrikrishnamani Tripathi, Varanasi: Chowkhamba Surbharati Prakashan, 1975.

Zaehner, R.C., *The Bhagavadgītā*, Oxford: Oxford University Press, 1969.

Secondary Works

Adiga, Malini, *The Making of Southern Karnataka Society, Polity and Culture in the Early Medieval Period: AD 400–1030*, Hyderabad: Orient Longman, 2006.

Agrawala, V.S., 'The Purāṇas and the Hindu Religion', *Purāṇa*, vol. VI, no. 2, 1964: 33–64.

Ahmad, Aijaz, 'Between Orientalism and Historicism: Anthropological Knowledge of India', *Studies in History*, vol. 7, no. 1, 1991: 135–63.

——, *In Theory: Nations, Classes, Literatures*, New Delhi: Oxford University Press, 1994.

Aiyangar, S.K., *A History of Tirupati*, Madras: C. Sambaiya Pantulu, vol. I, 1940–41.

Alexander, P.C., *Buddhism in Kerala*, Annamalainagar: Annamalai University, 1949.

Altekar, A.S., *The Position of Women in Hindu Civilization*, Delhi: Motilal Banarsidass, 1991.

Ambedkar, B.R., *Dr Babasaheb Ambedkar: Writings and Speeches*, vols I, III, V, edited by Vasant Moon, Bombay: Education Department, Government of Maharashtra, 1987–93.

——, 'Slaves and Untouchables', in *Dr Babasaheb Ambedkar: Writings and Speeches*, vol. V, edited by Vasant Moon, Bombay: Education Department, Government of Maharashtra, 1989.

——, *Annihilation of Caste: An Undelivered Speech*, edited by Mulk Raj Anand, New Delhi: Arnold Publishers, 1990.

Apte, V.M., 'Social and Economic Conditions', in R.C. Majumdar and A.D. Pusalker, eds, *The Vedic Age, The History and Culture of the Indian People*, vol. 1, Bombay: Bharatiya Vidya Bhavan, 1988; first edition 1951.

Apte, V.M., 'Religion and Philosophy', in R.C. Majumdar and A.D. Pusalker, eds, *The Vedic Age, The History and Culture of the Indian People*, vol. 1, Bombay: Bharatiya Vidya Bhavan, 1988; first edition 1951.

Awasthi, R., *Khajuraho ki deva pratimāyen*, Agra: Oriental Publishing House, 1967.

Bagchi, P.C., *Studies in the Tantras*, Calcutta: Calcutta University, 1939.

Bagchi, Subhendugopal, *Eminent Śākta Centres in Eastern India*, Calcutta: Punthi Pustak, 1980.

Bailey, H.W., 'Iranian Arya- and Daha-', *Transactions of the Philological Society*, 1959: 71–115.

Bakker, Hans, *Ayodhya*, Groningen: Egbert Forsten, 1986.

Banerjea, J.N., 'Vyūhas and Vibhavas of Viṣṇu', *Journal of Indian Society of Oriental Art*, vol. XIV, 1946: 56–59.

Banerjee, P., *Rāma in Indian Literature, Art and Thought*, Delhi: Sandeep Prakashan, 1986.

Basham, A.L., *The Wonder That Was India*, Calcutta: Fontana and Rupa, 1971.

——, *The Origin and Development of Classical Hinduism*, edited and annotated by Kenneth Zysk, Delhi: Oxford University Press, 1990.

Basu, Jogiraj, *India of the Age of the Brāhmaṇas*, Calcutta: Sanskrit Pustak Bhandar, 1969.

Benveniste, Émile, *Indo–European Language and Society*, London: Faber, 1973.

Berreman, Gerald D., 'The Brahmanical View of Caste', *Contributions to Indian Sociology*, n.s., vol. 5, 1970: 16–25.

Béteille, André, 'The Reproduction of Inequality: Occupation, Caste and Family', *Contributions to Indian Sociology*, n.s., vol. 25, 1991: 3–28.

Bhandarkar, R.G., *Vaiṣṇavism, Śaivism and Minor Religious Systems*, Varanasi: Indological Book House, 1965; first edition, 1913.

Bhattacharya, Benoytosh, *Indian Buddhist Iconography*, Calcutta: Firma K.L. Mukhopadhyay, 1958.

Bosch, F.D.K., 'The God with the Horse's Head', in *Selected Studies in Indonesian Archaeology*, The Hague: Martinus Nijhoff, 1961: 137–52.

Bose, N.K., 'The Hindu Method of Tribal Absorption', in *Culture and Society in India*, Bombay: Asia Publishing House, 1967.

Bouglé, Célestin, *Essays on the Caste System*, translated by D.F. Pocock, Cambridge: Cambridge University Press, 1971.

Briggs, G.W., *The Chamars*, London: Oxford University Press, 1920.

Brockington, J.L., *Righteous Rāma: The Evolution of an Epic*, Delhi: Oxford University Press, 1984.

Bühler, Georg, 'Review of Alberuni's *India*: An English Edition with Notes and Indices by Dr Edward Sachau', *Indian Antiquary*, vol. XIX, 1890.

Bulcke, (Father) Camille, *Rāmakathā*, Allahabad: Allahabad University, sixth edition, 1999.

Chakravarti, Uma, *Social Dimensions of Early Buddhism*, Delhi: Oxford University Press, 1981.

——, *Rewriting History: The Life and Times of Pandita Ramabai*, Delhi: Kali for Women, 1998.

Champakalakshmi, R., *Vaiṣṇava Iconography in the Tamil Country*, Delhi: Orient Longman, 1981.

——, 'From Devotion and Dissent to Dominance: The Bhakti of Tamil Āḷvārs and Nāyanārs', in R. Champakalakshmi and S. Gopal, eds, *Tradition, Dissent and Ideology: Essays in Honour of Romila Thapar*, Delhi: Oxford University Press, 1996.

Chanana, Dev Raj, *Slavery in Ancient India*, Delhi: People's Publishing House, 1990; first edition, 1960.

Chandra, K.R., *A Critical Study of Paumacariyaṃ*, Muzaffarpur: Research Institute of Prakrit, Jainology and Ahimsa, 1970.

Chatterjee, Partha, 'Claims on the Past: The Genealogy of Modern Historiography in Bengal', in David Arnold and David Hardiman, eds, *Subaltern Studies VIII: Essays in Honour of Ranajit Guha*, Delhi: Oxford University Press, 1994: 1–49.

Chatterji, S.K., 'Race-Movements and Prehistoric Culture', in R.C. Majumdar and A.D. Pusalker, eds, *The Vedic Age, The History and Culture of the Indian People*, vol. 1, Bombay: Bharatiya Vidya Bhavan, 1988; first edition 1951.

Chattopadhyaya, B.D., *The Making of Early Medieval India*, Delhi: Oxford University Press, 1994.

——, *Representing the Other: Sanskrit Sources and the Muslims*, Delhi: Manohar, 1998.

Chattopadhyaya, Debiprasad, *Religion and Society: Stephanos Nirmalendu Ghose Lectures, 1981, of Calcutta University*, Bangalore: Ma-Le Prakashana, 1987.

Chaube, R.K., *Proceedings of the Indian History Congress*, First session, Allahabad, 1938.

Chaudhuri, Nupur and Rajat Kanta Ray, 'Eros and History: Sahajiya Secrets and the Tantric Culture of Love', in Irfan Habib, ed., *Religion in Indian History*, New Delhi: Tulika Books, 2007.

Chhatry, D.B., *The Centres of India*, series 3, part VI-B, *Special Survey Report on Selected Towns*, Gauhati, 1971.

Choudhary, Pradeep Kant, *Rāma with an Axe: Myth and Cult of Paraśurāma Avatāra*, Delhi: Aakar Books, 2010.

Choudhury, P.C., *The History of Civilization of the People of Assam to the Twelfth Century AD*, Gauhati: Department of Historical and Antiquarian Studies, Government of Assam, 1959.

Chowdhury, Sujit, 'The Bodos: The Tribe for Whom History Failed', in Dev Nathan, ed., *From Tribe to Caste*, Shimla: Indian Institute of Advanced Study, 1997: 432–45.

Converse, Hyla Shuntz, 'The Agnicayana Rite: Indigenous Origin?', *History of Religions*, vol. XIV, no. 2, 1974: 81–95.

Dahiwale, S.M., 'The Broken Men Theory of Untouchability', in S.M. Dahiwale, ed., *Understanding Indian Society: The Non-Brahmanic Perspective*, Jaipur and Delhi: Rawat Publications, 2006.

Dalton, E.T., 'Notes on Assam Temple Ruins', *Journal of Asiatic Society of Bengal*, vol. XXIV, 1855.

Dange, S.A., *Vedic Concept of Field and the Divine Fructification*, Bombay: University of Bombay, 1971.

——, *Sexual Symbolism from the Vedic Ritual*, Delhi: Ajanta Publications, 1979.

Das Gupta, N.N., in R.C. Majumdar and A.D. Pusalker, eds, *The Struggle for Empire, The History and Culture of the Indian People*, vol. 5, Bombay: Bharatiya Vidya Bhavan, second edition, 1966.

Dasgupta, Biplab, 'Mode of Production and the Extent of Peasant Differentiation in Pre-British Bengal', *Social Scientist*, vol. XII, no. 8, 1984.

Datta, Bhabatosh, 'The Rāmāyaṇa in Bengal', in V. Raghavan, ed., *The Rāmāyaṇa Tradition in Asia*, Delhi: Sahitya Akademi, 1980.

Davis, Richard H., *Lives of Indian Images*, Delhi: Motilal Banarsidass, 1999.

Deliège, Robert, 'The Myths of Origin of the Indian Untouchables', *Man*, n.s., vol. 28, no. 3, 1993: 533–49.

——, *The Untouchables of India*, translated by Nora Scott, Oxford: Berg, 1999.

Derrett, J. Duncan, *Religion, Law and the State in India*, London: Faber and Faber, 1968.

Desai, Devangana, *Erotic Sculptures of India*, New Delhi: Tata McGraw–Hill, 1975.

Desai, Kalpana, *Iconography of Viṣṇu: In Northern India, Upto the Medieval Period*, Delhi: Abhinav Publications, 1973.

Deshpande, Madhav M., 'Genesis of Ṛgvedic Retroflexion: A Historical and Socio-Linguistic Investigation', in M.M. Deshpande and Peter Edwin Hook, eds, *Aryan and Non-Aryan in India*, Ann Arbor: Karoma Publishers Inc. and Center for South and Southeast Asian Studies, University of Michigan, 1979: 235–315.

——, 'Vedic Aryans, Non-Vedic Aryans and Non-Aryans: Judging the Linguistic Evidence of the Veda', in George Erdosy, ed., *The Indo–Aryans of Ancient South Asia: Language, Material Culture and Ethnicity*, New York: Walter de Gruyter, 1995: 67–84.

——, 'Aryan Origins: Brief History of Linguistic Arguments', in Romila Thapar, ed., *India: Historical Beginnings and the Concept of the Aryan*, New Delhi: National Book Trust, 2006: 98–156.

Deva, Krishna, *Temples of Khajuraho*, vol. I, New Delhi: Archaeological Survey of India, 1990.

Dharmapala-Frick, Gita, 'Shifting Categories in the Discourse on Caste: Some Historical Observations', in Vasudha Dalmia and H. von Stietencron, eds, *Representing Hinduism*, New Delhi: Sage, 1995: 82–100.

Dirks, Nicholas B., *The Hollow Crown: Ethnohistory of an Indian Kingdom*, Ann Arbor: University of Michigan Press, second edition, 1993.

——, *Castes of Mind: Colonialism and the Making of Modern India*, New Delhi: Permanent Black, 2006.

Doniger O'Flaherty, Wendy, 'The Submarine Mare in the Mythology of Śiva', *Journal of the Royal Asiatic Society of Great Britain and Ireland*, no. 1, 1971: 9–27.

——, 'The Images of the Heretic in Gupta Purāṇas', in Bardwell Smith, ed., *Essays on Gupta Culture*, Delhi: Motilal Banarsidass, 1983.

Dumont, Louis, *A South Indian Subcaste: Social Organization and Religion of the Pramalai Kallar*, Delhi: Oxford University Press, 1986.

——, *Homo Hierarchicus: The Caste System and its Implications*, translated by Mark Sainsbury *et al.*, New Delhi: Oxford University Press, 1988; first edition, 1966.

Dutt, Nalinaksha, 'Buddhism', in R.C. Majumdar and A.D. Pusalker, eds, *The Classical Age, The History and Culture of the Indian People*, vol. 3, Bombay: Bharatiya Vidya Bhavan, third edition, 1970.

Dutta, Sukumar, *Transactions of the Indian Institute of Advanced Studies*, vol. 1, Shimla: Indian Institute of Advanced Studies, 1965.

Dwivedi, Hazari Prasad, *Kabīr*, Delhi: Rajkamal Prakashan, eighth reprint, 2000.

Eliade, Mircea, *Yoga: Immortality and Freedom*, London: Routledge and Kegan Paul, 1958.

Erdosy, George, 'Ethnicity in the Ṛgveda, and its Bearing on the Problem of Indo–European Origins', *South Asian Studies*, vol. V, 1989: 35–47.

——, 'Language, Material Culture and Ethnicity: Theoretical Perspectives', in George Erdosy, ed., *The Indo-Aryans of Ancient South Asia: Language, Material Culture and Ethnicity*, New York: Walter de Gruyter, 1995.

Erndl, Kathleen M., 'The Mutilation of Śūrpaṇakhā', in Paula Richman, ed., *Many Rāmāyaṇas: The Diversity of a Narrative Tradition in South Asia*, Delhi: Oxford University Press, 1994.

Eschmann, Ancharlott, 'The Vaiṣṇava Typology of Hinduization and the Origin of Jagannātha', in A. Eschmann, H. Kulke and G.C. Tripathi, eds, *The Cult of Jagannath and the Regional Tradition of Orissa*, Delhi: Manohar, 1978.

Eschmann, Ancharlott, Hermann Kulke and Gaya Charan Tripathi, eds, *The Cult of Jagannath and the Regional Tradition of Orissa*. Delhi: Manohar, Delhi, 1978.

Farquhar, J.N., *Outline of the Religious Literature of India*, London: Milford, 1920.

Faulkes, Thomas, 'A Grant of Nandivarman-Pallavamalla', *Indian Antiquary*, vol. VIII, 1879: 273–84.

Fick, Richard, *The Social Organization in North East India*, translated by S.K. Maitra, Calcutta: University of Calcutta, 1920.

Fukazawa, Hiroshi, *The Medieval Deccan: Peasants, Social Systems and States: Sixteenth to Eighteenth Centuries*, Delhi: Oxford University Press, 1991.

Geetha, V., 'Rewriting History in the Brahmin's Shadow: Caste and the Modern Historical Imagination', *Journal of Arts and Ideas*, nos 25–26, 1993: 127–37.

Ghate, V.S., *Lectures on the Ṛgveda*, revised and edited by V.S. Sukthankar, Poona Oriental Series, no. 12, Pune, 1966.

Ghosh, B.K., 'Language and Literature', in R.C. Majumdar and A.D. Pusalker, eds, *The Vedic Age, The History and Culture of the Indian People*, vol. 1, Bombay: Bharatiya Vidya Bhavan, fifth edition, 1988, chapter XX.

Ghoshal, U.N., 'Hindu Theories of the Origin of Kingship and Mr K.P. Jayaswal', *Indian Historical Quarterly*, vol. I, 1925.

——, *A History of Indian Political Ideas*, Calcutta: Oxford University Press, 1996; first edition, 1966.

Ghurye, G.S., *Gods and Men*, Bombay: Popular Book Depot, 1962.

——, *Two Brahmanical Institutions: Gotra and Charana*, Bombay: Popular Prakashan, 1972.

Goetz, Hermann, *The Early Wooden Temples of Chamba*, Leiden: E.J. Brill, 1955.

Goldman, Robert P., *The Rāmāyaṇa of Vālmīki: An Epic of Ancient India*, vol. I: *Bālakānda*, Delhi: Oxford University Press, 1984.

Goldman, Sally J. Sutherland, 'Speaking Gender: *Vāc* and the Vedic Construction of the Feminine', in Julia Leslie and Mary MacGee, eds, *Invented Identities: The Interplay of Gender, Religion and Politics in India*, Delhi: Oxford University Press, 2000: 57–83.

Gombrich, Richard F., *Buddhist Precept and Practice: Traditional Buddhism in the Rural Highlands of Ceylon*, Delhi: Oxford University Press, 1991.

Gonda, Jan, *Change and Continuity in Indian Religion*, The Hague: Mouton, 1965.

——, *Vedic Literature: A History of Indian Literature*, vol. I, Wiesbaden: Harrassowitz, 1975.

Gopalachari, K., *Early History of the Andhra Country*, Madras: Madras University Historical Series, 1941.

Goswami, Sarat Chandra, *Introducing Assam Vaiṣṇavism*, Gauhati, 1946.

Gupta, Dipankar, 'Continuous Hierarchies and Discrete Castes', *Economic and Political Weekly*, vol. 19, no. 46, 1984; reprinted in Dipankar Gupta, ed., *Social Stratification*, Delhi: Oxford University Press, 1991.

——, 'From Varna to Jati: The Indian Caste System from the Asiatic to the Feudal Mode of Production', *Journal of Contemporary Asia*, vol. X, 1980: 249–71; reprinted in K.L. Sharma, ed., *Social Inequality in India: Profiles of Caste, Class, Power and Social Mobility*, Delhi: Rawat Publications, 1995: 159–91.

——, *Interrogating Caste: Understanding Hierarchy and Difference in Indian Society*, Delhi: Penguin Books, 2000.

Gupta, J.D. and B.N. Saraswati, 'Ploughs and Husking Implements', in Nirmal Kumar Bose, ed., *Peasant Life in India: A Study in Indian Unity and Diversity*, Calcutta: Anthropological Survey of India, Memoir No. 8: 25–34.

Habib, Irfan, 'Economic History of the Delhi Sultanate: An Essay in Interpretation', *Indian Historical Review*, vol. IV, no. 2, 1978: 287–303.

——, 'The Peasant in Indian History: General President's Address to the Indian History Congress', in *Proceedings of the Indian History Congress*, forty-third session, Kurukshetra, 1982.

——, *Interpreting Indian History*, Shillong: North-Eastern Hill University Publications, 1985.

——, 'Medieval Popular Monotheism and Its Humanism: The Historical Setting', *Social Scientist*, vol. 21, nos 3–4, 1993: 78–88.

——, *Essays in Indian History: Towards a Marxist Perception*, New Delhi: Tulika Books, 1995.

——, *A People's History of India 2: The Indus Civilization*, New Delhi: Tulika Books, 2002.

Habib, Irfan, ed., *Religion in Indian History*, New Delhi: Tulika Books, 2007.

Habib, Irfan and V.K. Thakur, *A People's History of India 3: The Vedic Age*, New Delhi: Tulika Books, 2003.

Hale, Wash Edward, *Asura in Early Vedic Religion*, Delhi: Motilal Banarsidass, 1986.

Hanumanthan, K.R. 'Evolution of Untouchability in Tamil Nadu, up to AD 1600', *Indian Historical Review*, vol. XXIII, nos 1–2, 1996–97.

Hardiman, David, *Histories for the Subordinated*, Delhi: Permanent Black, 2006.

Hardy, Friedhelm, *Viraha-Bhakti*: *The Early History of Kṛṣṇa Devotion in South India*, Delhi: Oxford University Press, 1983.

——, *The Religious Culture of India: Power, Love and Wisdom*, Delhi: Cambridge University Press, 1995.

Hart III, George L., 'The Nature of Tamil Devotion', in M.M. Deshpande and Peter Edwin Hook, eds, *Aryan and Non-Aryan in India*, Ann Arbor: Karoma Publishers Inc.

and Center for South and Southeast Asian Studies, University of Michigan, 1979.
Hazra, R.C., *Studies in the Upapurāṇas*, vol. I, Sanskrit College Research Series, No. 11, Calcutta, 1958.
Hegarty, James, 'The Plurality of the Sanskrit Mahābhārata and of the Mahābhārata Story', in D.N. Jha, ed., *Contesting Symbols and Stereotypes: Essays on Indian History and Culture*, Delhi: Aakar Books, 2013: 146–86.
Hopkins, E.W., 'Numerical Formulae in the Veda and Their Bearing on Vedic Criticism', *Journal of American Oriental Society*, vol. XVI, 1896: 275–81.
——, 'Pragāthikāni, I', *Journal of the American Oriental Society*, vol. 17, 1896: 23–92.
Horner, I.B., *Women under Primitive Buddhism*, Delhi: Motilal Banarsidass, 1990; first edition, 1930.
Hutton, J.H., *Caste in India: Its Nature, Function, and Origins*, Cambridge: Cambridge University Press, 1946.
Ilaiah, Kancha, 'BSP and Caste as Ideology', *Economic and Political Weekly*, vol. 29, no. 12, 1994: 668–69.
——, 'Productive Labour, Consciousness, and History: The Dalitbahujan Alternative', in Shahid Amin and Dipesh Chakrabarty, eds, *Subaltern Studies IX: Writings on South Asian History and Society*, Delhi: Oxford University Press, 1996: 165–200.
Inden, Ronald, 'Orientalist Constructions of India', *Modern Asian Studies*, vol. 20, no. 3, 1986: 401–46.
——, *Imagining India*, Oxford: Basil Blackwell, 1990.
Indian Antiquary, vol. 18, 1889.
Jacobi, H., *Das Rāmāyaṇa*, Bonn, 1893; *The Rāmāyaṇa* (English translation), Baroda: Oriental Institute, 1960.
Jain, Jyoti Prasad, *The Jaina Sources of the History of Ancient India (100 BC–AD 900)*, Delhi: Munshiram Manoharlal, 1964.
Jaini, Padmanabha S., 'Jina Ṛṣabha as an avatāra of Viṣṇu', *Bulletin of the School of Oriental and African Studies*, vol. XL, part 2, 1977: 321–37.
——, *Gender and Salvation: Debates on the Spiritual Liberation of Women*, Delhi: Munshiram Manoharlal, 1991.
Jaiswal, Suvira, 'Studies in the Social History of the Early Tamils', in R.S. Sharma and V. Jha, eds, *Indian Society: Historical Probings: In Memory of D.D. Kosambi*, New Delhi: People's Publishing House, 1974.
——, 'Review of *The Sword and the Flute*', *Indian Book Chronicle*, vol. I, no. 10, 1976: 147–49.
——, 'Caste in the Socio-Economic Framework of Early India', Presidential Address, section I, in *Proceedings of the Indian History Congress*, thirty-eighth session, Bhubaneswar, 1977: pp. 23–48.
——, *The Origin and Development of Vaiṣṇavism*, Delhi: Munshiram Manoharlal, 1981; first edition, 1967.
——, 'Women in Early India: Problems and Perspectives', in *Proceedings of the Indian History Congress*, forty-second session, Bodh Gaya, 1981: 54–60.
——, 'Semitising Hinduism: Changing Paradigms of Brahmanical Integration', *Social Scientist*, vol. 19, no. 12, 1991: 20–32.
——, 'Varna Ideology and Social Change', *Social Scientist*, vol. 19, nos 3–4, 1991.
——, 'The Changing Concept of Gṛhapati', in D.N. Jha, ed., *Society and Ideology in*

India: Essays in Honour of Professor R.S. Sharma, Delhi: Munshiram Manoharlal, 1996: 29–37.
——, 'Tribe–Caste Interaction: A Re-examination of Certain Issues', in Dev Nathan, ed., *From Tribe to Caste*, Shimla: Indian Institute of Advanced Study, 1997: 167–75.
——, 'Caste: Ideology and Context', *Indologica Taurinensia*, vols XXIII–XXIV, 1997–98: 607–19.
——, *Caste: Origin, Function and Dimensions of Change*, Delhi: Manohar, 1998.
——, 'Change and Continuity in Brahmanical Religion with Particular Reference to Vaiṣṇava Bhakti', *Social Scientist*, vol. XXVII, nos 5–6, 2000: 3–23.
——, 'Kosambi on Caste', in D.N. Jha, ed., *The Many Careers of D.D. Kosambi: Critical Essays*, Delhi: Leftword Books, 2001: 130–50.
——, 'Rāma-Bhakti', in J.S. Grewal, ed., *Religious Movements and Institutions in Medieval India, The History of Science, Philosophy and Culture in Indian Civilization*, vol. VII, part 2, Delhi: Oxford University Press, 2006.
——, 'Reconstructing History from the Ṛgveda: A Paradigm Shift?' *Social Science Probings*, vol. 18, no. 2, 2006: 1–17.
——, '*Dalit asmitā aur agenda jāti vināśa kā*', *Tadbhav*, vol. 15, 2007: 27–40.
——, 'The Making of a Hegemonic Tradition: The Cult of Rama Dasarathi', S.C. Misra Memorial Lecture, Indian History Congrees, sixty-seventh session, 2007.
——, 'Social Dimensions of the Cult of Rama', in Irfan Habib, ed., *Religion in Indian History*, New Delhi: Tulika Books, 2007.
Jamkhedkar, A.P., 'Ancient Strucures', *Marg*, vol. 37, part 1, 1986: 25–56.
Jha, D.N., *Ancient India in Historical Outline*, Delhi: Manohar, 1998.
——, *The Myth of the Holy Cow*, London: Verso, 2001.
——, 'Looking for a Hindu Identity', General President's Address, in *Proceedings of the Indian History Congress*, sixty-sixth session, Visva-Bharati, Santiniketan, 2006.
——, *Rethinking Hindu Identity*, London: Equinox, 2009.
Jha, D.N., ed., *Contesting Symbols and Stereotypes: Essays on Indian History and Culture*, Delhi: Aakar Books, 2013.
Jha, Vivekanand, 'Status of the Rathakāra in Early Indian History', *Journal of Indian History*, vol. 52, part 1, 1974: 39–47.
——, 'Stages in the History of Untouchables', *Indian Historical Review*, vol. II, no. 1, 1975: 14 –31.
——, 'Caṇḍāla and the Origin of Untouchability', *Indian Historical Review*, vol. XIII, nos 1–2, 1986–87: 4–7.
——, 'Caste, Untouchability and Social Justice: Early North Indian Perspective', *Social Scientist*, vol. 25, nos 11–12, 1997.
Joshi, N.P, 'Early Brahmanical Sculptures in Bharat Kala Bhavan', *Chhavi*, part I, Golden Jubilee volume (1920–70), Bharat Kala Bhavan: 179–80.
Karashima, Noboru, 'The Untouchability in Tamil Inscriptions and Other Historical Sources in Tamil Nadu', in Hiroyoki Kotani, ed., *Caste System, Untouchability and the Depressed*, Delhi: Manohar, 1977.
Karve, Irawati, 'Kinship Terminology and Kinship Usages in *Ṛgveda* and *Atharvaveda*', *Annals of the Bhandarkar Oriental Research Institute*, vol. XX, 1938–39.
——, *Yugānta: The End of An Epoch*, New Delhi: Sangam Books, 1974.
Katju, Markanday, 'Looking Back on the Caste System', *The Hindu*, 8 January 2009.

Kenoyer, Jonathan Mark, 'Cultures and Societies in the Indus Tradition', in Romila Thapar, ed., *India: Historical Beginnings and the Concept of the Aryan*, New Delhi: National Book Trust, 2006: 41–97.

Kinsley, David R., *The Sword and the Flute: Kālī and Kṛṣṇa: Dark Visions of the Terrible and The Sublime in Hindu Mythology*, Delhi: Vikas Publishing House, 1976.

Kirk, G.S., *Myth: Its Meaning and Functions in Ancient and Other Cultures*, Cambridge: Cambridge University Press, 1970.

——, *The Nature of Greek Myths*, Harmondsworth: Penguin Books, 1974.

Klass, Morton, *Caste: The Emergence of the South Asian Social System*, Philadelphia: Institute for the Study of Human Issues, 1980.

Kolenda, Pauline, 'Religious Anxiety and Hindu Fate', in E.B. Harper, ed., *Religion in South Asia*, Seattle: University of Washington Press, 1964: 71–81.

——, *Caste, Cult and Hierarchy: Essays on the Culture of India*, Meerut: Folklore Institute, 1981.

Kosambi, D.D., 'Origin of Brahmin Gotras', *Journal of the Bombay Branch of the Royal Asiatic Society*, vol. 26, 1950.

——, 'The Basis of Ancient Indian History', *Journal of the American Oriental Society*, vol. 75, 1955; reprinted in *D.D. Kosambi: Combined Methods in Indology and Other Writings*, edited by Brajadulal Chattopadhyaya, Delhi: Oxford University Press, 2002.

——, *Myth and Reality: Studies in the Formation of Indian Culture*, Bombay: Popular Prakashan, 1962.

——, *The Culture and Civilization of Ancient India in Historical Outline*, London: Routledge and Kegan Paul, 1965.

——, *An Introduction to the Study of Indian History*, Bombay: Popular Prakashan, second revised edition, 1985; first edition, 1956.

——, 'The Decline of Buddhism in India', in *Exasperating Essays: Exercises in Dialectical Method*, Pune: R.P. Nene, 1986; first edition, 1956.

——, *Exasperating Essays: Exercises in the Dialectical Method*, Pune: R.P. Nene, 1986; first edition, 1956.

——, *Combined Methods in Indology and Other Writings*, edited by Brajadulal Chattopadhyaya, Delhi: Oxford University Press, 2002.

——, 'Indo–Aryan Nose Index', translated from the Russian, 'Indo–Ariiskii Nosovoi Ukazatel', *Sovetskaya Etnografia*, 1958: 39–57; reprinted in *Combined Methods in Indology and Other Writings*, edited by Brajadulal Chattopadhyaya, Delhi: Oxford University Press, 2002.

Kosambi, Dharmanand, *Bhagavān Buddha*, translated by Shripad Joshi, Delhi, 1956.

Kotani, H., 'Ati-śūdra castes in the Medieval Deccan', in H. Kotani, ed., *Caste System, Untouchability and the Depressed*, Delhi: Manohar, 1997.

Kotiyal, H.S., 'Śūdra Rulers and Officials in Early Medieval Times', in *Proceedings of the Indian History Congress*, thirty-fourth session, Chandigarh, 1973: 80–87.

Küiper, F.B.J., 'An Austro–Asiatic Myth in the *Ṛgveda*', in *Mededalingan der koninklyke Nederlandsche Akademie van Wetenschappen*, vol. 23, no. 7, 1950: 163–82.

——, *Aryans in the Ṛgveda*, Amsterdam: Rodopi, 1991.

Kulke, Hermann, in Anncharlott Eschmann, Hermann Kulke and Gaya Charan

Tripathi, eds, *The Cult of Jagannāth and the Regional Tradition of Orissa*, Delhi: Manohar, 1978

——, *Kings and Cults: State Formation and Legitimation in India and South-East Asia*, Delhi: Manohar, 1993.

Kulke, Hermann and Dietmar Rothermund, *A History of India*, Delhi: Manohar, 1989.

Lahiri, Nayanjot, *Pre-Ahom Assam*, Delhi: Munshiram Manoharlal, 1991.

Lal, Vinay, *The History of History: Politics of Scholarship in Modern India*, Delhi: Oxford University Press, 2003.

Leacock, Eleanor, 'Introduction to Frederick Engels, *The Origin of the Family, Private Property and the State*', New York: International Publishers, 1977.

Lele, Jayant, *Hindutva: The Emergence of the Right*, Madras: Earthworm Books, 1995.

Lerner, Gerda, *The Creation of Patriarchy*, New York: Oxford University Press, 1986.

Leslie, Julia I., *The Perfect Wife*, Delhi: Oxford University Press, 1989.

Lorenzen, David N., 'The Kālāmukha Background to Vīraśaivsm: Studies in Orientology', in S.K. Maity, Upendra Thakur and A.K. Narayan, eds, *Studies in Orientology: Essays in Memory of Professor A.L. Basham*, Agra: Y.K. Publishers, 1988.

Lutgendorf, Philip, 'The Secret Life of Rāmacandra of Ayodhyā', in Paula Richman, ed., *Many Rāmāyaṇas: The Diversity of a Narrative Tradition in South Asia*, Delhi: Oxford University Press, 1992: 217–34.

——, 'Interpreting Rāmrāj', in David N. Lorenzen, ed., *Bhakti Religion in North India*, Albany: SUNY Press, 1995.

Macdonell, A.A., *Vedic Mythology*, Delhi: Motilal Banarsidass, 1963; first edition, 1897.

Mahalingam, T.V., 'Hayagrīva, the Concept and the Cult', *Adyar Library Bulletin*, vol. XXIX, 1965: 188–99.

Mainkar, T.G., *The Vasiṣṭha Rāmāyaṇa: A Study*, New Delhi: Meharchand Lachhmandas, 1977.

Majumdar, R.C., 'Eastern India During the Pāla Period', in R.C. Majumdar, ed., *The Age of Imperial Kanauj, The History and Culture of the Indian People*, vol. 4, Bombay: Bharatiya Vidya Bhavan, 1964.

Majumdar, R.C., ed., *The Classical Accounts of India*, Calcutta: Firma K.L. Mukhopadhyay, 1960.

Mani, Vettam, *Purāṇic Encyclopedia*, Delhi: Motilal Banarsidass, 1979.

Marglin, F.A., *Wives of the God–King: The Rituals of the Devadasis of Puri*, Delhi: Oxford University Press, 1985.

Masica, C.P., 'Aryan and Non-Aryan Elements in North Indian Agriculture', in M.M. Deshpande and Peter Edwin Hook, eds, *Aryan and Non-Aryan in India*, Ann Arbor: Karoma Publishers Inc. and Center for South and Southeast Asian Studies, University of Michigan, 1979: 55–102.

Mazumdar, B.C., *Orissa in the Making*, Calcutta: University of Calcutta, 1925.

Mehendale, M.A., 'Language and Literature', in R.C. Majumdar and A.D. Pusalker, eds, *The Age of Imperial Unity, The History and Cultural of the Indian People*, vol. 2, Bombay: Bharatiya Vidya Bhavan, 1951.

Mencher, Joan P., 'The Caste System Upside Down, or the Not So Mysterious East', *Current Anthropology*, vol. 15, no. 4, 1974.

Mendelsohn, Oliver and Marika Vicziany, *The Untouchables*, New Delhi: Foundation Books, 2000.

Menon, A.G. and G.H. Schokker, 'The Conception of Rāma Rajya in South and North Indian Literature', in A.W. van den Hock, D.H.A. Kolff and M.S. Oorts, eds, *Ritual, State and History in South Asia: Essays in Honour* of *J.C. Heesterman*, Leiden: E.J. Brill, 1992.

Meyer, Adrian C., 'The Indian Caste System', in *International Encyclopedia of the Social Sciences*, edited by David L. Sills, New York: Macmillan, 1968.

Michael, P.M., ed., *Dalits in Modern India: Vision and Values*, New Delhi: Sage Publications, 2007; first edition, 1999.

Mishra, D.P., *The Search for Laṅkā*, Delhi: Agam Kala Prakashan, 1985.

Misra, K.C., *The Cult of Jagannatha*, Calcutta: Firma K.L. Mukhopadhyay, 1971.

Misra, S.N., *Ancient Indian Republics*, Lucknow: The Upper India Publishing House, 1976.

Mitra, R.C., *The Decline of Buddhism in India*, Santiniketan: Visva Bharati, 1954.

Mookerji, Radha Kumud, 'Candragupta and the Mauryan Empire', in R.C. Majumdar and A.D. Pusalker, eds, *The Age of Imperial Unity*, *The History and Culture of the Indian People*, vol. 2, Bombay: Bharatiya Vidya Bhavan, sixth edition, 1990.

Mukherjee, Prabhati, *Beyond the Four Varṇas: The Untouchables in India*, Shimla: Indian Institute of Advanced Study, revised edition, 2002.

Murti, M. Srimannarayana, 'Sati in the *Ṛgveda*', *Journal of the Asiatic Society*, vol. 39, no. 1, 1997: 1–24.

Nagaraju, S., 'Emergence of Regional Identity and Beginnings of Vernacular Literature: A Case Study', *Social Scientist*, vol. 23, nos 10–12, 1995: 8–23.

Nagaswamy, R., 'Śri Rāmāyaṇa in Tamilnadu in Art, Thought and Literature', in V. Raghavan, ed., *The Rāmāyaṇa Tradition in Asia*, New Delhi: Sahitya Akademi, 1980.

Nandi, R.N., *Religious Institutions and Cults in the Deccan*, Delhi: Motilal Banarsidass, 1973.

——, 'Anthropology and the Study of Veda', *Indian Historical Review*, vol. XII, 1986–87: 153–65.

——, 'Archaeology and the Ṛgveda', *Indian Historical Review*, vol. XVI, 1990: 35–79.

——, *Aryans Revisited*, New Delhi: Munshiram Manoharlal, 2001.

Nandimath, S.C., 'Śaivism', in R.R. Divakar, ed., *Karnataka through the Ages*, Bangalore: The Government of Mysore, 1960.

Narayan, Badri, *Women Heroes and Dalit Assertion in North India: Culture, Identity and Politics*, New Delhi: Sage Publishers, 2006.

Narayanan, M.G.S. and Kesavan Veluthat, 'Bhakti Movement in South India', in S.C. Malik, ed., *Indian Movements: Some Aspects of Dissent, Protest and Reform*, Shimla: Indian Institute of Advanced Study, 1978; reprinted in D.N. Jha, ed., *Feudal Social Formation in Early India*, New Delhi: Chanakya Publications, 1989: 348–75.

Nath, Vijay, *Purāṇas and Acculturation: A Historio–Anthropological Perspective*, Delhi: Munshiram Manoharlal, 2001.

Neog, Maheswar, 'Hayagrīva Worship in Assam', *Journal of Oriental Research*, vol. XXII, 1954.

——, 'Buddhism in Kamarupa', *Indian Historical Quarterly*, vol. XXVII, 1957: 140–50.

Norman, K.R., 'Dialect Variation in Old and Middle Indo–Aryan', in George Erdosy,

ed., *The Indo-Aryans of Ancient South Asia: Language, Material Culture and Ethnicity*, New York: Walter de Gruyter, 1995: 278–92.
Oberoi, Harjot, *Construction of Religious Boundaries: Culture, Identity and Diversity in the Sikh Tradition*, Delhi: Oxford University Press, 1984.
Omvedt, Gail, *Buddhism in India*, New Delhi: Sage Publications, 2003.
Pal, Pratapaditya, *Vaiṣṇava Iconology in Nepal*, Calcutta: Asiatic Society, 1970.
Panikkar, K.N., Terence J. Byres and Utsa Patnaik, eds, *The Making of History: Essays Presented to Irfan Habib*, New Delhi: Tulika Books, 2000.
Parpola, Asko, 'The Coming of the Aryans to Iran and India and the Cultural and Ethnic Identity of the Dāsas', *International Journal of Dravidian Linguistics*, vol. XVII, no. 2, 1988: 85–215.
——, 'The Problem of the Aryans and the Soma: Textual–Linguistic and Archaeological Evidence', in George Erdosy, ed., *The Indo-Aryans of Ancient South Asia: Language, Material Culture and Ethnicity*, New York: Walter de Gruyter, 1995: 353–81.
Pathak, C.S., ed., *Nalanda: Past and Present*, Silver Jubilee souvenir, Nalanda, 1977.
Pathak, V.S., *Ancient Historians of India: A Study in Historical Biographies*, Bombay: Asia Publishing House, 1962.
Patil, Sharad, 'Problems of Slavery in Ancient India', *Social Scientist*, vol. 1, no. 11, 1973.
Patton, Laurie L., 'The Fate of the Female *Ṛṣi*: Portraits of Lopāmudrā', in Julia Leslie, ed., *Myth and Mythmaking: Continuous Evolution in Indian Tradition*, London: Curzon Press, 1996: 21–37.
Pfeffer, G., 'Puri's Vedic Brahmanas', in Anncharlott Eschmann, Hermann Kulke and Gaya Charan Tripathi, eds, *The Cult of Jagannāth and the Regional Tradition of Orissa*, Delhi: Manohar, 1978.
Pollock, Sheldon, 'The Rāmāyaṇa Text and Critical Edition', in Robert P. Goldman, ed., *Rāmāyaṇa of Vālmīki: An Epic of Ancient India*, Delhi: Oxford University Press, 1984.
——, 'Rāmāyaṇa and Political Imagination in India', *Journal of Asian Studies*, vol. 52, no. 3, 1993: 261–97.
——, *The Language of the Gods in the World of Men: Sanskrit Culture and Power in Premodern India*, Delhi: Permanent Black, 2007.
Prasad, B. Rajendra, ed., *Early Medieval Andhra Pradesh, AD 624–1000, Comprehensive History and Culture of Andhra Pradesh*, vol. III, New Delhi: Tulika Books, 2009.
Prasad, Pushpa, 'Female Slavery in Thirteenth-Century Gujarat', *Indian Historical Review*, vol. XV, nos 1–2, 1988–89: 269–75.
Przyluski, J., 'Satvant, Sātvata and Nāsatya', *Indian Historical Quarterly*, vol. IX, 1933: 88–91.
Pusalker, A.D., in R.C. Majumdar, ed., *The Age of Imperial Kanauj*, *The History and Culture of the Indian People*, vol. 4, Bombay: Bharatiya Vidya Bhavan, third edition, 1984.
Radhakrishnan, S., *The Hindu View of Life*, New York: Macmillan, 1973; first edition, 1927.
——, *Indian Philosophy*, Delhi: Oxford University Press, 1989; first edition, 1923.
Raghavan, V., 'The Rāmāyana in Sanskrit Literature', in V. Raghavan, ed., *The Rāmāyaṇa Tradition in Asia*, Madras: Sahitya Akademi, 1980.

Raheja, Gloria Goodwin, *The Poison in the Gift: Ritual Prestation and the Dominant Caste in a North Indian Village*, Chicago: University of Chicago Press, 1988.
Rai, G.K., *Involuntary Labour in Ancient India*, Allahabad: Chaitanya Publishing House, 1981.
Rajaguru, S.N., 'The Kalahandi Copperplate of Tuṣṭikara', *Journal of Andhra Historical Society*, vol. II, no. 2, 1974: 107–10.
Ramanujan, A.K., 'Three Hundred Rāmāyaṇas, Five Examples and Three Thoughts on Translation', in *Collected Essays of A.K. Ramanujan*, edited by Vinay Dharwadker, Delhi: Oxford University Press, 1999: 131–60.
Ramanujan, A.K. and Norman Cutler, 'From Classicism to Bhakti', in Bardwell L. Smith, ed., *Essays on Gupta Culture*, Delhi: Motilal Banarsidass, 1983: 177–214.
Ramaswamy, Gita, *India Stinking: Manual Scavengers in Andhra Pradesh and Their Work*, Chennai: Navayana, 2005.
Ramaswamy, Vijaya, 'Anklets on the Feet: Women Saints in Medieval Indian Society', *Indian Historical Review*, vol. XVIII, nos 1–2, 1990–91: 60–89.
——, 'Women in the Warkari Panth', *Indian Historical Review*, vol. XXII, nos 1–2, 1995–96: 77–104.
——, 'The Kuḍi in Early Tamiḷaham and the Tamil Women', in Dev Nathan, ed., *From Tribe to Caste*, Shimla: Indian Institute of Advanced Study, 1997.
Ramesan, N., *Temples and Legends of Andhra Pradesh*, Bombay: Bharatiya Vidya Bhavan, 1962.
——, *The Tirumala Temple*, Tirupati: Tirumala Devasthanam, 1981.
Rao, B.V. Krishna, *A History of the Early Dynasties of Āndhradeśa*, Madras, 1942.
Rao, M. Rama, *Ikṣvākus of Vijayapurī*, Tirupati: Sri Venkateswara University, 1967.
Rao, R. Subba, 'Scope of Anthropological Research in the Agency Division', *Journal of the Andhra Historical Research Society*, vol. I, part 3, 1926.
Rao, Rama, 'The Temples of Śriśailam', *Journal of the Andhra Historical Research Society*, vol. XXVI, 1966.
Rao, T.A. Gopinatha, *Elements of Hindu Iconography*, vol. I, part 1, Madras: Law Printing House, 1914.
Rau, Wilhelm, *Staat und Gesellschaft im alten Indien*, Wiesbaden: Harrassowitz, 1956.
——, *The Meaning of Pur in Vedic Literature*, München: Wilhelm Fink Verlag, 1976.
Raychaudhuri, H.C., *Political History of Ancient India with Commentary by B.N. Mukherjee*, New Delhi: Oxford University Press, 2000; first edition, 1970.
Reddy, Y. Gopala, 'Socio–Economic Tensions in the Coḷa Period', *Journal of the Oriental Institute*, vol. 29, nos 1–2, 1979: 74–84.
Renou, Louis, *The Destiny of the Veda in India*, Delhi: Motilal Banarsidass, 1965.
Richman, Paula, ed., *Many Rāmāyaṇas: The Diversity of a Narrative Tradition in South Asia*, Delhi: Oxford Univesity Press, 1992.
——, *Questioning Rāmāyaṇas: A South Asian Tradition*, Delhi: Oxford University Press, 2000.
Rocher, Rosane, 'British Orientalism in the Eighteenth Century: The Dialectics of Knowledge and Government', in Carol A. Breckenridge and Peter van der Veer, eds, *Orientalism and the Postcolonial Predicament: Perspectives on South Asia*, Delhi: Oxford University Press, 1994: 215–49.
Roy, Kumkum, *Emergence of Monarchy in North India: Eighth to Fourth Centuries*

BC *as reflected in the Brahmanical Tradition*, Delhi: Oxford University Press, Delhi, 1994.

Sahlins, Marshall D., 'The Segmentary Lineage: An Organization of Predatory Expansion', *American Anthropologist*, vol. 63, no. 2, 1961: 322–45.

——, *Tribesmen*, New Jersey: Prentice–Hall, 1968.

Sahu, Bhairabi Prasad, 'The Past as a Mirror of the Present: The Case of Oriya Society', *Social Science Probings*, vol. IX, nos 1–4, 1995: 8–23.

Sankalia, H.D., *Rāmāyaṇa: Myth or Reality?* Delhi: People's Publishing House, 1973.

——, '"The Aryan Enigma": Review of K.D. Sethna, *The Problem of Aryan Origin*', *The Times of India*, 13 September 1981.

Sarao, K.T.S., *Urban Centres and Urbanization as Reflected in the Pali and Sutta Piṭakas*, Delhi: Department of Buddhist studies, University of Delhi, second revised edition, 2007.

Sardesai, G.S., ed., *Selections from the Peshwa Daftar*, Bombay: Government Central Press, 1930–34.

Sareen, T.R., 'Slavery in India Under British Rule, 1772–1843', *Indian Historical Review*, XV, nos 1–2, 1988–89: 257–68.

Sarkar, H.B., 'The Migration of the Rāmāyaṇa Story to Indonesia and Some Problems Connected With the Structure and Contents of the Old Javanese Rāmāyaṇa', in V. Raghavan, ed., *The Rāmāyaṇa Tradition in Asia*, Madras: Sahitya Akademi, 1980.

Sastri, K.A. Nilakanta, 'The Cālukyas of Bādāmi', in G. Yazdani, ed., *The Early History of the Deccan*, vol. I, part IV, London: Oxford University Press, 1960.

——, *A History of South India*, Madras: Oxford University Press, third edition, 1966.

——, *The Coḷas*, Madras: University of Madras, 1975.

——, *Development of Religion in South India*, Delhi: Munshiram Manoharlal, 1992; first edition, 1963.

Sastri, K.A. Nilakanta, ed., *Comprehensive History of India*, vol. II, Madras: Orient Longman, 1957.

Sastry, P.V. Parabrahma, 'Society and Economy of the Sātavāhana Age', in *Early Historic Andhra Pradesh: 500* BC–AD *624*, edited by I. K. Sharma, *Comprehensive History and Culture of Andhra Pradesh*, vol. II, New Delhi: Tulika Books, 2008.

Schmidt, Hans-Peter, *Some Women's Rites and Rights in the Veda*, Pune: Bhandarkar Oriental Institute, 1987.

Schneider, David M. and Kathleen Gough, eds, *Matrilineal Kinship*, Berkeley: University of California Press, 1961.

Selvam, S., 'Sociology of India and Hinduism: Towards a Method', in S.M. Michael, ed., *Dalits in Modern India: Vision and Values*, Delhi: Sage, 2007.

Sen, Amartya, *The Argumentative Indian: Writings on Indian Culture, History and Identity*, Delhi: Penguin Books, 2005.

Sen, Dineshchandra, *The Bengali Rāmāyaṇas*, Calcutta: Calcutta University, 1920.

Sergent, Bernard, 'Three Notes on the Trifunctional Indo–European Marriage', *Journal of Indo–European Studies*, vol. XII, 1984: 179–91.

Sharma, B.N., 'Religious Tolerance and Intolerance in Indian Sculpture', in *Umesh Misra Commemoration Volume*, edited by B.R. Saksena, Allahabad: Gangaram Jha Research Institute, 1970: 657–68.

Sharma, J.P., *Republics in Ancient India*, Leiden: E.J. Brill, 1968.

Sharma, R.S., 'Material Milieu of Tantricism', in R.S. Sharma and V. Jha, eds, *Indian Society: Historical Probings, In Memory of D.D. Kosambi*, Delhi: People's Publishing House, 1974: 175–89.

——, 'Forms of Property in the Early Portions of *Ṛgveda*', in Diptendra Banerjee *et al.*, eds, *Essays in Honour of Prof. S.C. Sarkar*, Delhi: People's Publishing House, 1976: 39–50.

——, *Śūdras in Ancient India*, Delhi: Motilal Banarsidass, second revised edition, 1980.

——, *Material Culture and Social Formations in Ancient India*, Delhi: Macmillan, 1983.

——, *Origin of the State in India*, Bombay: Department of History, University of Bombay, 1989.

——, *Communal History and Rāma's Ayodhyā*, New Delhi: People's Publishing House, second reprint, 1990.

——, *Aspects of Political Ideas and Institutions in Ancient India*, Delhi: Motilal Banarsidass, third revised edition, 1991.

——, 'Material Background of the Genesis of the State and Complex Society in the Middle Gangetic Plains', *Social Science Probings*, vol. X, nos 1–4, 1993.

——, *Looking for the Aryans*, Hyderabad: Orient Longman, 1995.

——, *Perspectives in Social and Economic History of Early India*, Delhi: Munshiram Manoharlal, 1995; first edition, 1983.

——, 'Historiography of the Ancient Indian Social Order', in *Light on Early Indian Society and Economy*, Bombay: Manaktala, 1996: 1–18.

——, *The State and Varṇa Formation in the Mid-Ganga Plains: An Ethno-archaeological View*, Delhi: Manohar, 1996.

——, *Advent of Aryans in India*, Delhi: Manohar, 1999.

——, *Early Medieval Indian Society: A Study in Feudalization*, Hyderabad: Orient Longman, 2001.

——, 'Economic and Social Basis of Tantrism', in *Early Medieval Indian Society: A Study in Feudalization*, Hyderabad: Orient Longman, 2001.

——, *Economic History of Early India*, Delhi: Viva Books, 2011.

Sharma, S.R., *Jainism and Karnataka Culture*, Dharwad: Dharwad University, 1940.

Shastri, Ajay Mitra, *India As Seen in the Bṛhatsaṃhitā of Varāhamihira*, Delhi: Motilal Banarsidass, 1969.

Shastri, Biswanarayan, 'Rāmāyaṇa in Assamese Literature', in V. Raghavan, ed., *The Rāmāyaṇa Tradition in Asia*, Madras: Sahitya Akademi, 1980.

Shastri, Shakuntala Rao, *Women in the Vedic Age*, Bombay: Bharatiya Vidya Bhavan, 1969.

Shende, N.J., 'The Authorship of the Mahābhārata', *Annals of the Bhandarkar Oriental Research Institute*, vol. 24, 1943: 67–82.

Sheth, D.L., 'Caste and the Secularization Process in India', in Peter Ronald de Souza, ed., *Contemporary India: Transitions*, New Delhi: Sage, 2000: 237–63.

Shrirama, 'Untouchability and Stratification in Indian Civilisation', in S.M. Michael, ed., *Dalits in Modern India: Vision and Values*, Delhi: Sage, second edition, 2007: 45–75.

Shukla, Rama Kant, *Jainācārya Raviṣeṇa kṛta Padma-Purāṇa aur Tulasīkṛt Rāmacaritamānasa*, Delhi: Vani Prakashan, 1974.

Singh, Bhagavati Prasad, *Rāmabhakti men Rasika Sampradāya*, Balarampur: Avadha Sahitya Mandir, 1957.
——, *Rāma Kāvya Dhārā: Anusandhāna Aivam Anucintana*, Allahabad: Lokabharati Prakashan, 1976.
Singh, Kumar Suresh, *Tribal Society in India: An Anthropo-Historical Perspective*, Delhi: Manohar, 1985.
——, *People of India: An Introduction*, Calcutta: Anthropological Survey of India, 1992.
——, 'Tribe into Caste: A Colonial Paradigm (?)', in Dev Nathan, ed., *From Tribe to Caste*, Shimla: Indian Institute of Advanced Study, 1997.
Singh, Rajadeva, *Nirguṇa Rāmabhakti aur Dalita Jātiyān*, New Delhi: Vani Prakashan, 1998.
Singh, Ram Bhushan Prasad, *Jainism in Early Medieval Karnataka (c. AD 500–1200)*, Delhi: Motilal Banarsidass, 1975.
Singh, Sarva Darman, *Ancient Indian Warfare with Special Reference to the Vedic Period*, Leiden: E.J. Brill, 1965.
——, *Polyandry in Ancient India*, Delhi: Vikas Publishing House, 1978.
Singh, Sheo Bahadur, *Brahmanical Icons in Northern India*, New Delhi: Sagar Publications, 1977.
Sircar, D.C., 'Vaishnavism', in R.C. Majumdar, ed., *The Classical Age*, *The History and Culture of the Indian People*, vol. 3, Bombay: Bharatiya Vidya Bhavan, third edition, 1970.
——, '*Rāmāyaṇa* in inscriptions', in V. Raghavan, ed., *The Rāmāyaṇa Tradition in Asia*, Madras: Sahitya Akademi, 1980: 322–33.
Sjoberg, A., 'The Dravidian Contribution to the Development of Indian Civilization: A Call for Reassessment', *Comparative Civilizations Review*, vol. XXII, 1990.
Slotkin, J.S., 'On a Possible Lack of Incest Regulations in Old Iran', *American Anthropologist*, vol. 49, 1947: 612–15.
Smith, Brian K., *Reflections on Resemblance, Ritual and Religion*, Delhi: Oxford University Press, 1989.
Smith, Fredrick M., 'Indra's Curse, Varuṇa's Noose, and the Suppression of Women in the Vedic Śrauta Ritual', in Julia Leslie, ed., *Roles and Rituals for Hindu Women*, Delhi: Motilal Banarsidass, 1992: 17–45.
Sontheimer, Gunther-Dietz, *The Joint Hindu Family: Its Evolution as a Legal Institution*, Delhi: Munshiram Manoharlal, 1977.
Sparreboom, M., *Chariots in the Veda*, Leiden: E.J. Brill, 1985.
Srinivas, M.N., *The Changing Position of Indian Women*, Delhi: Oxford University Press, 1976.
——, 'The Dominant Caste in Rampura', in *The Dominant Caste and Other Essays*, Delhi: Oxford University Press, 1987.
Staal, Frits, 'The Science of Ritual', *Professor P.D. Gune Memorial Lecture*, first series, Pune: Bhandarkar Oriental Research Institute, 1982.
Stepan, Nancy Leys, '"Science" and Race: Before and After the Human Genome Project', in *Socialist Register, 2003: Fighting Identities: Race, Religion and Ethno-Nationalism*, edited by Leo Panitch and Colin Leys, Kolkata: K.P. Bagchi & Co., 2003: 393–414.
Sukthankar, V.S., 'The Bhṛgus and the Bhārata: A Text Historical Study', *Epic Stud-*

ies (VI), Annals of the Bhandarkar Oriental Research Institute, vol. 18, part 1, 1936: 1–76.

——, *On the Meaning of the Mahābhārata*, Bombay: Asiatic Society, 1957.

Sundaram, K., *The Simhachalam Temple*, Simhachalam: Simhachalam Devasthanam, 1969.

Sutton, Nicholas, 'An Exposition of Early Sāmkhya, a Projection of the Bhagavad-Gītā and a Critique of the Role of Women in Hindu Society: The Sulabhā-Janaka-Saṃvāda', *Annals of the Bhandarkar Oriental Research Institute*, vol. 50, part 1–4, 1999–2000: 53–65.

Talbot, Cynthia, 'Rudramā Devi, the Female King: Gender and Political Authority in Medieval India', in David Shulman, ed., *Syllables of Sky: Studies in South Indian Civilization in Honour of V. Narayana Rao*, Delhi: Oxford University Press, 1995: 391–429.

Tawney, C.H., tr., *The Prabandha Cintāmaṇi or Wishingstone of Narratives*, Calcutta: Asiatic Society, 1901.

Thakur, V.K., 'A Note on Vedic Agriculture', in D.N. Tripathi, ed., *A Discourse on Indo–European Languages and Culture*, New Delhi: Indian Council of Historical Research, 2005: 140–51.

Thapar, Romila, 'Dāna and Dakṣiṇā as Forms of Exchange', *Indica*, vol. 13, nos 1–2, 1976: 37–48.

——, *Ancient Indian Social History*, Delhi: Orient Longman, 1978.

——, *Exile and the Kingdom: Some Thoughts on the Rāmāyaṇa*, Bangalore: The Mythic Society, 1978.

——, *From Lineage to State: Social Formations in the Mid-First Millennium* BC *in the Ganga Valley*, Delhi: Oxford University Press, 1983.

——, 'The Historiography of the Concept of Aryan', in *India: Historical Beginnings and the Concept of the Aryan*, New Delhi: National Book Trust.

Thomas, Northcote W., 'Animals', in *Encyclopedia of Religion and Ethics*, vol. I, edited by James Hastings *et al.*, Edinburgh: T. & T. Clark, 1908–26.

Thurston, Edgar and K. Rangachari, *Castes and Tribes of Southern India*, Madras: Government Press, 1909.

Trautmann, Thomas R., 'On the Translation of the Term *Varṇa*', *Journal of the Economic and Social History of the Orient*, vol. VII, 1964: 196–201.

——, *Dravidian Kinship*, Cambridge: Cambridge University Press, 1981.

——, *Aryans and British India*, New Delhi: Vistaar Publications, 1997.

Trautmann, Thomas R., ed., *The Aryan Debate*, New Delhi: Oxford University Press, 2005.

Vajpeyi, Ananya, '*Śūdradharma* and Legal Treatments of Caste', in Timothy Lubin, Donald R. Davis, Jr. and Jayanth K. Krishnan, eds, *Hinduism and Law: An Introduction*, New Delhi: Cambridge University Press, 2010.

van der Veer, Peter, 'The Politics of Devotion to Rāma', in David N. Lorenzen, ed., *Bhakti Religion in North India: Community Identity and Political Action*, Delhi: Manohar, 1996.

Van Gulik, R.H., *Hayagrīva: The Mantrayanic Aspect of Horse-Cult in China and Japan*, Leiden: E.J. Brill, 1935.

Vansina, Jan, *Oral Tradition: A Study in Historical Methodology*, translated by H.M. Wright, London: Routledge and Kegan Paul, 1965.

Varadachari, K.C., *The Āḻvārs of South India*, Bombay: Bharatiya Vidya Bhavan, 1966.

Vaudeville, Charlotte, *Kabīr*, Oxford: Clarendon Press, 1975.

Venkataraman, K.R., 'A Note on the Kalabhras', *Transactions of the Archaeological Society of South India*, 1956–57: 94–100.

Venkataramanayya, N., and M. Somasekhara Sarma, 'The Kākatīyas of Warangal', in G. Yazdani, ed., *The Early History of the Deccan*, vol. II, part IX, London: Oxford University Press, 1960.

Vira, Raghu and Chikyu Yamamoto, *Rāmāyaṇa in China*, Sarasvati Vihar Series No. 8, Nagpur: International Academy of Indian Culture, 1955; first edition, 1938.

Wagle, N., *Society at the Time of the Buddha*, Bombay: Popular Prakashan, 1966.

Warder, A.K., *Indian Buddhism*, Delhi: Motilal Banarsidass, 1970.

——, 'Feudalism and Mahāyāna Buddhism', in R.S. Sharma and V. Jha, eds, *Indian Society: Historical Probings, In Memory of D.D. Kosambi*, Delhi: People's Publishing House, 1974.

Watters, T., *On Yuan Chwang's Travels in India*, edited by T.W. Rhys Davids and S.W. Bushell, vol. I, London: Royal Asiatic Society, 1904.

Weber, Albrecht, *On the Rāmāyaṇa*, translated by D.C. Boyd, London, 1873.

Weber, Max, *The Religion of India: The Sociology of Hinduism and Buddhism*, translated by Hans Gerth and Don Martindale, New York: Free Press, 1958.

Whaling, Frank, *The Rise of the Religious Significance of Rāma*, Delhi: Motilal Banarsidass, 1980.

Winternitz, M., *A History of Indian Literature*, New York: Russell & Russell, 1971.

Witzel, Michael, 'Early Indian History: Linguistic and Textual Parameters', in George Erdosy, ed., *The Indo-Aryans of Ancient South Asia: Language, Material Culture and Ethnicity*, New York: Walter de Gruyter, 1995: 85–125.

Yadava, B.N.S., 'Immobility and Subjection of Indian Peasantry in Early Medieval Complex', *Indian Historical Review*, vol. I, no. 1, 1968: 18–27.

——, 'Some Aspects of the Changing Order in the Saka–Kusana Age', in G.R. Sharma, ed., *Kuṣāṇa Studies*, Allahabad: University of Allahabad, 1968: 75–97.

——, *Society and Culture in Northern India in the Twelfth Century*, Allahabad: Central Book Depot, 1973.

——, 'Problems of the Interaction Between Socio–Economic Classes in the Early Medieval Complex', *Indian Historical Review*, vol. III, no. I, 1974: 43–58.

——, 'The Accounts of the Kali Age and the Social Transition from Antiquity to the Middle Ages', *Indian Historical Review*, vol. V, nos 1–2, 1978–79: 31–63.

Yi-Jing (I-Tsing), *A Record of the Buddhist Religion as Practised in India and the Malay Archipelago*, translated by J. Takakasu, Oxford, 1896.

Young, Katherine K., 'Hinduism', in Arvind Sharma, ed., *Women in World Religions*, Albany: SUNY Press, 1987.

Zelliot, Eleanor, *From Untouchable to Dalit: Essays on the Ambedkar Movement*, Delhi: Manohar, 1996.

Zvelebil, Kamil, *The Smile of Murugan: On Tamil Literature of South India*, Leiden: E.J. Brill, 1973.

Inscriptions and Dictionaries

Annual Reports of South Indian Epigraphy.

Apte, Vaman Shivaram, *Sanskrit–English Dictionary*, vols I–III, Poona: Prasad Prakashan, 1959.

Catalogue of the Kalā Sarvekṣaṇa Purātatva Saṅgrahālaya, No. 40, Jaipur.

Cousens, Henry, *List of Antiquarian Remains in the Central Provinces and Berar*, Calcutta: Archaeological Survey of India, 1897.

Dabaral, Shiva Prasad, *Uttarākhaṇḍa ke Abhilekh evaṃ Mudrā*, Gadhaval: Vīra-gāthā-Prakashan, Vikram Samvat 2047.

Epigraphia Indica, vols. V, VIII, X, XV, XXV, XXVIII.

Fleet, J.F., *Corpus Inscriptionum Indicarum*, vol. III, Calcutta: Government Printing, 1888.

Ghosh, A., ed., *An Encyclopaedia of Indian Archaeology*, vol. II, New Delhi: Munshiram Manoharlal, 1989.

Gopal, B.R. *et al.*, *Epigraphia Carnatica*, 1984.

Macdonell, A.A. and A.B. Keith, *Vedic Index of Names and Subjects*, 2 vols, London: John Murray, 1912.

Mahalingam, T.V., *Inscriptions of the Pallavas*, Delhi: Agama Prakashan, 1988.

Mirashi, V.V., *Corpus Inscriptionum Indicarum*, vol. IV, parts I and II, Ootacamund: Government Epigraphist for India, 1955.

Monier-Williams, Monier, *Sanskrit–English Dictionary*, Oxford: Clarendon Press, 1956.

Sircar, D.C., *Select Inscriptions Bearing on Indian History and Civilization*, vol. I, Calcutta: University of Calcutta, 1942.

——, *Indian Epigraphical Glossary*, Delhi: Motilal Banarsidass, 1966.

——, *Inscriptions of Asoka*, New Delhi: Publications Division, Ministry of Information and Broadcasting, Government of India, fourth edition, 1998.

Index

Primary Texts

Authors of Modern Works

General Index